Edgar G. Ulmer

ALSO EDITED BY
BERND HERZOGENRATH

The Cinema of Tod Browning: Essays of the Macabre and Grotesque (McFarland, 2008)

Edgar G. Ulmer

Essays on the King of the B's

Edited by Bernd Herzogenrath
Foreword by Arianné Ulmer Cipes

McFarland & Company, Inc., Publishers
Jefferson, North Carolina, and London

LIBRARY OF CONGRESS CATALOGUING-IN-PUBLICATION DATA

Edgar G. Ulmer : essays on the king of the B's / edited by Bernd Herzogenrath ; foreword by Arianné Ulmer Cipes.
    p.   cm.
Includes bibliographical references and index.

ISBN 978-0-7864-3700-9
softcover : 50# alkaline paper ∞

1. Ulmer, Edgar G. (Edgar George), 1904–1972.
I. Herzogenrath, Bernd, 1964–
PN1998.3.U46E57   2009
791.4302'3092 — dc22[B]   2008045683

British Library cataloguing data are available

©2009 Bernd Herzogenrath. All rights reserved

No part of this book may be reproduced or transmitted in any form or by any means, electronic or mechanical, including photocopying or recording, or by any information storage and retrieval system, without permission in writing from the publisher.

On the cover: Edgar G. Ulmer in the 1940s (Photofest)

Manufactured in the United States of America

McFarland & Company, Inc., Publishers
  Box 611, Jefferson, North Carolina 28640
  www.mcfarlandpub.com

To the memory of Edgar G. Ulmer

for Arianné
for Olomouc

Acknowledgments

A big THANX! to Janna "the-one-and-only-Jamni" Wanagas for her grrrreat help in this.

A big hearty "Diky!" to Andrea & Dorka of Tara Fuki ... you know why...

My sincere gratitude to the DFG, the Česko-Německý Fond Budoucnosti, the Židovské Muzeum v Praze, and the Goethe-Institute in Prague, without whose help this project would have been on a constant detour.

Table of Contents

Foreword by Arianné Ulmer Cipes — 1
Introduction: The Return of Edgar G. Ulmer
    BERND HERZOGENRATH — 3

Ulmer and Cult/ure
    BERND HERZOGENRATH — 23

Camera Obscura, or Moments of Broken Economy in
Edgar G. Ulmer's Films
    STEFAN GRISSEMANN — 39

The Ordinary Life of Ordinary People: *Menschen am Sonntag*
    PETRA LÖFFLER — 49

Ulmer's Anti-Syphilis Film: *Damaged Lives* and
Its Novelization
    MARCEL ARBEIT — 63

The Black Cat
    GREGORY WILLIAM MANK — 89

In Search of Jewish Identity
    SHARON PUCKER RIVO — 105

Moon of Alabama / *Moon Over Harlem*: African American
Culture and German Imaginations from Brecht to Ulmer
    FRANK MEHRING — 119

Detour's History/History's *Detour*
    DANA POLAN — 137

The Strange Woman: An Analysis with Gilles Deleuze's Notion
of the Impulse-Image
    JULIA MEIER — 150

The Logic of Contradiction and the Politics of Desire in *Ruthless*
    Reynold Humphries   159

The Man from Planet X
    Matthew Sweney   171

Camp, Art Film, Classical Hollywood Cinema and *Babes in Bagdad*
    Herbert Schwaab   183

The Pleasures of the "Not-Quite Movie": *Murder Is My Beat* and *Daughter of Dr. Jekyll*
    Ekkehard Knörer   196

Products of Circumstances
    Stefanie Diekmann   206

The Naked Dawn: Production, Sources, and *Mise-en-Scène*
    Bill Krohn   215

The Effects of the Displacement of Home in *Daughter of Dr. Jekyll*
    Michal Peprník   225

What You See Is What You Get: Ulmer and the Nudist Picture
    Petra Hanáková   236

Geocinema and Geophilosophy: *The Cavern*
    Philipp Hofmann   248

Ulmer in the Aquarium
    Adrian Martin   262

About the Contributors   279
Index   285

Foreword
ARIANNÉ ULMER CIPES

In one of the very last conversations my mother, Shirley Kassler Ulmer, and I had with Edgar G. Ulmer he expressed his fear that all of his work would some day disappear from the face of the earth. If this were true he felt his life was meaningless. Soon after, he had his final stroke. He was no longer able to speak, and both my mother and I assured him we would do everything possible to see that his work was preserved.

This collection of essays—for which the editor, Bernd Herzogenrath, has my full cooperation and authorization—and the interest of a new generation of film lovers more than thirty-five years after Ulmer's death represents our dream fulfilled.

There were many people who were responsible along the way. I would never have been able to preserve and collect many of his films without their assistance. It is impossible to note them all but a few outstanding examples that I cannot overlook must be mentioned.

Bill Krohn in 1983 set up the first large retrospective for UCLA's "King of the Bs." He became an indispensable partner in everything regarding the preservation and study of Ulmer. I am always grateful for his friendship and efforts.

Peter Bogdanovich was extremely important in introducing Ulmer to a new generation of directors and fans. He published his 1970 interview with Ulmer in the 1974 edition of *Film Culture* and later on in the 1975 *King of the Bs*, and finally in the 1997 *Who The Devil Made It*. Aside from his valued personal friendship, generosity and interest, he made it possible for our nonprofit company to produce the documentary *Edgar G. Ulmer—The Man Off-Screen*.

Sharon Pucker Rivo and Miriam Krant of the National Center for Jewish Film managed over many years of labor to preserve and restore all four of the Yiddish films made in the 1930s.

Thank you to every one of the many men and women who contributed to this book.

In closing I wish to thank the prime mover in the rebirth of Ulmer's works, Bernd Herzogenrath. He is the founding father of the 2006 ulmer-fest, and even sought out Ulmer's Olomouc birth home. He is the editor of this collection. His devoted dedication to the revival of Ulmer is invaluable.

I now believe that coming generations of film lovers will be able to enjoy the films of our father in the future.

> ARIANNÉ ULMER CIPES
> The Edgar G. Ulmer Preservation Corporation
> Sherman Oaks, California

Introduction: The Return of Edgar G. Ulmer

BERND HERZOGENRATH

Edgar G. Ulmer was the King of the B's, the B's King of Kings, what the French filmmakers of the *nouvelle vague* would later call an *auteur*, someone whose distinguished voice and highly individual handwriting stood out, a maker of *independent movies* before that category even existed. Let me open the curtain with some appraisal for an undeservedly almost forgotten director, who was only rediscovered in the 1950s by the French, and in the early 1970s by some young American filmmakers who were interested in the history of film and the dimly lit side streets of the Hollywood mainstream:

> [N]obody has ever made good pictures faster or for less money than Edgar Ulmer. What he could do with nothing ... remains an object lesson for those directors, myself included, who complain about tight budgets and schedules [Bogdanovich 559].

> Ulmer's camera never falters even when his characters disintegrate.... That a personal style could emerge from the lowest depths of Poverty Row is a tribute to a director without alibis [Sarris 143].

> Edgar G. Ulmer built a filmography like nobody else's. His only mainstream classic was the 1934 horror film *The Black Cat*, and even that is gloriously *outré*. Among film buffs, Ulmer is best known for his 1946 [*sic*] nightmare road movie *Detour*, but some of his more obscure B (or X) films are livelier. These movies come off as oddly sophisticated Saturday-matinee stuff; their campiness derives not from incompetence but from intelligence pushed to budgetary limits. Even at his worst, Ulmer was never less than the thinking man's Ed Wood [*New Yorker* November 16, 1998].

> Poverty Row. From this cinematic no-man's land, one expects no lavish, herculean masterworks. The most one can hope for are films that make the most of the modest resources and transcend their limitations of capital; films whose obvious budgetary shortcomings reveal the difficult conditions under which the filmmaker struggled to realize his/her vision, the financial obstacles

that were cleared by ingenuity and clever craftsmanship. One hopes for films that do not rest upon established techniques and premises, but rather explore (even if clumsily and sometimes with unsatisfactory results) the possibilities and promise of an art form whose limits are not often enough tested. There, Edgar G. Ulmer fulfilled these hopes, found absolution and made the films for which he is best remembered.... Yet, in those moments when the filmmaker fought ramshackleness with pure creativity, the unpolished gems that resulted remind us of the inventive spirit that first made photographs dance, make us aware of the mechanics of film construction, and ultimately reveal the cinema in its purest essence [Wood 24].

It's a shame Ulmer's name, as influential as he was, is not better known.... There was something more to an Ulmer picture. Mood was part of it, but it went beyond that, just like Orson Welles is more than deep focus and Hitchcock is more than suspense. It was something physical — the radical play of light and shadow, the sets that shouldn't make sense but do, the characters who make unwise and unhealthy decisions about their lives.... There's much more to Edgar Ulmer. He's an American classic, a real classic, like Joseph H. Lewis or Sam Fuller, whose life sounds a lot like one of his films — sometimes it wasn't too pretty, but it always had style" [Knipfel].

Ulmer was the son of Henriette Ulmer, *née* Edels, from Vienna, and Siegfried Ulmer, a socialist and Jewish wine merchant from Ivanovice na Hané. Ulmer was born in Olomouc — not in Vienna — because the Ulmer family was living there at the family property of Siegfried Ulmer's grandparents.

Ulmer spent part of his childhood in Vienna and Sweden. His father died in World War I, and his mother and the children went to Vienna to live with his mothers' parents. Immediately after the war, Edgar was sent to Stockholm and Uppsala for a year with the Hoover Commission. Returning to Vienna in 1920, he enrolled in the Academy of Fine Arts and studied with stage designer Alfred Roller, a close associate of the famous Max Reinhardt. And it is with Max Reinhardt that Ulmer — as stage designer and Reinhardt's personal artistic advisor — made it to America in 1924, where he immediately snapped at the first chance to work as a film director.[1]

Earlier, Ulmer had developed an appetite for staging, designing, production, and the world of movie-making. In 1920, Ulmer met Friedrich Wilhelm Murnau in Berlin and started working with him. According to the legend that Ulmer spread in the 1970 interview with American director Peter Bogdanovich, two years before his death, published in *Who the Devil Made It*, Ulmer worked as set designer and second director/assistant art director for all of Murnau's films — *Nosferatu, Finances of the Grand Duke, Sunrise, Faust, TABU*, and *The Last Laugh* — for which Ulmer even claimed to have invented the dolly shot, by having been inspired by a woman with a baby buggy (Bogdanovich 569). And not only that — the Ulmer legend has it that he worked with all the famous European directors of the '20s, on all the famous films — as set designer with Paul Wegener's *The Golem*, Fritz Lang's *Nibelungen* and *Metropolis*, Robert Wiene's *The Cabinet of Dr. Caligari*, with Mauritz Stiller and G. W. Pabst — Ulmer seems to almost single-handedly have given birth to German Expressionist Cinema — or, better, to Olomouc Expressionism.

Ulmer's first real film was *Menschen am Sonntag (People on Sunday)*, an important item in film history not only because it created something different at that time in 1929 — a kind of documentary film about a city — Berlin — with ordinary people, no actors, with very low budget, but shot "with an innovative impulse for freedom and fresh air" (Meisel 148) that set it apart from the studio films of the 1920s and that almost foreshadows the neo-realism of a Rosselini or the *nouvelle vague* — in fact, Truffaut later claimed Ulmer as one of his great inspirations. *People on Sunday* is also notorious for the fact that it brought together in one project people who later became big names in the movie industry: in addition to Ulmer, there was Robert Siodmak as co-director (*The Spiral Staircase*), the producer and director Fred Zinnemann of *High Noon* fame, the cinematographer Eugen Schüfftan, and, as script writer, Billy Wilder. Ulmer — fresh from Hollywood, where he was working with Murnau, and was already shooting two-reel Westerns for Universal studios — was welcomed to the project.

Thus, in the mid- to late 1920s Ulmer was commuting between Hollywood and Berlin, working for Universal Studios until the mid-'30s, doing a series of quick and cheap but brilliant "ethnic films" — four films that became classics of the Yiddish cinema, *Green Fields, The Singing Blacksmith, The Light Ahead*, and *American Matchmaker* — a Ukrainian film, *Natalka Poltavka*; plus a film with an all-black amateur cast, *Moon Over Harlem*. These films were always shot in four to eight days, with a minimum budget, a tenth of the Hollywood productions — for peanuts, that is, petty cash. In the first half of the 1940s, Ulmer became director with PRC — Producers Releasing Corporation — a small B-picture studio, for which Ulmer directed some of his best films, among them gems such as *Bluebeard, Club Havana*, and the noir-classic *Detour*, which film historians regard as "probably the greatest B ever made" (McCarthy and Flynn 23) or, "the cheapest really good film to come out of Hollywood" (Cameron 68). From the mid-'40s to the early '60s, Ulmer was desperate for projects. He again commuted between the USA and Europe — known as a director who can make something out of nothing, the ability in itself is highly valuable, the reputation, however, leads to the fact that he is mostly offered quite bad, cheap scripts and monumental costume dramas such as the Italian *Hannibal*, with Victor Mature. In 1964, Ulmer realized his last film, the anti-war drama *The Cavern*, under terrible financial and health problems — he suffered his first stroke. His last years were marked by the fear that nothing of his work would last — B-pictures were regarded as disposable objects, and were not conserved the way that big-budget productions were — and by more strokes, leaving him incapable of speaking. On September 30, 1972, Ulmer died at the Motion Picture Hospital in Woodland Hills, California. The motto on his gravestone reads: *Talent Obliges.*

Rediscovered by film buffs — critics and directors alike, in the 1950s in France (Truffaut, Godard, Tavernier) and in the 1970s in America (Peter Bogdanovich, Martin Scorsese) — Ulmer's name was being whispered to each other almost behind closed doors, passed on in an almost oral tradition, the password for a cult-following. As Myron Meisel stated in 1972, in an early and groundbreaking essay on Ulmer called "The Primacy of the Visual," "[f]or many years, scattered cults of film lovers had cherished the impossibility of his demented poetry in such forsaken projects as *The Black Cat* (1934), *Bluebeard* (1944), *Detour* (1945), *Ruthless* (1948), *The Naked Dawn* (1955), and *Beyond the Time Barrier* (1960), to name his best. Such cults thrived on those very titles that were certain to earn the reflex contempt of all 'serious' students of film ... *Girls in Chains* ... *Babes in Bagdad* [i.e., *of Bagdad*] ... and even (help us) *My Son, the Hero*" (Meisel 147) — and it is this very *reflex* that brought the contributors of this volume here, serious students of film nonetheless.

Not born in Vienna, as the legend would have it, Edgar Georg Ulmer was born on September 17, 1904, in ... Olomouc [then Olmütz]. When Truffaut and the critics of the *Cahiers du Cinéma* interviewed the man, he gave Vienna as his birth-place. Fashioning [and seeing] himself as a representative of European High Culture, Ulmer almost naturally felt the urge to repress provinciality. The ship manifests and visa papers on his entry to Ellis Island in 1924 show that Ulmer's last permanent residence may have been Vienna, but his birthplace was Olomouc.

Vienna may have sounded more urbane and chic, but in fact it really would have suited a film director soaked in the repertoire, style, and *mis-en-scène* of German Expressionism much better had the legend incorporated the fact — Olomouc, not Vienna. How *less* provincial can you get? Olomouc is where the Mozarts and Gustav Mahler stayed, where Ludwig Wittgenstein attended the school for artillery officers. Ulmer was born in what might be called a cradle of Modernism. Edmund Husserl was born in Prostějov, a stone's throw from Olomouc. Sigmund Freud was born in Příbor, North Moravia, also not far from Olomouc. In 1923, he wrote *The Ego and the Id*. You only have to walk Olomouc streets (or better — the byroads and back-alleys of the old city center), and you are *within* a German Expressionist set! The more pivo or slivovice you've had, the more forced your perspectives grow. Go to the Tourist Office and see the Hanacka Giant, Olomouc's closest to the Golem!

[ship manifest image]

This Ellis Island ship manifest lists Edgar G. Ulmer's arrival (entry number 2). Note Wien (Vienna).

Or, even better, enter the Ponorka (a local pub in Olomouc), and meet the complete Cabinet of Dr. Caligari. Try it, it's a fact! You even *become* the Cabinet of Caligari, once you're there.

The ulmerfest — this dream I had of a commemoration of Ulmer's work by lovers and scholars at the very *locus genii* — was born in 2003, when I learnt that my beloved Ulmer was born in my beloved Olomouc, and the idea of the ulmerfest came as

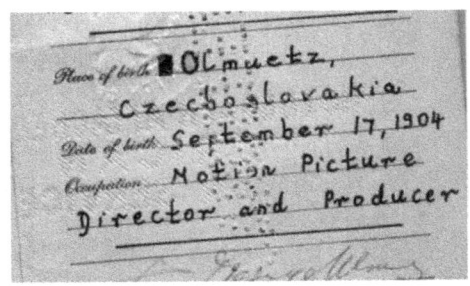

Ulmer's passport correctly cites his birthplace.

a natural response and finally took place in 2006.[2] After I contacted Arianné Ulmer Cipes to ask for her blessing — which she generously gave — I spent lots of quality time contacting and digging through archives, until, finally, I found what I had been looking for — the address of Ulmer's birth home in Olomouc. In 1904, the address was Resselgasse 1, Ort Neugasse. Today, the name is Resslova 1, in the part of town now called Nová ulice.

Ulmer was forgotten, rediscovered, and finally ended up a cult figure. He was and still is the nonconformist, non-classifiable filmmaker *par excellence*. He, the émigré director, represents the other History of the Cinema — not the history of powerful and canonized successes, but the counter-history of a minor and extremely agile cinema. In his text "Mediators," Gilles Deleuze, who unfortunately never mentioned Ulmer in his cinema books, seems to be talking about him at last: "A creator who isn't grabbed around the throat by a set of impossibilities is no creator. A creator's someone who creates their own impossibilities, and thereby creates possibilities.... All writers, all creators, are shadows" (133). All his life Ulmer straddled the shadowy line between art,

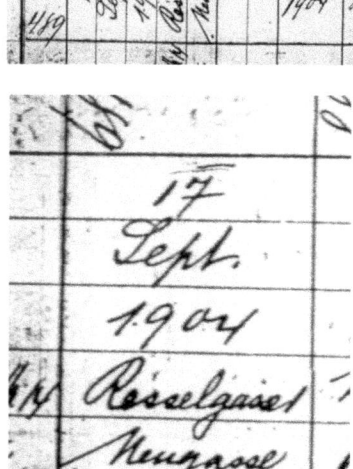

Ulmer's birth certificate with detail (above), enlarged (left)—showing birthdate and place as 17 Sept. 1904 Resselgasse 1[,] Neugasse (courtesy National Archives, Prague).

solid craftsmanship, and trash — a Ulysses of the cinema who was not destined to return home, but who, on his long voyage through various genres and film cultures, spanned the entire spectrum: cool modernity alongside lascivious speculation, cheap trash beside classic virtuosity. In Theodore Roszak's novel *Flicker*—which is about the life, art, and discovery of the fictitious filmmaker Max Castle, whose character is at least in part modeled on Ulmer, we read the following description of film: "[a] movie [is] a thin broth of illusion smeared across perishing plastic" (12). Ulmer's life and work was a dedication to that broth of illusion, he felt the irresistible urge to cook it according to ever new and yummy recipes of his own invention. And his daughter Arianné is devoted to keep that perishing plastic from doing exactly this.

The following essays will explore Ulmer's recipes for these broths of illusion. My own contribution analyses the interplay of cult and culture in Ulmer's oeuvre, the highly original mix of pulp cinema and high culture. As an independent filmmaker *avant la lettre*, with an influence on directors such as Peter Bogdanovich, François Truffaut, and others, Ulmer's films — always produced under high temporal pressure and on the limit of both financial and nervous breakdown — explore the oscillations between cult and culture, between the B-movies' cheap approach and his own European cultural background, merging low budget cinema with high art and culture.

It is these moments of broken economy that Stefan Grissemann focuses on in his essay. Ulmer's film work is characterized by this strange sense of economy: Made with breathtakingly meagre budgets by a free-lancing director who only temporarily even joined Hollywood's poverty row studios (but more often opted for complete creative liberty), those films openly document their desperate lack of material while trying to transform *deficiency* into *efficiency*. Even Ulmer's lesser films, frequently plodding in terms of narration and genre references, tend to feature remarkably transgressive images or scenes — moments out of time and taste, genuinely Ulmerian flashes of utter modernity and political intensity in spite of lacking means, bleak sets and hollow B-picture acting.

As one of the few remaining eyewitnesses of Ulmer's weird acuteness — aesthetically as well as ideologically — Ann Savage, star in his nightmarish masterpiece *Detour*, illustrates her director's quick, sometimes also improvisational way of working, his making do with only a week of shooting and ultra-low budgets, concentrating on a special cinematic toughness, on an unheard-of realism, thereby explicitly countering classical Hollywood's dominant beauty fetishism and studio stylisation: Fragments from an unpublished interview with Savage, conducted by Grissemann in 2001, highlight the author's analysis of Ulmer's unconventional methods and charismatic persona.

Ulmer's first film, shot in Germany, was the 1929 collaboration with Wilder, Siodmak, and Zinnemann, *Menschen am Sonntag (People on Sunday)*. This movie is widely known and accepted among film historians as an outstanding example of late German silent cinema, as well as it is famous for being an important early documentary. Petra Löffler's essay discusses these two different, sometimes even contradictory tendencies, which make the film an aesthetic hybrid of a very special kind, focusing on the historical conditions of the European Cinema as well as on Ulmer's connections to Hollywood at that time. For Ulmer's film, she argues, a concept of realism is important, which film historian Siegfried Kracauer has described as specifically cinematic. With this cinematic realism Ulmer was able to point out the shifts between working and leisure time which were typical for the Weimar Republic. Thus, the film shows how five ordinary people living in the German capital Berlin work and spend their leisure time on a lazy Sunday afternoon. To explore the rise of modern leisure culture and the role of modern mass media within this development, Löffler provides a historical framework by referring to Georg Simmel and Kracauer, and by focusing on Murnau's *Sunrise: A Song of two Humans* (1927) — a film on which Ulmer participated as an assistant of the set designer and art director Rochus Gliese. Löffler discusses the power and implicit self-reflexivity of Ulmer's film as a modern mass medium by comparing the medial capacities of film and photography. In her conclusion, she concentrates on important topics of the Weimar Republic that were left out by the film: the then-existing poverty of the lower working class and the inevitable rise of the fascist totalitarianism.

Marcel Arbeit's essay "Ulmer's Anti-Syphilis Film: *Damaged Lives* and Its Novelization" gives the complicated history of Ulmer's *Damaged Lives* (1933), the anti-syphilis dramatic movie for which he also wrote the screenplay with Donald Davis. The movie, commissioned and made under the auspices of the Canadian Social Hygiene Council, was supplemented with two screen lectures, delivered by Dr. Gordon Bates, the head of the Canadian Social Hygiene Council — one for men, and one for women. While in Canada and Great Britain the film was an immediate success, in the United States it was, immediately after its premiere in Boston on September 15, 1933, withdrawn by the Board of Censors.

Arbeit's essay describes the American approaches to venereal diseases and their treatment at the time when the movie was made, acknowledging it as a pioneering work, successful on both the educational and the artistic level. On the other hand, when the movie was finally released in June 1937, the cultural as well as social context was completely different: the crusade against VDs had reached a new, much more promising stage, and the topic ceased to be taboo and gradually infiltrated the sphere of art (Arnold Sundgaard's *Spirochete*). The four-year delay harmed Ulmer's film tremendously; still, it became a huge commercial success. Unfortunately, the American audience could not see the original version: the film was drastically cut. Also, the American Social Hygiene Council made Ulmer shoot a new documentary supplement, this time with the actor who played a VD specialist in the movie.

Arbeit discusses some of the scenes that were discarded, especially the crucial ones (the visit of Don, the young man who contracted syphilis, to an unqualified quack who took his money and gave him a wrong diagnosis; Don's strategies to protect his wife after he found out about his disease, etc.), and compares this abridged version (available now on DVD) with the original version, restored in the early 1990s by D.J. Turner, an archivist from the National Archives of Canada, and Robert Gitt of the UCLA Film and Television Archive.

Arbeit discusses the problem of the completeness of the movie with the help of C.J. Eustace's 1934 novelization of the film (*Damaged Lives: The Novel of the Film*), which has stayed unknown even among scholars and hard-boiled Ulmer fans. Eustace keeps Donald Davis's dialogues basically intact, which gives us a fair possibility to more than speculate about the missing scenes at the beginning of the movie (the archivists did not have the first and the last reels of the original eight-reel print).

The Black Cat, Hollywood's first historic union of Boris Karloff and Bela Lugosi, reigns today as Universal's most exquisitely twisted Golden Age horror film. It's a dark, hallowed and subversive masterpiece — one for which the film's director/adaptor/set and costume designer, Edgar G. Ulmer, performed professional penance for the rest of his life.

Based on primary research ranging from studio production records to interviews with the film's leading ladies to discussions with the Ulmer family, Gregory William Mank's essay tells the behind-the-scenes saga of this wildly daring film. The movie was Ulmer's virtual self-exorcism, surviving as one of the most vivid all-time examples of a Hollywood talent loose from his cage and running amok, personally and professionally. The chapter traces Ulmer's influences (both artistic and private ones) in crafting the film, his near-magical accomplishment on an absurdly small budget and mercilessly tight schedule, his sexual harassment of a starlet in the film that is rather a horror story in itself, and the exile he suffered in the wake of the film's shooting. Mank's essay details not only the perverse and nightmarish images of this milestone horror classic, but the brilliance and demons of Edgar G. Ulmer that haunt this remarkable film.

Ulmer directed four Yiddish language feature films in the New York area between 1937 and 1941. During this period, as Sharon Pucker Rivo's essay shows, his Jewish identity was greatly influenced by the intellectual Jewish milieu, his close acquaintances and neighbors, and his association with Yiddish actors and writers. Although he was a declared atheist, his background as a Jew from Vienna, his early childhood experiences, and his first-hand knowledge of the dangers of German antisemitism made him strongly identify as a secular Jew and heightened his awareness of the looming danger to Jews during this period.

The first Yiddish film, *Green Fields*, based on a play written by Peretz Hirschbein and adapted to the screen by Hirschbein and Ulmer, opens in a house of prayer with three traditional Jewish students heard chanting Hebrew prayers. This serious scene locates the film in the world of Eastern European Jewish orthodoxy. Ulmer's next two films, *Singing Blacksmith* and *The Light Ahead*, are based on classic Yiddish texts which reflect the same milieu of traditional Jewish life in the Pale of Settlement. Ulmer's final Yiddish feature film, *American Matchmaker*, set in an upper class New York neighborhood, focuses on characters who are assimilated, modern and Americanized. Interestingly, traditional Jewish values reappear to pave the way for happiness and a meaningful life for the leading character in this romantic comedy.

Ulmer's four Yiddish feature films have become classics in a genre where most of the directors were from the world of theatre with little experience in the world of cinema. The artistic value of Ulmer's films stand as a landmark. In addition, Ulmer's four Yiddish feature films demonstrate his knowledge of Jewish history and reflect his respect for Jewish practices and sensibilities even though he was an avowed atheist. Rivo's essay provides a brief overview of Ulmer's Jewish background and examines the content and individual scenes from the four Yiddish feature films to illuminate his Jewish values and beliefs.

Ulmer's Yiddish films were not his only contribution to the issue of ethnic cinema — his *Moon Over Harlem* (1939) stands out as the first film with an all black cast. In his essay, Frank Mehring analyzes Ulmer's visual and musical innovations of *Moon Over Harlem* through the lens of cultural hybridity and postcolonial fantasies. Thus, the shifting functions of African American culture on both sides of the Atlantic will become apparent. The imaginary constructions of the cultural other in the oeuvre of Bertolt Brecht and Edgar Ulmer emerge as representative examples. Particularly, jazz music served as a stimulus to fantasize about black Manhattan. African-American music and dances infused the paralyzed German cultural life after World War I with the vital power of modern American entertainment. Both artists worked closely with composers to fuse their dramatic visions with musical counterparts in their respective media, namely musical theatre and film. Brecht and his collaborator Kurt Weill created Germanized jazz songs like "Moon of Alabama" for the most revolutionary opera of the Weimar Republic, *Aufstieg und Fall der Stadt Mahagonny* (*Rise and Fall of the City of Mahagonny*, 1930). In the case of Ulmer, the collaboration with the African American composer Donald Heywood resulted in a unique film about black culture. Working outside the Hollywood system, he was able to avoid its deploring racial codifications. *Moon Over Harlem* is the first film with an all black cast by a white director about African American culture that denounced the racial stereotypes of coons, Uncle Toms, mammies, black bucks, and pickaninnies. Music offered a crucial means to subvert and resist racial representations in Hollywood. Thus, both opera and film function as means of subversion and resistance fuelled by German imaginations of the American cultural other.

In his essay "*Detour*'s History/History's Detour," Dana Polan examines the interpretative moves and rhetorical strategies by which most criticism of Edgar Ulmer has operated to render him as an auteur—some sort of special artist who transcends B-movie making's economic constraints to create supposed works of high art. Such criticism has recourse to a set of regular strategies: valorization of stylistic eccentricities as marks of intentional artistry, association of Ulmer with famous figures in the arts, thematic interpretation, and so on. The essay proposes that at the very least the auteurist discourse on Ulmer needs to be tempered by historical analysis of the production history of his films. Polan's essay looks at the production files for *Detour* (1945) at the Academy of Motion Picture Arts and Sciences as well as the original novel by Martin Goldsmith to outline the credits and contributions in the film's creation. The point is not to deny the historical interest of *Detour*—quite the contrary, the essay argues that the film is a prime example of the downbeat genre of film *gris*—but to argue that that historical interest and value have to be disentangled from a romantic discourse of auteurist genius.

Julia Meier's essay on *The Strange Woman* (1946) analyzes Ulmer's film from the perspective of the conceptual tool box of the French philosopher

Gilles Deleuze. Ulmer's melodrama *The Strange Woman* (1946) deals with the fast rise and fall of the main character, Jenny Hager (Hedy Lamarr), who is a beautiful, young woman. The setting of the film is Bangor, Maine, USA, a rising industrial city in the early 1820. Jenny derives from the underprivileged class in town, but she already knows as a little girl that she will find a way to escape poverty by means of her blossoming sexual power: "I'm going to be beautiful!" she promises to herself. As a young woman she quickly rises to the upper class by driving several men into death and despair.

In the film it becomes evident that all of Jenny's crucial actions seem to depart from elementary impulses rather than from contemplative intelligence. With reference to the works of Deleuze, Meier explores the impulsive dynamism of *The Strange Woman*, with special emphasis on the concept of the *impulse-image*. She argues that Ulmer does not depict the psychopathology of the main character and the moral ambivalence between good and evil, but rather captures and makes visible the energetic dynamism of primordial drives that manifest themselves in crucial situations within the real world.

Another movie where the interplay between impulses and intelligence is a predominant issue is Ulmer's *Ruthless* (1948). Written by Gordon Kahn, who was one of the Hollywood Nineteen in 1947 and was blacklisted in 1951, *Ruthless* is a denunciation of an economic system which enables bankers and speculators to grow rich by showing no concern for the community. Apparently, the title refers to the central character, Vendig, but in reality a close friend and assorted bankers and investors are also implicitly condemned by the film.

As Reynold Humphries shows, what the script and Ulmer's particularly astute and imaginative direction succeed in doing is simultaneously to highlight the pathology of Vendig's character in Freudian terms and to encourage the spectators to interpret this pathology as socially and economically overdetermined. *Ruthless* achieves this by presenting Vendig's obsession with success at any price as a value instilled in him by his father (a pathetic failure) and by showing how the father of his childhood sweetheart, Martha, makes a social and economic investment: paying for Vendig's education in exchange for a promise to marry his daughter, whom Vendig has saved from drowning. Vendig follows this financial logic to its conclusion, on the one hand by ditching those who gave him a start in life and business in favor of more influential people, on the other hand by transforming women into commodities to be exchanged on the market for ever-increasing power and wealth. At every turn, therefore, he is presented as carrying on a long tradition which he always takes literally (never let anyone stand in your way). Ulmer's use of close-ups, framing and point-of-view shots skillfully place the spectators in relation to the characters and enhance their knowledge of the latter and their motives. In particular, the director's highly unusual use of the flashback eliminates the notion of a character who narrates in favor of a discourse which gradually but implacably deconstructs the individual and the attendant ideology of individualism. At the same time the script puts in Vendig's mouth expressions that don't quite sound right but which translate the true nature of his desire.

According to Matthew Sweney, *The Man from Planet X* (1951) is not only one of Edgar Ulmer's best films, it is also a classic of science fiction, due primarily to the art design and its refusal to have a pat ending. Nor does it have a standard villain — instead, the film portrays the alien as the Other, but also as a Man. Primitive attempts at communication lead to tragic consequences. Yet the question remains — How to read the Other? It is a question which has no answer, and it is this question that the audience is left with, rather than a final kiss. Sweney's examines analyzes the film's plot, as well as the visual structure of the film, and provides background information as to the film's purported locale, the Orkney island Burray. Sweney's analysis helps to elucidate some of the complexities inherent in its choice which bolster the film's plot. The film is heavy on atmosphere — so heavy, it is a topic of discussion in the film. The film has seemingly no precedents, though there are some aspects it shares with Ulmer's own *The Black Cat*.

Herbert Schwaab's essay deals with questions of camp and the art film in Ulmer's *Babes in Bagdad* (1952). Trained in European high culture of the 1920s, Ulmer was never able to reconcile his artistic ambitions and his work for film, leaving behind an output of films ranging from minor classics of film noir to exploitation movies. Schwaab's analysis is based on the notion that film art itself is at times as ambivalent as Ulmer's cinema, which the following example may indicate. In his famous book *Film as Subversive Art*, Amos Vogel constantly crosses the line between popular, underground and art cinema. Film critic J. Hoberman defines the concept of vulgar modernism in one of his essays, which he uses for a progressive art form operating within popular culture, epitomized in films such as the highly self-reflexive comedy *Hellzapoppin* (1941). Joan Hawkins refers to the close relation between the highest and the lowest ranks of film culture. The masterpieces of European art cinema are put together with exploitation films and B-movies in mail order catalogues for connoisseurs of trash cinema: Godard's *Weekend* and similar films find themselves on the same pages as *The Werewolf and the Yeti* or *Zontar, the Thing from Venus*. This blurring of boundaries between high and low shows the ambivalence of avant-garde art. Ulmer himself proves this ambivalence in an interview from the early 1960s, as he reproaches Godard and the nouvelle vague for the use of shocking and disgusting images: "It's just like in a horror movie!" But Ulmer himself, operating mostly at the margins of and not within classical Hollywood cinema, very often had to use the same effects in his films. The extreme sadism of *The Black Cat* could hardly be equaled by the films of the nouvelle vague. Does that mean that neither Ulmer nor Godard deserve to be called true artists? Based on the concept of camp, which found its best known definition in the essay "Notes on Camp" by Susan Sontag, Schwaab's essay refers to the natural ambiguity of popular texts, turning them into ideal objects for subversive reading strategies. Users of camp, excluded from the common grounds of high culture, attribute meaning and complexity to specific texts. The excessiveness of style and acting, the exotism and artificiality of its settings, lend campy films not only ambiguity but an air of defamiliarization as well. Campiness in films can be read along the lines of a Brechtian or formalist and therefore modernist aesthetics.

Moments of campiness can be found in many of Ulmer's films, such as in the acting of *The Black Cat,* the melodramatic setting of *Strange Illusion* and *Strange Woman,* the exotism of *Isle of Forgotten Sins,* and in the genre-transgressions of *L'Atlantide.* According to Schwaab, these films gain their complexity from their campiness, and Ulmer becomes campy because he is too ambitious. Schwaab mainly focuses on the exotist *Babes in Bagdad,* one of the lesser known and least acknowledged films in Ulmer's work. As there are no valid criteria for intended progressive, modernist and subversive art, and because art works best whenever it becomes the unintended by-product of the artist's ambitions and excessive want of communication, even a film such as *Babes in Bagdad* can be turned into a rewarding and sustainable experience for both, cinephilia and theory. The campiness of Ulmer's films not only allows for reading against the grain of a common held culture or offers alternative texts for subordinated reading formations, but challenges our concepts of film art. Blurring the boundaries between the high and the low, Ulmer becomes the object of incessant fascination for lovers and scholars of film.

Schwaab's use of the term "camp" resonates with Ekkehard Knörer's idea of what he calls the "not-quite" movie. In his essay, Knörer focuses on Ulmer's *Murder Is My Beat* (1955) and *Daughter of Dr. Jekyll* (1957). Knörer sketches the collaborative contexts of these films, written by notorious campsters Aubrey Wisberg and Jack Pollexfen and shows how Ulmer's films do not, however, really fit into the context of pure camp or bland genre exercises suggested by his collaborators' careers. Placing the two films in the two genres they usually are supposed to belong to, i.e. noir and horror, and attempting to unfold the logic of repetition and variation implied in the idea of genre can yet again not really explain what makes these two Ulmer films special. The question Knörer tries to answer, then, is as specific as it is general. Specific insofar as he asks: What are my moments of pleasure in these two films by director Edgar G. Ulmer, films that certainly are no masterpieces? And general insofar as he tries to explain these pleasures as the pleasures that only a certain, but certainly not unique kind of movie can offer. These are strangely discontinuous movies that never really add up to unified wholes; movies in which quite a few sequences seem to come out of nowhere; movies in which there certainly is something like a continuous narrative, but it seems of little consequence, as it is disrupted by more or less blatant non sequiturs. Or perhaps one should rather say "not-quite-sequiturs." This, Knörer argues, might even be a perfect term for this kind of film: the "not-quite" movies; movies that do not quite fit into a generic field, movies that do not quite make sense, movies that are to be taken not quite seriously, but are not quite ridiculous either. Knörer's pleasure with these two Ulmer movies then is something like the pleasure of the "not-quite," the pleasure of the intriguing imperfection. There is, according to Knörer, something more general to learn from that experience. What makes virtual worlds feel real for us is that we know about our investment, but that we don't realize that we do. The very personal moments of pleasure in certain sequences of *Murder Is My Beat* and *Daughter of Dr. Jekyll* are moments exactly of the realization of this knowledge. It is a very gentle realization, though. The films — in contrast to all kinds of avant-garde works — quite obviously do not want to produce this realization. They want to hold together but are, against their intentions, falling apart. The spectator thus finds herself in two places at the same time, inside and outside, and her pleasure seems to derive from this strangely mixed experience.

It is exactly this strangely mixed experience that Stefanie Diekmann's "Product of Circumstances" critically explores in relation to three closely linked topics that seem to be central to understanding of what is interesting about Ulmer's work.

The three topics are those of authorship, signature, and that of the body of work. Authorship in Ulmer — or simply: Ulmer's authorship — presents itself as a rather difficult issue. While Ulmer, in his interview with Peter Bogdanovich, claims credit for many famous films made in Weimar Germany and in 1920s Hollywood, these claims are largely unsupported. Moreover, in his Hollywood period and also during his time in New York, co-operation played an important part in Ulmer's work as a filmmaker and it is yet to be established how much of the style or atmosphere of his films should be attributed to the work of artists like Eugen Schüfftan (light, camera) or Leo Erdody (composer) with whom he collaborated on a number of films. Attempts to cast Ulmer as a typical Hollywood *auteur* should be treated with reserve because they tend to underplay the formative influence of the constraints and difficult circumstances that were part of nearly all of his projects.

The essay's title "Products of Circumstances" refers to the observation that this may be a case where circumstances actually acquire authorial force. Therefore, for Diekmann, signature in Ulmer appears not just as the recognizable signature of one filmmaker-*auteur* but also as the visible mark(s) left on a film by his co-operators, by such constraints as tight schedules, very low budgets and makeshift settings, and, last but not least, as the — less visible but still present — marks of the very different agendas that came together or clashed or both in the making of an Ulmer picture. To a certain extent, this makes Ulmer's films exemplary (film being the collaborative, commercial business it is) but some of them, especially the ethnic pictures, are quite exceptional with regard to forces and actors they brought together.

The concept of the body of work is interesting insofar as two very different tendencies in the treatment of Ulmer's work can be observed. One is the tendency that works towards completion (the rediscovery of Ulmer was largely a matter of recovery and restoration of his films); the other is the tendency that works towards fragmentation, focusing on a very limited number of very short clips to explain the merits of Ulmer a filmmaker. Again, the tension between these tendencies is, to a certain extent, exemplary for film studies; but in the case of Ulmer it meets with a set of curiously pre-fragmented and disconnected pictures.

The Naked Dawn (1955) led to Ulmer's recognition in Europe when it premiered at the Venice Film Festival, but its production remains shrouded in mystery. As Bill Krohn shows, the study of production documents at the Universal Archives, University of Southern California, and the history of the script, written by blacklisted screenwriter Robert Zimet, permits us to isolate the contribution of the director to the film, using the concept of *mise-en-scène* as interpretation. Zimet's interpretation of his source, Maxim Gorki's early short story "Chelshak," is erased and replaced by the director's interpretation of the structure of the story as transmitted to him by the screenplay alone. Formal choices (particularly in the kitchen and cantina scenes), the treatment of the Betta St. John character and Ulmer's anxious relationship to the influence of his master, F.W. Murnau, all contribute to the creation of a work of film art that reads Zimet, Gorki and Murnau: readings, as Krohn shows, that are the film.

Michal Peprník's examination of *Daughter of Dr. Jekyll* (1957) deals with the questions of home and displacement in Ulmer's work. Ulmer has managed to mystify film scholars as regards his place of birth. Although his birth home has finally been located, the consequences on Ulmer's film art still deserve a close examination. Peprník discusses this act of public mystification here as an act of displacement, which has had an impact on the choice of Ulmer's scripts and his personal approach and style. The concept of displacement is approached from the point of view of another famous personality, born in Moravia, the Eastern part of the Czech Republic, Sigmund Freud. Peprník's essay focuses on the defamiliarization of home into a haunted place in *Daughter of Dr. Jekyll*, a retake of R. L. Stevenson's novella *The Strange Case of Dr. Jekyll and Mr. Hyde* (1886). The recurrence of this motif is taken as an evidence that Ulmer himself became haunted by this archaic memory of his home in Olomouc, a place which he in a public gesture erased (though privately acknowledged), and used such motifs as pretext for exorcising the old spirits (ghosts) of the place.

The strategy of defamiliarization of the main heroine's home includes a surprisingly high degree of uncanny elements, such as we find in Freud's essay on "The Uncanny." Peprník argues with Freud that the effect of the uncanny stems from the suppression of a familiar, archaic content and takes the form of recursive patterns, and ontological ambivalence. These forms were also found in Ulmer's film: fearful repetitions, which deprive the subject of the control over one's own mind and body, springing from the archaic fears of and desires for an omnipotence of thoughts, and a clever manipulation of ontological ambivalence.

This ontological ambivalence might be put to a stop in Ulmer's nudist film *The Naked Venus* (1958), because here, as Petra Hanáková argues, "What you see is what you get!" ... but is it? Hanáková approaches Ulmer's *The Naked Venus* as representative of a genre in which the body, its social meanings and control become the site for negotiation and performance of the politics of the visual. The nudist film is torn within a paradoxical conflict between what is being *said* about its images and what is actually *shown* and offered for specific purposes; these two levels interact and struggle with each other. The genre of the nudist film is here read as a flawed palimpsest, in which the process of scraping away the original images is not fully achieved and far from fully overwritten by the text of the film's communicated message. *The Naked Venus* goes in some respects beyond its genre — rewriting the exploitation film as a moral tale and an implicit critique of the perverse nature of a certain type of American family. The director recasts the nudist genre as a legal drama, significantly personalizes the central nudist protagonist, and in the end, puts on trial the perverse gaze of the hypocritical American family and its misuse of the legal system. Here, the stark contrast between images and their status as evidence is laid out and presented as the main theme of the film. Furthermore, nudism here is not the initiator of the main conflict, but merely a side effect and an "aggravation" for the main character. More than a nudist film, *The Naked Venus* is yet another representative of an ambiguous morality play so typical for Ulmer's oeuvre. While the right to freedom is in the nudist films very often connected to the vision of the American dream, for Ulmer, this freedom is illusory, and the space of the American family is as terrifying as the places of his horror films. We may read *The Naked Venus* as Ulmer's commentary on the genre itself, exposing the paradox inherent in the overt message of the films.

In his essay on Ulmer's last film, Philipp Hofmann utilizes the geophilosophical approach of Gilles Deleuze and Félix Guattari as developed in their book *A Thousand Plateaus* for a reading of *The Cavern* (1964) in which, through the violent forces of the Second World War, a fundamental structural and spatial change takes place for the protagonists, who are caught in a cave whose entrance/exit has collapsed. To survive, the heterogeneous group of people has to re-organize its social structure: the members (divided by class, nationality, gender, social as well as military rank) have to adapt to the geological givens of the cave. In the final chapter of *A Thousand Plateaus*, Deleuze and Guattari describe two philosophical key concepts which they express in the geological terms "striated" and "smooth" space. These two kinds of spaces can be mapped onto Ulmer's film: much of the film's dynamics is grounded on the tension between the smooth and the striated and in the resulting force-field that the protagonists find themselves in. In *The Cavern* the characters have to find new modes of being in space and for space, they are pushed past a crisis threshold and exposed to intensities that have the force to crack them up, to completely de-organize the subject. "The State war machine," as part of which they have entered the cave, is becoming destratified, leading to deterritorializations, new couplings and unlikely friendships among and beyond nationalities and political parties.

The last word of this anthology is with Adrian Martin. His essay "Ulmer in the Aquarium" questions some of the ways in which viewers are likely to automatically approach and view the films of Edgar G. Ulmer. To begin with, Martin looks at what could called the "big but," or the equivocation reflex that filters into many writings on this director, even some of the most fannish or appreciative: the tendency to say that his films are good (even great) but, implicitly, they could have been much better if only they had professional actors, tighter scripts, better resources, and so on. In this view, Ulmer is seen as the brave *maudit* artist who constantly triumphed over adversity, over impossible circumstances and budgets, bringing merely his special touch to otherwise insignificant assignments. Martin goes on to argue that the criticism of Ulmer must liberate itself from such thinking, but that this is no easy matter. Hence, a prologomena to a proper study of Ulmer is required, in which matters of aesthetic-cultural taste and judgment are severely questioned, even replaced by a new, different kind of aesthetics. To this end, the type of normative criticism which underlies much work on Ulmer is discussed at some length. Normative criticism rests upon — often quite unconsciously — very constricted and restrictive, even repressive, standards of excellence in art and culture: the well-made film, the well-told story, three-dimensional psychological characterization and the realistic acting codes necessary to express this. The first part of Martin's essay concludes with a positive example of Ulmerian critique: the writing of French critic Jacques Lourcelles in his *Dictionnaire des films*, who finds in the example of Ulmer's film *Club Havana* (1945) an instance of Ulmer's cosmic viewpoint upon humanity.

The second section of Martin's essay considers Ulmer within the context of B cinema. Again, it is a matter of considering B cinema in itself as the site or realm of a new, very different aesthetic — not to judge it, explicitly or implicitly, as the poor brother of proper A cinema. In this light, two critics who are Ulmer specialists are considered: the American Bill Krohn and the Australian William Routt. For Krohn, carrying over ideas of the advanced film theory of the '70s from the avant-garde into the B realm, Ulmer's films are the example of a practice of heterogeneity. For Routt, B cinema poses the possibility of a flat, neutral, literal cinema that questions our received notions of artistic expressivity in cinema, as well as our tendency to neat moral interpretations. This section concludes with a consideration of a certain kind of exciting non-psychology typical of Ulmer's films.

The last section takes up one particular cinematic figure in Ulmer: that of the aquarium shot, the type of image in which the director crams as many human figures as possible, and holds such a frame even as the actors and the

The city of Olomouc honored director Edgar G. Ulmer with a plaque on the house in which he was born. The artist is Bohumil Teplý.

camera are in movement. The theory of Alain Bergala concerning the aquarium aesthetic in cinema is canvassed. Then the question is posed: what are we to make of Ulmer's remarkable penchant for aquarium shots? Is it a motif to be interpreted, a key to be deciphered, a spectacle to enjoy, a signature to be prized? Ultimately, it is a question of auteurist method as it might be applied to Ulmer, and here, too, a reconsideration of the standard procedures is required. Finally, Ulmer's auteur vision as expressed in the aquarium shot might best be understood as a matter of artistic will, in a strong and powerful philosophic sense.

Ulmer's work thus still has the power to fascinate, to invite admiration and critical reception. It is the hope of this editor and his contributors that Ulmer's work will continue to do so.

One evidence of the combination of past, present in future is the fact that Ulmer, finally, has come home. In 2006, on occasion of the *ulmerfest*, the city of Olomouc commemorated her native son with a memorial plaque — the King has returned at last!

Notes

1. For the biography of Ulmer, I have relied on the meticulously researched book by Stefan Grissemann.
2. For info about the ulmerfest 2006, see www.uni-koeln.de/phil-fak/englisch/abteilungen/berressem/herzogenrath/ulmer/index.htm, last accessed April 4, 2008.

Works Cited

Bogdanovich, Peter. "Edgar G. Ulmer." *Who the Devil Made It: Conversations with Legendary Film Directors*. New York: Ballantine, 1998, 558–604.
Cameron, Ian, and Elisabeth Cameron. *Dames*. New York: Praeger, 1969. qtd. in "Detour." Danny Peary. *Cult Movies. The Classics, the Sleepers, the Weird and the Wonderful*. New York: Gramercy, 1981, 68–70, 68.
Deleuze, Gilles. "Mediators." *Negotiations. 1972–1990*. New York: Columbia University Press, 1995, 121–34.
Grissemann, Stefan. *Mann im Schatten. Der Filmemacher Edgar G. Ulmer*. Wien: Paul Zsolnay Verlag, 2003.
Knipfel, Jim. "Fate Stuck Out Its Foot: The Struggles of Edgar G. Ulmer." The *New York Press*, 1998, *www.missioncreep.com/slackjaw/1998/ulmer.html*
McCarthy, Todd, and Charles Flynn, editors. *Kings of the Bs: Working Within the Hollywood System: An Anthology of Film History and Criticism*. New York: E.P. Dutton, 1975.
Roszak, Theodore. *Flicker. A Novel*. New York: Summit, 1991.
Sarris, Andrew. *The American Cinema: Directors and Directions, 1929–1968*. Chicago: University of Chicago Press, 1985.
Wood, Bret. "Edgar G. Ulmer: Visions from the Second Kingdom." *Video Watchdog* 41 (1997): 23–31.

Ulmer and Cult/ure
BERND HERZOGENRATH

In one of the most famous scenes of John Ford's *The Man Who Shot Liberty Valance*, a newspaper editor and journalist, Maxwell Scott, utters the memorable line: "This is the West, sir. When the legend becomes fact, print the legend." In the movie, this line and attitude guarantees that the legend Tom Doniphon, played by John Wayne, is in fact the Man Who Shot Liberty Valance — even though he might not be. This line could also serve as a motto for John Ford, the director, who secured himself a place in the Pantheon of America's Greatest Mythmakers with his Westerns. This line — "When the legend becomes fact, print the legend" — is also a perfect epitaph for one of the most prolific [and, for that matter, in inverse proportion] most forgotten filmmakers of the twentieth century, and if a legend, printed or otherwise, is the founding stone for a cult, than we definitely have a cult-figure here. We are speaking of Edgar G. Ulmer.

The first film to discuss is Ulmer's second real American feature film — not counting the Westerns he had shot as an assistant director. After *Damaged Lives* — a film about venereal disease, released in 1933, Ulmer directed *The Black Cat* for Universal Pictures in 1934. It is with this movie the discussion starts about cult/ure — that is, the connection between cult in its basic sense, and culture. Ulmer was a very cultured man, proud of his education and knowledge of European high culture, and it is in fact the inoculation of that high culture into his B-movies that turns these films into something else, staging strange dissonances between European high culture and American trash cinema. For instance, Ulmer based his film plots on Shakespeare's *Hamlet* (in *Strange Illusions*), or used lots of classical music, such as Brahms and Beethoven, for his film scores — in his film *Carnegie Hall* (1947), he even attempted to create a monument for classical music, and a bow to "some of the world's greatest artists of that time," as the opening credits declare, artists such as Jascha Heifetz, Arthur Rubinstein, Fritz Reiner and Leopold Stokowski. In his biography of Ulmer, *Mann im Schatten* (*Man in the Shadows*),

Stefan Grissemann writes that Ulmer was "a philosopher out of curiosity. Fascinated by Calvin, Hegel, Luther, by Greek Mythology, by Thomas Mann, Schiller and Goethe, Molière, painting, ballet and architecture and — most of all — by Classical Music" (Grissemann 95, my translation). And J. Hoberman concedes, "[f]ar from artless, Ulmer was, if anything, too arty. He created 'atmosphere' with a vengeance. Moreover, Ulmer had *kultur*" (Hoberman) — Ulmer, it seems, is himself situated at the cusp between cult and culture.

So, how to define culture, and how to define cult? The word *culture* is etymologically derived from the Latin words *colere* and *cultus*, meaning to inhabit, to cultivate, and to worship. Thus, *culture* relates to specific *human* activities. In 1871, Sir Edward Burnett Taylor, the British anthropologist, proposed the following definition of culture: "culture or civilization, taken in its wide ethnographic sense, is that complex whole which includes knowledge, belief, art, morals, law, custom, and any other capabilities and habits acquired by man as a member of society" (Taylor I: 1). In general terms, culture is thus equated with civilization — a concept that developed in Europe through the eighteenth and nineteenth century, pointing at differences between the European powers — the Old World — and the colonies at the margins of the Empires. According to this thinking, one can classify some countries as more civilized than others, and some people as more cultured than others. Thus some cultural theorists have actually tried to eliminate popular or mass culture from the definition of culture. Matthew Arnold, e.g., saw culture as simply as "pursuit of our total perfection by means of getting to know, on all the matters which most concern us, the best which has been thought and said in the world" (Arnold 6), and labeled all that did not fit into his category as anarchy and chaos. Culture thus is intimately linked to social cultivation and the progress and refinement of human behavior. In practice, then, culture refers to high goods and activities such as *haute couture* and equally *haute cuisine*, art sanctified by being put into a museum, classical literature and music, etc., and the word cultured is a tag for people who are in the know. Using "culture" in this way represses the use of this word in its plural form —"cultures." In this definition, distinct cultures do not exist, there is only a single standard of refinement suffices, against which one can measure all groups — people with different customs from those who regard themselves as cultured do not usually count as "having a different culture," but class as "uncultured," or sometimes as "more natural" ... sounds positive, but works according to the same exclusionary logic.

This ambivalent stance towards nature from within a civilization and a cultural system has been at the heart of Sigmund Freud's analysis of dichotomy of nature and culture. Freud, who also was born in Freiberg (now Příbor),

Moravia, not far away from Olomouc, observed that nature and instinct had been and must be forever subordinated in order that civilization might thrive and endure which is commonly known as civilization thesis. In his late texts *The Future of an Illusion* (1927) and *Civilization and Its Discontents* (1929), Freud elaborated an understanding of the functional character of culture. In *The Future of an Illusion*, he stated that "the principal task of civilization, its actual *raison d'être*, is to defend us against nature" (*Illusion* 194). In the same way that Freud "scorn[s] to distinguish between culture and civilization" (*Illusion* 184), nature can be read as both animals, flora and fauna and instincts. In addition to the view of culture as function, Freud explicitly acknowledges a master-slave mechanics at work, in which culture is imposed on the individual: since "every individual is virtually an enemy of civilization ... one gets ... an impression that civilization is something which was imposed on a resisting majority by a minority which understood how to obtain possession of the means to power and coercion" (*Illusion* 184–5). Since "every civilization rests upon a compulsion to work and a renunciation of instinct" (*Illusion* 189), these restrictions are responsible for the ineradicable frustrations and hostility against the cultural Law. The resulting sense of guilt is seen by Freud as "the most important problem in the development of civilization ... the price we have to pay for our advance in civilization is a loss of happiness through the heightening sense of guilt" (*Discontents* 327). The progress of culture and civilization is thus reciprocal to the repression and erasure of instincts and nature.

The antagonism between nature and culture as Freud analyzed it in *Discontents* has usually been interpreted following the suggested model of a "simple" inside/outside opposition: either nature is the incarcerated inside, oppressed by cultural laws and restraints, or culture is the closed community of reason in danger to be overswept by an alien, destructive outside. So, in the final analysis,

> civilization is a process ... whose purpose is to combine single individuals, and after that families, then races, peoples and nations, into one great unity, the unity of mankind.... These collections of men are to be libidinally bound to one another. Necessity alone, the advantages of work in common, will not hold them together. But man's natural aggressive instinct, the hostility of each against all and of all against each, opposes this programme of civilization.... And now, I think, the meaning of the evolution of civilization is no longer obscure to us. It must present the struggle ... between the instinct of life and the instinct of destruction, as it works itself out in the human species.... [T]he evolution of civilization may therefore simply be described as the struggle for life of the human species [*Discontents* 313–4].

In an earlier attempt to explain the origin of culture, to narrate the primal scene of the development of civilization and society as such, Freud employed a somewhat different approach with regard to the nature/culture dichotomy.

In his 1913 text *Totem and Taboo*, Freud, following Darwin, relates the beginnings of culture and civilization to a primal horde. Though basically a kind of mythical narrative, to be sure, the myth of the beginning of all myths, Freud himself describes this method of the origin of exogamy and thus of the foundations of a society as historical. Freud follows this hypothesis through other writings such as *Group Psychology and the Analysis of the Ego* (1921) and *Moses and Monotheism: Three Essays* (1934–9). In this later text, in which Freud applies his theory of the primal horde to a (sacred) text, he goes from the assumption that such a text does not represent historical truth, but that such a text in fact bears the trace of its very repression. Freud supposes a primal patriarch, a "violent and jealous father who keeps all the females for himself and drives away his sons as they grow up" (*Totem and Taboo* 202). This father, completely free and independent, was "the 'superman' whom Nietzsche only expected from the future" (*Group Psychology* 156). His libido without limits whatsoever, this primal father may occupy the nature/instinct position in the later dichotomy. Society and culture begin with the act of "killing ... the chief by violence and the transformation of the paternal horde into a community of brothers" (*Totem and Taboo* 154). This cultic sacrifice can thus be seen as the prototype of the cruelty at the heart of every civilization, of the in-/un-human event that has to be repressed. Since the group of brothers had not only feared, but also loved and respected their father, a "sense of guilt made its appearance.... The dead father became stronger than the living one had been.... What had up to then been prevented by his actual existence was thenceforward prohibited by the sons themselves" (*Totem and Taboo* 204–5). Thus, the killing of the father and the following remorse over this outburst of primitive, libidinal energy instigated the laws and restrictions of culture. Nature and the primitivism of a pre-cultural state become a necessary component of culture itself, not its counterpart. The antagonism is here seen not so much as a result of a progressing over-culturation and thus repression, but as the very foundation of culture. But, the very condition of a culture's common origin somehow seems to be the erasure of that origin as real.

Another paradox arises, logical and temporal: before the law, there had been no consciousness of guilt. How then can this feeling of guilt have been the cause of the foundation of that very law, and the killing of the father have been the cause for remorse? It is here that a curious temporal structure arises that seems to be at the heart of all attempts to tell the origin: any linear narration from its beginning necessarily has to posit the point of origin, has to present it as chronologically earlier, although with respect to its representation, it is later and has to be constructed, since it is exactly the missing of the origin that makes any attempt of reconstruction necessary and possible in the first place. Any distinction between before and after belongs to the symbolic and thus cultural register, that is, already to the after of nature and origin. The spatial inside/outside opposition is thus revealed to be ultimately based on a temporal paradox: the origin of a given culture can only be invented in retrospect, is a belated effect of that very culture which is said to be founded on it.[1] And it is here that the notion of "cult" neatly fits in. Deriving from the same etymological root — the Latin *cultus* — it reveals its close proximity with culture and the religious connotation and function at the heart of that concept. *Cultus* — cult and culture — originally is the whole of religious practices and rites, literally the care and worship owed to the Gods and the shrines. However, with the overriding system of monotheism that Freud equates with civilization — in particular: Christianity — the word cult became distinguished from culture and was assigned a pejorative meaning. Two definitions of cult from Merriam-Webster seem particularly relevant for this Colloquium — a) "a religion regarded as unorthodox or spurious," and b) "great devotion to a person, idea, object, movement, or work (as a film or book); especially: such devotion regarded as a literary or intellectual fad; a usually small group of people characterized by such devotion." Since basically any religion based on worship could classify as a cult, it is basically the question of who has the authority to classify something as orthodox religion or culture on the one hand, and as unorthodox and spurious cult on the other hand — here we have again the belated effect that Freud pointed out — only the fact that one cult poses as culture assigns to the other the pejorative cult-status ... which then, in turn, can be claimed as a badge of honor almost. And here the religious and secular notions of cult collide: a cult in the secular realm — in a time when Art has become the substitute for Religion — is exactly such a "great devotion to a person, idea, object, movement, or work (as a film or book)," but as something proudly "unorthodox or spurious." And even if I do not want to equate Freud's nature — drives and the libido — with cult, I think one might venture to say that a cult following not only thrives on that libidinous love to an almost fetish-object (film, book, etc.), but is also attached to objects (films, books, etc.) that display an amount of energy, libidinousness, of *intensity* that characterizes it as unorthodox in that it is too energetic for cultured culture (which is based on repression) — exactly Matthew Arnold's chaos and anarchy. With that in mind, let us turn to Ulmer's film *The Black Cat*.

At first sight, *The Black Cat* seems to be the typical Universal Horror movie, in the vain of Tod Browning's *Dracula* (1931) or James Whale's *Frankenstein* (1931), not the least because of the performances of Boris Karloff and Bela Lugosi, the first of seven monstrous collaborations. True as it may be on one level, there's more to it. Limited by the genre-restrictions of the Hollywood B movie, Ulmer nevertheless managed to produce a personal work of art, an underground avant-garde film. Considered individually, the seemingly dissonant elements Ulmer brought together seem as if they couldn't possibly make sense in one film. The plot, dream-like and inconsistent, is secondary to atmosphere and overall effect. As Raúl Ruiz has noted in his *Poetics of Cinema*, films such as *The Black Cat* break up into "a series of situations, each with a life of its own" (Ruiz 85). Yet, in spite of the disturbance of the linear mind that *The Black Cat* presents, it comes together with surreal harmony, makes sense emotionally. A student of Murnau's, almost on a par with his master in his accentuation of visual design touches and his use of *chiaroscuro*, the play of light and shadow, Ulmer could convince Universal chief "Junior" Laemmle to give him "free rein to write a horror picture in the style we had started in Europe with *Caligari*" (Bogdanovich 575). Laemmle agreed on that experiment and allowed Ulmer an unusual amount of creative control over the project — on the condition that the movie be titled *The Black Cat*, after the Poe tale, for "commercial reasons" (Bogdanovich 576).

Honeymooning in Hungary, on their way to Visegrád, American crime fiction writer Peter Alison and his wife Joan share their train compartment with the psychologist Dr. Vitus Verdegast, a courtly but tragic man who is returning to the remains of the town he defended before becoming a prisoner of war for fifteen years. [A brief aside — Peter and Joan Alison were the role models for Brad and Janet in *The Rocky Horror Picture Show*, another cult classic.] When their hotel-bound bus crashes in a mountain storm and Joan is injured, the travelers seek refuge with Werdegast's old friend Hjalmar Poelzig in the ultra-modern and fortress-like house the architect Poelzig has built over the site of a World War I battlefield massacre in the Carpathians.

As a former commander, Poelzig had escaped the former Fort Marmoros and abandoned his troops. As Werdegast spits out, "You sold Marmoros to the Russians. You scurried away in the night and left us to die." As Poelzig and Werdegast engage in a battle of minds, Werdegast discovers that Poelzig not only has Werdegast's late wife's dead body preserved in the house but has also married Werdegast's daughter. Poelzig and Werdegast now engage in a game of chess for the soul of Joan, whom Poelzig wants to sacrifice in a Satanist ceremony. Poelzig thus is the High Priest of a Satanic Cult. (We actually see the architect with the book *The Rites of Lucifer* for bedside reading). On a striking Expressionist set, Poelzig leads a stylized Black Mass. The first group Satanic ritual ever seen on the screen, this scene would have an enduring influence, eventually becoming a staple of almost every movie concerning black magic — see e.g. Kubrick's *Eyes Wide Shut* (1999). With his usual sense of humor, Karloff improvised the impressive sounding Satanic invocation he intones, by stringing together a few phrases from his college Latin. Consequently,

Poelzig's Satanic litany includes calendar mottos such as *Cum grano salis* (with a grain of salt)—one almost waits for *In vino veritas* (in wine there is truth).

Werdegast manages to rescue Joan Alison, the intended sacrifice, to get hold of Poelzig, and finally blows up the whole mansion.

Now, the clash (and complication) of cult and culture becomes evident on various levels. First of all, the movie merges a distinctly European sensibility (of high culture) and aesthetics (see the wonderful detached camera tracking shot that prefigures Resnais' *L'Année Dernière à Marienbad* [1961]) with a highly sensationalistic narrative (the Hollywood B-picture). Not only the location (Hungary, the Carpathians) and the broad and highly distinct accents of the two main actors make the film sound European (Karloff's and Lugosi's voices are almost arranged like instruments in an orchestra—in addition, the music underlies literally *all* of the movie ... this picture makes a deep bow to the tradition of the silent movie). No—the film score blasts "European High Culture" into your face—variations on themes of Tschaikowsky, Chopin, Liszt, and the ominous tones of both Schubert's *Unfinished Symphony* and Bach's *Toccata and Fugue in D minor* add music and commentary to a narrative of which presented "a veritable catalogue of human corruption. Sadism, shades of incest, revenge, murder, torture, voyeurism, Satan worship" (Brunas/Brunas/Weaver 78)—a punch in the priggish faces of the Apostles of the Moral Standards, the Guardians of the Hays Code that called for films only that "will affect lives for the better." As Noah Isenberg points out, the struggle between cult and culture—personified in Poelzig and Werdegast, can be read "as an instance of the émigré director engaging the cultural fears and fantasies of his new country yet captivating his audience by drawing on aesthetic conventions of the old" (Isenberg 9)—e.g. classical music, or the highly artificial Bauhaus set.

Yet, things are even more complex. Poelzig, the cultist, appears as a highly cultivated man. In fact, the constructivist design of his house, and his Zen-like wardrobe, the pure geometrical patterns that are everywhere in his house, not only parallel the geometry of the Satanic Church, with its cross:[2] the whole over-cultured ambience reads like a translation of rituality—in this case: cultist rituals—into space and architecture. Culture is a continuation of the cult with other means—culture is a petrified version of a cult. Another case in point is the fact that Poelzig and Werdegast play chess for Joan's life. Chess is the translation of war into culture. This is almost a metonymic detail only, since the whole mansion of Poelzig is built on the remnants of a battlefield that still haunt the house, and also built on a foundation in which cultic rituals still take place—almost like building a Christian Church on the remnants of a Heathen Temple, as if to channel off the intensity and translate it into something static.

On the other hand, there is Werdegast, who, as the anti-cultist, might stand for culture here. And again, things are not that easy. After he has rescued Joan from the Satanists, he gets hold of Poelzig, and we witness the following scene. Werdegast wants to skin Poelzig alive, like an animal, "slowly — bit by bit." In this scene, where Werdegast, as it were, wants to strip off Poelzig's mask of culture, deep down to the flesh — he starts by tearing Poelzig's Zen-like wardrobe into pieces — Werdegast himself is transformed into a cultist, eyes wide open, ecstatic facial expression, trying to ritually flay his enemy.

The Black Cat can almost be read as an echo of Freud, and even as anticipating Adorno and Horkheimer's argument in *Dialectic of Enlightenment* that when culture and reason becomes technocratic, there is the danger of reverting to barbarism ... and thus of the move from Poelzig to Hitler. Rational thinking and progress become manipulative, a tool for domination — the historical reference point here is of course German fascism, and Ulmer, as a Jew, was definitely highly sensitive to what was going on in Germany at the time — note that the historic Marmoros was a Jewish district, close to Mateszalka, where one of the biggest concentration camps in Hungary was built ten years later, and that one of the Satanist's in the script — in a scene that was later cut — was called Goering. The name Poelzig refers to Hans Poelzig — who not only designed the film-sets for *The Golem*, but who, as an architect, was the teacher of Albert Speer, and built the IG-Farben building in Frankfurt. As Erik Ulman has noted with regard to some of Ulmer's films, there is often "a persistent if shadowy link between civilization and sickness" (Ulman) — a fitting observation for a Jewish intellectual in the first quarter of the twentieth century. As Ulmer's daughter remembers, Ulmer "had based most of his thinking on the great minds of the German language, only to find that it led to a stupid monster of an Austrian painter named Hitler. For the rest of his life he tried to understand how civilization could end up in barbarism" (qtd. in Gallagher).

After *The Black Cat*, Ulmer left Universal — the fact that he had an affair with Shirley Alexander, who was at that time married to Carl Laemmle's nephew, and who became Ulmer's wife a year later, might have been a decisive factor — the "aesthete of the Alps"[3] became a *persona non grata*.

Another film to focus on is *Bluebeard*, a film Ulmer did for PRC in Los Angeles, in Poverty Row — the small studios at the limit and in the shadow of Hollywood, home of the B-pictures, nudies and cheapies in 1943, approximately ten years after *The Black Cat*. In the meantime, Ulmer has made himself a reputation for doing pictures cheap and fast — he could shoot a movie in a week or less, at the cost of $8,000 to $20,000, for a weekly salary of approx. $250 (to get figures into perspective, the production costs of a film such as Universal's *Dracula* cost about $355,000, shot in about eight to nine weeks).

However, one should not parallel Ulmer's fall into the rock bottom of the film industry with the bleak doom and fatalism of his most famous films, such as *Detour*. Ulmer, in fact, did not work as a mere hack director, paid by PRC. He actually "*chose* to make these films" (Meisel 149), pumping his own money into the productions, if necessary, even when living almost on the margin of his own subsistence. What Ulmer valued highest was absolute creative control, integrity of vision, to have to make no compromise in his artistic endeavor—Hollywood could not give him that, but PRC could, and did. Thus, the almost non-existence of budget had to be substituted by enthusiasm and ideas—in fact, one might say that budgetary limitations in fact *produced* this creativity, brought it to light. Ulmer later claimed that working in these poor circumstances preserved his freedom to make these personal and obsessive films: "I didn't want to be ground up in the Hollywood hash machine" (Bogdanovich 592).

Bluebeard is set in early nineteenth century Paris, and is the story of Gaston Morel (played by John Carradine), a painter and puppeteer. A serial-killer is afoot in Paris, strangling young women with a black tie and drowning them in the Seine. A young *modiste*, Lucille, falls in love with Morel, who invites her to one of his puppet-shows. Soon after, we find that Morel himself is the killer, driven by an uncontrollable urge to kill women who were in fact models for his paintings. Thus, the question of whodunit is transferred to the question if Morel will kill Lucille as well, and to a depiction of a more complex character. When Gaston's latest victim is recognized in one of his works at an exhibit, inspector LeFevre uses Lucille's sister, Francine, a police detective, as bait in a scheme to trap the mysterious, unknown painter who kills his models—she poses as the model for a painting commissioned by a rich art lover. Morel kills her, but later confesses to Lucille that he is in fact the serial-killer Bluebeard. After he almost kills Lucille, too, he drowns himself in the Seine.

The character of Gaston Morel is played by John Carradine, a Shakespearean theater actor, who was prone to portray eccentric characters with a stylish exaggeration. In his more restrained performance of Gaston Morel, he demonstrates that he is able to temper his techniques and plays Morel as a complex character driven by his obsessions, but who also feels guilt and wants to avoid killing. His rich voice, with registers both authoritative and velvety mellow, is a crucial part of the illusion. Ulmer embellishes the role, pulls us into Morel's psyche, with some of the best photography in any of his films (again by master cinematographer Eugen Shüfftan). During flashback scenes, the director re-creates the intensity of Morel's character and the terror of his victims with long sequences of weird angles and forced perspectives. He avoids dwelling on the details of murder, preferring shock-cuts to a close-up of Morel's wild eyes followed by the slumping of a body.

A French-language poster for *Bluebeard* (courtesy Edgar G. Ulmer Preservation Corporation).

Originally intended as Universal's follow-up to *The Black Cat*, with Boris Karloff in the leading role, Ulmer, quite fittingly for his career, would have to wait 10 years before actually filming *Bluebeard*. With PRC, Ulmer was able to put many personal idiosyncrasies into it, such as his love of opera and the puppet-play. And it is here we get the inevitable "Ulmer-twist" for this film, again intro-

The opening credits matte for *Bluebeard* (courtesy Edgar G. Ulmer Preservation Corporation).

ducing European High Culture into American genre/cult — even trash — cinema. In addition to the film score, which consists of episodes of Mussorgsky's *Pictures at an Exhibition*, in various variations on the theme, Ulmer introduced an extended presentation of a scene from Gounod's opera *Faust* as enacted by Gaston's marionettes. This puppet opera is a classy sequence and an excellent example of something that goes well beyond what would normally be expected from a low-budget film director. PRCs boss, Leon Fromkess, was not particularly happy as Ulmer insisted on that scene. In the end, however, Ulmer got his way and embarked on his usual six-day production schedule to complete the film. Ulmer acted as his own production designer on *Bluebeard* (as ever so often). He put much effort in designing the puppets, and used his trademark mattes and miniatures to open and close *Bluebeard*. The film begins with a series of paintings of Paris behind the credits, followed by an image of Notre Dame and the Seine, and then focuses on a miniature of a bridge over the river before cutting to his first shot of a woman's body floating in the water.

Using these painted backgrounds and theater costumes, the stage-feel nonetheless adds to the claustrophobic air of melancholy that hangs over the film. The movie ends with a climactic chase over the roofs of Paris. Despite the fact that the rooftop props were almost pathetically make-shift and barren, Ulmer again turns this defect into an asset, shooting the set at crazy angles and makes an almost Expressionist statement, not unlike to the chase in *Cabinet of Dr. Caligari*.

Later, almost at the end of the movie, we witness the following scene, flashback included, in which Morel explains himself to Lucille. With its *chiaroscuro* style, the film itself is almost a flashback to the times of the old Gothic Horror Films, shot in a time when the studios aimed at showing modernity. Note Morel's puppets, who project haunting shadows on the wall, almost like dead persons dangling from the gallows.

Note also that the hellfire which was present at the end of the puppet scene also flickers here, in the scene between Morel (Faust) and Lucille (Marguerite). In this scene, we learn that an emotional experience in his past leads Morel to strangle each model once he has painted them. His search for an ideal of beauty — his failure to find it, that is — causes him to go into a trance-like state and strangle those who fail to measure up. And it is here that the play within the play — or play within the film of *Faust* makes perfect sense. Like Poelzig in *The Black Cat*, Morel has entered a mephistophelean pact in order to conserve beauty, to find truth — however, representation, the painting, coincides with the destruction and cancellation of the thing itself, the real body, as the source of the painting, which may indeed point the finger at the crux of culture, as Ulmer sees it.

There is a similar architecture at work in *Bluebeard* as in *The Black Cat*— due to the fact that it was intended to shoot them back to back, there is good reason to see them as part of a duo. In *The Black Cat*, there was the modernist and highly cultured upper part of the Poelzig mansion, situated on top of the cellar where the rites of the Satanic cult were performed. In *Bluebeard*, we have the whole city of Paris, represented by artists, fashion designers, rich art patrons, built on top, as it were, of the underground sewage system, were Morel, the Bluebeard, disappears after his murders, and from where Lamarte's place — the realm of the art industry — can be directly accessed. Like in *The Black Cat*, culture and — if you will — sub/culture, the realm of the cult, defined as the unorthodox, interpenetrate each other. Note also that this spatial topology perfectly mirrors the Hollywood hierarchy of the big productions and the B-pictures — and the interpenetration being exactly that which Ulmer aimed at.

Thus, both the threesome Morel-Faust-Poelzig and the threesome Morel-Faust-Lamarte evoke that inseparable interpenetration of cult and culture, of drives and civilization. Lamarte, the art dealer, is in fact the ever tempting Mephistopheles to Morel's Faust, and he pushes Morel to more and more paintings, being perfectly aware of Morel's inclination and the soon-to-be fate of the models, but does not care, since he benefits from that.

Morel himself had in fact abandoned painting for puppeteering — a less

Opposite: **The underground sewage system of Paris, where Morel disappears after the murders.**

lethal practice, since Morel is in control here, he holds the strings, while as a painter, he was always at the mercy of his fascination — or, waning of fascination — for the model. There is an important analogy here — when the camera focuses on the marionettes in the puppet scene, it follows the strings, higher, up to the place where the puppeteers are, and moves just a small instance higher — to indicate that human beings themselves are also puppets, played by ... by what? Ulmer's *Detour* has the memorable quote: "God or Fate or some mysterious force can put the finger on you or on me for no good reason at all." It seems as if human beings are played by fate. However, that would be too easy a comment by Ulmer, a man who never succumbed to fate, or to circumstances. As Tag Gallagher has noted, Morel — and in fact all of Ulmer's broken heroes — cannot be simply regarded as mere victims of fate. In *Bluebeard*, Morel's murders are not only, as he wants us to believe, results of his traumatic search for beauty — they are also motivated differently, as when he kills his former assistance, because she found out about his killings. Thus, "a mindset that blames fate is already villainous for Ulmer. Ulmer's failed people reject every grace offered them. They end up voids — black holes of egomania" (Gallagher).

For Ulmer, than, cult and culture — the unorthodox and civilization — go hand in hand, need each other. While there is always the danger that the sickness of culture makes it revert to barbarism, culture is built on that unorthodox, on drives — and establishes itself by draining, petrifying, ultimately killing it. The cult not only presents a danger to culture, it is also the source of life for culture — a vitality that Ulmer wants to preserve. It is only by completely succumbing to fate — as the inevitability of drives, the unorthodox, ultimately, the *excluded* of culture — that this outside becomes dangerous and sick. In contrast, Ulmer votes for the active interpenetration of those two realms, reviving the mere rituals of culture by intensity, and refining the intensity of the unorthodox by controlled infusions of High Culture. In his reconciliation of representation (culture) and the source/the body (cult), Ulmer seems to follow Heinrich von Kleist, who in his "On the Marionette Theater" — how fitting! — has a dancer claim that marionettes are not spiritless; it is rather that in fact "even th[e] last fraction of mind ... could indeed be removed from the marionettes, their dance transposed wholly into the realm of mechanical forces" (Kleist). Affectation — culturization, that is, even over-culturization — is an effect of the body being separated from, out-of-tune with, the soul, the fact that "the soul (*vis motrix*) is located at any point other than the center of gravity of a movement" (Kleist) — representation/culture has lost its touch with the source of life, has in fact killed it. As a consequence, to bring the marionette to live, "the puppeteer [has to transpose] himself into the center of gravity of the marionette ... by dancing," that is, he has to link himself to his center of gravity, in order to counter "disorders that consciousness [culture! B.H.] could produce in the natural grace of humankind" (Kleist).

Ulmer, who loved the Classical Arts, brings culture to life again by linking it with cult, with the unorthodox, the trashy — and thus graces the unorthodox, the trashy. As Alexander Horwath, director of the Austrian Film Museum in Vienna, has recently noted, Ulmer's "free and brash way of merging European education with sensationalistic stories, all this proves that cinema does not have to follow the traditional arts" (Horwath). It is admirable that Ulmer, who had worked in "the least fertile soil" and "had chosen the most impossible of terms ... had functioned as a true artist" (Meisel 152) — yet it is tragic that this man should have been almost forgotten for such a long time.

This brings to mind the memorable final line of *Ruthless* — the film that is regarded as Ulmer's *Citizen Kane*: "He wasn't just a man. He was a way of life."

Notes

1. On this issue, see also Derrida.
2. The cross is actually the double cross of the Hungarian Coat of Arms.
3. Universal's epithet for Ulmer (see Mank 47).

Works Cited

Arnold, Matthew. *Culture and Anarchy*. 1882. Repr. New York: Macmillan, 1960.
Bogdanovich, Peter. "Edgar G. Ulmer." *Who the Devil Made It: Conversations with Legendary Film Directors*. New York: Ballantine, 1998, 558–604.
Brunas, Michael, John Brunas and Tom Weaver. *Universal Horrors: The Studio's Classic Films, 1931–1946*. Jefferson, N.C.: McFarland, 1990.
Derrida, Jacques. "Before the Law." *Jacques Derrida. Acts of Literature*. Ed. Derek Attridge. New York, London: Routledge, 1992, 181–220.
Freud, Sigmund. "Civilization and Its Discontents." *Civilization, Society and Religion*. Harmondsworth: Penguin Freud Library, 1991, 12: 244–340.
_____. "The Future of an Illusion." *Civilization, Society and Religion*. Harmondsworth: Penguin Freud Library, 1991, 12: 179–241.
_____. "Totem and Taboo." In: *The Origins of Religion*. Harmondsworth: Penguin Freud Library, 1991, 13: 43–224.
Gallagher, Tag. "All Lost in Wonder: Edgar G. Ulmer" *www.latrobe.edu.au/screening thepast/firstrelease/fr0301/tgafr12a.htm*, last accessed April 10, 2008.
Grissemann, Stefan. *Mann im Schatten. Der Filmemacher Edgar G. Ulmer*. Wien: Paul Zsolnay Verlag, 2003.
Hoberman, J. "Low and Behold: Edgar G. Ulmer." *Village Voice*, November 17, 1998.
Horwath, Alexander. Interview in Michael Palm's documentary *Edgar G. Ulmer — The Man Off-Screen* (2004).
Isenberg, Noah. "Perennial Detour: The Cinema of Edgar G. Ulmer and the Experience of Exile." *Cinema Journal* 43: 2 (Winter 2004), 3–25.

Mank, Gregory William. *Karloff and Lugosi: The Story of a Haunting Collaboration.* Jefferson, N.C.: McFarland, 1990.

Meisel, Myron. "The Primacy of the Visual." In *Kings of the Bs. Working Within the Hollywood System. An Anthology of Film History and Criticism.* Eds. Todd McCarthy and Charles Flynn. New York: E.P. Dutton, 1975, 147–52.

Ruiz, Raúl. *Poetics of Cinema.* Trans. Brian Holmes. Paris: Editions Dis-Voir, n.d.

Taylor, Edward B. *Primitive Culture. Researches into the Development of Mythology, Philosophy, Religion, Art, and Custom.* 2 vols. 1871; reprint ed., Gloucester, Mass.: Peter Smith, 1958.

von Kleist, Heinrich. "On the Puppet Theater." *http://academic.udayton.edu/bradhume/hst348/Kleist.htm*

Ulman, Erik. "Edgar G. Ulmer." *www.sensesofcinema.com/contents/directors/03/ulmer.html*, last accessed April 10, 2008.

Camera Obscura, or Moments of Broken Economy in Edgar G. Ulmer's Films
STEFAN GRISSEMANN

> There was no pressure at all. Edgar got what he wanted, and he got it in one take. He would do a master shot and then come in and take close ups. We never had a retake. That was it. When we finished a scene or whatever, the shot, he would say, "Print it"—and he'd smile a little smile, turn around and get ready to set up the next shot. That's how we just kept moving. Benny Kline was the cameraman. He could just read Edgar's mind, I mean, it was perfect. He was a very experienced cameraman, very good.
> —Ann Savage

Ann Savage's account of shooting *Detour*, almost six decades after the fact, paints a laconic picture of Edgar G. Ulmer's directing skills: portrait of the artist as self-confidence personified. That was Ulmer's method: no-nonsense filmmaking, nothing to think about twice, set it up, put it on. That's how most of his films were made—as quick operations, with up to 25 shots a day, a cinema literally *on the run*. Not everything works in his movies—nor could it at that pace. But he tried to make his visions work, aiming at stylistic condensation even when he knew he dealt with heavy-handed melodrama or talkative thrills. "Broken economy" is a term that seems fit to highlight Ulmer's strange take on narrative efficiency, on ultra-low budget cinematic elegance. Nevertheless, any debate of that special economy at work in Edgar G. Ulmer's films in less than 300 pages has to become something of a *chase*, a movement in fast-forward through a very few images and themes, artistic bits and set pieces. This essay is therefore basically limited to three areas, three fields that can be perceived as definite strengths of Ulmer's film work. One: his ever-intact potential for surprising visual and narrative solutions; secondly: the strange documentary value in many of his films; and finally: the sometimes breathtaking minimalism of his *mise-en-scène*.

> As I understand it, *Detour* was six days shooting, of which I only had three and a half. I don't come in until halfway into the film, so six days probably is the truth. Everything worked, it was perfect. I don't even recall any retakes except at the very end, where Tom apparently hadn't studied his lines too well and kept blowing. But with Edgar, I never had retakes [Savage, interview].

Speaking of economy: *Money* as a topic is an excellent, if somewhat perverse basis for approaching Ulmer, since it provides a sort of negative folio on which to outline the artistic personality of a filmmaker who kept doing his work not *because of* but *in spite of* the (lack of) money behind it. Borrowing a phrase from Martin Goldsmith's pulp novel *Detour*, Ulmer himself seems to have voiced his contempt for the capitalistic nightmare the world around him has become: In one of those highly personal movie moments Ulmer loved to infuse his films with, in a scene early on in the Goldsmith-adaptation *Detour*, a disillusioned Tom Neal asks himself what money was anyway. He comes up with a sobering answer: "a piece of paper with germs crawling on it."

In a moment of disenchantment over David Lean's *Dr. Zhivago*, the critic Andrew Sarris pointed out that if you were to give an Edgar G. Ulmer three years and a budget of millions of dollars, he would turn out twenty films — and (very probably) quite a few of them substantially better than Lean's epic romance. Ulmer is, in fact, a singular case, a *complete* filmmaker in the sense of the word: a man being initiated and socialized as an artist by German expressionism *and* documentary filmmaking, by his complicity with Murnau *and* his participation in the Berlin city symphony *People on Sunday*, that he co-directed in 1929.

During the four decades that he made films, Ulmer kept going back and forth between the extremes of expressionistic stylization and the higher authenticity of documentary filmmaking. The artificial aspects of his work have been well described: the sinister world of the *The Black Cat*, the obliquely painted backgrounds of *The Light Ahead*, the silent movie mise-en-scène in the period piece *Bluebeard*. Ulmer's fierce attempts at realism however have, I feel, not been worked on properly as yet: From the very beginning of his career, from *People on Sunday* onwards, there's a red thread of documentary reality in his film work. He celebrated open nature in *Green Fields* and *Cossacks in Exile*—and he did so even more passionately in his other Ukrainian film: in the beautiful, relaxed outdoor movie *Natalka Poltavka*. He obviously adored to let natural light and wide landscapes interfere with his otherwise quite calculated way of directing: In the middle of one of his short subjects that deal with the perils of tuberculosis, a film called *Another to Conquer* (made in 1941 on a Navajo reservation in Arizona), Ulmer interrupts the flow of fiction with a long sequence of working processes, with a gaze on how men, women and children go about their daily duties, how they perform the cleaning of sheep under the big sky, in the fields and in the water.

Quite a similar scene occurs in Ulmer's World War II jazz operetta *Jive Junction*: In order to realize their dream of forming a jazz band for the American boys who serve in the war, a gang of kids helps to pick oranges in a grove. Ulmer gets carried away, showing what seems to be archive material of peasants in their fields, of the miracle of work in their own land, not unlike some corresponding moments in revolutionary Soviet cinema. More clinical documentary filmmaking can be seen in *Damaged Lives:* Ulmer shows a gallery of syphilitic people in medical care, one after the other, with hyperrealistic intensity. In the famous noir *Detour* there's yet another weird moment of documentation, a sort of close-up on the conditions of telecommunication. When the hero calls his faraway bride, we see women at work plugging and unplugging telephone lines, we see the wire expanding over vast landscapes, connecting the East with the West Coast: a shot, completely unnecessary, even plodding from a simple narrative point of view, but indispensable for a director with the intention of telling stories in new, strange ways — by incorporating technical reality and invisible human interaction in an otherwise very efficiently directed tale of fate and doom.

Ulmer's revolutionary mind — the role he insisted on playing as the lone fighter, the free spirit in a universe of industrial image- and filmmaking — quickly led him to a position of radical liberalism, of contempt against reactionary attitudes concerning sex, war and religion, and to an almost surrealistic contempt for the bourgeoisie itself: *I Pirati di Capri*, a film he shot in Italy in the late forties, shows that contempt clearly — you can see and feel Ulmer's enthusiasm for breaking rules (in every sense of the word: formally and ideologically). And Ulmer never simply executed the scripts he was working on, not even under the very real pressure by time and budget; rather, he elaborated on his screenplays on the spot. He was not averse to using improvisation on the set; he liked to invent things as he went along. Some of his most famous scenes were done that way: To visualize the internal disintegration of his hero, a murderer against his own will, in *Detour*, right after the strangling of Vera, Ulmer lets the camera curiously track around the room creating blurred images, a world out of focus.

> I think that was Edgar's idea, all of this. I don't believe that was in the script. Vera was just supposed to fall against the wall somewhere — in my script [Savage].

The sheer minimalism of *Detour* is that film's most brilliant special effect: Its narrative and visual abstractness — it makes use of only a handful of sparse sets to depict the infernal downfall of all of his characters — is a given in Ulmer's style. Apparently nobody felt any need to discuss the absolute scantiness on the set.

> Edgar was so busy moving from shot to shot each day. Everything was good, so there was no reason to discuss anything that might come up from an actor's point of view. We had never any conversations like that. We just met in the morning, we were prepared, and we went to work. That was it [Savage].

It actually doesn't really matter which of his films you choose to study: In each and every instance Ulmer's cinema opens up a whole cosmos, a vast empire of signs and meaning, of names, lines and traditions. Consider, for example, the case of *Moon Over Harlem,* a social drama that Ulmer directed in the winter of 1938, in presumably just four days, for barely 8000 dollars, with an all-black cast. Ulmer brought in a guy named Jack Kemp as his cutter, who also collaborated on the first three of Ulmer's Yiddish films of that period. Almost ten years later that very same Jack Kemp will be directing a single film, entitled *Miracle in Harlem,* a rare, treasured work of black independent cinema. In Kemp's only piece of fiction, a young actor called William Greaves will appear, who — nineteen more years later — will be serving as director of an underground classic of African-American film, the 1967 *Symbiopsychotaxiplasm: Take One,* one of the most influential black films of all time. So Ulmer's *Moon Over Harlem* in fact was something of a first step, a bridge between the low-budget B-film of the thirties and the distant era of Blaxploitation cinema of the seventies.

Ulmer has been writing film history (mostly of course: underground film history) as he moved along, with breakneck pace, from project to project: a man not merely of culture, as he loved to emphasize wherever he could, but — more to the point — a man of several different cultures, going back and forth between remote social spheres, a true filmmaker of minorities.

Undoubtedly he strongly identified with his characters: He shared their views, he was literally in their shoes. Like most people he portrayed, Ulmer had to make do with next to nothing. He shot some of his films with almost no retakes, no resources at all, just like that: do it and get away with it. That method shaped his sense of tight filmmaking, his desire for elliptical directing. This tendency can be demonstrated most clearly in some of the death scenes Ulmer staged — and not just the famous strangling sequence of Ann Savage in *Detour.* In the final minutes of the brilliant *Club Havana,* for example, made for poverty row studio PRC in 1945, a girl is shot, in front of a nightclub, in pitch black night. In that scene the girl is behind the steering wheel of her car, trying to distract a waiting killer, trying to keep him from murdering an innocent man. She flashes the lights of her car, irritating the man with the gun, who blindly fires towards the driver's seat. His shot breaks through the glass of the windscreen — and the forehead of the woman. There's no music, just a gunshot, breaking glass and a dead girl, in a series of events in what feels to be only a split second: The quickness, toughness and utter clarity of that scene strongly contrasts with the visual euphemisms on which American thrillers in the forties generally relied on. If seen today, the outrageous modernity of Ulmer's depiction of a violent, a deadly moment can be quite physically felt.

"Well, it's true, there are things that can be so ugly there's a certain beauty to them," Savage said.

The villain in *Moon Over Harlem*, a gangster called Dollar Bill — a most significant name in an Ulmer film, by the way — finally meets death in a cool little scene that boasts an almost documentary shock value. Bill, gunned down by members of an antagonistic gang, dies on a dirty floor in a run down place. The way Ulmer shows Bill's corpse instantly reminds one of historical police photography: a strangely authentic, ugly image, deglamorized to the maximum, complete with a zoom that seems to prefigure sixties cinema rather than conforming to the visual styles of the late thirties.

If one were to concentrate only on the death scenes in Edgar G. Ulmer's body of work, it would seem that this director had been tirelessly assembling a rather morbid collection of those particular scenes: eccentric instants of exitus. It is easy to locate further examples: One tightly staged oddity can be found in *Daughter of Dr. Jekyll*, a film created in the mid-fifties, largely conventional in its methods — except for two scenes. Ulmer again demonstrates his inclination for weird little murder arrangements, in this case involving a girl in underwear and an old gramophone — a marvelous moment that seems completely out of tune with the rest of the film: the implicit depiction of a horrible crime, Hitchcock-style with even an air of Bresson. But more than anything else it is an Ulmerian flashback to *Detour*'s famous central killing scene. An anonymous girl is unexpectedly visited at her home, she screams, falls, is horribly killed off-screen and remains lifeless on the floor of her apartment. The record she had been playing is stuck, producing weird noises beside her dead, half naked body. The primitive beauty of this short sequence is in itself enough to testify to Ulmer's artistic refinement.

There's a second wonderful scene in *Daughter of Dr. Jekyll*, standing out from clumsy re-enactments of Victorian horror imagery and bad, long-winded dialogue: It depicts the heroine's murderous nightmares, showing "reality" and dream in superimposition, insinuating modern art more than Hollywood's poverty row. Ulmer's *Daughter of Dr. Jekyll* is nevertheless anything but a masterpiece: With almost provocative carelessness he sets his brilliant visual touches apart from the explicitly sloppy procedures in less exalted scenes.

In a breakfast scene that takes place in a supposedly dark old house in the middle of nowhere, in a foggy landscape, one can clearly see standard model passenger cars from the fifties go by outside the window in the background: Ulmer did not shoot his film in a studio, but in an old building on Sixth Street in Beverly Hills, near Hancock Park. And obviously he didn't care if anybody noticed that or not.

Edgar Ulmer is an unpredictable artist: Behind the sarcasm that drives some of his pictures, he also cultivated, almost candidly, a *melodramatic* nature, most evident in his — highly emotionally charged — recurrent use of mirrors and water. Sydney Greenstreet, one of the character actors in *Ruthless,* is forced by a cold, loveless wife to take notice of his own repulsiveness in a grand, luxurious mirror; Hedy Lamarr, conversely, admires her own beauty on the slightly trembling black surface of water in *The Strange Woman;* girl-killer John Carradine paints his last model by her mirror image in *Bluebeard*; and Tom Neal in *Detour* has to find Ann Savage accidentally killed by him on the bed of a cheap motel; as he enters the room, he is visually doubled, literally split in two: We see him standing still, frozen in shock, over the corpse — and we also see an tilted, twisted image of him and his victim in the mirror in the back of the room.

> After consulting Benny Kline who ran the camera on this track, Edgar asked me: "Ann, do you think that you could pick up the phone and run with it, get through the door, fall onto the bed and get this thing wrapped around your neck?" I said "Yes, I can" — and I did it with the camera and Edgar. Then we shot it. We shot it only once, and it was just perfect. Wasn't difficult, no retake. Edgar did move in later and showed her on the bed lying across this way, when Tom comes into the room and realizes he has strangled her by trying to break the cord under the door [Savage].

French filmmaker Bertrand Tavernier, an ardent admirer of Ulmer's work since the late fifties, has noted the value of surprise in the work of the Viennese-American filmmaker. It is true: The Ulmer touch is constituted not so much by themes or styles, but rather by surprise and irritation. By the breaking of the taboo, the rejection of the ordinary, the happy return to insanity: In a body of work ranging from cheap Hollywood westerns to Ukrainian folk musicals to Italian swashbucklers and French fantasy films there is virtually no other connecting element than the visionary impulsiveness of its creator.

Only very few of Ulmer's movies are consistent in themselves, most of them are rather dangerously unbalanced compositions, unevenly built, often a little inept, as far as storytelling is concerned — and overproduced, as far as music is concerned. But even the most unambitious of his films will always get to the point of sudden interest, to a bizarre scene or image, that no one ever could have foreseen. Edgar G. Ulmer is a director of moments out of time. Such an instant happens, very literally, in the rather outrageous finale of the science-fiction-epic *Beyond the Time Barrier*, where youthful hero Robert Clarke returns home from his voyage through time and space with a horribly wrinkled face — an old, dying man: a brilliant make-up effect, again totally incongruous with some of the more pedestrian effects in that film.

Like all directors who take their medium seriously, Edgar G. Ulmer loved to watch — especially things that weren't meant for his (or anyone's) eyes: Voyeuristic pleasures are central to Ulmer's cinema. *The Naked Venus*, released in 1958, starts with a very programmatic sequence, with the registration of an intimate, uncovered scene — that is: two young women in the nude and two lusty men with a camera in the open nature. *The Naked Venus* is a highly personal piece of cinema — not only due to the fact that Arianne, Ulmer's daughter played one of the lead characters in the film: In this story the avowed nudist Ulmer comments on conservative resistance. The picture, even though it is labeled a "nudie" to this day, is not about the exploitation of naked women, as one might suspect, but about a true discussion of moral dilemmas, American family values and political perspectives. With Ulmer, the horror of traditional family life — as it is in fact connected to trauma and destruction — is always right underneath the coating of false love and fake harmony. In *The Naked Venus* a vampiric mother talks to her fearful son who has just come back from the war. It's a night scene, long and devoid of any ornament, verbally or visually. Mom is happy about her highly decorated son's success in Korea ("You did fine. You got all the medals"). She does not — or does not want to — notice the deep fear that still shakes him when he remembers the war. There's a certain rawness to that scene, even furthered by the amateurish B-movie acting: an uncanny, abysmal sequence, modern and classical at once.

Later on, a pig-faced judge representing narrow-minded, late fifties America inquires about the dubious liberalism of the war veteran's young wife: "Did she actively practice nudism?" he asks in one of his cross-examinations, as if to remind us of recent US-bigotry, of Senator McCarthy's witch hunt. As usual, Ulmer goes for the dark, the ugly side.

> The very first day of shooting, we were in the car — and you know, this was a very strange woman to play, she had to look weird and ugly. That was another unusual thing: to allow your leading lady to look so ugly. Because the studios — all of us had been under contract with studios — would all tell you the same thing: They did not wanna allow their women actresses to be anything but beautiful. And they made us so beautiful, beyond our wildest dreams — what those wonderful cameramen and make-up people could do for you! It's just remarkable. Anyway, so here comes *Detour*, and Vera is described as looking as if she's just come off the dirtiest freight train in the world, which she probably did. But the make-up people had done my hair very nicely,

apparently the hairdresser hadn't realized that I was supposed to look so dishevelled, but anyway, Edgar came along after they had combed me out and everything looked so pretty, and he said "This will never do." There was a large jar of cold cream on the dresser. He just said "Mess it up, put some cold cream through her hair." Well, actually it looked just like some of the hairdos that you see today! Stringy, as if hadn't been combed in weeks. But that's exactly what they did to me, and they put dirt on my face. Buddy Westmore of the Westmore family — wonderful make-up family — actually smeared dirt on my face, and then I was dressed badly. Matter of fact, Edgar at one point in the scene had my sweater pinned, cause it was so loose and didn't show any of my figure — not that it was that great or anything — so they pinned in the back, so they could pull the sweater tight [Savage].

Women are the prime drive in Edgar G. Ulmer's pictures. He enjoys watching and staging them more than conforming to the Hollywood set of rules on how to decently show women on screen. One thoroughly weird — and deservedly famous — Ulmerian set piece can be seen in the radically antidramatic western *The Naked Dawn*: Betta St. John takes a shower in front of her house, and Ulmer revels in those precious moments by focusing on outlandish little details — the water running down the legs of the girl, an idling chicken beside her, the shiny white towel she wraps herself into. A counterpart to that scene is contained in *The Cavern*, where Rosanna Schiaffino is having a bath with a goat by her side — only not in open air anymore but trapped in a darkened cave. Like the girls in the prelude to *The Naked Venus*, she is secretly observed by a voyeur in the distance: Ulmer himself shares that position.

A connoisseur of female passion — that's what film director Ulmer is. A strong scene of implied sadomasochistic hysteria, only about a minute long, occurs in *The Strange Woman*: Hedy Lamarr is abused und punished; she is cruelly whipped, but as she endures it with dignity there is also a confused passion to be seen in her face. Cinema according to Edgar G. Ulmer is a test laboratory for extreme human fervor — but above all it's a question of rhythm.

> When I came to the line "What did you do with his body?" I spoke it — and Edgar stopped me saying "No, no, no." Then he snapped his fingers very quickly: What he was telling me without saying anything was that he wanted me to speed up my delivery. By doing that he added another dimension to Vera's characterization. He brought out a psychosis. By that tempo. I kept that tempo all through the film — with the exception of one scene where she's maudlin and drinking on the sofa, feeling sorry for herself of course.
>
> It was hard to generate that anger at times. Actually that was one of the reasons my voice was so thin in *Detour*. I had to go down in my seat, because Tom and I were about the same height, he was not a real tall man. So Edgar asked me to make myself seem smaller, which I did, but it cut off my diaphragm, you know? You really should be speaking from the diaphragm

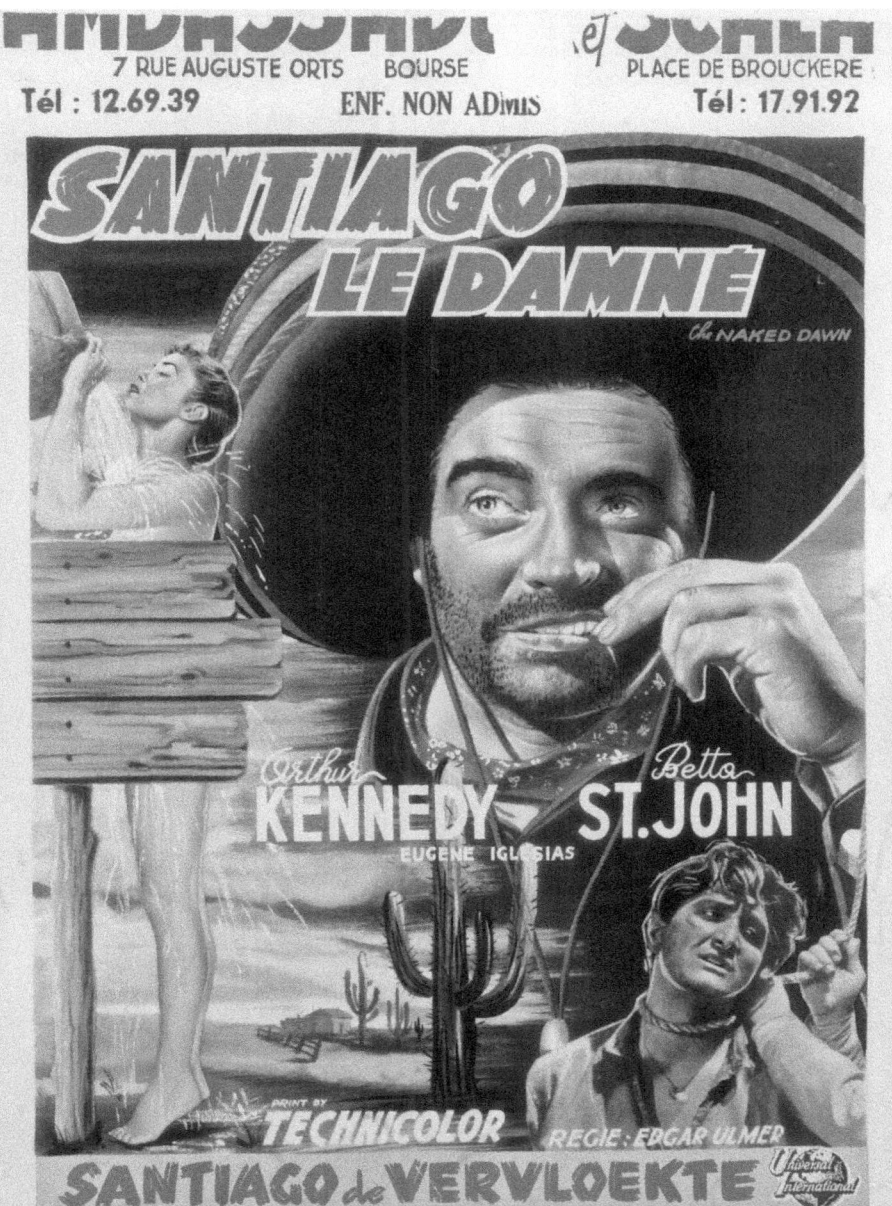

A Belgian poster for *The Naked Dawn* (*Santiago le Damné/Santiago de Vervloekte*) features Betta St. John showering (courtesy Edgar G. Ulmer Preservation Corporation).

especially when you're angry and you should get all this volume. But I couldn't do it, and I was kinda short of breath. I was so tense just talking from up here through clenched teeth, so I was strained. But that was good for the part [Savage].

Perhaps Ulmer's extravagant style, his own private *Arte povera*, is best appreciated with another quote from Martin M. Goldsmith's novel *Detour*, published in 1939 — a line that didn't make it into the movie; it might well serve to define and celebrate both Edgar G. Ulmer's precious way of working and — in fact — cinephilia itself. Goldsmith wrote: "What's a little dust and a few dirty dishes when you're in love."

Works Cited

Savage, Anne. Personal interview, July 2, 2001, Sherman Oaks, Los Angeles, Calif.

The Ordinary Life of Ordinary People: *Menschen am Sonntag*

PETRA LÖFFLER

> *Jeder heutige Mensch hat einen Anspruch, gefilmt zu werden.*
> —Walter Benjamin

Menschen am Sonntag (1929, *People on Sunday*) is widely known and accepted amongst film historians as an outstanding example of late German silent cinema, as well as being a famous important early documentary. Siegfried Kracauer, for instance, in his *Theory of Film* from 1960 states that the film is a "remarkable semi-documentary" (44). The emerging filmmaker Robert Siodmak started the project together with his brother Kurt. Edgar G. Ulmer returned from Hollywood, where he had been living since the mid-twenties, and soon became co-director of the film. The screenplay was written by Billy Wilder and was based on a reporter story from Kurt Siodmak, but beside Wilder, who was working as a newspaper journalist during that time, Ulmer was also mentioned as co-author. Eugen Schüfftan,[1] who would later become famous, was responsible for cinematography. His assistant was Fred Zinnemann and the original soundtrack was composed by Otto Stenzeel.[2] As a "remarkable semi-documentary," *Menschen am Sonntag* combines two different tendencies: aesthetic invention on the one hand and pure recording of reality on the other. As a cinematic experience of a special kind, it is a hybrid consisting of elements from feature film and documentary.

At the end of the roaring twenties, when the film was being shot, there already existed a highly developed language of silent cinema. It consisted of different kinds of camera focus, modes and conventions of cutting and montage, of light atmospheres, facial expressions and gestures, of the aesthetics of props and set design. Nevertheless, *Menschen am Sonntag* was made in an even more realistic style than other productions at the time, because with only one exception, the film was shot outside the studios. As a low-budget-film, it doesn't employ professional actors. It rejects melodramatic action performed by well-known stars, and focuses instead on the ordinary life of ordinary people living in the German metropolis of Berlin. As Kracauer has argued in his book *From Caligari to Hitler*, back in those days, "German film-makers cultivated a species of films presenting a cross-section of some sphere of reality. ... They were the purest expression of New Objectivity on the screen" (181). The main prototypes for this kind of cross-section film were *Die Abenteuer eines Zehnmarkscheins* (1926, *The Adventures of a Ten-Mark-Note*), which was directed by Berthold Viertel, and Walter Ruttmann's famous film *Berlin. Die Sinfonie einer Großstadt* (1927, *Symphony of a Great City*).

The aesthetic conventions generated by a realistic recording of reality created a new genre: the so-called reporter story film (Reportagefilm). *Menschen am Sonntag* is said to be one of them: As a contemporary critic pointed out after the film's release, it was a pure realistic work in the spirit of the "Berliner Blätter — a specific journalistic genre, which portrays individual lives and fates in the urban jungle of the metropolis" (Grissemann 50). The silent film was finished in December 1929 and premiered on February 4, 1930, at a theater on the famous Kurfürstendamm. The critics were overwhelmed and very enthusiastic about this "little drama about our Sunday luck, the true record of our life" (qtd. in Grissemann 55). Nevertheless, after this last experience with the silent film culture in Germany, the 24-year-old Ulmer returned to Hollywood and its synthetic studio world (see Grissemann 56).

To call *Menschen am Sonntag* a "true record of our life" makes it part of a cinematic aesthetic, which was referred to as documentary at the time — a term that English film critic John Grierson was said to have given its theoretical meaning a few years before in his review of Robert Flaherty's film *Moana* (1926). In his article for the *The New York Sun,* Grierson stated that Flaherty's film has, besides its beauty, a "documentary value" because of its true "visual account of events in the daily life of a Polynesian youth and his family" (Jacobs 25).

Work and Leisure

Like the documentary *Moana, Menschen am Sonntag* first of all draws our attention to the everyday life and especially to the ordinary leisure activities of young people living in a big city. As the social historian, Kaspar Masse, in his survey of the rise of modern mass culture, pointed out, at the turn of the new century film, light fiction, technically recorded entertainment music and public sports events had found a place in the average life of the urban lower classes (see 78).[3] From that time onwards, the medium film was often seen as an ideal vehicle for entertainment — the metropolitan film palaces were the preferred localities for the masses to celebrate the "cult of distraction."[4]

Therefore it is not surprising that urban culture and leisure itself became an issue in feature films, too. Even in its early years, silent films often showed urban traffic, crowds of passer-bys and various places of entertainment, such as cafés, film theaters and Luna Parks. There was, not only in the well-known films of the Lumière brothers, a great interest in the velocity of urban life and a sympathy for motion in every possible (human or technical) manifestation. This interest is most obviously represented in the so called panorama films or travelogues, which offered "a variety of vistas across the city space, from panoramic perspectives to street-level views" (Bruno 20). As Giuliana Bruno put it, being a "product of the era of the metropolis and its transits, film expressed an urban viewpoint from its very inception" (18). The rise of modern mass culture, including the general availability of modern mass media such as gramophones, film theaters and the illustrated press, is represented in the film by the Siodmak brothers and Ulmer. The makers of *Menschen am Sonntag* were very sensitive to this special language of cinema: They often installed the camera as the ideal apparatus for transporting this language on streets, at traffic junctions, railway lines or subway stations, where it "observes" and records all motions of traffic vehicles and movements of passers-by.[5]

In addition, their choice of characters is very typical for the social groundwork of the Weimar Republic. They all belong to the petty bourgeoisie: the taxi driver Erich Splettstößer, the model Annie Schreyer as his lazy lover, the traveling wine trader Wolfgang von Waltershausen, who meets the film extra Christl Ehlers at a busy corner near the station "Bahnhof Zoo" and asks her on a date for the next day, a Sunday, and not to forget her friend, the record seller Brigitte Borchert, who will accompany Christl to meet Wolfgang.

The opening credits show the real names and professions of the main characters. This is done for the purpose of a realistic cinematic experiment that wants to explore what real young people with different professions actually do in their leisure time. These people are connected through neighborhood, friendship or the shared desire to make new acquaintances. Thus, Wolfgang visits his neighbors, Annie and Erich, in their apartment on Saturday evening and asks them on a trip to Nikolaussee on the following Sunday with his new acquaintance Christl and her friend Brigitte. While the lazy Annie spends the whole day in the couple's apartment, the other four make the trip to Lake Nikolassee, a popular meeting point close to the city. They

> **Menschen am Sonntag,**
> ein Film ohne Schauspieler.

> Erwin Splettstößer
> fährt die Taxe IA 10088.

> Brigitte Borchert,
> hat im letzten Monat
> 150 mal die Platte:
> „In einer kleinen Konditorei"
> verkauft.

The credits display the real names and professions of the characters.

have fun swimming, listening to music, flirting with each other, having a picnic, and boating on the lake before they return to the city in the early evening. While focusing on the activities of the group relaxing at the lake, from time to time the camera returns to the solitary sleeping Christl and the realm of the city streets, where few people spend their Sunday leisure time. This is — in few words — the whole "story" of the film. Through this complexity of two parallel narrations, *Menschen am Sonntag* shows a great diversity of localities inside and outside the city landscape and creates a display of the site specificity of urban life: a choreography of modern living spaces. The realism of common and well-known localities, such as the Bahnhof Zoo and the Nikolassee, play an important role for the "documentary value" (John Grierson). This was attributed to the film by the audience as well as by critics.[6]

Grierson's description of Robert Flaherty's *Moana* as a "documentary" fits in with Ulmer's film in another way. The actors are non-professionals and are not playing characters in the way one would expect it from a feature film. The makers have claimed that no rehearsal was necessary for the scenes and sometimes the crew didn't know what to do until the morning of the shooting. The participants of the filmic experiment play only themselves: common people with ordinary lives. Brigitte Borchert, for instance, works in a music shop selling gramophones and records in real life as well as in the film. She owns a gramophone and a collection of records, which she takes with her on the Sunday trip. The professions and hobbies of the others — mannequin, taxi driver, traveling salesman and film extra, representing professions typical for the mobile, mass media shaped urban culture of the Weimar Republic — are also related to the mobility and mediality of modern city life.[7] The film cast exhibits behavior that is typical for a specific class of people — the petty bourgeoisie — with common leisure activities like going out to see a film, sitting in a café, dancing or making a trip to the countryside. This is what the characters share with other average people of their specific class and period of time.

Menschen am Sonntag exhibits the theme of urban sites and a topology of its inhabitants. The film draws attention to the patterns of culture[8] and the social life of the average man in Twentieth Century Germany between the two World Wars. These vary from such tribal rites as cleaning the streets or washing the car on Saturday afternoons, to pure leisure activities like dancing, sports, a trip to the countryside or playing with the kids on Sunday. The greatest part of the film is reserved for this Sunday relaxation. The film's final scene takes place on a Monday morning where crowds of people are shown going to work again and the suggestion is that they can't wait for the next Sunday to arrive. It was again Sigfried Kracauer who created a mosaic of these often marginalized cultural patterns in his Feuilleton-novel "Die Angestellten" (The White-Collar Workers), which was first published in 1929 in the *Frankfurter Zeitung*— the same year in which Ulmer and his friends were shooting their film.[9]

Since the second half of the nineteenth century, there has existed a strict division between work and leisure in Western societies. Working hours became regulated, with a fixed beginning, end, and breaks in between (see Rabinbach 32). Leisure became in itself an important part in the everyday life of the working classes, to recover from overwork, physical and mental exhaustion or even illness. A vast repertoire of commercial amusements flourished around the end of the nineteenth century including the vaudeville, the magic lantern show, and acrobatics, among others. It was the nineteenth century socialist Paul Lafargue, who in 1880 wrote a scandalous vindication of the worker's right to laziness in *Le Droit à la paresse*. In his treatise, Lafargue denounced the protestant capitalist dogma of work as the ultimate way for the proletarian to achieve contentment or even happiness.

At the same time, new types of leisure and entertainment were emerging in the cities, and the new business of the leisure and entertainment industry was emerging. This industry produced a remarkable change not only in American society, but in Western societies, too. Ben Singer argues that cities "had never been nearly as busy as they became just before the turn of the century" because of the "sudden increase in urban population..., the escalation of commercial activity, the proliferation of signs, and the density and complexity of street traffic" (Singer 73). Apart from these efforts of modernization and industrialization, Singer marks its effects on more ephemeral parts of modern life: "As the urban environment grew more and more intense, so did the sensations of commercial amusement. Around the turn of the century, an array of amusements greatly increased the emphasis placed on spectacle, sensationalism, and astonishment" (88). What is really new about these amusement tools to him is that "the new prevalence and power of immediate, gripping sensation defined a fundamentally different epoch in popular entertainment" (88).

This new epoch is also characterized by a special interest, shared by all working people, in new modes of entertainment to fill their leisure time. In the twenties and thirties the weekend therefore became the status of a social institution (see Masse 134). Hits like "Wochenend und Sonnenschein" (Weekend and Sunshine) emphasize this new status, and exhibitions like "Das Wochenende" (The Weekend), organized in 1927 by the Berliner Messe-Amt, showed new tendencies in weekend architecture available to ordinary people.

Siegfried Kracauer has argued in his sociological description of the white-collar workers' culture in the Weimar Republic that the large-scale saloons that want to capture their customers by means of exotic decorations and cheap amusements are "Asyle für Obdachlose" (asylums for the homeless) (see Kracauer, 1971, 95). For Kracauer, these amusement halls, which he called "Pläsierkasernen" (95) (barracks of amusement), follow the same ideology of rationalization that has occupied the space of capitalist production and circulation of commodities. These localities, which renewed the nineteenth century tradition of variety shows, would satisfy the thirst of the masses for glamour and distraction. He also observed that for the white-collar workers, there exists only a small gap between business and entertainment activities: "Aus dem Geschäftsbetrieb in den Amüsierbetrieb ist ihre unausgesprochene Devise" (95). The historian, Kaspar Masse, characterized the young people of the incipient Twentieth Century as more open-minded and as having various interests and on the lookout for new kinds of leisure and sensations (see 77). These are the ideal customers of the modern amusement temples. The social function of leisure and common activities is emphasized by the masses and their positive effects on society are highlighted. He resumes that modern nations finally grew together by sharing the same rituals of leisure time (see 76).

Important films concerned with the relationship between work and leisure and modern city life at that time are René Clair's *Paris qui dort* (1923), Fritz Lang's *Metropolis* (1926), Walther Ruttmann's *Berlin. Die Sinfonie einer Großstadt* (1927), Friedrich Wilhelm Murnau's first American feature film *Sunrise: A Song of two Humans* (1927), King Vidor's *The Crowd* (1929) and Alberto Cavalcanti's *Rien que les heures* (1929). As films that work out the "correspondence between city space and film space" (Bruno 21), they stand for the modernity of filmic expression. Ulmer's *Menschen am Sonntag* was predominantly modeled on Murnau's *Sunrise*.[10] Ulmer, employed at that time as an assistant art director by the Fox film company, participated in *Sunrise* as an assistant to the set designer and art director Rochus Gliese. Before he settled in Hollywood in 1923 or 1924 (there is no exact data available), he had met Murnau for the first time in Berlin in the early twenties. From that time on he was very impressed with Murnau's genius.

Apart from the aesthetic differences between documentary and melodramatic film styles, there are obvious similarities between Ulmer's and Murnau's films in more than one respect. There are two significant scenes in *Sunrise* that demonstrate the similar interest of both filmmakers concerning the differences between urban and rural landscapes and the shapes of modern city life: firstly, there is the scene in which the couple, after their reconciliation, enters the big city in a railway carriage, and secondly, their joyous rendezvous in a big Luna Park at night.

Murnau's film focuses on traffic junctions with crowds of passer-bys, street cafés and leisure areas as specific sites of urban culture. The extremely mobile camera of Charles Rosher and Karl Struss in these scenes is typical of the whole film and Murnau's artistic ambitions. We encounter the modern city and its transport network, its traffic and rush hours, featuring railways, trams and streetcars. In Murnau's *Sunrise* velocity plays an important role and creates special effects generated by the moving camera. In the first scene, the camera is inside the railway carriage with the protagonists and is as instable as they are. Like the famous "phantom rides" of the era of single shot-films, it follows every change and even the most subtle movements in the direction of the railway. In Siodmak's and Ulmer's *Menschen am Sonntag* the camera, however, is more static. It often shoots from a stable, fixed point of view which is situated further away. Many times the camera shows or widens to panoramic views — such as when it shows the floating crowds of people from a point far away.

In *Sunrise*, the dynamic expression of the moving images is rather subtle and quite different from the floating, but more stable camera of Ulmer's cameraman Eugen Schüfftan. In *Sunrise*, which was shot in the Fox film studios, Murnau focuses on common leisure activities in the metropolitan atmosphere of a crowded Luna Park.[11] The Luna Park scene at night in Murnau's film especially is a sophisticated arrangement of various body movements and camera motions — something Siegfried Kracauer has called "the mass ornament" (see Kracauer, 1927). *Menschen am Sonntag*, in contrast, was shot in the open air in real locations in and around the German capital. Ulmer centers on natural leisure and sports activities in the countryside outside the metropolis. The different approaches of the two filmmakers also mark the cultural difference between rural country life and vibrant city life as different living spheres. The Germans, one has to remember, love spending their weekends in the countryside. Especially shortly after the Great Depression they appreciated the rural landscape for the cheap and healthy relaxation it offered, while the American metropolitan society seemed to prefer Luna Park and its exaltations.[12]

What is really surprising, however, is that Ulmer's *Menschen am Sonntag* left all institutions of commercial amusement out of his film. Instead, it celebrates "natural" leisure environments and prefers the open air of the landscape around the metropolis. Thus, the film methodically neglects the urban localities of commercial entertainment which are connected with city life: an empty little carousel, children playing, and the entrance to a Luna Park are all that is seen in one sequence, while Murnau's *Sunrise* celebrates the desires and sensations offered by the flickering lights of the Luna Park at night.

Another scene is even more significant in terms of excluding common entertainment localities: the film introduces the main protagonists Erich and Annie making arrangements over the phone to meet the coming Saturday evening. Annie wants to go out for a movie, Erich agrees, but later, at home, they start an argument about which film they should go see. Erich makes fun of his wife's adoration of a male film star, whose photographic portraits adorn an entire wall of their apartment. Annie, in return, mocks her husband's fancy for his favored female actor, which is — not very surprisingly — Greta Garbo. The argument ends with a sadistic destruction of all the portraits, and so their planned evening in a movie theater is cancelled. They stay at home, the offended Annie throws herself onto the bed and Erich plays cards with his friend Wolfgang. This humorous, slightly grotesque scene criticizes the commercialization of leisure activities, which is all too common for the first decades of the Twentieth Century.

Film or Photography

Menschen am Sonntag offers an insight to one day of the ordinary lives of five people, who all belong to the petty bourgeoisie and who live in the city of Berlin. Kracauer has pointed out that the film "draws attention to the plight of the 'little man'" (Kracauer 1947, 189). In my opinion, *Menschen am Sonntag* is also a portrait of the Weimar Republic, its culture and its people. Therefore it is comparable to August Sander's photographic album *Antlitz der Zeit* (*Face/Countenance of Time*), part of his larger project *Menschen des 20. Jahrhunderts* (*People of the Twentieth Century*). Sander's album was first published in 1929, when Ulmer and the Siodmak Brothers were shooting the film. Sander's photographic series was seen as a kind of sociological research project, as the writer Alfred Döblin stated in his preface to Sander's book. Over a period of more then 20 years, the German photographer collected portraits of men and women, children, teenagers and elderly people of all social classes and spheres including farmers, workers, craftsmen, sportsmen, secretaries, teachers, artists, industrialists, revolutionists, representatives, unemployed and even blind persons — to name only a few (there is no ranking suggested in this list of people here). Sander's aim was to create a visual summary of all human types of German society at that time dating back to the early twentieth century. He was convinced that the traditional structures of society were changing. Sander observed these changes and the rise of new professions, social roles and personalities. That is why he named his ambitious project *Menschen des 20. Jahrhunderts* (*People of the Twentieth Century*). The title of the first issue of his photographic series was a clear expression of his sociological approach. "Antlitz" in German does not only mean face, but also summary or overview. The importance of Sander's book for the understanding of the German culture of the Weimar Republic is all too evident. The journalistic resonance was remarkable, and the book was controversially discussed by well-known critics and intellectuals. For more than one reason, Ulmer's and Siodmak's film has much in common with Sander's ambitious project. There is one important scene in *Menschen am Sonntag* which is even directly connected with photography as a medium of sociological research. At the same time they share the aesthetic ambition to record reality itself, to create a living portrait of their time and their contemporaries.

In his description of that scene, Kracauer, in his book *From Caligari to Hitler*, marks the effect, which the interruption of the filmic movement caused by the photographic recording process:

> In one sequence, a beach photographer is busy taking pictures which then appear in the film itself. They are inserted in such a way that it is as though the individuals photographed

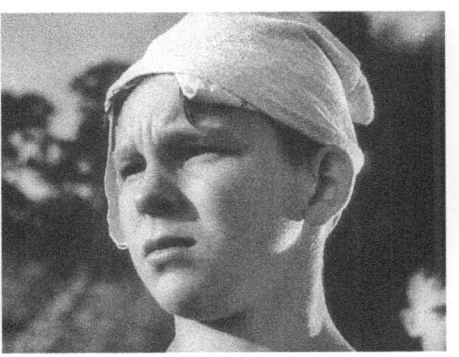

The images of people at the beach are placed so that they appear motionless in the film.

have suddenly become motionless in the middle of an action. As long as they are moving they are just average individuals; having come to a standstill however, they appear to be ludicrous products of mere chance. (44)

For the film critic Kracauer, the only medium able to capture life or living persons is film because of its ability to capture motion. But photography, he claims, shows no more than a short and often grotesque impression of these persons. The photographs don't seem to show them as individuals, their photographed faces seem nothing more than grimaces.[13] Whether these photographed people are "average individuals" or "ludicrous products of chance" depends for him first and foremost on the way they are represented through a medium — either through motion picture (*"temp duré"*) or still photography (*"temp espace"*). For Kracauer and his concept of filmic realism, the photographed persons seem to be real only in the time capturing motion picture.[14]

Maybe Siegfried Kracauer, in analyzing these portraits, was too close to his subject to see nothing more than its inherent potential for the unnatural grotesque. They could rather been seen as the same kind of sociological research as the well-known photographic series "Antlitz der Zeit" of August Sander (see Löffler, 2002).

Like in Sander's cycle, most of the characters in Ulmer's film aren't professional actors — with one remarkable exception. As part of the photographic session in the film, Valeska Gert and other more or less well-knows actors or charges of the Weimar Cinema pose in front of the eye of the camera.[15] They are, and they show what was called a "Filmgesicht," the face of a film star. Yet, these "Filmgesichter" (see Löffler, 2006), persons far removed from the ordinary, are mixed up with all the other average people shown in the film. They appear within the series showing a naked baby, a laughing boy and many different faces of men and women from the bourgeoisie and the working classes, such as the typical intellectual with his clear-cut glasses, the wannabe film diva with her fur boa, the bourgeois lady with the elegant hat, the secretary with the bob haircut, the beer drinker with the Kaiser-Wilhelm-moustache, the working class woman, the waiter, the sportsman, the working class girl with glasses, the tattooed man with bad teeth.... At the same time they recall bygone times of motion picture culture — the days where the screened film began with a frozen image.

Sander's photographs are full body portraits; Schüfftan's shots only show the faces. All of these cinematic-photographic pictures of faces are extreme close-ups and must be strictly separated from inserts of examples of artistic studio photography and its soft-focus portraits at the end of the series, which echo the wall plastered with posters of film stars in the apartment of Annie and Erich. This implies a sort of comment on medial and aesthetic changes, which are related to photography *and* film and which are related to the upcoming doctrine of realism, too. The film's intention to portray a huge range of the members of a society is based — like Sander's photographic project — on sociological typologies like class, race and gender.

The City Is the Star

In achieving this, the film is also (and not only in the prologue) a portrait of the city, of Berlin as a metropolis, its social structure and cultural patterns. There is no need, on my part, to stress that it is far more realistic in its approach than, for instance, Fritz Lang's film of the same name (*Metropolis* 1927). The city itself becomes a main character — consisting of space filled by lots of nameless inhabitants, countless passers-by, and anonymous working crowds. The earlier cross-section film *Die Abenteuer eines Zehnmarkscheins* was reviewed by a critic in 1928 as follows: "There is a fascinating shot of the villain sitting in the window of a café. Trams, buses and passers-by are reflected in the plate-glass. The city is intent on doing something."[16] In this quotation the city achieves the power to act like a human being — its fate being entirely self-created.

"The city is the star" — Stefan Grissemann also stresses this argument about *Menschen am Sonntag* in his autobiography of Edgar G. Ulmer: "a floating world in motion, pulsating like an organism, circulating" (Grissemann 51).[17] The camera focus imitates this perspective of urban city life (51).[18] Grissemann describes *Menschen am Sonntag* as "a 'symphonic' urban montage of passing house fronts, wide avenues, and gigantic billboards" (Grissemann 53).[19] To him, however, the film's empathy for the beautiful details of everyday life reveals a blind spot. It totally neglects the social plight of the lower classes just after the Great Depression. It is for this blind spot that Grissemann criticizes the "eclecticism" of Siodmak's and Ulmer's film. This is his reason for seeing the film as a mere polemic essay, and sometimes even as a caricature (53). Nevertheless, this is only one side of the medal. Unlike Murnau in *Sunrise*, Ulmer's film doesn't show (in the same way he doesn't show unemployment, poverty or illness) the glamorous side of a metropolis or even the common places of commercial entertainment. The city is "alive" only because of the power of its inhabitants, which is — as the film suggests — renewed every Sunday. Only through this is the city characterized as an organism and a real living sphere.

But what is really fascinating about *Menschen am Sonntag* is, as an American critic wrote after seeing the film for the first time in 2006, what you do not see:

This is Germany in 1930. They've just come out of a devastating economic post-war period, and they're newly into the world-wide depression. Hitler is lurking in the wings, waiting for his big chance. Yet we see hordes of happy people in Berlin living simple pleasant lives. It's eerie.... We see very little of the grinding poverty and desperation which Hitler was able to exploit, so I'm a bit skeptical about the supposed realism of the film. We don't see the ground that made a totalitarian dictatorship possible. The whole social environment we see on the screen is so benign and content, that I'm wondering what these young filmmakers were really thinking. Were they out of touch, indulging in wishful thinking, or just young and inept?[20]

Whatever we think of the filmmaker's intention, *Menschen am Sonntag* draws a too friendly image of the living environment of the petty bourgeoisie in the Weimar Republic. From this point of view the film itself is an instant photography in more than one respect. It shows only a lucky part of social life, and this part only in one very special moment of time. This is where the film's unconscious irony lies: *Menschen am Sonntag* reveals itself as a snapshot.

Notes

1. Schüfftan moved to France in 1933 to escape the Nazis and in 1940 to the United States. He received the Academy Award for black and white cinematography in 1977 for *The Hustler* and is the Inventor of the Schüfftan Process for optical special effects.

2. The original film did not survive World War II intact, and the musical score was lost completely. What we have has been assembled from the remaining fragments found in Germany and various countries around Europe.

3. "Vor dem Weltkrieg noch fanden Film, populäre Literatur, technisch reproduzierte Unterhaltungsmusik und Schausport einen Platz im Alltag der städtischen Unterschichten. Die moderne Massenkultur begann ihren Siegeszug."

4. Cp. Siegfried Kracauer's famous statement in his 1926 essay "Kult der Zerstreuung. Die Berliner Lichtspielhäuser" (Cult of Distraction. On Berlin's Picture Palaces). In: Siegfried Kracauer. *Das Ornament der Masse. Essays*. Frankfurt a. M.: Suhrkamp 1979, 311–7.

5. In his review of Karl Grune's film *Die Straße* (*The Street*, D 1923) Siegfried Kracauer has characterized the city street as the arena of the phantom character of modern life (see Siegfried Kracauer. *Werke*, Bd. 6.1.: *Kleine Schriften zum Film 1921–1927*, 56).

6. See for instance Kracauer (1997), 252.

7. For this argument see Siegfried Kracauer. *Die Angestellten*, Frankfurt a. M: Suhrkamp 1971, 65, where he declares that the conformism of the life of the lower white-collar workers in the big cities leads to the formation of normal types — professional images, which are echoed in magazines and films.

8. I use this term in the anthropological sense Ruth Benedict gave it in her book *Patterns of Culture* of 1934.

9. In his book, Kracauer attempts a unique look at the lives of white-collar-

workers living in the German capital to figure out the "Exotik des Alltags" ("the exotics of everyday-life"). He declares that despite the sheer numbers of the hundreds of thousands of white-collar workers in the streets of Berlin less is known about their life than about that of primitive tribes: "Hunderttausende von Angestellten bevölkern täglich die Straßen Berlins, und doch ist ihr Leben unbekannter als das der primitiven Volksstämme..." (Kracauer, 1971, 11).

10. Starring Janet Gaynor, who won an Academy Award in 1929 for Best Actress, and George O'Brien. The cameramen Charles Rosher and Karl Struss also won an Academy Award for their cinematography with an extremely mobile camera. Rochus Gliese was nominated for Best Art Direction.

11. See also Walker Evans' photographs of crowded urban places like Coney Island (*Walker Evans at Work*, London: Thames and Hudson, Reprint 1994, 24–5, and. 34–7: empty Luna Park). The Coney Island amusement complex opened in 1895 — in the same year the Lumière brothers introduced their cinematographe to the public.

12. Cp. the following article in a German magazine: "Mehr und mehr zieht heute der Mensch wieder auf das Land. Die ersten Anregungen hierzu gab der Sport, der die Wohltat des Aufenthalts und lebendiger Bewegung in der freien Natur entdeckte. Neuerdings haben die negativen Einwirkungen des modernen Großstadt- und Bürolebens auf die Gesundheit und zuletzt auch die finanzielle Notlage der Menschen zur Erkenntnis geführt, daß die wirkliche Erholung und wahre Lebensfreude am billigsten und bekömmlichsten in der Landschaft zu finden sind" (*Frau und Gegenwart*, no. 10, 1932/33, 273).

13. Kracauer sees photography as being connected with „the world of death in its independence from human beings", and according to him a photographic archive only collects "the last elements of nature alienated from intention" (see Siegfried Kracauer: "Die Photographie." *Das Ornament der Masse*, Frankfurt a. M. 1977, 38). For a more in-depth discussion of Kracauers thinking on these topics see: Miriam Hansen. "Decentric Perspectives: Kracauer's Early Writings on Film and Mass Culture." In: *New German Critique* 54 (Fall 1991): 47–76.

14. See also the relevant sentences on *Menschen am Sonntag* in Kracauer's *Theory of Film*: "...snapshots of the bathers, taken by a photographer on the spot, are inserted in different places; and the snapshots snatch from the flow of movement precisely such bodily postures as are bizarre and in a sense unnatural. The contrast between the bustling bodies and the poses they assume in the cut-ins could not be stronger. At the sight of these rigid and ludicrous poses the spectator cannot help identifying motionlessness with lifelessness and, accordingly, life with movement... (44)."

15. The other named actors are: Kurt Gerron, Heinrich Gretler, Ernö Verebes.

16. Blackstone: "The Adventures of a Ten-Mark-Note." In: *Close Up*, Now. 1928, 59–60; quoted in Kracauer (1947), 182.

17. "eine Welt im Fluß, in Bewegung, quasi organisch pulsierend, zirkulierend" (my translation, P.L.).

18. "Der gleitende Blick auf Berlin fällt aus fahrenden Autos und den oberen Etagen doppelstöckiger Busse oder von fernen Aussichtspunkten aus: Man sucht hier stets entweder das Mittendrin oder das Privileg des Überblicks."

19. "eine 'symphonische' urbane Montage aus vorbeiziehenden Hausfassaden, großzügigen Alleen und überdimensionierten Werbetafeln."

20. *http://www.imdb.com/title/tt0020163* (last accessed on Jan 08, 2008).

Works Cited

Benedict, Ruth. *Patterns of Culture*. Boston: Houghton Mifflin, 1934.
Blackstone. "The Adventures of a Ten-Mark-Note." *Close Up, Now* (1928): 59–60; quoted in Kracauer (1947): 182.
Bruno, Guiliana. *Atlas of Emotion. Journeys in Art, Architecture, and Film*. New York: Verso, 2002.
Evans, Walker. *Walker Evans at Work*. London: Thames and Hudson, Reprint 1994.
Frau und Gegenwart 10 (1932/33).
Grissemann, Stefan. *Mann im Schatten. Der Filmemacher Edgar G. Ulmer*. Wien: Zsolnay Verlag, 2003.
Hansen, Miriam. "Decentric Perspectives: Kracauer's Early Writings on Film and Mass Culture." *New German Critique* 54 (Fall 1991): 47–76.
Jacobs, Lewis. *The Documentary Tradition*. New York/London: W.W. Norton & Co., 2. ed., 1979.
Kracauer, Siegfried. *Theory of Film. The Redemption of Physical Reality*, Princeton: Princeton UP, 1997.
———. *From Caligari to Hitler. A Psychological History of the German Film*, Princeton: Princeton UP, 1947.
———. "Kult der Zerstreuung. Die Berliner Lichtspielhäuser." Siegfried Kracauer. *Das Ornament der Masse. Essays*. Frankfurt a. M.: Suhrkamp, 1979, 311–17.
———. *Werke*. Bd. 6.1.: *Kleine Schriften zum Film 1921–1927*. Frankfurt a. M.: Suhrkamp, 2004.
———. *Die Angestellten*. Frankfurt a. M: Suhrkamp 1971.
———. "The Mass Ornament (1927)." *New German Critique* 5 (Spring 1975): 67–76.
Löffler, Petra. "'Ein Dichter sieht aus wie ein Chemiker.' Das Gesicht in der Fotografie." Stefan Andriopoulos and Bernhard Dotzler (eds.). *1929. Beiträge zur Archäologie der Medien*. Frankfurt a. M.: Suhrkamp, 2002, 132–57.
———. "Das Filmgesicht. Die Rede vom Gesicht im frühen Film." Wolfgang Beilenhoff, Marijana Erstic, Walburga Hülk, Klaus Kreimeier (eds.). *Gesichtsdetektionen in den Medien des zwanzigsten Jahrhunderts*. Siegen: Universitätsverlag, 2006, S. 25–51.
Masse, Kaspar. *Grenzenloses Vergnügen. Der Aufstieg der Massenkultur 1850–1970*. Frankfurt a. M.: Fischer, 1997.
Rabinbach, Anson. *The Human Motor. Energy, Fatigue, and the Origins of Modernity*. New York: Basic Books, 1990.
Singer, Ben. "Modernity, Hyperstimulus, and the Rise of Popular Sensationalism." Leo Charney and Vanessa R. Schwartz (eds.). *Cinema and the Invention of Modern Life*. Berkeley/Los Angeles/London: U of California P, 1995, 72–99.

Ulmer's Anti-Syphilis Film: *Damaged Lives* and Its Novelization
Marcel Arbeit

In the United States, with its traditional myth of self-made men who build their careers from scratch just by their own diligence, skills, and perseverance, physical health was always an issue of vital importance. To live up to the American Dream, and safely avoid the American nightmare, a bright mind is usually not enough — one also needs a strong, healthy body. Still, the diseases are here, and they arrive on wings and depart on foot. The United States had its deadly flu epidemic in 1918 and 1919 and desperately tried to reduce the number of polio and smallpox cases.

As the number one killer in the period between the world wars was tuberculosis, in 1938 the New York–based National Tuberculosis Association initiated a new project, a series of educational films about the perils of the disease and its cure, as well as the new diagnostic methods. One of them, *Goodbye, Mr. Germ* (1940), even contained animated sequences in which a TB germ explains through a microphone and special radio to a scientist (who then passes the information on to his two curious children and a parrot) how it lives in the human body, what helps it proliferate, and what destroys it. The young patient through whose case the film demonstrates the different stages of the contagious disease is called Edgar, like the director of the film: Edgar G. Ulmer.

Ulmer made five other films on tuberculosis between 1938–1940 for the National Tuberculosis and Health Association. They were targeted at different age and ethnic groups: children and adults, African Americans, Hispanic Americans, and Navajos on the reservation. But tuberculosis was not the only contagious disease Ulmer was making films about. Five years before his first anti-tuberculosis documentary he made a dramatic film about a dangerous venereal disease hardly anyone talked about in public — syphilis. It was released in 1933 under the title *Damaged Lives*.

Syphilis: The American Scourge, the American Taboo

According to Owsei Temkin, syphilis was considered an American illness, first detected in Europe in about 1495, having been brought there by the crew of Christopher Columbus — then Charles VIII's soldiers spread it throughout the continent (524). As social historian Allan M. Brandt writes in *No Magic Bullet: A Social History of Venereal Disease in the United States since 1880*, well into the 1830s many doctors considered syphilis and gonorrhea "manifestations of the same disease" (9). When they started to be treated as separate diseases, it did not take long before the three stages of syphilis were discovered, and some serious conditions, including partial or complete paralysis and insanity, earlier considered to be unrelated illnesses, were attributed to syphilitic infections. When the grave effects of the disease on the lives of families, ranging from sterility to demented children, were recognized, there was an increasing call for pre-marital medical examinations. However, Puritan America made a medical issue into a moral one, and imposed an embargo on fully informative accounts of the symptoms, stages, and consequences of venereal diseases. Even when some magazines were courageous enough to lift the taboo, their readership showed their disgust and their wish to stay in a state of sweet ignorance. Brandt gives some alarming examples: when in 1906 the *Ladies' Home Journal* "published a series of articles on venereal disease" it "lost some 75,000 subscribers" (24). Six years later an educational pamphlet for young girls containing references to venereal diseases was found obscene, and confiscated (see 24). During World War I the situation improved for patriotic reasons — the anti–VD campaign could save the health and lives of American soldiers — and by 1919 the U.S. Public Health Service was openly advocating the provision of sex education in schools (see 26).

However, in the 1920s "America had returned to the Victorian era; the conspiracy of silence regarding these diseases had been reconstituted" (129). One of the results was the withdrawal by the Public Health Service of all the anti-venereal disease documentary films, used in the campaign against syphilis and gonorrhea during and shortly after the war, including the most famous of them, *Fit to Fight* (dir. Edward H. Griffith and Lewis Milestone, 1919) on the ground of obscenity (124). Syphilis was referred to euphemistically as "rare blood disease" (23), "social disease" (32), or, when a concession induced by the progress of science seemed to be necessary, a "genito-infectious disease"

(137). It was considered to be "a disease of the 'other,' be it the other race, the other class, the other ethnic group" (23). The establishment of the Committee for Research in Syphilis in 1928 was a flash in the pan, but the formation of the Cooperative Clinical Group, consisting of the directors of five major U.S. clinics specializing in the cure of VDs, a year later, the task of which was "to establish uniform treatment regimens for a variety of syphilis-induced ailments" (130), did bring some results. Yet, according to Brandt, medical reports estimated that by "the early 1930s one out of every ten Americans suffered from syphilis" and each year "citizens of the United States contracted almost half a million new infections" (129). Although the data were later found much exaggerated (see 149), the real numbers were high enough to be more than alarming. In 1933, the year when Ulmer's *Damaged Lives* was made, the universal blood-serum tests for syphilis, developed as early as 1906 by the German bacteriologist August von Wassermann and his colleague Albert Neisser, were still not being used in the U.S.A. for the screening of the general populace.

From the very beginning syphilis was treated with mercury — orally, topically, or in vapor baths — and, later, by potassium iodide, vitriol, and even guaiacum, a West Indian wood (Temkin 524). The cures, besides being painful, had numerous side effects and could at best relieve patients of their symptoms, not the disease itself. The side effects were intensive and severe, but the general public, including the patients, especially lower-class ones, usually considered it "a punishment for their sins" (524). In addition to that, people believed that "a therapy considered effective by both doctor and patient [...] had to elicit some outward, empirical effect" (Brandt 12). Among such empirical effects belonged, for example, lost teeth or severe hemorrhaging of the bowel (12). In 1909 the immunologist Paul Ehrlich (together with Sahachiro Hata) invented Salvarsan (arsphenamine), an arsenic compound applied intravenously. It was effective, but at the same time highly toxic, which made the treatment somewhat risky and postponed the universal acceptance of the medicine well into the 1920s (40–1). But even after the introduction of Salvarsan, or its less toxic successor Neosalvarsan, the treatment of syphilis was a long and unpleasant procedure until penicillin was discovered in 1943.

Damaged Lives: *A History*

In 1933, Columbia Pictures of Canada, Columbia's Canadian distributor, was commissioned to make a film against syphilis for Weldon Pictures (see Turner). Consequently, Ulmer and Donald Davis wrote a screenplay about a rich boy, Don (Lyman Williams), who, during a one-night affair with a girl named Elise (Charlotte Merriam)[1] introduced to him by his business associate, contracted the disease and passed it on his fiancée Joan (Diane Sinclair), whom he had married in the meantime and who had borne his child. The movie, first titled *Dark Waters*, and at one stage even *Happy Ending* (see Turner, cited also in Grissemann 59), was finally released as *Damaged Lives*, a title that would fit many other Ulmer movies as well. It was shot in April 1933 in Hollywood, probably at Educational Studios, as a Canadian-American co-production (see Turner).[2] The movie was first shown in Toronto on May 22, 1933 and in London on August 18 of the same year. Both in Canada and in Great Britain the film was shown with a supplement: a screen lecture in which Dr. Gordon Bates, the Head of the Canadian Social Hygiene Council, who was the clinical supervisor on the movie, explained the dangers and perils of syphilis with the help of diagrams and illustrations. Ulmer made two versions of this supplement, both now lost, one for men and one for women, as in Ontario the film was at first shown to segregated audiences: to women on Mondays, Wednesdays, and Fridays, and to men on Tuesdays, Thursdays, and Saturdays (Turner, cited also in Grissemann 62). When, after some time, this practice was abandoned, only the version originally intended for women was used (see Turner); three months later in London the movie was open to a mixed audience from the very beginning.

The anonymous London *Times* reviewer praised *Damaged Lives* especially for its educational impact: "[T]o see it is to realize afresh the tremendous power of the cinema for direct propaganda of any kind; a discovery which for many years seems to have been exploited only by the great Russian producers" (8). The only flaw, according to the reviewer, was that the moral was tacked onto the dramatic story "from the outside" (8). In this British critic's opinion, the film fortunately transcends its genre, as it "was not made by militant hygienists but by workaday professionals who have produced a film in the ordinary way" (8).

Boston was chosen as the place of the film's American premiere. Although in 1933 it was not common for the U.S. media to promote a work of art dealing with such a topic, the *Boston Globe* still ran an advertisement campaign for the movie and, after its premiere on September 15, 1933, at the Majestic Theater, printed two rave reviews. In the first of them, which appeared on September 16, the reviewer especially appreciated the way in which the authors managed to combine their artistic and educational goals: "It is the sort of film in which the absolute silence of the audience is perhaps the best tribute. [...] It is a dramatization in which something unusual is introduced — a film in which an important branch of medical science — personal hygiene — has been dramatized in an effective way" (8).[3] The second review, which appeared three days later, by Harleigh Schultz, focused on the artistic merits of the film, exaggeratedly calling it "the most amazing product of all the sound screen" (10), at the same time praising all the leading actors for their screen performances.

However, the actors were not the only ones who enjoyed critical acclaim; others also received their due portion of praise: "I cannot but admire the deep sincerity with which producers, author, director and cast carry through: not once is there a false note, a jarring tone" (10). The Boston showing was also the world premiere of a brand new film lecture: the American Social Hygiene Association, putting its name on the head credits instead of the Canadian one, which sponsored the production of the film, asked Ulmer to shoot a new supplement to the movie with Murray Kinnell, the actor who, in the film, played Dr. Leonard, a VD specialist, as they did not want a Canadian doctor in that role. Unlike its two twenty-nine-minute Canadian counterparts, the American supplement (which, according to the 1937 *New York Times* review, took only twenty minutes) has survived until the present (see Turner). In spite of the involvement of the American Social Hygiene Association and the critical praise, the outcome was predictable: the first Boston screenings were also the last ones for a long time.

The New York State Board of Censors banned the film and the ban was lifted after the intervention of the American Social Hygiene Association, which appealed to the New York State Board of Regents, as late as June 1937 (see J. T. M. 26, Grissemann 62).[4] The involuntary delay harmed the film tremendously, as the social and cultural context changed considerably during those four years. While in 1933 Ulmer's movie could be seen as a breakthrough in the fight against venereal diseases, in 1937, when the anti–VD campaign was well under way, it became just one of many attempts to make the public more enlightened and sensitive toward the omnipresent danger. That is why the promotion of the movie put aside the educational purposes which stood at the birth of the film, and focused on its scandalous reputation and dramatic qualities: the New York poster presented it as a shocking and sinful film, the slogan of which said: "His life of debauchery brought disease to his wife." What complicated the reception of Ulmer's movie even more was that, instead of the original 1933 film, the exact length of which, as far as we know, has never been announced, the audience could see only an abridged 61-minute version (the running time given in *Variety*) lacking some of the crucial scenes. The severely cut version had its premiere on June 12, 1937, at the Central Theater (Broadway at 47th Street), New York City (see D.J. Turner and Arianné Ulmer Cipes). Nevertheless, as in other similar cases, the previous ban made it an immediate success: according to J. Hoberman, it earned $1.4 million (135). American reviewers did not find the film shocking or even immoral, and, while not ignoring its undeniable artistic qualities, they returned the discussion to the educational role the film could fulfill. For example, in *Variety* Hobe Morrison wrote: "Certainly there is nothing obscene or immorally suggestive about the film. Rather, it may serve to educate a certain section of the public on how to combat the diseases" (13).

Damaged Lives was exceptional among Ulmer's films in more than one aspect. It was one of the few movies where he was credited as a co-writer; he was notorious for having every film-making skill except writing. It was also the only Ulmer film followed by a novelization, the book *Damaged Lives: The Novel of the Film*, published by Putnam & Co. in Great Britain in February 1934. Its author was Cecil John Eustace, a British-born Canadian writer who later became a president of J.M. Dent & Sons, the largest publishing house in Canada and a subsidiary of the London company.[5] Besides the story, the book also contained an introduction by S. Neville Rolfe, the Secretary-General of the British Social Hygiene Council, which supported the distribution of the film in Great Britain, serving a similar role to the one of the screen lectures supplementing the film — Rolfe interpreted the movie from a medical point of view and explained the behavior of the major characters, as well as its consequences. But the introduction, mentioned even on the copyright page, was not the only bonus the readers got. After the conclusion of the novel, there was an informative article by Dr. Drummond Shiels, Medical Secretary of the Council, explaining the main activities and listing the recent achievements of the Council; the article was preceded by a list of the Council's current officials, as well as by an enumeration of the major aims and objectives of the Council. The novel remains to the present — as the original screenplay did not survive — the only available source where not just the complete storyline but also the original dialogues could be found, as Eustace, while logically substituting the film images with more or less lengthy descriptions, kept the dialogues almost intact. According to our present knowledge, neither Ulmer, nor Donald Davis, who wrote all the screen dialogues, had any direct share in the novelization; still, the minor differences in dialogues between the film and the novelization strongly suggest that Eustace worked with the original screenplay and ignored the insignificant changes the director or the actors made during the shooting, such as, for example, changes in word order, unnecessary repetitions, or even occasional slips of the tongue. There is no evidence that he himself changed any of the dialogues; the only suspicious distinction is the systematic replacement of the then fashionable American "swell" ("swell time") by "wonderful" (77) or "great" (82).

Because of the lack of information about the original version of the story, *Damaged Lives* was undeservedly considered a minor film for a long time. Eustace's book remained generally unknown even to the most dedicated Ulmer fans and, in addition to that, when Alpha Video Classics finally released the movie on DVD, it was the abridged 1937 version. While in 1933 Schultz praised Diane Sinclair as "conviction itself" and Lyman Williams as "a romantic lead worth the attention of the studios, a lad with vast personality, good voice, and even good looks" (10), seventy years later Grissemann had only harsh criticism for them: "The problem of the film is the (main) protagonists: Williams, Sinclair and Merriam are prototypes of second-league Hollywood actors. Nothing about them can be believed, not even once in the (spare) dramatic moments" (61, my translation). However, when Grissemann writes about "the psychological weaknesses of the screenplay" (61, my translation), it becomes obvious that the incompleteness of the available version played a crucial role in his condemnation.

In 1958 the movie was re-released under the new title *The Shocking Truth*, but its real new life began in October 1990, when D.J. Turner, an archivist from the National Archives of Canada, arrived at the UCLA Film and Television Archive to assist Robert Gitt in its restoration. While the two surviving incomplete American prints, one from the Library of Congress and the other held by the UCLA, were not enough when combined to reconstruct the film in its completeness, the major discovery of six reels (two through seven) of the original eight-reel version in Canada (see Turner and Gitt) finally made possible the restoration of the movie close to its original length as shown in Toronto in 1933; the running time of the restored version is 69' 27". The addition of eight minutes and twenty-seven seconds of the previously cut out footage removed from the film the logical lapses and psychological inconsistencies of the abridged version and allowed viewers at last to perceive the movie as a valuable film drama, not just a curiosity. The restored film had its premiere at the UCLA's Fifth Annual Festival of Preservation in 1993 where D.J. Turner personally introduced it.[6] The common effort of the two institutions deserves great credit, and even Arianné Ulmer Cipes, the director's daughter, highlighted the fact that it was the first time that a Canadian archivist had collaborated with a foreign archive in a film restoration (see Ulmer Cipes).

In the following analysis of the movie I will use both the restored and the abridged versions of the movie, as well as Eustace's novelization. I will try to explain why the abridged 1937 version, the only one American film viewers could become familiar with before 1993, although both a commercial and educational success, could not fully achieve its goals. For that purpose, some basic facts about the progress in the crusade against venereal diseases in the U.S. between 1933, the year of the movie's premiere, and 1937, the year of its belated release, will be given. I will also discuss the scenes which seem to have survived only through Eustace's novelization. With the help of Eustace's novel, I will attempt a reconstruction of the scenes at the very beginning of Ulmer's movie, i.e. from the missing first reel of the eight-reel print (the eighth reel, also missing, should not contain any surprises).

Damaged Lives *as a Prophylactic Movie*

In his book about the history of venereal diseases, Brandt gives the most frequent model of how syphilis is spread, "an inevitably repeated scenario, in which a married man, or one about to be married, would visit a prostitute and acquire a venereal infection. Ignorant of the nature of his new affliction, he would infect his wife; soon pregnant, she would pass the disease to the newborn" (14). This reads like a synopsis of *Damaged Lives*, and the screenwriters used that pattern for a good reason. Syphilis and gonorrhea were, even at that time, considered by the public to be lower-class urban diseases, which moral citizens could easily avoid if they secured their sexual partners' fidelity. They were also seen as "foreign" diseases transmitted primarily by immigrants, although this theory was never supported by facts (20). The main problem was an ethical dilemma doctors faced: when they diagnosed a venereal disease, should they keep the medical secret, or warn the spouse of the afflicted of a possible contamination?

The best known literary work discussing this dilemma and its consequences for family life was Eugène Brieux's *Les Avariés* (1901), a French play about syphilis in high society. The play, published in English under the title *Damaged Goods* in 1911 (in John Pollock's translation), introduced a wealthy man who decided to ignore the diagnosis, passing the disease on to his wife who, instead of accepting medical help, joined him in his irresponsible behavior and exposed both her child and a hired wet nurse to the danger. Upton Sinclair, a writer who frequently addressed the issues of physical and mental hygiene in his works, wrote a novel based on that play in 1913, and its Alexander Butler's screen version of 1919 seems to be the first dramatic film about a venereal disease. But there was a need for an original, American story, which would scare the audience, but also show contemporary medicine in a good light, which would give a few warning words, but then proliferate hope. Ulmer and Davis tried to perform the task according to their best abilities.[7]

Don and Joan, the protagonists of *Damaged Lives*, are an upper-class couple; Don is even the heir to a large and prosperous steamship company. The beginning of all their troubles lies in the hesitation of Joan to marry Don. When Don becomes a respectable executive, Joan has no pragmatic reasons for postponing the marriage, and by doing so she assumes her share of guilt for Don's disease — according to the screenwriters, it goes without saying that as a married man Don would resist the temptation of the beautiful Elise Cooper, who is not a prostitute, but the sustained lover of a rich, and much older, businessman.[8] Don's surrender to Elise's charms echoes the arguments of Shiels, who emphasized that the most dangerous age in this aspect comes between puberty and what he calls "marriageable age." Shiels advocated early marriages because married people were, in his opinion, less likely to be promiscuous, and consequently, had a better chance to stay free of venereal diseases (218). Many years later, Brandt extended this argumentation to premarital sex as well, claiming that when "more young women engaged in premarital sex, the prostitute became something of an anachronism" (128).

In *Damaged Lives*, this is also the attitude of other characters: Don's friend and family doctor Bill Hall (Jason Robards), a happily married father of a three-year-old son, and his wife Laura (Marceline Day). When Laura asks Joan what she is waiting for, Joan fails in making her point clear: "I know — it's terrible. But it isn't Donny's fault. It's just — oh, I don't know" (58). Later, Bill brings up the subject again, being much more ominous this time:

> BILL: Joan — why do you insist upon waiting so long?
> JOAN: But, Bill, what possible difference could it make?
> BILL: Maybe none — but maybe it would make a lot of difference [comp. Eustace 93].

Joan later realizes her share of the guilt and when Don admits his one-night stand with Elise, not only does she forgive him, but she also agrees to marry him immediately at a two-dollar wedding without any family members or guests. Joan does not care about the infidelity of Don's body; she is interested only in the loyalty of the heart of her fiancé:

> DON: Last night at that stupid party I met a girl named Elise Cooper —
> JOAN: Donny — are you in love with her?
> DON: No. But that doesn't make any difference.
> JOAN: It does, it does.... Don't you see —
> DON: I want you to know.
> JOAN: No. If you love me — it's all that matters. Donny, you do — still?
> DON: Yes.... More than ever. I know that now so surely — [comp. Eustace 97].

The matter is closed but Davis and Ulmer show that it should not have been. Joan was not any more aware of the danger of venereal diseases than Don, consenting to sexual intercourse with him right after the hasty wedding, and the punishment came early: she bore not only Don's child but also his syphilis. Not that a wedding cures all in other cases: another British specialist, S. Neville Rolfe, was aware of that, but he stayed optimistic:

> No one suggests that the maintenance of continence until a late marriage age is easy, but with a right attitude of mind towards sex and satisfying ideal supported by an understanding of methods which will assist its achievement it is not only possible but actually practiced by many young men and women of to-day [13].

Davis and Ulmer made a great effort not to put the guilt squarely on Don only; that is why they explained the circumstances of Don's infidelity in such great detail. Elise was a companion of Nat Franklin (Harry Myers), the head of the Franklin Steamship Line Company, who invited Don to an informal evening business meeting, during which he wanted to discuss the protection of freight rates against price-cutting competitors; the preference of a night of business to an evening at the theater with Joan was even approved by Don's father, himself a decent family man.

The story pinpoints the factors that contributed to Don's moral failure. The main one is the use of alcohol, a widely discussed theme in the early 1930s when Prohibition was approaching its end; the Twenty-First Amendment to the Constitution was finally ratified on December 5, 1933, only three months after the Boston premiere of *Damaged Lives*. Don, Nat, and Elise go first to Kitty's, a cabaret where alcohol is illegally sold, and then to the house of a rich friend of Nat's, which Don at first considers to be a speakeasy. When Nat leaves with another woman and Don and Elise, both tipsy, decide to "go places," they have some drinks in a tough-looking joint with a bouncer at the entrance, and when they end up in Elise's luxurious penthouse flat, they

Elise (Charlotte Merriam) offers a toast to Don (Lyman Williams) at her penthouse: "Here's to you and me" (courtesy UCLA Film and Television Archive and National Archives of Canada).

promptly pour a drink from her well-stocked bar. The alcohol makes Don and Elise playful, uninhibited, and irresponsible — the day after, however, hangover and self-disgust take over. In opposition to the wild events where jazz music also contributes to the excessively relaxed atmosphere, a game of bridge with family friends and theater-going are given as examples of proper entertainment for well-to-do young people.

When Don receives a call from Elise Cooper and is asked to pay an urgent visit to her, he has no idea why it should be a life-or-death matter. Elise, who tried to commit suicide after she found out that she had contracted syphilis from Nat, is extremely hysterical. She does not have any idea that the disease can be successfully cured, and warns Don, who has arrived promptly, not to go near her or touch her. As Grissemann notices, she does not even find the courage to name the disease, referring to syphilis only as "it" (60). When Don finally understands, he does not believe his bad luck:

> DON: I don't believe you. You hear me, I don't believe you. You're lying to me. A thing like that couldn't happen to me — it's impossible. It just couldn't [comp. Eustace 115].

He repeats the same when Bill and, later, Dr. Leonard, the specialist to whom Bill takes both him and his wife, tell him the diagnosis. The fact that

Don (Lyman Williams) can't believe what happened: "It's impossible" (courtesy UCLA Film and Television Archive and National Archives of Canada).

one mistake is enough to ruin a person's life both physically and psychologically is reiterated constantly in the movie. After Dr. Leonard sends the unhappy couple home from his clinic, promising that he will start their cure next week, he says to Bill: "I feel for that boy. After all, if he slipped once, he's not like the rest of them, who are only getting what they asked for [...] Bill, I can cure that young couple physically, I think, but I'm afraid for them [...] They're so likely to lose faith with a world they thought beautiful ... and with each other" (comp. Eustace 169–70).

The scene, which has the highest informational and educational value, is set in Dr. Leonard's sanatorium, where Bill took Joan and Don. At the clinic, Don and Bill — joined by cinema viewers — observe patients in different stages of the illness, each in one of the examination rooms. Dr. Leonard's guided tour of his workplace is the true medical climax of the movie, and for the health counselors the rest of the story might be only an excuse for these five minutes. Dr. Leonard opens the doors of one examination room after another, and introduces to the depressed Don worse and worse stages of the disease the young man has just developed. It is a kind of shock treatment, but also a sideshow attraction; Grissemann was right when he noticed that the syphilitic patients in the rooms were exhibited like freaks (see 61). In the case of venereal diseases a scared patient is an obedient patient, and that is why the doctor (as well as the director working for a hygiene council) must turn the screw gradually but fasten it as tight as possible.

The introduction of the show is not so bad: the first noticeable symptom of the disease is a sore that might not appear at all or stay almost invisible and unrecognized. Then comes a rash that gradually vanishes, but if the treatment is non-existent or neglected, in a few years the real horrors follow: locomotoric ataxia, paralysis, affliction of the central nervous system, and if the patient is a pregnant woman, then defective and mentally retarded syphilitic children who face an early death or life in an institution. By showing it in a naturalistic way, the movie industry can repay its share of guilt about the proliferation of venereal diseases because, as Shiels wrote, "the constant sex appeal presented in cinema pictures and modern books and magazines made ignorance a great danger" (215). That is why the presentation of ugliness instead of sex appeal, and horror instead of light entertainment, can have the desired healing effect. Consider the conclusion of Dr. Leonard's tour:

> You see the woman. She's a shocking case. She's had seven children. She didn't know that she was infected until she took the blood test. We checked up on her children. One of them is dead. But of the six living, one is partially blind and deaf, one deaf and dumb, one crippled, one idiot, the fifth mentally defective, and an eighteen-month-old baby is also syphilitic.

Dr. Leonard's lecture is one of the rare instances when the scene in Eustace's novelization differs substantially from the film. There are two possible reasons for this: either Eustace, instead of the film as released, used an original screenplay, as I suggested earlier, or he, usually so meticulous in copying the speeches of characters, surrendered to the temptation to make the doctor's monologues even more impressive. Thus the woman introduced at the end of the tour has in the book version eleven children instead of seven, of which five did not survive, and "her husband died of general paralysis of the insane, which is invariably caused by the disease" (Eustace 163–64).

An even more radical change comes in the case of another patient, a middle-aged man with a lurid rash on his leg, who is just being treated by a doctor. In the movie Dr. Leonard says:

> What a curious coincidence. This infection was contracted innocently, too. Years ago from a kiss. The primary sore was neglected (*sic*) for a cold sore and the treatment was neglected.

In the novel there are two different patients: the one who contracted the disease through a kiss is a "young girl with a lip sore" (Eustace 161), while the story of the man with the ugly-looking rash on his arm (not on his leg) is

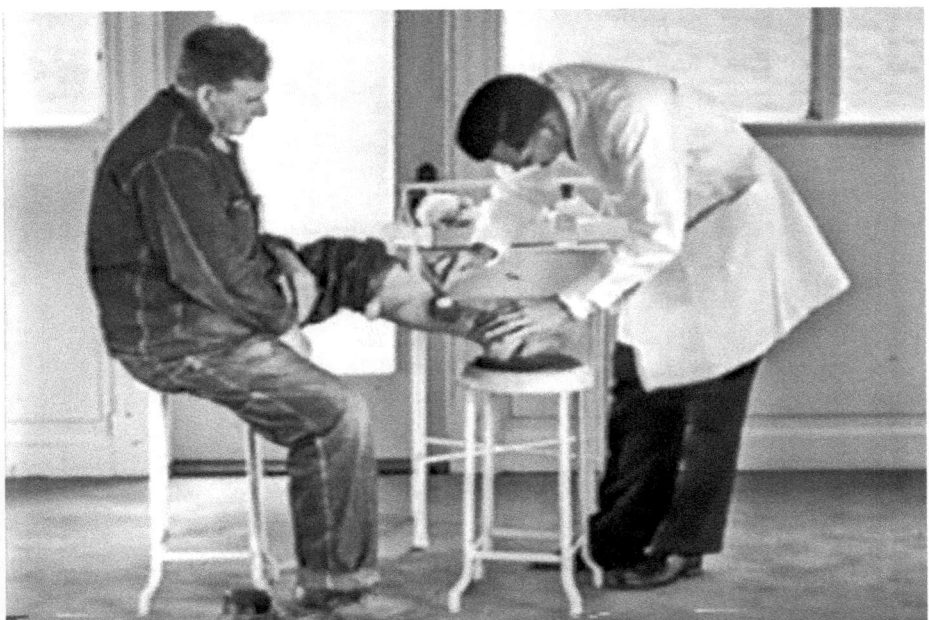

The doctor treats a man with a rash, who also "contracted innocently" (courtesy UCLA Film and Television Archive and National Archives of Canada).

never revealed. Only one of Dr. Leonard's patients — one in the third stage who had been "with a street-walker" (comp. Eustace 162) — is presented as immoral; the rest are victims of ignorance and the irresponsible behavior of others.

The social stigma that came with syphilis and gonorrhea often prevented people suffering from the diseases from looking for qualified medical help. The acknowledgment of a possibility, although rare, of "innocent" contagion had enormous psychological value, as it was the first step in persuading VD patients to visit a doctor. The patients badly needed a guarantee that they would not be ostracized from society, and their hypothetical innocence could be a shield even to those who led an immoral life and originally decided to stay silent about the source of their disease. The goal of health workers was to address such people's sense of responsibility and explain to them that their hesitation to consult a surgeon and to tell the true story could result in irreversible harm to other people, especially their former and current partners and their offspring. That is why many physicians supported the myth of contamination in various extra-genital ways, which science later proved as next-to impossible: according to them, one could get syphilis through "[m]etal drinking cups attached to public water fountains, eating utensils, towels and bedding [...], whistles, pens, pencils, toilets, medical procedures, tattoos, and toothbrushes" (Brandt 21). In *Damaged Lives*, besides the possibility of being contaminated through a kiss, another innocent way of transmission is described: "Playing bridge one night at a friend's house, he borrowed a pipe. The friend, of course, was already infected" (comp. Eustace 161). A quarter of a century later, in 1959, a doctor in an American educational film on venereal diseases, *The Innocent Party*, commissioned by the Kansas State Board of Health (re-released on DVD as a bonus to *Damaged Lives*) tells a careless young man who had sex with an "easy woman" unambiguously and bluntly that the possibility of getting it "from a toilet seat is similar to being hit by a meteor."

The task of hygienists was not only to make infected people seek medical help, but also to encourage the patients' confidence in medicine and make them believe in the possibility of a full recovery. *Damaged Lives* succeeded in this point: for example, the *New York Times* reviewer appreciated the fact that the film "stresses hope; there is assurance of the ability of medicine to deal with it if a fair chance is given; there is a pooh-poohing of the fiction that these things invariably leave ineradicable stains" (26).

When Elise Cooper, the blonde seductress, found out about her disease, she committed suicide; fortunately, not before she told Don about the infection, which at that time had already passed on to Joan and endangered the couple's unborn child. Suicide among venereal patients was very common:

that is why Dr. Leonard makes such an effort to explain to Don and Joan that their condition can be successfully treated:

> It's been neglected too long, but to-morrow we will start a course of treatments. Both you and your wife must continue regularly with these treatments for a period of two years, at the end of which [time] *I think I can safely say* you will both be cured [comp. Eustace 167, emphasis mine, the word in brackets not in the novelization].

The loophole in Dr. Leonard's otherwise optimistic pronouncement was pertinent: in the pre-antibiotic 1930s the arsenical compounds supplied intramuscularly or intravenously on a weekly basis usually "alternated with injections of bismuth to reduce the chance of toxic reaction" (Brandt 131), and the following regular after-treatment tests, including lumbar punctures, did not make the two-year period any walk in a rose garden. For poorer patients, the cost of the treatment would also be a problem: according to Brandt, in the early 1930s a complete cure at a private clinic (such as Dr. Leonard's) would cost "between $305 to $380, but could range as high as $1000" (131).

At the end of the movie Ulmer and Davis emphasized again how important full access to the facts about venereal diseases is, for the public as well as for those who already suffer from them. Don, who was exposed to Dr.

Joan (Diane Sinclair) between two unfriendly looking nurses in *Damaged Lives* (courtesy UCLA Film and Television Archive and National Archives of Canada).

Leonard's captivating tour, never thought of committing suicide, while Joan, who did not hear the lecture, planned to asphyxiate both herself and her husband with gas, despite Dr. Leonard's assurance that her child would be born normal. Such reasoning brought her closer to the hysterical and suicidal Elise than she would ever think: even the facial expressions of both women, confronting the fact of their disease, are similar.

Damaged Lives *in 1937:*
Too Late and Too Incomplete

The belated U.S. premiere of *Damaged Lives* in June 1937 came amidst rapid changes in the field of venereal disease research and treatment. While in November 1934 Thomas Parran, Jr., the New York State Health Commissioner, was ordered by the Columbia Broadcasting Company not to mention syphilis and gonorrhea in his radio address, in October 1936 his picture appeared on the cover of the issue of *Time* magazine that dealt, among other things, with his hygienic strategies in that field (Brandt 122–23). At that time Parran, a former chief of the Venereal Disease Division of the Public Health Service, was a freshly appointed surgeon general whose article about venereal diseases, supplemented with graphs and charts, was even reprinted in *Reader's Digest* (Brandt 138). Parran asked for confidential blood tests, immediate treatment for the contaminated, the duty to locate all the contacts of VD patients, compulsory examinations before marriages and in pregnancies, and proper sex education (Brandt 139–40). As Brandt pointed out, while in the early 1930s newspapers and magazines hardly dared to mention venereal diseases, in 1937 "the Pulitzer Prize Committee accorded an honorable mention to the New York *Daily News*" for its "campaign covering venereal diseases and prophylaxis" (141).

In 1937 Wassermann tests became a fashion of the season. According to Brandt, there were days in Chicago when ten to twelve thousand people were tested (152). Thus Ulmer's movie, which could have been the vanguard of the crusade against syphilis in 1930s America, served its purpose better in Canada and in Great Britain, while in the United States, due to its ban, it came to people's awareness too late — at the time when the campaign was in full swing. Only one year later, in Chicago and later in Boston, Seattle, and Philadelphia, people rushed to see Arnold Sundgaard's *Spirochete* (1938), a two-act theatrical "living newspaper" and "fictionalized documentary" on the history of the treatment of syphilis, and had themselves tested in the lobby during the intermission (Brandt 152).

The sad fact that *Damaged Lives* was severely bowdlerized definitely did not improve its position on the hygienic front. Sometimes it is impossible to guess why some parts of the film were cut. The most important missing scenes, which only Gitt and Turner returned to their place, describe Don's hesitation about how to cope with his disease, after Elise committed suicide and the police investigated his relationship with her, and subsequently his decision not to tell his best friend, the doctor, and seek unqualified medical help instead. These scenes are crucial for both the development of the story and its educational value, as they show exactly what people should not do after they find out about their diseases.

When Bill returns home from police headquarters, he must face not only his wife and his father but also his mother and Aunt Sylvia, the latter two not appearing in the 1937 version of the movie at all. Although they do not know about Don's disease, they found out about his affair and the scandalous suicide of Elise from the newspapers — the headline says "Shipowner's Son Sees Sweetie's Suicide" (see Eustace 120). Like Joan, they express their unconditional support for Don, offering help. Being ashamed to confess to his loved ones, Don, in a belated and futile outbreak of responsibility, pretends that he does not love his wife any more. The following dialogue, which serves as a revision of the above-quoted conversation in which Joan forgives Don his infidelity after being assured that it was only lust, not love, which brought him to Elise's bed, was also absent in the version the American audience could see in 1937:

JOAN: Did you love her? I'm just trying to understand, Donny, that's all. Don't you see, I've got to understand.
DON: Sure I loved her. What about it?
JOAN: Donny.
DON: Well, what are you going to do about it?
JOAN: Nothing, Donny. What is there to do?
DON: I don't care what you do. But I'm through, see? I'm going away somewhere, [I don't know where,] but I'm going alone. Do you understand?
JOAN: Donny, Donny — what are you saying?
DON: Listen, Joan, you might as well understand it once and for all. [I'm through with you.] I don't love you any more. Maybe I never did. Anyhow, I'm through now and I'm going [comp. Eustace 123–24, sentences in brackets not in the film].

Having abandoned his crying wife, Don strolls along the streets, until, on a park bench hastily vacated by a couple who did not want to sit next to a depressed stranger, he finds a copy of the *New York Bulletin*, and inside the advertisement of a Doctor Hortonn (in Eustace's book Horton): "Men! Are You Suffering? Quick Relief and Guaranteed Cure for Any Blood Disorder. YOU CAN BE CURED!" After a cut we can see Don in Dr. Hortonn's office. Everything there is arranged to increase the patients' confidence in the doctor's methods: his room is large and airy, his nurse immaculate-looking, and the doctor himself well-dressed and friendly (see Eustace 127–28). After an unspecified examination, Don is assured that there is nothing to worry about and is asked to pay $100. After the auspicious verdict of Dr. Hortonn, the elated Don hurries to ask his wife for forgiveness and tell her how much he loves her.

In Eustace's novelization the scene is longer. Dr. Horton coaxes Don into his office in an assuring voice: "The only way we can tell, Mr. Bradley, is by a medical examination. You need an expert's advice, and fortunately for you I am the man you need" (Eustace 129). Except the last part, there is nothing wrong with this statement, but Don, who desperately wants to hear good news, does not wonder that the results of the examination that might have even involved a blood test (the doctor takes a sample to his laboratory situated next to his office) come in only a few minutes. The cutting of this scene — its beginning cannot be found even in the restored version — goes against any logic, as it unmasks the strategies of the fake "specialists" preying on the fear of people to consult their intimate problems with a doctor they know.

In the 1937 version, Harrison Greene who plays Dr. Hortonn, does not appear on the screen at all, and the name of the character is mentioned only once. When Don tells Dr. Leonard that he did look for medical aid and found Hortonn's name in the newspapers, Dr. Leonard replies: "I know. One of those advertising specialists. I've heard that story before — other people have been to him, and to other fakirs (*sic*) like him" (comp. Eustace 156).

In his introduction to Eustace's novelization, Rolfe explicitly stressed that "more than a cursory look-over is necessary" to properly diagnose a venereal disease and continues with an example that warns against those who are not able to recognize the disease and take money for false hope, as well as against the equally dangerous charlatans who, in contrast, pretend that a healthy person has developed a complicated condition:

> The organisms that cause these diseases have to be sought for under the microscope or have their effects discovered in a test tube. Of course, it is quite possible [...] that quacks, knowing that the public expects blood tests, actually do take a specimen of blood from their victims! In India they have been known to hold half a sheet of blotting paper up to the window in front of the patient on which the spot of blood has been dropped, and pretend to find the spirochaete! Then they gravely tell their victim that an expensive course of treatment is necessary, which they can give [8].

The omission of the scene in Dr. Hortonn's office in the U.S.–released version is even more illogical when we realize that in the 1920s and the early 1930s such quacks were more a threat in the United States than in Great

Britain, where the Venereal Diseases Act made any attempts at treating such diseases by non-qualified people illegal as early as 1917, and any infringement of that law was strictly monitored and duly punished (Shiels 211).

In the early 1920s some American surgeons believed that the three most frequent mortal diseases, i.e. syphilis, tuberculosis, and cancer, were, in fact, only modifications of one of them: syphilis. Albert Abrams, who claimed to have discovered a diagnostic method using the "radio activity" of blood and became so popular that even Upton Sinclair, the famous author of *The Jungle*, wrote a laudatory article on him and his methods, "The House of Wonder" (1922), lectured:

> [Y]ou never find blood in which there is either carcinoma, sarcoma, tuberculosis, or dementia, that you do not also find the reaction of some form of syphilis. This disease turns out to be the basic source of our worst troubles; lurking in our blood in forms hitherto unrecognized, and in places not accessible to other researches [Sinclair 14].

According to Abrams, a Boston doctor who captured the attention of both the general and scientific public by his diagnoses from small samples of patients' blood sent to him (yes, on blotting paper), sometimes without any information about the people's symptoms or even their age or sex, there were two types of syphilis: a congenital one, for which the irresponsible behavior of our predecessors was responsible, and an acquired one, which people could contract through inoculation (Sinclair 10). Abrams claimed that because every illness had its own, unique, vibratory rate, he could diagnose them easily, running the blood sample through his special diagnostic equipment. This included a holder with three electrodes; on two of them the sample was placed, while the third one was connected to the forehead of a healthy human being through a set of three apparatuses called the "rheostatic dynamizer," "vibratory rate rheostat," and the "measuring rheostat." After the diagnosis was made, Abrams claimed he could cure a disease simply by exposing the person to "appropriate vibratory waves" from another invention of his, an "oscilloclast" (see Van Vleck).

At the time when Ulmer's movie was made, medicine in the U.S. was even further advanced in its conversion into a full-fledged "health industry." Nancy Tomes, exploring the "transformation of patients into consumers" (522), describes how the process in which the idea that "when it comes to health and health care, the normal economics on the production of goods and services in a modern market economy did not apply," was losing its validity, and how the conditions for the aggressive competition of doctors for patients were being created (522). Such competition, which included medical advertising, re-opened space for unqualified healers and different kinds of frauds of Dr. Hortonn's kind, whose era seemed to have terminated around the 1880s.

In *Damaged Lives*, the fatal consequences of Dr. Hortonn's trickery become obvious immediately after Don's next meeting with Joan, who found solace at the Halls'. Although Joan is angry at Don, again she shows her ability to forgive practically anything in the course of a few minutes, and later, in their king-size bed, she betrays to Don her sweet secret: she is pregnant. The scene, romantic and playful, is interrupted by the telephone. It is Marie, their neighbor from the apartment downstairs, pregnant with twins, who in the middle of the night calls Joan to ask whether her unborn children might be harmed when she disobeyed her doctor's instructions and took a bath. This is the first humorous scene of the film, and its non-inclusion in the 1937 version deprives it of the tension coming from the contrast between what we can see on the screen, and what we know about the main characters' health condition. To take a hot bath might not be ideal for the pregnant Marie, but the danger is nil compared to Joan's serious and undetected condition. The last third of Ulmer's film works skillfully with the polarization between humor and tragedy, but the American audience in 1937 did not have much opportunity to laugh during the screenings, unlike its 1933 predecessor. The restored print also re-introduces a comic scene in which the happy Don announces to his image in the mirror: "Congratulate me! I'm going to be a father" (see Eustace 141); later, a similar mood characterizes the reactions of family members, as well as Peter and Laura Hall, to Joan's pregnancy. However, Don's narcissistic gesture betrays his double nature as well: the loving husband and prospective father, and the macho who has the right to cheat on his fiancée only because she postponed their wedding day.

The comedy returns at the very end of the film, when Marie calls again to inquire whether eating pickles can harm her unborn babies. This scene was impossible to cut, as it resulted in the climax: it made Don and Joan realize that there is no reason to give it up. Still, without the context of the previous comic scenes it contributed to the cut version's fragmentariness, and left the viewers puzzled as to who this new character, that "fool woman" who supposedly appeared "again" (comp. Eustace 201), might be.

There is a similar problem in the 1937 version with another comic character, Captain Olaf Jensen (Vic Potel), or, better to say, with his absence, but in this case it is necessary to consult the novelization.

Novelization and the Beginning of Don's Story

Both the abridged 1937 version and the restored version of *Damaged Lives* start with the piercing sound of a cargo steamer under the credits (the restorers added one more shot). Then, after a cut, we can see New York with its skyscrapers and finally an office, where Donald Bradley, Sr. is just announcing through loudspeakers that his son is now the executive vice-president of the company. Don speaks in a very loud voice and as his first order he makes a certain Olaf Jensen captain; then his father scolds him for shouting: "I do wish you'd remember, son, that you're not on the ship one of the crew now." Even in the restored version, this is the only hint that Don ever worked as a sailor. In the abridged version no Jensen is mentioned afterwards, and the American audience had no chance to find out that he was Don's strict but reliable superior, a ship's mate of Swedish origin. In the restored version Jensen does appear in person: he gives the young couple a Swedish wooden cradle as a token of appreciation; unfortunately on the same day when they find out about their venereal disease which can harm the unborn child.

Jensen, who pronounces Donny's name as "Yonney," and his own name as "Yensen," may act as a clumsy and good-hearted sea-wolf who is pondering whether he can find his ship in "such a funny place — they call it Brooklyn I think" (comp. the different word order in Eustace 190), but the fact that he invaded the privacy of the Bradleys and reminded them of the danger their disease means for their child, makes the story even more tragic. In a preceding scene, Bill Hall prevented his little son from kissing Joan, giving her a clear sign that, despite the optimistic predictions of Dr. Leonard, her and Don's isolation will be long-term and on all sides.

However, Jensen does not enter the story as a remainder of Don's failure to protect his wife; he appears at its very beginning, in one of the scenes missing even in the restored version of the film. With the first reel missing and Eustace's novelization as the only source for the complete story, there is no certainty that the version released in 1933 contained the scenes, but it is more than a possibility: without them the story loses its structure and, judging after the continuity in the restored version, identical with the one in Eustace's book, both screenwriters were too careful to keep so many ends loose.

Jensen's very first sentence is, symbolically, "Steady ... Did ye year vat I say — steady!" (Eustace 26). He is referring to the cargo steamer arriving after an almost two-year-long journey with such destinations as Bombay, Port Said, Singapore, and Calcutta, but it would also be a piece of good advice for Donald, whom Jensen considers to be just an ordinary sailor signed on in Bombay. Jensen has no idea that Donald is the only son of the rich owner of the Bradley Steamship Co., who wants to taste "real life" before settling down as a New York businessman, and as his superior, he threatens him that he will not allow him to go ashore. When Donald laughs, Jensen, feeling offended, starts a friendly fight. Even when Donald, already changed into expensive civilian clothing, is leaving the ship to greet his fiancée, who came to meet him in a chauffeured Rolls-Royce, Jensen calls after him: "Where do you think you going in them swell clothes? ... Lend a hand with dat gangway and then I lock you up in the coal bunk" (Eustace 32).

In the next scene Joan takes the fight with Jensen as one of the reasons for postponing her wedding with Don. As the existence of this scene has been practically unknown in the U.S., I will quote it almost in full:

> DON: What's the matter, honey? You're crying.
> JOAN: I don't know. I'm happy, and I'm unhappy. Donny, you've been fighting again.
> DON: Sure. Why not? It was only with old Jenny. Do you know what, Joan? If ever I get a chance, Jenny's going to be captain of one of our ships. He's a great head, that chap.
> JOAN: Well, why do you fight with him? You know I hate it.
> DON: Oh well. Love me, Joan?
> JOAN: You know I do, Donny.
> DON: Well — marry me.
> JOAN: Donny, dear, don't be absurd.
> DON: Do I look as though I'm acting absurdly?
> JOAN: Of course you don't, darling. But you do, you know.
> DON: Well, why do you try to put me off? When's it going to be?
> JOAN: Are you serious, Donny?
> DON: Gee, Joan, you get me all burned up. Now listen here, young lady — we've stalled around long enough. Ever since Hector was a pup we've talked about getting married. Well, now I mean business. When will you marry me?
> JOAN: Yes, Donny, I know. But —
> DON: Well, let's not talk any more about it. Let's do it. We'll stop at the City Hall on the way uptown. Now there's an idea for you. We can surprise dad —
> [...]
> JOAN: There you are — you can't be serious even when I am. After all, you've been out of college for nearly two years now — and they've been wonderful years, romantic, adventurous. I know. But I can't marry you, dear, until you settle down and go to work.
> DON: All right. I've changed my mind — I'm not going home. I'm going to work. To my father's office, please [Eustace 34–37, only dialogues cited].

The scene characterizes both Don and Joan as naïve children from rich families — for Don life is just an adventurous game, while Joan obviously thinks that it can be carefully and responsibly planned into the slightest detail.

It is no coincidence that the main character of a story about venereal diseases is introduced at first as a sailor; according to statistics, the most endangered groups are all-male communities far from home, e.g. sailors and soldiers. Great Britain, as a marine superpower, had more experience with infected sailors than the United States: the British National Council for Combating Venereal Diseases, founded in 1914, established free and discreet treatment centers in all the important ports of the world through an international agreement (Shiels 212).

The most risky parts of the world in this aspect seemed to be the West Indies, Hong Kong, Singapore, Ceylon, and Mediterranean colonies where prostitution flourished and no one checked the hygienic conditions. There were at least attempts to regulate prostitution, but the Colonial Office had partial success only in some of the areas, namely Ceylon, the Straits Settlements, and Hong Kong. It is therefore obvious that Don, during his two years at sea, had many opportunities to sleep with prostitutes and contract a venereal disease, but, fortunately, his sense of adventure was lacking in this point; he was faithful to his fiancée, thinking more about family wealth than about sex. The disease hit him where he expected it least, and therefore was more vulnerable to erotic temptation: in New York, among the rich and the educated — and, which is even more important, when he cheated on Joan for the first and last time.

Don returned from the journey as a true businessman, which he proves immediately to his father, who is strictly against giving important positions in the company to undeserving relatives. When Don arrives at his father's offices to ask for a position in the family firm, Mr. Bradley, Sr. informs him bluntly that "[j]obs are scarce" (Eustace 41), but a few minutes later the boy miraculously solves a serious problem the company faces — one of the ships is stuck in Hong Kong without any cargo and because of a strike on shore, she would have to return home "in ballast" (42). Don sends the ship to Bombay, as when he was there, he had made a deal with the Elliman Salt Mines, according to which the company guaranteed a cargo for any of the Bradley ships that might be sent in their direction. Consequently, his father softens: "Here's your office, son. If it's work you want, I'll see that you get plenty of it" (45).

Without these scenes it is impossible to understand why Donald "will have complete charge of all ships" (comp. Eustace 46) and who the Jensen, promoted to Captain of the *Atlantic* (in the novelization the *Hulva*), is. To emphasize the simple relationship between the woman's hesitation to marry the man and the man's infidelity that often results in a venereal disease, there is one more dialogue about marriage, proving that Joan maneuvers even after her beloved receives a well-paid and respectable job:

DON: Well, don't you believe me now?
JOAN: I don't know, dear. I guess so.
DON: When will you marry me?
JOAN: How about June?
DON: How about to-morrow?
JOAN: Nope.
[...]

DON: What more do you want? Look, I'm settled down. Father is serious about this. I know it sounds funny. But father is giving me my chance. I'm a big business man now, Joan, all tied down to my desk. What more can I do?
JOAN: You can wait, Donny. Besides, I want a June wedding.
DON: Why June?
JOAN: I don't know. Just want it that way, that's all [Eustace 46–47, only dialogues cited].

This conversation makes even more obvious that Joan is not the pragmatic woman waiting reasonably for her beloved's maturation that she occasionally seemed to be, but a whimsical little girl, who, in most cases, simply does not know. That is why a knowledge of the two dialogues, which probably did not survive in their film form, is crucial for an understanding of why Joan is later not presented simply as an innocent victim, but, more ambiguously, as both a casualty and an accomplice. Part and parcel of the hygienic point of view is the attempt to abstain from useless moralizing, common among the American neo–Victorians. They concentrated primarily on men and the widespread myth that they need more sex "to maintain their physical and psychic health" than women (Brandt 26), and took women, save for prostitutes, automatically as victims. These neo–Victorians, mostly approaching the problem from religious positions, would rather eradicate the danger by a ban on any extra-marital sex, and took the threat of venereal diseases "as a powerful control on immorality" (Brandt 27). In the 1930s, it was already more than clear that hypocrisy and moralistic clichés contributed to the proliferation of the diseases, instead of reducing the number of cases, and that pre-marital sex was not a moral plague, but a valid prophylactic instrument. From the novelization it is obvious that there was no sex between Don and Joan prior to their wedding: on the ship, Don muses only over a kiss he received from his fiancée two years earlier.

After Gitt and Turner's efforts at the restoration of the film came to fruition, it finally became possible, with the help of Eustace's novelization, to make an attempt at reconstructing the story as Davis and Ulmer originally wrote it. This will at last enable film scholars to discuss the role of Ulmer's film in various cinematic, broadly cultural, and social contexts without spending too much time on speculations as to what was the artists' intention and what was a mere omission or a censor's cut. A decent analysis of the aesthetic qualities of the movie is still waiting to be written, but even our investigation, although it used the comparison of the restored version, the abridged version, and the novelization of the movie primarily to highlight the story's educational and hygienic merits, tried hard not to shift out of sight the screenwriters' narrative skills and the director's film-making qualities.

Notes

1. The anonymous reviewer for the *Boston Globe* confused the actresses and praised for the role of Elise, the blonde seductress, Marcelline (*sic*) Day, who played the part of Laura Hall.
2. Grissemann claims that the film was made "at General Service Studios in Hollywood (at that time still Metropolitan Studios)," not realizing that when the shooting of *Damaged Lives* started, at the end of March 1933, the studios were already renamed (Grissemann 61, my translation). In addition to that, D. J. Turner, consulting the correspondence of Dr. Gordan Bates from that time, discovered that the set was, in all probability, at Educational Studios (see Turner).
3. The reviewer also suggests that the story "has taken five years adequately to dramatize and portray on the screen" (8), which is highly improbable given the fact that Ulmer received the commission as late as in 1933.
4. Grissemann follows J. T. M., the *New York Times* reviewer, erroneously giving the name of the organization as the American Social Hygiene Society (62).
5. C. J. Eustace, a later convert to Catholicism and contributor to periodicals such as the *Commonweal* and the *Catholic Record* (his pen name there was "The Fisherman"), thought that science, following needs of human bodies rather than souls and often forgetting about the moral order derived from the laws of God, should be subject to religion. *Damaged Lives* obviously got his attention for its focus on ethical problems but his "novel of the film," showing the necessity for the scientific treatment of venereal diseases, also proves that he was not strictly anti-science. See Kuffert 117–18.
6. Facts provided by D. J. Turner in an e-mail of 3 Apr. 2008 (according to Turner, identical information was sent in November 2002 to Grissemann). D.J. Turner also provided me with access to the restored version of *Damaged Lives,* and, in his e-mail of 30 July 2008, he turned my attention to several often-repeated errors and omissions concerning the film. Without his valuable help my essay could never have been written.
7. A new film version of *Damaged Goods* by Phil Goldstone appeared in 1937 (the premiere was on 22 May, three weeks before the re-release of Ulmer's film), inviting a comparison with *Damaged Lives.*
8. As the credits do not give the characters' names, reviewers misspelled Elise as Alyce, copying the mistake from each other.

Works Cited

Brandt, Allan M. *No Magic Bullet: A Social History of Venereal Disease in the United States since 1880.* Revised ed. Oxford: Oxford University Press, 1987.
"The Coliseum—'Damaged Lives.'" Rev. of *Damaged Lives,* dir. by Edgar G. Ulmer. *Times* (London) 21 Aug. 1933: 8.
Eustace, C. J. *Damaged Lives: The Novel of the Film.* London: Putnam & Co., 1934.
Gitt, Robert. "RE: Edgar G. Ulmer's Damaged Lives." E-mail to Marcel Arbeit, 16 Apr. 2008.
Grissemann, Stefan. *Mann im Schatten: Der Filmemacher Edgar G. Ulmer.* Wien: Paul Zsolnay Verlag, 2003.
Hoberman, J[im]. "Low and Behold." *Village Voice* 17 Nov. 1998: 135.
The Innocent Party, dir. uncredited. Kansas State Board of Health, 1959. DVD. Alpha Video Classics, [n.d.].

J. T. M. Rev. of *Damaged Lives*, from a story by Don Davis and Edgar Ulmer. *New York Times* 14 June 1937: 26.

Kuffert, L. B. *A Great Duty: Canadian Responses to Modern Life, and Mass Culture, 1939–1967*. Winnipeg: University of Winnipeg Press, 2002.

"Majestic Theatre — 'Damaged Lives.'" Rev of *Damaged Lives*, dir. by Edgar G. Ulmer. *Boston Globe* 16 Sept. 1933: 8.

[Morrison], Hobe. Rev. of *Damaged Lives*, dir. by Edgar G. Ulmer. *Variety* 16 June 1937: 13.

Rolfe, S. Neville. "Introduction." *Damaged Lives: The Novel of the Film*. By C. J. Eustace. London: Putnam & Co., 1934. 7–20.

Schultz, Harleigh. "Bold Stroke in Movie Proves Keen Drama." *Boston Globe* 18 Sept. 1933: 10.

Shiels, Drummond. "What the British Social Hygiene Council Is and Does." *Damaged Lives: The Novel of the Film*. By C. J. Eustace. London: Putnam & Co., 1934. 209–221.

Sinclair, Upton. "The House of Wonder: An Account of the Revolutionary Discovery of Dr. Albert Abrams, the Diagnosis of Disease from the Radio Activity of the Blood." *Pearson's Magazine* 48 (June 1922): 9–17.

Temkin, Owsei. "Therapeutic Trends and the Treatment of Syphilis before 1900." *The Double Face of Janus and Other Essays in the History of Medicine*. Baltimore: Johns Hopkins University Press, [1977]. 518–524.

Tomes, Nancy. "Merchants of Health: Medicine and Consumer Culture in the United States, 1900–1940." *Journal of American History* 88.2 (Sept. 2001): 519–47.

Turner, D.J. "DJT/DAMAGED LIVES." E-mails to Marcel Arbeit, 3 Apr. 2008; 30 July 2008.

Ulmer, Edgar G., dir. *Damaged Lives*. 1933. Abridged version. Weldon Pictures, 1937. DVD. Alpha Video Classics, [n.d.].

_____. *Damaged Lives*. Weldon Pictures, 1933. Restored by Robert Gitt and D.J. Turner. Preserved by UCLA Film and Television Archive and the National Archives of Canada, [1993].

Ulmer Cipes, Arianné. "Re: DAMAGED LIVES." E-mail to Marcel Arbeit, 8 Mar. 2008.

Van Vleck, Richard. "The Electronic Reactions of Albert Abrams." *American Artifacts* 39 (1998–99), *http://www.americanartifacts.com/smma/abrams/abrams.htm*, last accessed April 8, 2008.

The Black Cat

Gregory William Mank

> *WILD! WEIRD! WICKED!*
> *B-r-r-r-r-r-r! You'll see things you never WILL forget!... but you'll love it!*
> — Publicity for *The Black Cat*

It was in Hollywood, in 1934, that Edgar G. Ulmer crucified the Devil.

Of course, it wasn't actually a crucifixion — it was a skinning alive on a rack — but it was close enough. The arms-stretched, half-naked victim was Boris Karloff, world-famous as Frankenstein's Monster, made up here to look like a fey Lucifer as Ulmer boldly (and blasphemously) made Satan a Christ symbol. His scourger was no less than Bela Lugosi, Dracula-as-hero — a nicely subversive touch.

It was only one in a repertoire of defiant, perverse and unforgettably nightmarish images that an on-the-loose Edgar Ulmer strikingly brought forth into the light in *The Black Cat,* Universal's historic first union of Karloff and Lugosi. The horror classic reigns as Ulmer's most famous film, the only one where he had his wicked way at a major studio (if one accepts Universal as a major) and surely one of the most vivid all-time examples of a Hollywood talent free from his cage and running amok, professionally and personally. Ulmer's film about "the modern incarnation of Satan" is a wild and revealing self-exorcism, and in its course he:

- Defied the Production Code by presenting a Black Mass, complete with a cockeyed cross.
- Further thumb-nosed the Code by presenting the skinning alive scene.
- Weaved necrophilia, incest, and cat phobia into his witch's brew of a story.
- Sneaked in a shot where the heroine's dress flew up in the back and exposed her panties.

Crucifying the devil: Dr. Vitus Werdegast (Bela Lugosi) skins alive Hjalmar Poelzig (Boris Karloff) in the baroque climax of *The Black Cat* (from the collection of Gregory William Mank).

- Sexually harassed a starlet in baroque manner that haunted her until her death almost 70 years later.
- Fell in love with an in-law of Carl Laemmle, Sr. (the founder of Universal), lured her away from her husband, eventually married her — and became the victim of a monolithic Hollywood blackballing.

Indeed, come the night of the premiere of *The Black Cat* at Hollywood's Pantages Theatre, and Ulmer was *persona-non-grata*, uninvited to the opening of Universal's hit of the season, a film he had masterminded from adaptation to Bauhaus sets, from costumes to classical musical score. Perhaps it was inevitable. *The Black Cat* is so aberrant and exotically horrific that the 1934 cinema colony only could have presented its director with professional exile or a straitjacket.

Yet today, *The Black Cat* rules as Universal's most exquisitely twisted horror film — so hallowed that it was possibly worth it that Edgar G. Ulmer virtually performed professional penance for his dark masterpiece for the rest of his life.

* * *

> "My father was a gremlin! He could go between being very scary and being very funny. He loved to scare people — it's a Germanic thing — and if I was bad as a little girl, he'd tell me the 'ooflydoof' (he invented language!) was going to come out of the closet and get me! It really scared me, but it's a very funny word, right?" [interview, Arianné Ulmer Cipes].

Horror was the flagship attraction of Universal City, California — appropriately.

The studio, nestled under the mountains of the San Fernando Valley, actually had the look of a California boomtown set up in Transylvania's Borgo Pass. Its founder, "Uncle Carl" Laemmle, was a 5'3" Bavarian immigrant whose bald, wizened hobgoblin appearance perfectly suited his status as Universal's "mountain king," and whose failing prostate caused his teenage son "Junior" to trot behind him carrying a tin pail bucket (see Gabler). Junior grew up to become Universal's "Crown Prince," whose job as General Manager was a twenty-first birthday gift from his shamelessly nepotistic dad. The heir had produced the classic *All Quiet on the Western Front* (1930), winning the Best Picture Academy Award, yet Junior himself was no prize. He was a legendary hypochondriac who wore Kotex in his pants (interview, Shirley Ulmer) because he feared his penis might catch cold and battled with his dad, who — General Manager job be damned — still sometimes passed off his filled bucket to Junior to dump.

In 1988, Shirley Ulmer recalled her days as a Laemmle relative-by-marriage:

> In 1933, I married Max Alexander, "Uncle Carl" Laemmle's nephew, and worked at Universal as a script clerk (we're called "script supervisors" today!). Universal was an eccentric studio, and "Uncle Carl" was an eccentric, dear, crazy old man — let's face it.... It was amazing! At the big Laemmle estate in Benedict Canyon, every Sunday, we all came into the dining room, maybe 24 strong — all relatives. We were not allowed to speak or sit until Uncle Carl had made his entrance. Since he was always fighting with his son, poor Junior, and his daughter Rosabelle, I finally got the seat of honor at the table, next to Uncle Carl [interview].

One of the sources of trouble between Laemmle Sr. and Jr. was horror. Uncle Carl labeled such films as "morbid," but had to acknowledge that Universal's two legendary hits of the 1920s were *The Hunchback of Notre Dame* and *The Phantom of the Opera*, both starring Lon Chaney. Junior's flirtations with the shadowy side of cinema had spawned 1931's *Dracula*, starring Bela Lugosi, and *Frankenstein*, starring Boris Karloff — sensations that became modern folklore, spooking old man Laemmle while saving the studio. The complexities between the mountain king and his crown prince ran dark and deep.

Junior Laemmle had little ability to pursue a project past his initial fascination, but he had an uncanny flair for selecting the right talent to capture the vision. Tod Browning had directed *Dracula*, the recovering alcoholic giving the film a crawlingly evil hangover aura, complete with Texas armadillos creeping around a Transylvania castle. James Whale, who'd created his own aristocratic Hollywood "self" by imitating the gentleman lovers he'd known in London, had brought a deeply personal feel to *Frankenstein* and its "I have created a Monster!" credo. Of course, Browning was "the Edgar Allan Poe of the Screen," while Universal was all-hailing contract director Whale as a "genius," so their engagements had made show business sense.

However! Come *The Black Cat*, the first epic screen union of Boris Karloff and Bela Lugosi, and Junior indulged a truly daredevil instinct in selecting a director. His choice was 29-year old Austrian Edgar G. Ulmer who, for all his work in European and Hollywood cinema, had never directed a major feature. Ulmer himself claimed he got the job because he was part of the "so-called intellectual crew" (as he put it) who hung around Junior. The director's future wife claimed he won the reins of *The Black Cat* because he was Junior's "unofficial psychiatrist" and due to the fact that Junior, possibly sexually ecumenical, "had a crush" on the man. Other accounts claim that the young director had wanted to direct *Little Man, What Now?* but had to settle for set designer, losing the director job to Academy Award-winning Frank Borzage, and that the front office owed him an assignment.

All of these factors surely played a part. But perhaps the most potent reason Junior Laemmle hired Edgar G. Ulmer to direct *The Black Cat* was because he wanted to produce a horror show that would truly amaze and appall Laemmle Sr. Junior unlocked the closet and let loose the "ooflydoof"—trusting that once the old man saw what Ulmer had wrought, he'd never have time to aim for the bucket.

* * *

I rave, I rape, I rip, I rend...
— from Aleister Crowley's *Hymn to Pan*.

On January 13, 1934, Louella Parsons announced that Karloff would star for Universal in *The Black Cat*, based on Poe's 1843 horror tale. Four days later the Universal "family" gathered for Uncle Carl's 67th birthday. Celebrating celebrities enjoying the cake included Margaret Sullavan, Ken Maynard, and, on the right hand of the founder, Boris Karloff. Lurking in a back row: Edgar Ulmer.

By this time Ulmer had landed the job on *The Black Cat*. Set to direct a horror film at Universal surely made Ulmer feel like a kid proverbially loose in a candy store and he merrily plunged into all aspects of the production.

For the obsessive services of its director/story adaptor/set and costume designer, Universal paid Ulmer $150 per week.

Tossing away Universal's three previous scripts based on *The Black Cat*, Ulmer remembered his days and nights on 1920's *Der Golem*, and Gustav Meyrinck, who'd written *Der Golem* as a novel. Ulmer told Peter Bogdanovich that Meyrinck

> was contemplating a play based upon Doumont, which was a French fortress the Germans had shelled to pieces during the First World War. There were some survivors who didn't come out for years. And the commander was a strange Euripides figure who went crazy three years later when he was brought back to Paris, because he had walked on that mountain of bodies [Bogdanovich 389]

Meanwhile, Ulmer had a *simpatico* collaborator — Peter Ruric, who wrote for *Black Mask* magazine, as well as screenplays. Described as "a blond, bearded member of the Malibu Beach crowd, taken to wearing ascot scarves" (Fischer), Ruric faced a rocky future, including his cigarette girl wife jumping out the window of their third story Hollywood apartment in 1940 (she merely injured her arm) and an alcoholic demise in a cheap North Hollywood apartment in 1966. Ruric would receive solo credit on *The Black Cat's* screenplay (despite Ulmer's ideas) and his salary for the film far surpassed Ulmer's own compensation, with Ruric also serving as the film's dialogue director. One by one, Ulmer tossed his concepts into the witch's pot that he and Ruric were stirring. Doumont became Fort Marmaros — described in the film as "the greatest graveyard in the world!" Ulmer paid homage to *The Cabinet of Dr. Caligari* via the film's tragic hero, Dr. Vitus Werdegast, a mad psychiatrist, suffering from cat phobia. He honored *Der Golem* with Thamal, Werdegast's giant mute servant.

For a dash of topical horror, Ulmer looked to the headlines.

"The Wickedest Man in the World" was the soubriquet of Aleister Crowley, a Satanist who, with a shaved head and sharpened teeth, proudly proclaimed himself "The Beast of the Apocalypse." Born in England in 1875, the son of hysterically religious parents, Crowley had been the inspiration for Somerset Maugham's 1908 story *The Magician* (later adapted into a 1926 film, directed by Rex Ingram). A wealthy heir, mountain climber, writer, poet, chess player, sex maniac, drug addict and high priest, Crowley professed a Rabelaisian theology: "Do what thou wilt/shall be the whole of the Law."

Crowley "peaked" in 1920, when he founded the Abbey of Thelema in a farmhouse in Cefalu, Sicily. There, with his "Scarlet Woman" mistress, the gaunt, wild-eyed Leah Hirsig, Crowley celebrated all variety of depraved rites and enjoyed a bedroom he called "The Room of Nightmares." One witness reported a Black Mass in which the "Scarlet Woman" performed bestiality with a goat. In February of 1923, an Oxford undergraduate named Raoul Loveday died, possibly due to drinking the blood of a sacrificial cat at Crowley's temple. There was a wild public scandal, and Benito Mussolini exiled Crowley from Sicily. In 1932, artist Nina Hamnett, the model for Henri Gaudier-Brzeska's sculpture "Laughing Torso," wrote in her memoir (also titled *Laughing Torso*) that's she'd been an acquaintance of "the Beast," that he was "supposed" to have practiced Black Magic at his abbey in Cefalu, that a baby was said to have mysteriously disappeared, that Crowley had a goat, and that the villagers "were frightened of him." Crowley, who'd squandered most of his inheritance, decided to sue. "The Beast" was preparing his lawsuit at the very same time Universal was concocting *The Black Cat* (see Sutin).

The raving, raping, ripping and rending of Aleister Crowley fascinated Edgar Ulmer — becoming the influence that truly made *The Black Cat* a horror film. Yet there was also a private influence that fueled part of the bitter passion he brought to this film: his recent divorce.

* * *

> I'd describe my mother as a femme fatale — very attractive.... She was a "Fanchonette," one of the Fanchon and Marco dancers who danced at the Paramount Theatre in Los Angeles, and quite a lot of other places, including Silent movies. She was a tiny little woman, 5' tall, with very dark hair and almost black eyes, a great beauty, known for her gorgeous legs. Clara Bow didn't have very pretty legs, and when they shot Clara Bow's legs, those were my mother's legs.... I remember her showing me how to do the Charleston — a very mean Charleston! She was a flapper, absolutely [interview, Joen Mitchell].

After her father's death in 1972, Arianne Ulmer sought a half-sister via an early marriage her father rarely discussed. Ironically, the sister found *her* over twenty years later after reading Bogdanovich's collection of director profiles and interviews, *Who the Devil Made It?* (that reprinted his Ulmer interview from *Kings of the B's*). The first wife's name was Joen Warner, and she'd wed Ulmer at the mission in Riverside August 21, 1926. Their daughter Joen was born December 15, 1929.

Edgar and Joen honeymooned at Lake Arrowhead, where Ulmer was working with F.W. Murnau filming *Sunrise*. Intriguingly, Joen resembled Margaret Livingston, *Sunrise*'s dark, vampy "Woman from the City," who nearly destroys the pastoral bliss of George O'Brien and Janet Gaynor. As Joen Mitchell recalls, her parents were divorced "by the time I was three or four years old" — which would have been shortly before *The Black Cat*. Her mother eventually married a man from rural Montana ("very different from my father," says Joen) and died in 1988. Joen met Edgar Ulmer only once — when she was 17 ("My mother had to make contact with my father as part of a financial settlement for past child support, and he wanted to see me"). The unhappy marriage apparently left lasting scars on both man and wife, and Ulmer named his imperiled heroine of *The Black Cat* "Joan."

By the way, Joen Mitchell has seen *The Black Cat*. Her impression? "It gave me the creeps," she laughs. "I don't like creepy things. I'm anti-scary, creepy things!"

In addition to his other labors on *The Black Cat*, Ulmer did a considerable bit of hand-holding for both stars as the film approached its shooting date. Karloff, back at Universal after powerful character roles in RKO's *The Lost Patrol* and Twentieth Century's *The House of Rothschild*, was reluctant to be a bogeyman again, and Ulmer tantalized him with his costume designs — "He felt in these duds," recalled Ulmer, "he could employ a sort of 'out-of-this-world' appearance" (*Modern Monsters*). Lugosi came from New York, abandoning a scheduled play to join *The Black Cat*— his inclusion was a studio afterthought — and he and Ulmer conferred in German (which Lugosi still found more familiar than English) as the actor, also fearful of horror typecasting, campaigned for his role to be as sympathetic as possible.

How did Ulmer get this far with so perverse a premise for his nightmare film? Well, Uncle Carl and Junior had taken the train to New York at the end of January to discuss Universal's next season with the sales representatives. Sr. came back in mid–February, while Jr. stayed a bit longer in the Big Apple to see some plays, and would not arrive back in L.A. until February 24. This left the supervisory preparation to E. M. Asher, who'd served in a similar capacity on the "U" horrors *Dracula, Frankenstein* and *Murders in the Rue Morgue*. Asher, as Shirley Ulmer remembered, had a strange habit: he'd meet Ulmer for story conferences while sitting on the toilet.

"There'd be Asher," Shirley laughed, "having a 'b.m.,' holding up the script and saying to Edgar, 'I've read it — and I think it's *great!*'"

Destined to help capture the warped vision of *The Black Cat* was John J. Mescall, the gifted (but sadly alcoholic) cinematographer whose most famous credit would be James Whale's *Bride of Frankenstein*. Shirley Alexander — who'd recently fallen in love with Edgar Ulmer ("I fell in love with Edgar the first time I met him — the first time I *heard* him") — was delighted to get work on *The Black Cat* as an assistant to the script girl.

The final story bore a resemblance to Poe only in its passionately mad fervor. Modern Lucifer incarnate Hjalmar Poelzig (KARLOFF, as Universal top-billed him, surname only) hosts mad-for-revenge Dr. Vitus Werdegast (Bela Lugosi) at Fort Marmaros, which Poelzig had commanded — and betrayed — during the war. Poelzig had stolen Werdegast's wife Karen and not only has killed her (and displays her cadaver hanging in a vertical glass coffin in his cellars), but has married the daughter of Werdegast and Karen —

a sylph also named Karen (blonde Universal starlet Lucille Lund). Caught as pawns in the "game of death" are stranded-in-the-night newlyweds Peter Alison (David Manners, classically handsome romantic hero of *Dracula* and *The Mummy*) and his bride Joan (auburn-haired Jacqueline Wells, later known professionally as Julie Bishop, who'd recently played *Hamlet's* Ophelia at the Pasadena Playhouse). Also on hand for the macabre festivities: Harry Cording as the hulking Thamal, and Egon Brecher (whom Ulmer had known when Brecher was managing director of the Vienna Theatre) as Poelzig's beetle-browed major domo. The 65-minute film builds to Poelzig killing stepdaughter/wife Karen, a Black Mass with Poelzig as high priest and Joan as virgin sacrifice *du jour*, Werdegast saving Joan and skinning Poelzig alive, and our dark hero sending the newlyweds out into the night as he sets off the old dynamite, blowing up Fort Marmaros — and himself.

Monday, February 26, 1934: a potentially disastrous day for *The Black Cat* arrived as Ulmer, Ruric and Asher had a pre-shooting meeting with Joseph Breen, czar of the Production Code Administration.[1] Breen followed up that day with a letter of warning to Universal, citing two major problems. The first was the skinning of a man alive, and the second was the killing of a cat. Actually, Breen advised caution on 19 different points of *The Black Cat* script. Among them: a photographer at the opening wedding (an episode cut from the script) could not be presented as homosexual; "Czech Slovakians" (*sic*) could not be referred to as "people who devour the young"; the shot of Poelzig in bed with a naked woman ("and all it implies") should go; the scene of Karen hanging in the glass coffin was a no-no; there could be no indecent exposure of Joan in the shower; the devil worshippers could not be identified as German, nor could they show "any suggestion of homosexuality or perversion;" the inverted cross at the Black Mass was "definitely inadvisable;" the celebration of Poelzig's Black Mass should "avoid any suggestion of a parody on any church ceremony." Still, the greatest trouble was the "too brutal and gruesome" climactic skinning alive of Poelzig.

"This entire sequence is a very dangerous one...," warned Joseph Breen.

Storms and casting trouble caused "the Big U." to set back starting dates on four pictures — including *The Black Cat,* now set to begin March 2. On February 28, Universal re-submitted its script for *The Black Cat* to Joseph Breen, the opening wedding episode deleted. As for Breen's many concerns, one of his watchdogs reported that Ulmer had merely eliminated the "Czech Slovakians" line (actually, the script now claimed "Tasmanians are the ones who devour their young"), and removed Ulmer's description of the inverted cross — "although a cross of some type is still used," carped the reader.

"As for the skinning alive scenes," the Breen Office noted, "they remain unchanged."

Boris Karloff as the modern Lucifer in *The Black Cat* (from the collection of Gregory William Mank).

Despite the announced postponement, *The Black Cat* jumped the gun and began shooting Wednesday, February 28, 1934, the same day Universal had re-submitted the script to the Breen office. Ulmer had not waited for Breen's reply.

The film was already coming to pass.

* * *

That's when the horror started — and it wasn't in the script, believe me!
— interview, Lucille Lund.

The budget was only $91,125.00 — 25 percent of which was studio overhead — and the shooting schedule only 15 days (see *The Black Cat* Production Papers). For the young Edgar Ulmer to have such overnight control, however, could only have been intoxicating.

As the Luciferian high priest Poelzig, Karloff was truly a lisping, leering horror. In his satanic hairdo, festooned eyebrows and black lipstick, he didn't resemble a devil as much as he did a kinky "Satan" at a Weimar Berlin cabaret Halloween party, hell-bent on snaring first prize. Between scenes, Karloff was a jolly devil too — merrily ruining takes by saying "Boo!" to the camera, charming leading lady Jacqueline Wells ("an extremely bright, beautifully educated man, every inch the gentleman," she remembered [interview, Jacqueline Wells]) and singing Cockney ditties to Lucille Lund ("Karloff was darling!"). Ulmer praised Karloff as "Very charming ... a very fine actor. Five star." Indeed, in one of the finest moments in *The Black Cat*, Karloff felinely lisps to Wells of Lugosi, "He has an intense and all-consuming horror — of cats!" — his spine-tingling delivery sexy, sinister and sacrilegious, all at once. "...Karloff had this Goddamned lisp!" laughed Shirley Ulmer, who had high praise for Karloff personally and professionally. "We had a terrible time, because he couldn't say "black cat" — he'd say, "black cath!"

Lugosi, too, was at his best, his Dr. Vitus Werdegast a superb tragic hero. The actor overcame his anxieties about Karloff's scene-stealing ("when he realized I didn't go in for such nonsense, we became friends," recalled Karloff [see Roman]) and Universal's machinations (the studio had unceremoniously dumped him after Karloff's triumph in *Frankenstein*). Ulmer carefully controlled Lugosi's penchant for overacting, understanding his stage origins. "Supernatural, perhaps," intones Lugosi in one scene with masterfully foreboding pauses. "Baloney, perhaps not. There are many things — under the sun!"

Ulmer directed both stars as if conducting an orchestra — actually waving a baton as they acted their scenes. And he accented Lugosi's good looks, much to the delight of the star himself, who'd exult when seeing *The Black Cat* in his late years, "My, what a handsome bastard I used to be!" (interview, Hope Lugosi).

Shirley Ulmer, there on the set every day as assistant script supervisor, believed Lugosi a bit intimidated by Karloff and resentful of the friendship he enjoyed with Ulmer. If so, it was all for the best — in the Karloff vs. Lugosi scenes, the dramatic sparks fly.

There was Karloff's daily 4 P.M. tea break and various frivolities, such as a Universal "Black Cats Parade," with Karloff and Lugosi as judges. All the while, Ulmer crafted the most truly horrific of Universal's Golden Age shockers — defying the Breen office on virtually every point. He showed Poelzig in bed with the (implied) naked Karen. He hung Karen's mother (also Lund) in the glass coffin. He shot his Black Mass, complete with cockeyed cross and cockamamie Latin prayers ("*Cum grano salis*," i.e., "with a grain of salt," etc.). And he pulled all stops, delivering the "very dangerous" skinning alive scene unforgettably — Karloff, stripped to the waist and arms stretched on a rack, a crucified Lucifer, yelping like a skinned cat, Liszt's *Devil Sonata* booming on the soundtrack, Lugosi so sadistically into the scene that he garbles his English in the release print "(promising to skin Boris 'flowly' when he meant 'slowly')." This scene alone, with its madly askew religious twist, reigns as one of the most wildly daring images in all of cinema.

As scripted, the scene was even more baroque — Karloff's skinned pulp of a body wriggling off the rack and oozing its way across the cellar floors to attack the mockingly laughing Werdegast. The scene was likely never shot, but complete verity of that now appears lost to the ages.

All in all, Ulmer directed his opus like a man possessed, which might not have been far from the truth. He masterfully mixed his fascination with post-war "soul-dead" casualties with sadism, necrophilia and insanity, keeping the show rip-roaring along, almost meeting the absurdly skimpy schedule and barely exceeding the mercilessly tight budget. He provided an aura of supercharged erotica to the film that still glistens in the work today, making virtually any serious analyst of the work wonder what was going on in the mind and soul of the man who so deliriously masterminded it.

Indeed perhaps the most illuminating insight into Edgar G. Ulmer as he directed *The Black Cat* came from the blonde, beautiful starlet who played "Karen," Lucille Lund. In 1991, over 57 years after the film's production, she revealed in an interview with this author the sexual harassment she suffered at the hands of her director.

Lund's luminously tragic Karen is remarkable. "My father *loved* angels — very baroque angels — and everything that was Gothic," says Arianne Ulmer. "...in *The Black Cat,* Lucille Lund looks like a Christmas angel. Absolutely." In her flowing blonde hair and the black negligee she wears late in the film, Lund also suggests Rapunzel after a shopping spree at Frederick's of Hollywood, and Ulmer — who had created her "look" for *The Black Cat*— clearly found her bewitching. The "horror," as Lund put it, began in what she called the "glamour boudoir scene" with Karloff. She was concealed below her neck under the satin sheet, and Ulmer made her wear a sheer net one-piece bathing suit. "You'll notice I'm well under the sheet in *The Black Cat,*" said Lund.

"Well, if you'd been in the 'thing' I had on, you would have pulled the sheet up too!"

As Lund rejected Ulmer's overtures — "We would be a combination like Dietrich and Von Sternberg," he promised — he became "very sadistic." In the scene in the glass coffin, Ulmer had Lund hanging from a hook by her hair and swinging in a pair of canvas panties under her costume strung to wires. Trussed up in the crystal casket, Lund couldn't move — and Ulmer spitefully sent everyone to lunch while he left her hanging there. "I couldn't get out!" remembered Lund with a shudder. "I couldn't do *anything*!"

Finally, come the scene where Lugosi finds the dead Karen on the slab, Ulmer cruelly tightened the curvature around Lund's neck — and again sent everyone to lunch. The trapped starlet began bleeding from the mouth, but this time was saved — Harry Cording, "Thamal," saw her in distress and rescued her from the slab. There's little surprise that Lucille Lund soon retired from films and had never even told her grown daughters of this nightmare episode at the time of her 1991 revelation.

Did the rampant demons of *The Black Cat* truly get under Ulmer's own skin? Did he believe the director of a horror film should provide his own share of horror?

Whatever the dynamic, Edgar Ulmer completed *The Black Cat* Saturday, March 17, 1934, one day over schedule. The film had its desired effect — Shirley Ulmer recalled that Uncle Carl Laemmle "almost had a heart attack" when he saw the rough cut and on March 25, three days and nights of emergency, front office-mandated retakes began. New bits and pieces of footage accented Lugosi's "good guy" nature, diminishing his climactic mania and empowering Werdegast as a force for good. Yet even here, Ulmer was irrepressibly defiant. It was during the retakes that he added the episode in which Karloff's Poelzig, stroking a cat, prowls through the cellars of Marmaros, his own kinky kingdom of Hell, and eyeballs the dead women who, *à la* the dead Karen, hang in glass coffins. The six anonymous starlets earned $12.50 each for being part of this necrophiliac fantasy, portraying the embalmed and preserved past sacrifices of Poelzig. "The sex scene of all sex scenes!" laughed Shirley Ulmer in 1988. Amazingly, the scene survived in the release print.

Indeed, that *The Black Cat* ever saw release at all is a dark miracle. The Satanism plot was depraved enough, but the garnish Ulmer added was almost as strikingly subversive. Prior to the chess game, Karloff teasingly touches the breast of a chess queen. As Manners and Wells flee the cellars, the back of the heroine's sacrificial gown flies up (an "accident" that must have been contrived by the director) and we get a shadowy peek at her panties. And as the newlyweds flee the soon-to-explode Fort Marmaros, the preserved virgin runs, wearing a black cape presumably swiped from one of the devil worshippers and showing a 1934 Pre–Code flash of thighs, lingerie and black high heels — surely Edgar G. Ulmer's idea of *Female-in-Excelsis*. Reminded 63 years later of her kinky cape and semi-striptease, Jacqueline Wells just laughed. "Probably, by that time, we were getting near the end — it didn't matter!"

Laemmle Jr. was delighted with what Edgar G. Ulmer had wrought and the chill it had given Laemmle Sr. Ulmer worked with Heinz Roemheld on classically scoring the film, with splashes of Beethoven, Bach, Brahms, Chopin, Schubert, Tchaikovsky and of course Liszt (who had his own fascinations with the devil). On April 2, the Breen office screened the film and Breen sent Universal a letter, not only giving the green light but actually congratulating the studio and Ulmer on the finished product. Ten days later, April 12, *The Hollywood Reporter* announced Edgar Ulmer would direct Universal's *Bluebeard*, probably to star Karloff, promising "an elaborate production."

Instead, what happened was worthy of a nighttime soap opera. Uncle Carl Laemmle learned that his in-law Shirley, once his "pet" at the Sunday meals, had fallen in love with Ulmer. That she had "betrayed" the Laemmles was bad enough — that the recipient of her affections was the man who'd directed *The Black Cat* was unforgivable. The mountain king banished both sinners from Universal City, and the April 21 *Hollywood Reporter* gave the whitewashed account that Ulmer had decided to "freelance."

The Black Cat premiered at the Hollywood Pantages Theatre, May 3, 1934. Karloff and Lugosi were there, with their wives, but not Ulmer or Shirley, whom he'd marry in 1935. "Karloff and Lugosi make improper faces at each other," noted an aghast *Hollywood Reporter*. The film had its critical admirers — *The Washington Post* headlined its review "A Masterpiece of Suspense." Most of the reviews, however, resembled the tone of *Time* magazine's (May 28, 1934): "with that grisly bout of Satanism, [Karloff and Lugosi] swing into action, shrieking, shooting, skulking, fainting, sprinting, cursing and puffing.... Silly shot: the Black Mass, with Karloff intoning Latin gibberish."

There was censorship trouble internationally — including Ulmer's native Austria, that banned the *The Black Cat* outright ("Because religious feelings are hurt by the broad showing of the devil service and by the fact that one main figure, an Austrian, is shown as [a] military traitor and main criminal, thus offending the national feeling of the people"). Maryland, Ohio and Chicago cut the shadow shot of Bela skinning Boris, and all dialogue relating to the skinning. Yet the laugh was on the critics and the censors. In June of 1934, the trade paper *Harrison's Reports* ran a listing of Hollywood releases, including 26 Universal products from the last half of 1933 through the first part of 1934. Of the 26, *The Black Cat* was one of only four Universals to rate an unqualified "Good" at the box office — along with John Stahl's *Only Yes-*

terday ("Very Good"), James Whale's *The Invisible Man* ("From Very Good to Good"), and William Wyler's *Counselor At Law* ("Good").

The Black Cat was a treasure trove of blessings for many associated with it. The film provided Karloff his most slyly sinister role, Lugosi his most dashingly sympathetic one, David Manners his personal favorite of his trio of horror classics (though he claimed to have "hated" all of them [interview, David Manners]) and Jacqueline Wells the leading man she respected most (Karloff). Junior Laemmle had goaded his father and Universal had made a pile of money. Even Lucille Lund, who trembled at the very title of *The Black Cat*, was pleased when her little daughters eventually found her old publicity pictures from the film and—believing she looked like a fairy tale princess—loved displaying them.

For Edgar G. Ulmer, however, the only prize came in posterity. Laemmle Sr. and Jr. lost Universal in 1936 to usurpers and Uncle Carl died in 1939, but even with the demise of the mountain king, the curse of *The Black Cat* loomed and lingered over Ulmer. The casting into Hollywood Purgatory was

Director Edgar G. Ulmer, left, with Bela Lugosi on the set of *The Black Cat* (from the collection of Gregory William Mank).

a life sentence, but Edgar Ulmer, in his defiant way, decided he enjoyed Purgatory's perks — freedom, challenge, and personal identity. Surely no major studio would have allowed him to direct *Bluebeard* (the old Universal title, filmed in 1944 with John Carradine, who had played a bit part as the Black Mass organist in *The Black Cat*) or *Detour* (1945) in the way he fashioned those films at PRC.

Was *The Black Cat* worth the wrath? Perhaps so. It survives as a beloved horror epic of Hollywood's Golden Age, a three-ring circus of Karloff, Lugosi and bastardized Poe, with Ulmer its demonic ringmaster. Rarely has any horror film been so strikingly personal, so radiant with both the artistry and the torment of the film's prime mover. As Arianné Ulmer Cipes says:

> What do I see of my father in The Black Cat? Well, first of all, the Bauhaus influence. When Karloff's stroking the lady bronze piece, our house had elements of this — bronze statues and such, that were part of our everyday living. Of course, the music is very much a part of my father. There's the deliberate modulation of Bela Lugosi's voice, which in some ways is very similar to my father's extremely deep voice and heavy, thick accent. And my father, with his great eyes and incredible voice, had an erotic quality about him — as does the film. When I see The Black Cat, it's chemically right, it's familiar — like I'm in the presence of people who are my own skin!

Note

1. All information here about *The Black Cat's* censorship trouble before and after its release comes from the Margaret Herrick Library of the Academy of Motion Picture Arts and Sciences.

Works Cited

The Black Cat Production Papers, Universal Collection, University of Southern California.
Bogdanovich, Peter. "Edgar G. Ulmer." Todd McCarthy and Charles Flynn (eds.). *Kings of the Bs*. New York: E.P. Dutton, 1975, 376–409.
Fischer, Dennis. "*The Black Cat*." *Midnight Marquee Actors Series, Boris Karloff*. Gary J. Svehla and Susan Svehla (eds.). Baltimore, MD: Midnight Marquee, 1996.
Gabler, Neal. *An Empire of Their Own*. New York: Crown, 1988.
Lugosi, Hope. Telephone interviews, Honolulu, HI, July 15 and August 12, 1993.
Lund, Lucille. Telephone interview, Malibu, CA, November 19, 1991. All quotes and information from Miss Lund come from various interviews with the author on telephone and at her Malibu home, 1991 to 1998.
Manners, David. Interview, Pacific Palisades, CA, July 31, 1976.
Mitchell, Joen. Telephone interview, Valley Center, CA, September 27, 2001.
Modern Monsters magazine, 1966.
Roman, Robert C. "Boris Karloff." *Films in Review*, August/September 1964.

Sutin, Lawrence. *Do What Thou Wilt: A Life of Aleister Crowley*. New York: St. Martin's, 2000.
Ulmer, Shirley. Telephone interviews, Los Angeles, March 8 and March 24, 1988.
Ulmer Cipes, Arianné. Telephone interview, Sherman Oaks, CA, September 13, 2001.
Wells, Jacqueline (aka Julie Bishop). Telephone interview, Mendocino, CA, April 3, 1997.

In Search of Jewish Identity
Sharon Pucker Rivo

Edgar G. Ulmer directed four Yiddish language feature films in the New York area between 1937 and 1941. During this period of his life, his Jewish identity was greatly influenced by the intellectual Jewish milieu, his close acquaintances and neighbors, and his association with Yiddish actors and writers. Although he was a declared atheist, his background as a Jew from Vienna, his early childhood experiences, and his first-hand knowledge of the dangers of German antisemitism made him strongly identify as a secular Jew and heightened his awareness of the looming danger to Jews during this period. Ulmer's four Yiddish feature films demonstrate his knowledge of Jewish history and ritual and reflect his respect for Jewish practices and sensibilities. This essay will provide a brief overview of Ulmer's Jewish background and examine scenes from the four Yiddish feature films to illuminate his Jewish values and beliefs.

Edgar George Ulmer was born in Olomouc (Moravia) during the summer of 1904 to Siegfried Ulmer and Henrietta Eisenstein Ulmer at the home of his maternal grandmother Sally Eisenstein (Ulmer's birth-home was found in 2005 by Bernd Herzogenrath, it is located in the Resselgasse 1 in what is now the Czech Republic). Edgar was the eldest of 4 children. Edgar had a *bris* (Jewish circumcision ceremony) but no *bar mitzvah* or formal Jewish education (personal communication with Arianne Ulmer Cipes).

The Ulmer family lived in Vienna and spent summers at the Eisenstein's home in Olomouc. Siegfried, a vintner, was a cultured man with socialist leanings and the family was financially stable. The family fell on hard times, however, after Siegfried's unfortunate death from injuries sustained in World War I.

According to Edgar Ulmer's daughter Arianne, two important early experiences influenced Ulmer's attitude toward his Jewish heritage. Due to economic hardship following the death of the father, Edgar's mother allowed the two oldest Ulmer children to be sent to Sweden in 1919. Edgar, then aged 15, together with his sister Karola, spent a year in Stockholm and Uppsala, Sweden, under the auspices of either the Hoover commission or a Jewish Agency where they lived with a Jewish family. His brother Max and sister Elvira were sent to Holland. Edgar later remembered being forced to wear a yellow star and the feeling of being singled out from the rest of the population.

When Edgar returned to Vienna, he was befriended by the Schildkraut family. Joseph Schildraut, a contemporary of Edgar, came from a well placed Romanian family who strongly identified as Jews. During his teenage years, Edgar spent a great deal of time in the Schildraut home where he was introduced to great books of literature and to Jewish writings. It wasn't long before Edgar became enamored with the world of theatre and culture.

While he began as a student of architecture, Edgar soon broke into the film industry. As a teenager he worked as a set designer for the Austrian director Max Reinhardt. In 1923, Ulmer came with Reinhardt to the United States with the play "The Miracle," which opened on Broadway. In the mid 1920s he was contracted as an art director by Universal Pictures. Ulmer shuttled between Berlin and Hollywood, finally settling in Hollywood in the early 1930s. In 1934 he directed the highly successful horror film *The Black Cat* for Universal Pictures.

Following his marriage to an Episcopalian woman, Edgar was baptized. A few years later he met Shirley Kassler (later Castle), the wife of a much older man, Max Alexander, a B-picture producer at Universal and nephew of powerful Universal Pictures president Carl Laemmle. When Edgar and Shirley fell in love, Edgar was ostracized from Universal Pictures and essentially blackballed from working in Hollywood. At this juncture Ulmer and Shirley relocated to New York City in search of work. Shirley, originally from New York City, had a strong sense of her Jewish heritage. It was Shirley's mother who pushed Edgar to return to his Jewish roots. Over the next few years he directed an assortment of independent "ethnic" feature films, including a quartet of Yiddish-language talkies that have since become classics.

Soon after Edgar and Shirley arrived in New York, they moved into a Jewish neighborhood where they became friendly with a host of Jewish intellectuals, writers, and theatre people. These new attachments ultimately led to Edgar's involvement with the production of *Green Fields*, the first Yiddish feature film which he directed, in 1936. By the mid–1930s, the Yiddish theater boom had kick started an expanding — and profitable — Yiddish cinema. *Al Chet* ("I Have Sinned") and *Yiddle with His Fiddle,* Polish Yiddish film imports, were big financial successes in 1935 and 1936, respectively.

Yiddish cinema—a direct offshoot of the Yiddish theatre—began as early as 1911 (with the film *L'Chaim*), in Russia and ended with the last Yiddish feature film produced in 1949, in New York City. Around one hundred Yiddish feature films were made in Russia, Poland, Austria, and America with the golden age between 1935 and 1939 when dozens of professional productions emerged from Warsaw and New York City. The films, like the plays, existed outside the traditional orthodoxy of the religious Jewish community because they dealt with secular themes and issues. The religious establishment banned all forms of theatre and entertainment, except for the *Badkhan* who performed at weddings and the *Purimsphiler* who entertained during Purim celebrations. Ironically, even though the Yiddish language films were shunned by the orthodox community, the films' content almost always reinforce traditional Jewish values and ethics.

The first three Yiddish films that Ulmer directed, *Green Fields* (1937), *The Singing Blacksmith* (1938) and *The Light Ahead* (1939), were based on classic Yiddish plays and literature set in the old world of Eastern Europe. They each dramatize life in the small rural Jewish communities at end of the nineteenth century when Jewish life flourished even amidst rabid antisemitism. The films focus on internal issues of family conflict, community strife, poverty, love and romance, and all three films are infused with a strong sense of Jewish practice and tradition. The last Yiddish film directed by Ulmer, *American Matchmaker* (1940), is set in America and offers a completely different milieu and sensibility. Interestingly, even with its comic critique of the *nuevo riche*, this film contains strong and positive Jewish thematic material. All four of Ulmer's films were made primarily for Jewish audiences, specifically America's new Jewish immigrants and their children, as well as for the large Jewish market in Europe before the outbreak of World War II.

The Ulmers lived in the same neighborhood as Peretz Hirschbein and his wife and Edgar wanted to helm the film production of Hirschbein's well known play *Green Fields* written in 1916. Ulmer later recalled, "I had a very favorite script, a play which [Peretz] Hirschbein wrote called *Grine Felder* [*Green Fields*, 1937]. So I went to see Hirschbein because he wouldn't give the play to anybody" (Bogdanovich 578). Ulmer and Hirschbein worked for six months adapting the successful stage play for the screen (personal communication with Arianné Ulmer Cipes). The screenplay contains a very important addition to the original play: the film's opening scene in which the protagonist, the young Yeshiva student Levi Yitskhok, announces his decision to abandon the house of study and prayer to venture out into the "real world" in search of "true Jews." This semi-autobiographical material was added by Hirschbein. It sets up the central thesis for the work and plays a pivotal role in understanding the importance and success of the film.

The opening scene of *Green Fields* unfolds as follows:

1st STUDENT: Where are you going?
   In search of a brighter synagogue?
   Better Jews, Levi Yitskhok?
LEVI YITSKHOK: No it's not that.
2nd STUDENT: God's grace is here, in the synagogue.
1st STUDENT: The light of truth is everywhere, one need not search for it afar.
LEVI YITSKHOK: The light of truth is everywhere, but one must still search for it.
1st STUDENT: What is the rush? Wait a while.
LEVI YITSKHOK: It's daybreak.
2nd STUDENT: He'll lose his way.
1st STUDENT: He who seeks the truth will find it.

Hirschbein insisted that his good friend Jacob Ben-Ami, who had played the leading role on stage, be involved in the production. "Hirschbein insisted I couldn't make the picture if Ben-Ami didn't play the lead," Ulmer later explained. "The night before I started shooting I got Ben-Ami out by giving

From left, Herschel Bernardi (back to camera), Helen Beverly, Michael Goldstein, Isidore Cashier and Saul Levine in *Green Fields* (courtesy National Center for Jewish Film at Brandeis University, www.jewishfilm.org).

Levi Yitskhok (Michael Gorin, right) and the son of a farmer (Herschel Bernardi) in *Green Fields* (courtesy National Center for Jewish Film at Brandeis University, www.jewishfilm.org).

him the co-credit as co-director" (Bogdanovich 208). Although Ulmer did not speak Yiddish, he understood a great deal because of his native German. Jacob Ben-Ami was hired as dialogue coach and assisted with the direction of the actors even though Ulmer soon acquired enough Yiddish to manage. The film was shot on a farm in New Jersey in five days, followed by a week of shooting in a studio in Fort Lee, New Jersey.

Ulmer took great care in augmenting the dialogue with an increasingly sophisticated visual vocabulary. As Levi Yitskhok takes his first steps out into the real world, into the sunlight which will illuminate his new life, a rich light shines through the door. Levi leaves the dark, dank, stifling world of the orthodox house of prayer, respectful of learning and tradition but anxious to discover the new "Jewish worker" who respects the land and the manual labor it takes to make it flourish. This contemporary Zionist philosophy permeates the film and provides a sweet pastoral flavor for the love story which blossoms between Levi and Tsina.

There are numerous scenes in *Green Fields* which reveal and reinforce a respect for Jewish learning and practice. In the scene when the men prepare to eat dinner, they wash their hands, say blessings over the food, and treat the learned scholar with reverence and respect. When Tsina falls from a tree while picking apples, the young scholar recites the Talmudic rules applying to the eating of the first fruits of the season.

The extraordinary success of *Green Fields*—(it played for eight weeks in downtown New York City at the Squire Theater)—prompted Ulmer's next Yiddish film production, *The Singing Blacksmith* (see Hoberman 250). Ulmer re-teamed with his *Green Fields* producer Roman Rebush for the production, which was based on a classic Yiddish romantic play *Yankl der Schmidt* by David Pinski. The film stars the popular cantor and Yiddish entertainer Moishe Oysher as a swashbuckling, uncultured blacksmith married to the lovely and demure Tamara and tempted by a former flame. Although Jewish religious practices are not as prominent as in *Green Fields*, the Jewish traditions of matchmaking, family solidarity, and respect for learning are present throughout the film. Interestingly, Pinski's dual focus on hard labor and book learning, respecting both the common worker and the Talmudic scholar, mirrors Ulmer's own approach to life. Ulmer, a hardworking and inventive artist, had limited formal education and no Jewish education, and a reputation as a ladies man.

Probably the most significant film created by Ulmer is the lesser known Yiddish feature *The Light Ahead (Di Klyatshe*, or *Fishke der Krumer)*. The film, based on two short stories *Di Takse (The Tax on Kosher Meat)* and *Fishke the Lame* by the renowned author Mendele Mokher Sforim (S.Y. Abramovitch), was adapted by Chaver Pahver. This film embodies and nourishes the Jewish soul. The film is a sharp and biting critique of the negative elements in organized religion — the misuse of community funds for special interests, the archaic rules which create havoc for the common man, the excesses of the leaders, and the rigidity of some of the laws. At the same time, the film preserves a rare glimpse and respect for Jewish learning and ethical behavior. There is a wonderful scene in the *yeshiva* (house of prayer) when two of the students who are studying ask Mendele "where is Thursday" because as students who are fed by local patrons they have no place to eat on Thursday. The restorative power of the Sabbath is celebrated in the wordless scene during which the poverty-stricken lovers sip soup and noodles from the same bowl, shielded for a moment from the cruel poverty of the *shtetl*. The film discredits the archaic world of superstitions, greed, rigidity, stereotyping, and

Opposite top: Helen Beverly portrayed Tsina the farmer's daughter in *Green Fields*. **Bottom:** Moishe Oysher stars as the singing blacksmith (both photographs courtesy National Center for Jewish Film at Brandeis University, www.jewishfilm.org).

Top: The blacksmith's wife, Tamara (Miriam Riselle, left), Moishe Oysher, right, and the cast. *Above:* The matchmaker (Anna Appel) and the blacksmith (Moishe Oysher) (both photographs courtesy National Center for Jewish Film at Brandeis University, www.jewishfilm.org).

Top: Edgar G. Ulmer, standing, directing his actors on the set of *The Light Ahead*. *Above:* The German expressionist set for *The Light Ahead* (both photographs courtesy National Center for Jewish Film at Brandeis University, www.jewish film.org).

uneducated bigotry of this religious community in the heart of rural Eastern Europe.

The Light Ahead, produced in 1939, is inculcated with a sense of doom and an acute awareness of the increasing antisemitism overtaking Europe. Although set at the turn of the century, the film offers a veiled warning against the dangerous forces Ulmer had witnessed first hand in Austria and Germany. According to his daughter, Ulmer's fear of the Nazis and fascism permeated and effected his entire life. Is the film's title, then, ironic or optimistic?

Mendele's speech at the window speaks for Ulmer as well as the author:

> How beautiful is the moon!
> With quiet calm you move across the blue sky.
> And God's great world spins out it's length and breath....Without end or limit.
> And scattered over the globe are little Jewish cities (*stetlach*)
> Oye!!
> Thousands of years you gaze down upon them, You see their wretchedness, their misery — and keep silent.
> Silent so many thousand years....While you listen to their sighs.
> You hear their groans in persecutions and massacres.
> And you keep silent. Oh, like a sick child to its mother will I lament to you!
> Oh Mama
> Oh, How it hurts!
> How can one look on and keep silent?
> How long will they torture us?
> When will there be an end?

Ulmer's last Yiddish film, *American Matchmaker (Amerikaner Shadkhn)* is undoubtedly the most Jewish of his Yiddish films. Shirley Castle (Edgar's wife) wrote the film based on a story by her cousin Gustav H. Heimo. Produced in 1940 and set in contemporary New York, specifically on the Grand Concourse in the Bronx, *American Matchmaker* is a far cry from the Eastern European *shtetl* of Ulmer's previous films in both geography and content. In Ulmer's spin on the Art Deco comedy, popular during the period in Hollywood, a wealthy, urban Jew, Nat Gold, played by the talented Leo Fuchs, struggles with romantic entanglements and an increasing crisis of identity in a world of affluence and assimilation. After seven unsuccessful engagements, Gold eventually becomes a *Shadkhn* or Jewish matchmaker, finding a bride and his Jewish identity.

Opposite top: Helen Beverly and David Opatoshu as young lovers in *The Light Ahead*. Bottom: In *The Light Ahead*, a wedding takes place in the cemetery in an attempt to ward off cholera (both photographs courtesy National Center for Jewish Film at Brandeis University, www.jewishfilm.org).

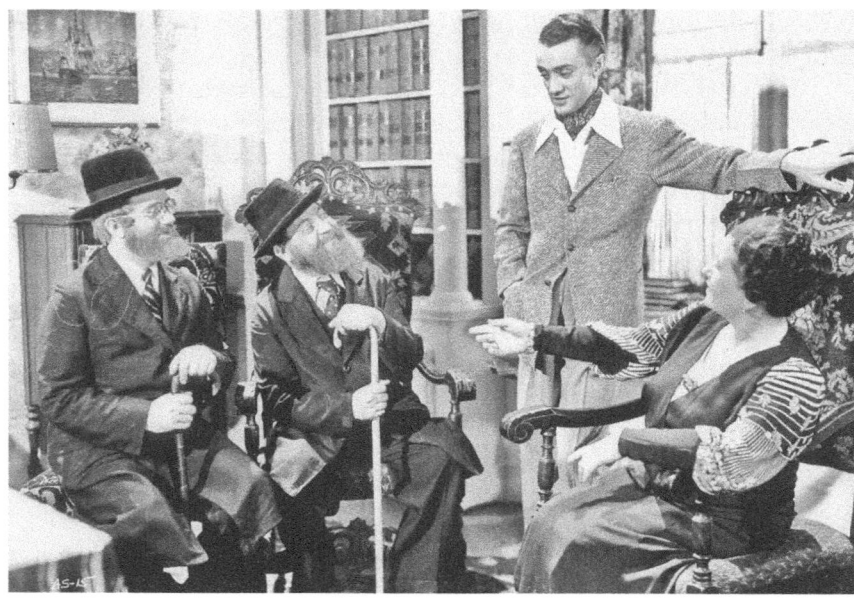

Top: Nat Gold (Leo Fuchs, standing) is a wealthy New Yorker in *American Matchmaker*. *Above:* Gold (Leo Fuchs) becomes a matchmaker and is confronted by boycotters (both photographs courtesy National Center for Jewish Film at Brandeis University, www.jewishfilm.org).

Leo Fuchs gets down to work as the matchmaker (courtesy National Center for Jewish Film at Brandeis University, www.jewishfilm.org).

Gold's transformation from a bon vivant, debonair, assimilated Americanized businessman to a happy and fulfilled traditional marriage broker stunningly endorses the need for American Jews to respect their Jewish roots and religious heritage.

In 1941 Ulmer returned to Hollywood where he made a host of low-budget genre films, of which 1945's *Detour*, now considered one of the greats of film noir, is certainly his most well known. His final movies were produced in Europe. Ulmer never returned to producing or directing Yiddish feature films; that phase of his life was over and the audience for the Yiddish films, both in America and Europe, was gone. In Europe the Nazis destroyed the vast majority of the Yiddish-speaking world and in America a large percentage of the Yiddish-speaking population moved to the more affluent suburbs, leaving behind their mother tongue and the Yiddish theatre. Many years after World War II, Edgar Ulmer returned to Europe with his daughter Arianne and together they visited the grave of his parents. Arianne remembers that

Edgar recited the *kaddish* (Jewish prayer for the dead) at their graveside and, according to Jewish custom, they placed a pebble on the cemetery monument to witness their visit. This Jewish son of a vintner from Olomouc left his mark on the Jewish world and on cinema history with his wonderful Yiddish language feature films, four invaluable gems.

Works Cited

Bogdanovich, Peter. "Edgar G. Ulmer." *Who the Devil Made It: Conversations with Legendary Film Directors.* New York: Ballantine, 1998, 558–604.

Hoberman, J. *Bridge of Light. Yiddish Film Between Two Worlds.* New York: The Museum of Modern Art; New York: Schocken Books, 1991.

Moon of Alabama / *Moon Over Harlem*: African American Culture and German Imaginations from Brecht to Ulmer

FRANK MEHRING

Bertolt Brecht and Edgar Ulmer were fascinated by American popular culture. Particularly jazz music functioned as a stimulus to fantasize about the cultural "other." African-American music and dances infused the paralyzed German cultural life after World War I with the vital power of modern American entertainment. Both artists worked closely with composers to fuse their dramatic visions with musical counterparts in their respective media, namely musical theatre and film. Brecht and his collaborator Kurt Weill created Germanized jazz songs like "Moon of Alabama" for the most revolutionary opera of the Weimar Republic, *Aufstieg und Fall der Stadt Mahagonny* (*Rise and Fall of the City of Mahagonny*, 1930). In the case of Ulmer, the collaboration with the African American composer Donald Heywood resulted in a unique film about black culture. Working outside the Hollywood system, he was able to avoid its deploring racial codifications. *Moon Over Harlem* (1939) represents the first film with an all black cast by a white director about African American culture that denounced the racial stereotypes of coons, Uncle Toms, mammies, black bucks, and pickaninnies. Ulmer's visual and musical innovations of *Moon Over Harlem* will be analyzed through the lens of cultural hybridity and postcolonial fantasies. This essay will explore the changing social meanings of fictionalizing African Americanness following the symbolic figurations described by Ed Guerrero:

The social and political meanings of "race," of course, are not fixed but are matters of ongoing construction and contestation; whether in volatile debate or subtle transactions, the negotiation of racial images, boundaries, and hierarchies has been part of our national life from its very beginnings. The turbulent power of race is evinced by the varieties of ways in which the images and historical experiences of African Americans and other people of color are symbolically figured in commercial cinema [Guerrero 41].

The poster art of *Moon Over Harlem* emphasizes the "all-colored cast." The final product however, represents a construction and contestation of black representations in film by a white German *émigré*. The following questions will be addressed: How does Ulmer represent African American life within the urban setting of Harlem? How does the film incorporate a new sense of self–respect in the wake of the Harlem Renaissance? What is the function of music and how does it relate to standard Hollywood musical melodramas? Ulmer's *Moon Over Harlem* transfers the German discourse about overcoming allegedly outdated theatrical concepts during the Weimar Republic to the American context. Ulmer set out to create a counter–narrative to traditional Hollywood representations of African Americans in film musicals such as *The Jazz Singer* (1927), *The Littlest Rebel* (1935), or the successful Herb Jeffries films featuring the "singing cowboy" in *Harlem on the Prairie* (1937), *Two-Gun Man from Harlem* (1938), or *Harlem Rides the Range* (1939). German musical theatre of the 1920s and early 1930s served as a foil for Ulmer's filmic visions. He admired Brecht and even claimed to be his friend (Grissemann 138). While there is insufficient evidence to prove a close personal relationship between the two artists, a structural comparison of the *The Rise and Fall of the City of Mahagonny* and *Moon Over Harlem* can reveal how the artistic innovations in musical theatre during the Weimar Republic shaped Ulmer's representation of "black Manhattan" in the late 1930s.

Neue Sachlichkeit *and Cultural Evocations of Harlem*

The evocation of the moon in *Mahagonny* and the film *Moon Over Harlem* signifies the hopes and dreams of a better future. In the song "Moon of Alabama," originally written and composed for the *Mahagonny Songspiel* (1927) and later reworked into the full-scale opera *Rise and Fall of the City of Mahagonny*, the moon is described as being "green." The atmosphere fits stereotypical representations of the American South on colorful kitsch postcards. The sentimental line "we now must say good bye" creates temporal and spatial contrasts when the Alabama prostitutes leave their hometown to head into a new direction: the fantastic city of Mahagonny "where everything is allowed." As so often in Brecht's Germanized visions of the United States, there is an element of simultaneity encoded. On the one hand, "America" appears [as] a country haunted by capitalism, greed, and social injustice. On the other hand, Brecht saw the great potential of cultural plurality within the U.S. democratic environment and its energy-driven society.[1]

The performance of "Moon of Alabama" functions as a provocation within the European concept of "high" art and opera on four levels: setting, lyrics, characters, and the music. The moon guides several prostitutes from Alabama like the star of Bethlehem to the anarchic city of Mahagonny. The holy trinity of modern entertainment rules supreme: sex, booze, and boxing. The English language features prominently in the [German] opera libretto creating intentionally awkward Pidgin English rhyme schemes such as "Alabama" and "Mamma."

> Oh Moon of Alabama
> We now must say good-bye,
> We've lost our good old Mamma
> And must have Whisky
> Oh you know why
> [Brecht/Weill 46].

In Ulmer's Harlem, the moon is connected to the nightlife of Black Manhattan with its glamorous entertainment scene and criminal subcultures. In the opening sequence, the moon shines like yet another light bulb over the illuminated city streets and their entertainment advertisements. While both visions of the cultural "other" focus on the ruling power of money and show business as the essence of American culture, theatre and film offer different solutions to come to terms with looming anarchy. Music provides revealing subtexts to dialogues, *mis-en-scènes*, and plot developments. Here, clues for resistance, the deconstruction of "false binaries" (Lipsitz 216), and socio-political change can be found, which link Harlem to [the] fictitious city of "Mahagonny."

Ulmer and his composer Heywood tell their story about murder, crime, social recognition, and entertainment culture like a modern opera. *Moon Over Harlem* follows the budding love affair of the young African American couple Sue (Izinetta Wilcox) and Bob (Earl Gough). They try to survive in the gangster stricken world of Harlem. Sue quits school in order to make a living as a chorus girl in one of the Harlem nightclubs. Bob campaigns for a political position in order to bring justice, order, and wealth to Harlem. Sue's widowed mother Minnie (Nora Green) marries the shady control freak Dollar Bill (Bud Harris) whose gangster friends blackmail shopkeepers in Harlem. After Sue and Bob announced their engagement, Dollar Bill accuses Bob of paying for his education by living off women. Sue is forced to promise that

"Alabama Song" sheet music, copyright ©1928 by Universal Edition A.G., Wien/UE 8900).

she will never see Bob again. In order to make ends meet, she takes on a job at Broadway Slick's Plantation nightclub. Her mother continues to believe that Dollar Bill is an honest grocer. With the appearance of Fats (Alec Lovejoy), a new gangster from Detroit moved in on the Harlem rackets. When he demands $ 15,000 from Dollar, he has his wife Sue killed to set an example. In the end, Dollar Bill is killed by a gang of mobsters. Instead of improving the living conditions in Harlem, they take Dollar Bill's place. From now on, they will control the streets of Harlem with similar brutality. Despite the escalation of violence, the movie ends on an optimistic note for a new generation of African Americans: Sue and Bob gaze over the streets of Harlem knowing that the socio-cultural situation needs to be changed by a strong person with leadership qualities. The film suggests that Bob might be such a leader.

The narrative of *Moon Over Harlem* is introduced, interrupted, and framed by musical elements comparable to the musical episodes, which Brecht and Weill employed to comment on the action on stage. What Brecht describes as "epic theatre" does not necessarily translate into "epic film" in Ulmer's *Moon Over Harlem*. Ulmer refrains from alienating the viewer from the action on screen or offering non–realistic set designs. However, like in *Mahagonny*, the action is interrupted through musical numbers. Both productions feature a strong political message. They work with contrasts and use music beyond the means of intensifying emotional empathy. In *Moon Over Harlem*, the soundtrack functions as a commentary on African American cultural expressions. Thus, structural similarities between Brecht's concept of *Zeitoper* and Ulmer's ethnic film become apparent.

In his "Notizen und Entwürfe zu den Anmerkungen zur Oper *Aufstieg und Fall der Stadt Mahagonny*," Brecht explains that the opera was conceived on the basis of several songs which then were connected through dramatic action (Brecht/Weill 134). These songs were highly unusual within the structural confinements of opera. Weill had been experimenting with American dance music and jazz idioms earlier. In respect of *Der Zar Lässt Sich Photographieren* (*The Tsar Has His Picture Taken*, 1928), Weill explains that the "composition is an illustration of the effect of modern jazz upon opera [...]. I didn't sit down to write jazz for its own sake, but rather opera for its own sake. In so doing I naturally found myself running into jazz as an expression of our time."[2]

Brecht and Weill were among those who openheartedly embraced new impulses from the United States in the early '20s. For them, "America" was associated with Charlie Chaplin and Buster Keaton's slapstick, Wild West movies, boxing and auto racing, technological progress, and a successful entertainment industry that spanned from Broadway to its musical distribution systems on film, radio, and gramophone records. The latest dance steps and jazz music conveyed the aura of newness, freshness, and artistic freedom. For the first time in history, American artistry seemed culturally superior to that of the Old World. In his diary Brecht expressed his boredom with German culture and its artistic paralysis.[3] Society had degenerated into misplaced farmers, a fat middle class and weak intellectuals. The only hope lay across the Atlantic in the United States.[4]

One of the visual innovations of Brecht's "epic theatre" rested on a rather simple but highly effective idea. Brecht moved the orchestra from the invisible space in front of the theatre curtain onto the stage making it an integral part of the theatre production. In *Mahagonny*, Weill uses both a symphonic orchestra in the traditional orchestra pit and a jazz band on stage. These positions of musical sources correspond in Ulmer's film to music being played on and off-screen. In addition to the visual setting of the orchestra, Weill changes the musical style by introducing what was then called "Gebrauchsmusik" to the high art of symphonic opera music. Thus, American sounds and rhythms confront an operatic tradition that seemed to be paralyzed by nineteenth century conventions. "We have tried to create a musical style, which is able to satisfy the musical needs of a broad spectrum of people without giving up the substance of its artistry [...]. In our music we want to provide a means for the contemporary person to express him-/herself and this citizen should speak to many people" (Brecht/Weill 160).[5]

In his essay "Die Neue Oper" from 1926, Weill set out to free opera from the dominating influence of Richard Wagner's concept of a *Gesamtkunstwerk*, namely to create a unity of effect by fusing musical leitmotifs with dramatic narrative and set design (Brecht/Weill 148). Instead of striving for aesthetic immersion, Brecht and Weill separated the individual art forms. Jazz served as a tool for his unconventional strategy. It became a signifier of the "rhythm of modern times" emphasizing speed, urbanity, simultaneity, anarchy, and the American way of life. In *The Tsar Has His Picture Taken*, Weill utilized jazz music for the first time as a new element within his wide range of compositional techniques. The subtitle "A Tragic Revue" refers to the popular musical genre, which had already successfully woven modern American dance steps and lyrics into its fabric. Weill played with a foxtrot tune. He altered its harmonic structure so that along with chromatically complex vocal lines it became a part of the classical texture. Weill perfected this technique in *Mahagonny*, where he erased the borderlines between "high" and "low" musical cultures completely.

In an interview, Weill explained that he and Brecht knew about the fantastic elements they brought to the project. "For every age and part of the world, there is a place about which fantasies are written. In Mozart's time, it was Turkey. For Shakespeare, it was Italy. For us in Germany, it was always America" (Weill 16). Brecht's and Weill's fictionalized versions of American big city life brought an element of popular entertainment culture to the world of German opera. These musical and theatrical innovations produced a site of doubleness, namely of the fantastic and the factual. The notion of "America" derived its meaning from an imaginary transfer in the sense of reception theory. How does Ulmer's use of music relate to this concept?

The Functions of Music in Moon Over Harlem

The growing attention, which the two major studios, Metro-Goldwyn-Mayer and Twentieth Century–Fox, paid to films, in which sympathetic "Negroes played a part" (quoted in Bogle 137), appealed to Ulmer for various reasons. As a Jewish German immigrant and artist ostracized from the Hollywood community he could empathize with the status of second-class-citizens, which African Americans strongly felt. In the wake of the Harlem Renaissance and the increasing popularity of jazz, African Americans produced independent films allowing Ulmer to find a new venue for his artistry. His collaboration with African American actors offered an opportunity to come to terms with the distorted images of blacks to which he had been exposed during the Weimar Republic. Working outside the Hollywood formula, Ulmer saw a chance to continue on his quest to confront aesthetic conceptions of "high" and "low" in the United States. Despite his commercial interests, he refrained from cashing in on black movie stereotypes such as the tragic mulatto, the coon, mammy or brutal black buck. Neither did he follow the major Hollywood genres of mystery, melodrama, musical or western like *Harlem on the Prairie* (1937), *Harlem Rides the Range* (1939), or *Dirty Gertie from Harlem* (1946).[6]

For his musical melodrama on life in Harlem, Ulmer uses jazz idioms as an important element to tell his story. The score is not limited to Broadway arrangements or Tin Pan Alley tunes to showcase popular sentiments. Unlike Brecht and Weill, the use of jazz should not only present the popular fantasies of "primitivist modernism" to feed on white fantasies of the African American "other." Ulmer's complex use of jazz and representation of African Americans in Harlem creates a nexus of white European and black American aesthetics. Thus, *Moon Over Harlem* emerges as an exemplary case of what Sieglinde Lemke describes as a "dialectical formation of an aesthetic and cultural identity" in America (Lemke 9). Vernacular music represents an integral part of his gaze on Harlem families and gangsters. Like a cultural anthropologist in the sense of Franz Boas and Zora Neale Hurston, Ulmer reconnects the blues, fox, or Charleston with social functions in African American lives. Thereby, he produces a space in-between the whitewashed versions of African American culture in the American entertainment industry and idealized constructions of authentic African American vernacular culture.

In *Moon Over Harlem*, music enters or disrupts the narrative flow on six different levels.

1. Leitmotifs in the credit sequences (overture and coda).
2. Vernacular music on screen during social occasions such as weddings and funerals.
3. Stylized musical Broadway numbers in night club scenes.
4. Popular jazz music from the radio.
5. Classical music played on screen.
6. Film score arrangements for heightened emotional effect.

Ulmer was obsessed with music, both in his personal life and in his films. Shortly before his work on *Moon Over Harlem*, Ulmer claims to have worked with director Leopold Stokowski on Walt Disney's feature animation Film *Fantasia*, which was released in 1940 (Grissemann 245–6). This revolutionary animated musical featured discrete six-channel sound recordings of classical and modern music ranging from Bach's "Toccata and Fugue" in D Minor or Beethoven's "6th Symphony" to Stravinsky's "Rite of Spring" and Mussorgsky's "A Night on Bald Mountain" to accompany onscreen visualizations. Ulmer's love for music can be traced back to some of his earliest efforts of the sound era. Despite producer Carl Laemmle's harsh resistance, Ulmer ordered a five-piece orchestra for his expressionist Hollywood horror film *Black Cat* (1934) to play variations of well-known classical themes derived from Bach, Beethoven, Chopin, Liszt, Schubert, and Tchaikovsky. In these cases, music served to heighten the mood suggested by the images and to provide his "Caligari"-like figures with a sense of European stylishness. Not only does the modernist castle stand upon a battlefield with corpses; Ulmer's classical music cues also firmly root these characters in the European past. While the narrative was confined to Hollywood conventions, Ulmer's visual and musical design opened up new aesthetic venues.

With *Jive Junction* (1943), Ulmer produced a propaganda film using swing music as a means to support the war effort. In *Bluebeard* (1944), he cut the action to a long passage from Charles Gounod's opera "Faust" (1859). *Carnegie Hall* (1947) blends contents and form in a vision of portraying the experience of music.[7] In *Detour* (1945), by now a classic *film noir*, music serves as a narrative bridge between the protagonist, a luckless piano player, and a cynical story about unfulfilled love. The jazzy interpretation of "I can't believe that you're in love with me" played on a record in a music box triggers a remarkable shift from the reality of a Reno diner to a subjective narrative.

In *Moon Over Harlem*, the function of music is more complex. In the most literal sense, music plays different characters independent of the actual actors. Music is heard in the background, played on screen, or represented by modern mass media like radios or gramophones. Ulmer's credit sequence functions like an operatic overture. The multi-facetted arrangement of sights and sounds of Harlem is significant in many ways. It exhibits similarities with the so-called German jazz operas such as Ernst Křenek's *Jonny spielt auf* (1927), the Zeitoper *Aufstieg und Fall der Stadt Mahagonny*, and experimental films of *Neue Sachlichkeit* such as Walter Ruttmann's *Berlin: Sinfonie der Grossstadt* (1927) and Ulmer's own documentary effort in Berlin entitled *Menschen am Sonntag* (1930). The cinematic overture consists of two parts: a credit sequence and a series of shots displaying Harlem at night.

A rectangular sign surrounded by a string of light bulbs identifies the New Jersey based Meteor production studio followed by the title "Moon Over Harlem." While the credits appear, Ulmer introduces four paintings in the

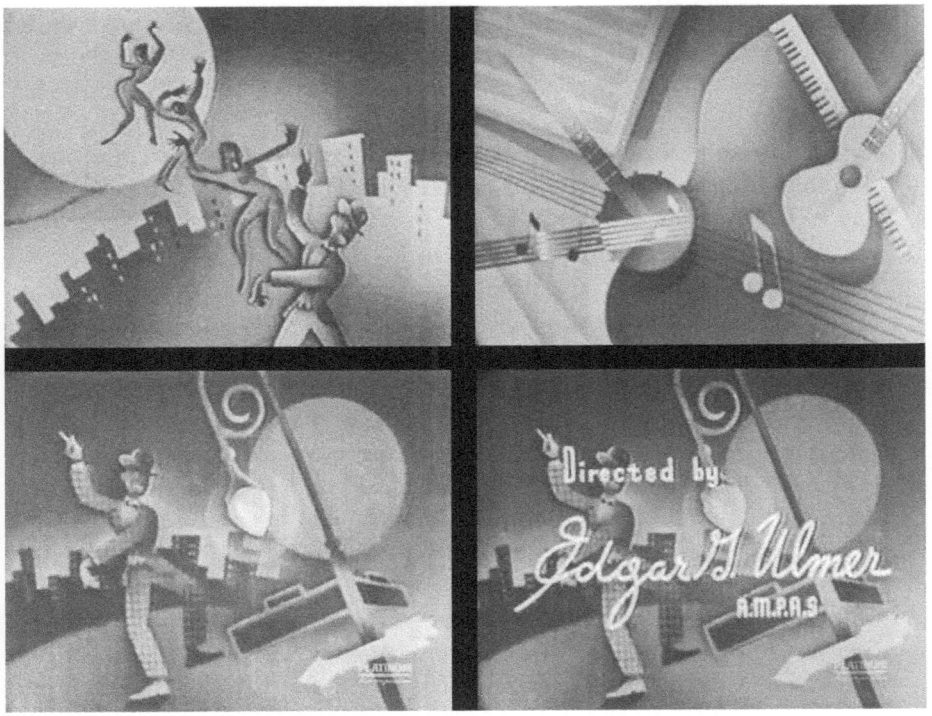

The credit sequence, *Moon Over Harlem*.

background. They highlight typical features of the Harlem music scene: first, a line of female dancers moving energetically towards the moon in the night sky; second, a skyline of houses in black Manhattan; third, a montage of instruments typical of Harlem jazz bands; and fourth, a lonely street scene with a lamp.

The music provides a *tour de force* of those melodies and rhythms, which will later appear in various scenes of the film. In the overture, rhythms and melodic lines jump energetically without harmonic bridges. The music shifts gears from a fast-paced Charleston to a dreamy blues and back again. This disruptive sound creates excitement und suggests an impulsive nightlife of uptown Manhattan. A similar disjoint piece of music can be heard in *Detour* when Al Roberts plays in a New York bar. Here, highbrow and lowbrow converge in a mix of Brahm's "Wiegenlied," a Chopin waltz, wild jazz improvisations and a hammering boogie-woogie. After two minutes and twenty seconds, the *Moon Over Harlem* credit sequence changes to a series of documentary shots, while the music is repeated from the beginning. The camera pans from the moon down into the proverbial "heart of Harlem" to which the metaphorical tagline of the movie poster "ripped from the heart of Harlem" alludes. In accordance with the musical montage, the film jumps into a wild ride of images depicting significant Harlem streets and buildings, among them the Savoy Ballroom, the Apollo Theatre Broomsteins, and Lennox Avenue with numerous cars and busses passing by. The tilted camera angle emphasizes transition and increases the effect of being lost inside a whirlwind of action. The scenes contrast stylized sketches of a glitzy Harlem to a dark documentary style suggesting authenticity.

Ulmer inscribes himself as a German Jewish *émigré* in some of the street signs on Lennox Avenue. The technique of cultural inscription emerges also in the artwork of the credit sequence and the movie advertisement poster. The sketches of the credit sequence hark back to the work of another German immigrant. Trained in Munich at the Kunstakademie (Royal Academy of Fine Arts), where he studied with Franz von Stuck, and the Kunstgewerbeschule (School of Applied Arts) under the guidance of Julius Diez, the painter and designer Winold Reiss had moved to the United States in 1913. Fascinated by non–western cultures, he contributed innovative paintings to the founding document of the Harlem Renaissance: the special issue of *Survey Graphic* (1925), which was later re–edited, enlarged and published as an anthology under the title *The New Negro* (1925) by Alain Locke. The collection was an exercise in a new race pride, self–awareness, and self–respect by celebrating African American culture. Reiss's portraits of leading members of the artistic movement created a foil, which became an important source for African American artists.[8] While his most prominent follower, Aaron Doug-

Winold Reiss. *Dawn in Harlem* (1925). Ink on Paper. 20" x 15." Reproduced with the kind permission of the Reiss Estate.

las, chose to combine African images of ritual dances and jungle wild life with race pride in New York, some elements of Ulmer's credit sequence pay homage to the more stereotypical icons of Harlem entertainment. These visual renderings extend beyond Reiss to Otto Dix's "Metropolis" vision of the African-Americanization of Berlin in the 1920 celebrating jazz, dance and jazz instruments. Again, Ulmer inscribes his own German identity into the very first sequences, only to deconstruct these white fantasies and come closer to an African American perspective on the every-day life of Harlem. Similar forms of cultural inscriptions and cultural hybridity can be found in the Reiss-like renderings of Harlem rooftops in the poster art of *Moon Over Harlem*.

Ulmer's audiovisual symphony of Black Manhattan leads into the exposition of the plot by moving from the outside city life to the particular setting of an African American marriage in Minny's apartment. Here, the family and wedding guests are present to witness the blessings of the priest. The acoustic link is provided by the famous black clarinet player Sidney Bechet. The camera finds him on the left side of the room playing a jazzy hymn for the newlyweds. Thus, the sounds of Harlem move from off screen right into the frame and onto the stage. When one of the guests demands a blues song, Ulmer displays the richness of African American musical culture with its specific functions. Music is not only entertainment or distraction for urban middle class slummers but an integral part of rituals and celebrations in African American social life.

The scenes in the Harlem dance clubs might be pure escapism leaving the peculiar jazz traditions of black culture behind to satisfy the [audience with] whitewashed versions of African American music created by the likes of Paul Whiteman, Irving Berlin, Cole Porter, and George Gershwin. Ulmer contrasts Broadway entertainment, symphonic swing, or popular dance songs from Tin Pan Alley with the private lives of African Americans. As early as the 1920s, Harlem bars became an attractive venue for white artists. In turn, black culture and Broadway entertainment merged. The central musical number of *Moon Over Harlem*, "Teach me how to sing again" by Heywood, highlights the theme of cultural contrast. The song builds on Broadway style melodies lacking typical jazz qualities like improvisation, call-and-response patterns, or rapid rhythm variations. Alluding to movie sequences from *King of Jazz* (1930) or *Broadway Melody of 1938* (1937), the *mis-en-scène* features a 20 member symphonic orchestra called "Christopher Columbus and his Swing Crew" and a line of chorus girls who join into a grand vocal finale to reprise the title line.

The scene is preceded by the lead singer Sue sitting at a grand piano in the living room of her mother. She passes easily from one musical genre to another. Following the notion of W.E.B. DuBois that cultural education will provide a key for acquiring self-confidence and dignity for the "New Negro,"

The *Moon Over Harlem* poster emphasizes the all-black cast and offers Reiss-like renderings of rooftops.

Image from the "Teach Me How to Sing Again" sequence.

Ulmer suggests that African Americans need not be confined to a single form of musical culture. Instead, Sue shows that a new generation in Harlem feels comfortable expressing herself through Broadway melodies, African American vernacular music, and classical music.

Another remarkable scene, which makes effective use of music as a critical subtext, shows the young couple Sue and Bob

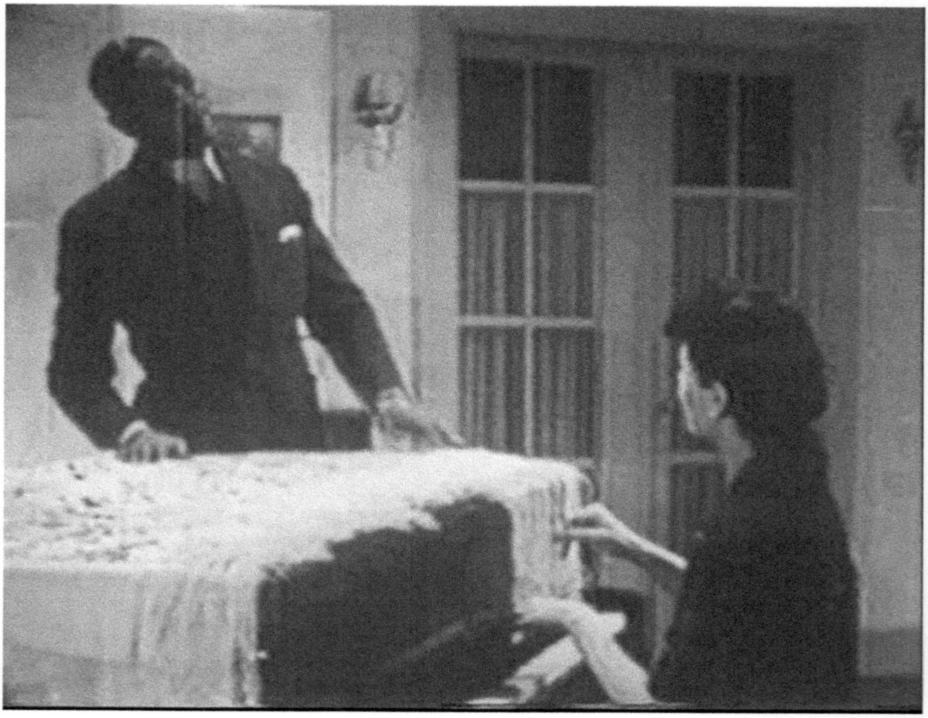

Dollar Bill and Sue at the grand piano in *Moon Over Harlem*.

outside of Harlem in a car up on a hill with a fictitious backdrop of the New York skyline. Like in Ernst Křenek's opera *Jonny spielt auf*, in which radio and loudspeakers bring jazz music to remote areas in the Alps, "Harlem" and its musical spirit constantly accompanies the couple in *Moon Over Harlem*. They enjoy their remoteness by listening to the song "My Hope Chest of Dreams" (1939) on the radio. This composition is another trademark of composer and lyricist Heywood written explicitly for the film. Thereby, Ulmer creates almost without effort another striking instance where music is part of the story telling. The idea goes back to experiments in Weimar musical theatre, and particularly Weill's "Tango Angele" in *The Tsar Has His Picture Taken* from 1927.

In the last musical sequence of *Moon Over Harlem*, Ulmer returns to the setting of the opening shots of the film during the wedding, albeit now under opposite emotional connotations. At the end, family and friends congregate to mourn the death of Minnie who was shot accidentally by the mobsters during their pursuit of Dollar Bill. Ulmer creates an elaborate shot avoiding any cuts to amplify the solemn scene of the multi-layered musical mourns of "Amen" and "Hallelujah." Music takes on the function of social glue and spiritual self-empowerment. The hymn harks back to the gospel repertoire of African American musical traditions. Shot in a documentary-like style, happiness and sadness appear side by side, expressed in the same room, by the same people, in the same city. The audio-visual representation is full of dignity and respect for the traditions of African Americans.

The sense of authenticity, which permeates Ulmer's film about life in Harlem, becomes all the more striking when compared to other films, which focus on jazz music. One of the most influential American films of the sound era was also its first, called *The Jazz Singer* (1927). Contrary to expectations, this film is rooted in the minstrel tradition with the protagonist played by renown vaudeville actor/singer Al Jolson. The white actor appears in blackface singing songs, which were all composed in the Tin Pan Alley style by white musicians. Among them were "Blue Skies" (Irving Berlin), "My Mammy" (Walter Donaldson), [or] "My Gal Sal" (Paul Dresser). Ulmer, in contrast, uses jazz to pay homage to black vernacular culture and subvert such Hollywood depictions of black musical culture.

Conclusion

In Germany, Brecht and Weill used English lyrics and (Germanized) jazz music to infuse "high" art forms with "low" art elements. "America" became a signifier for artistic innovations within a democratized sphere of entertainment. Ulmer's strategy in the United States followed opposite venues. His use of different musical genres, popular entertainment music, Broadway and authentic black jazz, gospel, or blues provides a subtext for the film's sociopolitical agenda: turning Harlem into a representative urban setting for a new generation of African Americans. Thereby, Ulmer gives voice to the "New Negro" of the Harlem Renaissance. Within a democratic entertainment culture, popular music ruled supreme. Therefore, Ulmer blended vernacular and classical elements to infuse American popular culture such as the musical melodrama with elements inspired by European aristocratic traditions. This process turns the efforts of Brecht and Weill upside down. "Moon of Alabama" and *Moon Over Harlem* represent transatlantic efforts of confronting "high" and "low" art within different entertainment systems.

Brecht instrumentalizes Hollywood representations of "America" to overthrow paralyzing conventions in European musical theater. In *Moon Over Harlem*, Ulmer used music to subvert and resist racial representations in Hollywood. Thus, both opera and film function as means of subversion and resistance fuelled by German imaginations of the American cultural "other." For Ulmer, escapist entertainment and high-minded socio-political tracts about racial issues in the United States did not need to be opposites. In *Moon Over Harlem,* he used generic forms to generate social change. What George Lipsitz deconstructed as false-binaries in "blaxploitation" films also applies to Ulmer's "race film." "In many cases, foregrounding race did more than desegregate previously all-white genres. Rather, the prominence of race called the generic form itself into questions" (Lipsitz 216–20). Ulmer's transatlantic background made him keenly aware of the color-line in the United States. While *Moon Over Harlem* is a film with an "all black cast," the white immigrant director used the foregrounding of race to subvert the Hollywood formula of race-films of the 1930s. Like the *Zeitoperas* of Brecht and Weill in the Weimar Republic, Ulmer turned to music as a means to deconstruct false binaries, which he encountered both in Germany as well as the United States.

Notes

1. See, for example, Parmalee's discussion of Brecht's sources for his complex vision of "America," in particular Brecht's reading of Erich Mendelsohn's photographic essay *Amerika: Bilderbuch eines Architekten* (1926) (Parmalee: 1981, 70–73).

2. "Berlin Opera Mingles Auto Horn, Films, Jazz. Ultra-Modern Piece, 38 Scenes, Lasting Hour, Brings Applause and Hisses." *New York Times.* 3 (March 1927): 23. Reprinted in David Farneth with Elmar Juchem and Dave Stein (eds.). *Kurt Weill. Ein Leben in Bildern und Dokumenten.* Transl. Elmar Juchem. Berlin: Ullstein, 2000, 70.

3. "It is a good, medium-sized country, the pale colors and planes are beautiful in it, but what inhabitants! A degenerate peasant class, whose coarseness however gives birth to no fabulous monster, but only to a quiet bestialization, an obese mid-

dle class and a dull intelligentsia! There remains: America!" ["Wie mich dieses Deutschland langweilt! Es ist ein gutes mittleres Land, schön darin die blassen Farben und die Flächen, aber welche Einwohner! Ein verkommener Bauernstand, dessen Rohheit aber keine fabelhaften Unwesen gebiert, sondern eine stille Vertierung, ein verfetteter Mittelstand und eine matte Intellektuelle! Bleibt: Amerika!"]. Bertolt Brecht, *Gesammelte Werke: Werkausgabe Edition Suhrkamp.* 20 vols. Frankfurt am Main: Suhrkamp, 1967. Vol. 20. 10. Transl. Patty Lee Parmalee.

    4. "In the young men you/have not corrupted/America awakens." ["Und in den Jungen, die du/nicht verdorben hast/Erwacht Amerika!"]. Ibid.

    5. "Wir haben deshalb den Versuch unternommen, eine Musik zu schaffen, die auch das Musikbedürfnis breiterer Bevölkerungsschichten zu befriedigen vermag, ohne ihre künstlerische Substanz aufzugeben. [...] Wir wollen in unserer Musik den Menschen unserer Zeit sprechen lassen, und er soll zu vielen sprechen." English translation Frank Mehring.

    6. Some white writers and directors used pseudonyms to enter into the market of films with an "all black cast." See Bogle, 107–8. However, as Thomas Cripps demonstrates, the simple equation that blacks would root enthusiastically for protagonists in an "all black film" proved to be a false "great myth" (Cripps 171). Similar patterns of white patronage emerged in the early 1970s. In the era of "blaxploitation" films, the issue of African American agency was complicated by directors, editors, producers, or crews who often were white. For the function of agency and the construction of blackness in 1970s movies see Harry M. Benshoff, "Blaxploitation Horror Films: Generic Reappropriation or Reinscription?" *Cinema Journal* 39.2 (2000): 31–50.

    7. For further descriptions of music in these films see the Ulmer biography *Mann im Schatten* by S. Grissemann.

    8. While Winold Reiss was interested in the primitivist movements of his time, his paintings, however, cannot be subsumed under the four types, which Robert Goldwater identified as the "primitivism of the subconscious, "romantic primitivism," "emotional primitivism," and "intellectual primitivism" (Goldwater 3). Instead, Reiss's portrait painting can be described as "anthropological primitivism." See my article "The Unfinished Business of Democracy: Transcultural Confrontations in the Portraits of the German-American Artist Winold Reiss." *American Artists in Munich: Artistic Migration and Cultural Exchange Processes.* Christian Fuhrmeister, et al. (eds.). Munich, 2008.

Works Cited

Benshoff, Harry M. "Blaxploitation Horror Films: Generic Reappropriation or Reinscription?" *Cinema Journal* 39.2 (2000): 31–50.

Bogle, Donald. *Toms, Coons, Mulattoes, Mammies, and Bucks: An Interpretive History of Blacks in American Films.* New York: Viking, 1973.

Brecht, Brecht. *Gesammelte Werke: Werkausgabe Edition Suhrkamp.* 20 vols. Frankfurt am Main: Suhrkamp, 1967.

_____, and Kurt Weill. *Brecht/Weill. "Mahagonny."* Fritz Hennenberg and Jan Knopf (eds.). Frankfurt am Main: Suhrkamp, 2006.

Cripps, Thomas. *Slow Fade to Black: The Negro in American Film, 1900–1942.* New York: Oxford University Press, 1977.

Farneth, David, with Elmar Juchem and Dave Stein (eds.). *Kurt Weill. Ein Leben in Bildern und Dokumenten.* Translated by Elmar Juchem. Berlin: Ullstein, 2000.

Goldwater, Robert. *Primitivism in Modern Painting.* New York and London: Harper and Brothers, 1938.

Grissemann, Stefan. *Mann im Schatten: Der Filmemacher Edgar G. Ulmer.* Wien: Paul Zsolnay Verlag, 2003.

Guerrero, Ed. *Framing Blackness: The African American Image in Film.* Philadelphia: Temple University Press, 1993.

Kowalke, Kim H. "Kurt Weill's Amerika/America." Hermann Danuser and Hermann Gottschewski (eds.). *Amerikanismus Americanism Weill: Die Suche nach kultureller Identität in der Moderne.* Schliengen: Argus, 2003, 9–15.

Lemke, Sieglinde. *Primitivist Modernism: Black Culture and the Origins of Transatlantic Modernism.* Oxford and New York: Oxford University Press, 1998.

Lipsitz, George. "Genre Anxiety and Racial Representation in 1970s Cinema." Nick Browne (ed.). *Reconfiguring American Film Genres, History, and Theory.* Los Angeles: University of California Press, 1998, 216–20.

Mehring, Frank. "'The Unfinished Business of Democracy:' Transcultural Confrontations in the Portraits of the German-American Artist Winold Reiss." Christian Fuhrmeister et al. (eds.). *American Artists in Munich: Artistic Migration and Cultural Exchange Processes.* Munich: Deutscher Kunstverlag, 2008 (forthcoming).

Parmalee, Patty Lee. *Brecht's Ameria.* Columbus: Ohio State University Press, 1981.

Weill, Kurt. "*Alabama-Song*" aus "*Aufstieg und Fall der Stadt Mahagonny.*" Gesang und Klavier. Wien und Leipzig: Universal Edition, 1930.

_____. *Der Zar Lässt Sich Photographieren.* Wien und Leipzig: Universal Edition, 1927.

_____. "I am an American." *"I am an American" Radio Series.* Broadcast on September 9, 1941. RGA 9794. Washington: National Archives.

Detour's History/ History's *Detour*

Dana Polan

"'What was money?,' I asked myself. 'A piece of paper crawling with germs.'" Whenever *Detour* is shown, at this point the audience reacts with an enthusiasm usually reserved for football. Frequently, the spectators quote the best lines before the actors say them. According to traditional standards, *Detour* is not a work of art. Nevertheless, it is a great example of cinematic discourse, a paramount laboratory for semiotic research into textual strategies. Moreover, it has become a cult movie.

The title of this essay—*Detour*'s History/History's *Detour*—is presented as a way of investigating the cult status of this widely reputed Ulmer film. This essay will look at the ways in which criticism and traditions of cinephilia have constructed an image for *Detour*, the ways in which critical and cinephiliac discourses have framed the conditions for the film's reception and thereby imputed a particular and often fixed identity to it. Inspiration comes from a little book by the intellectual historian Dominick La Capra, *Madame Bovary on Trial* from 1982. Looking at the novel's obscenity trial in 1857, La Capra argues that a judicial hearing for a cultural work involves not only a legal decision but aesthetic ones—decisions that can be consequent for the destiny of the work and the way it is received in history. For instance, as La Capra shows, the lawyers in the *Madame Bovary* case invoke a number of aesthetic precepts that could seem obvious and even natural but in the case of an experimental work like Flaubert's novel are quite ideologically overloaded. Thus, whatever side they're on and whatever personal views of the novel they may have, the lawyers agree in a series of assumptions: that an artistic work's title is a direct guide to its subject, that point-of-view is easily assignable in narrative works, that a work radiates a morality (whether positive or negative) and does so in emphatic fashion, that synopsis of plot is an appropriate first step in critical analysis, that there is a direct line from textual point of view to authorial point of view — that, therefore, the cultural text is ultimately best understood as an expressive emanation of an author's personal vision. One of the most insightful aspects of La Capra's study of aesthetic assumptions in the trial has to do with his demonstration that such assumptions were common to prosecution and defense alike. Whatever their views on the obscenity or not of the book, both agreed on art's necessary relation to morality and meaningfulness and both agreed that a work became meaningful through the willful agency of a strong authorial presence and voice. There is the art work but there is also for the reception of that work a set of socially shared assumptions, relatively independent of personal taste or conviction, that determine in fact how that work is to be construed and, over time, granted its identity or set of identities.

Much of the critical and cinephiliac writing on *Detour* is also a way of framing it in advance, putting it on trial, so to speak, and, in this case, deciding for its positive value and thereby constructing it as an aesthetic object of a particularly strong sort. Following are some of the aesthetic presuppositions that drive the discourse on Ulmer and *Detour*. As with the obscenity trial for Flaubert's novel, the issue is not whether the interpretations of *Detour* are wrong or right but how they come about, what strategies of approaching the film enable it to be interpreted as it is and to be granted the aesthetic virtues it is said to have. Despite differences of emphasis and interpretation from writer to writer, there has been a consistency of overall assumption in writings on Ulmer. And despite the ways in which cinephiliac or fan discourse and academic film discourse often are presented as in opposition, the two frequently meet in an implicit or not-so-implicit auteurism that can set up a problematic distinction between those who see the specialness of the director and those who ostensibly miss it. This can be particularly troublesome in academia where, despite the emphasis on pedagogy as open learning, it is clear that the professor can in subtle ways tell students what he/she wants — what sort of aestheticization to engage in — and where ironically it is all too easy for students to succeed by mimicking back to the professor the gestures of aesthetic valorization he/she prefers. Such subtle (and sometimes not so subtle) signaling to students of the desired performative activity — in this case, interpretation and, specifically, auteurist interpretation of a particularly valorizing sort — especially merits analysis in the case of the study of Edgar Ulmer since anyone who has taught *Detour* likely has had the common experience of promoting the film's virtues, admittedly rough in a B-aesthetics sort of manner, only to realize the students simply think of it as cheesy or even silly. The tendency is to force the students to try to think of the film as great even as they demonstrate they don't feel it is.

Detour can productively be examined outside the discourse of cheesiness as a quite trenchant and gray vision of small-minded, dead-end lives at the beginning of the postwar period. But it's not so much that the students are misguided in their response as that they are not being offered effective guidance pedagogically by an aestheticizing approach that asserts the brilliance of the B-movie without arguing it and that adopts auteurist hyperboles to laud a work that doesn't perhaps necessitate appreciation so much as analysis. Telling the students *Detour* is great doesn't make it great.

The regularity of aesthetic attitudes in most writings on Ulmer is suggested with the second half of my title: History's *Detour*. This refers first of all to the ways in which the aesthetic presuppositions of auteurism can frequently work to block historical reflection around film. The newest spurt of interest in Ulmer — represented by new books that range from biographies to critical studies of individual films and by conferences and other events of rediscovery and reevaluation — can help us revise some of the historical record and, even more, lead us to recognize how much historical research is detoured by cultism, cinephilia, and auteurism. We can always uncover more historical detail but so long as we do not interrogate the framework in which we do research, we risk closing ourselves to some of the things that history can tell us, we risk making our own historical research irrelevant. At some fundamental level indeed, auteurism can be inimical to historical study: whatever we discover about production will not in any critical way revise the fundamental assumption that the director is an expressive force who transcends the limiting factors in history. Our understanding of cultural production is still in thrall to an aesthetic ideology that imagines there is the grubby world of facts, the world of material necessity and constraint, and then there is a shift into another realm — one of magic — through an ineffable mystery of creativity. It is possible to theorize and study historically the specific role of directors. Individuals are situated in history in ways that enables them to interact with that history in particular and irreducible ways. Remember Jean-Paul Sartre's famous aphorism: "[Paul] Valéry is a petit-bourgeois intellectual, no doubt about it. But not every petit bourgeois intellectual is [Paul] Valéry" (56). But there is nothing in that idea that requires a notion of genius or magical creativity. Quite the contrary, as Sartre's own existential biographies of figures such as Flaubert suggest, it can be a spur to conducting very precise material history of the conditions artists arise out of and react against in biographically singular ways. The director can be studied and his/her functions within a mode of production can be unpacked but only insofar as those are divorced from the assumption that directors are auteurs.

But given the auteurist conception of artistic expression as a wondrous act beyond reason, historical research can often seem secondary — something that doesn't really touch the essential and mysterious core of creation. In many ways, auteur analysis still operates in the realm of assertion — the assertion, in particular, that the evidence of genius is without argument — literally without argument — evident. Remember, for instance, Jacques Rivette's famous (or infamous) assertion about Hawks's *Monkey Business* and his blurring of evidence and proof: "The evidence on the screen is the proof of Hawks's genius: you only have to watch *Monkey Business* to know that it is a brilliant film. Some people refuse to admit this, however, they refuse to be satisfied by proof" (126). Not so far from this is a recurrent rhetoric in Ulmer criticism in which quality is not so much argued as subtly (or not so subtly) asserted. For instance, dogmatic assertion frequently shows up by the introduction, into simple and seemingly neutral declarative sentences, of unexamined, value-laden adjectives that enable acts of judgment to slide delicately and even surreptitiously into the analysis. For example, for Tim Pulleine writing on *Detour* in *Films & Filming*, "there is, for instance, an astonishing moment of chiaroscuro lighting as Al wishfully visualizes his girl Sue in the big-time as a band singer." The key word here is "astonishing"— an assertion of aesthetic accomplishment that shortcuts the work of careful argument. The word impels agreement by the very fact and act of its very expression — we are being asked to take the astonishing qualities of the shot for granted — and begs the question of why it is astonishing (personally, I find it not much different from images we might find in other Hollywood films of the time) and the extent to which it is exceptional or not within the standard operating procedures of the studio system and the B-system of the moment.

On the one hand, auteurism, at most, when faced with new details in the historical record that reveal divisions of labor and contribution, retreats to a faith in those realms of production that only the director would be in control of. That is, it admits that other workers make their contributions to the film but that the director has his/her inviolate realm of ultimate creativity. Thus, to take a typical case, to respond to the claim that the published scenario reveals that Martin Goldsmith is the true auteur of *Detour*, one website cinephile looks for directorial flourishes that exceed the screenplay: "Ulmer ... invented the idea during the climax of moving the camera in and out of focus over the objects in the hotel room after the murder" (Anderson). In other words, the screenwriter does the job of coming up with the bare bones of the narrative but it is the director who fleshes it out in ways that give the story its real aesthetic value. A similar auteurist gesture will be to admit stylistic weaknesses in Ulmer but consign and constrain them to limited areas that he is felt to have no affinity with. This, then, allows all the greater valorization of those areas that are imagined to be Ulmer's forte and in which he shines. For example, John Belton acknowledges that Ulmer is not strong in action sequences but then attributes this to the director's affinity for non-active psychology and introspection: "Ulmer's characters are rarely shown as the initiators of action; rather, they are most often presented with an object, character, event, or situation to which they react. Ulmer's action sequences are awkwardly staged and edited..., but his reaction shots are eloquent and beautiful" (344). And of course a related gesture is to take what seems like a weakness and reinterpret it as a strength. There is, for instance, a recurrent approach to Ulmer acting that takes deadness of performance — what for a general public would seem bad acting — and reads it affirmatively as in keeping with a thematics in Ulmer of characters deadened by worldly experience.

On the other hand, a more aggressive and expansive auteurism will imagine that no factual discovery drawn from the historical record of a film's production can contravene the fundamental premise of the director's transcendent power: whatever the history of production, there comes that mysterious moment when the facts are transcended and given new valence by the director's special force of genius and creativity. For instance, it is noteworthy that Martin Goldsmith's screenplay suggests that certain shots use rear projection, a staple of B-movie production. But for a strong auteurism, historical facts of production and the magic of esthetic expression can exist in separate and inviolate realms. In such a perspective, the practicalities of the former never falsify the wondrous accomplishments of the latter. Thus, the auteurists persist in attributing the use of rear projection to an intentional choice on Ulmer's part in keeping with his supposed interest in rendering the world as insubstantial and dream-like (or nightmare-like). We might compare this to the auteurist vindication of the painted backdrops in Hitchcock's *Marnie* which are interpreted in this context as signs also of the insubstantiality of the world Marnie has grown up in: in both cases, an unrealistic effect that the viewers may likely notice and that comes from budgetary constraints is re-interpreted to become a comment on the unreality of the fictional world of the film *for the characters who inhabit it* (rather than for the viewers watching it). Insofar as one common concern and tactic of auteurism is to valorize and look for signs of self-reflexivity in film, and insofar as the auteur's ultimate commitment in this view becomes that of commitment to the art of cinema itself against all concerns for social theme or political commitment, the strongest auteurs will be those whose films, whatever their subject, are really about cinematic seeing. Even though Goldsmith's screenplay includes the track into the rear view mirror that enables Al to reflect back on Sue as he drives Haskell's car, any number of essays will see the mirror scene as *Ulmer's* reflection on cinematic vision and memory.

It's not that Ulmer might not have as one of his personal, even authorial, preoccupations a concern with self-reflexivity, with cinematic seeing, and with the rendering of a fictional universe as insubstantial. No doubt, it could be possible logically for Goldsmith to have had reasons for suggesting rear projection that would differ from the reasons that Ulmer might have had in deciding to follow Goldsmith's script suggestion and shoot with rear projection. But it's illogical to assume that Ulmer came up with the very idea of rear projection (rather than a personal meaning assigned to it by him) when the historical record suggests that the origin of the idea came from someone else.

For what it's worth — and to encourage more rigorous research into the various contributions by the film team to production history — following are just a few of the facts of production revealed in the Production Code Administration file at the Margaret Herrick Library of the Academy of Motion Picture Arts and Sciences. My purpose is not to offer a full history but to suggest that any such history — any attention to concrete practices of film production, *including necessary attention to the concrete and irreducible contribution that directors make in their place in the division of labor*— offers an advance over an auteur theory that is really not so much a theory — since that would be testable against history — as a dogma asserted in advance of any actual engagement with films and the narrative of their production. To the extent that we can reconstruct a production history, we may be able to specify the contributions of directors in ways that actually recognize those contributions than fantasize about them in ways that actually do disservice to the often very real struggles directors (and other creative workers) engage in to bring their works of art to fruition.

On November 1, 1944, the Breen office (PCA) responded to Producers Releasing Corporation about a 16 page synopsis for *Detour* which appears to have closely followed Goldsmith's novel (in which there is an additional narration by Sue who has been seduced by an actor in Hollywood and eventually throws him over for her career). Some of the Breen office suggestions are incorporated into the final film: for example, it is Breen who asks that Al be seen being picked up at the very end by the police rather than getting away. Breen often made recommendations of add-on end scenes about the moral rightness of the universe and of the effective workings of the law and justice within it as a way supposedly of compensating for prior moments of immorality and lawlessness, and the abrupt addition to the ending of *Detour* can help explain how, in an instant before, Al had said that he was going to get away with murder and then doesn't. (Ironically, if Breen sees the final scene as offering a last-minute moment of compensatory moral values, the Ohio censor board would find the addition itself to be troublesome insofar as the idea of a mysterious but inevitable fate that will infallibly bring the lawless to justice, as expressed in Al's last line of narration, could seem to challenge deistic models of the universe. For the Ohio board, there was something too random about the ineffable workings of destiny presented here.) At the same, we should note — and this is in keeping with recent research on the Breen office and the Production Code as a site of complicated negotiation rather than outright repression — that not all Breen stipulations are met: for example, Breen said that Al and Vera could not be seen registering as man and wife in the hotel in LA and must have separate rooms.

On December 29, 1944, PRC submitted to Breen a one-page treatment that was much closer to the script versions that would now follow than to Goldsmith's original novel. The revelation of Sue's doings in Los Angeles (she had an affair while away from Al, for instance) had been eliminated but there was now a framing story of Sue marrying a gangster named Dillon while Al is in the diner remembering his tale. There was also a subplot in which Al and Vera wander LA looking for people who owed Haskell money (including, in a pointed irony, Dillon). By February 13, Breen had approved a script (still with the marriage ceremony frame) but was asking for any glimpse of Vera's body to be kept "to a flash," again something that does not seem to have really been adhered to. On May 26, 1945, PRC told Breen that the main character's name is now Al Roberts and that the subplot of Al trying to collect on his debts had been taken out. The film went into production in June and the release print was evaluated by the PCA in August (amusingly, Al was judged on the PCA evaluation score sheet to be both "sympathetic" and "unsympathetic" while Vera is nothing but "unsympathetic").

What do we do with production history such as this? It reminds us that the end result of any Hollywood act of movie-making — even for a film like *Detour* that bears on the screen all the marks of B-movie impoverishment — is an activity of compromise, negotiation, and struggle even, with multiple forces and factors all working to impose a range of identities on the film. Auteurism too often acts as an unstoppable machine of aesthetic valorization, a machine that at its strongest constructs itself as non-falsifiable. It imagines the facts of production history as irrelevant to its appreciation of authorial accomplishment. Ulmer criticism operates generally as a series of regularized tactics and assertive gestures. And it does so in defiance of such histories of compromise and division of labor that may mean that the director is certainly in charge but is only one creative force among others.

Any number of common features distinguish auteurist dogmatism. First, there is the sheer fact of regularity and repetition themselves. It is striking in reading *Detour* criticism to see the same lines, the same analyses, the same anecdotes endlessly enacted. For example, any number of essays rehearse the same facts about Ulmer's life and argue its parallels with Al's own career trajectory (the desire to be the sort of artiste who can play Carnegie Hall but who can also make a go of it in Hollywood). A new stage of research will allow us to move beyond many of the *idées reçues* in Ulmer criticism but we need to recognize that their tenacity comes from aesthetic needs deeper than that of a simple setting straight of the historiographical record. Biographical criticism, for instance, frequently mentions Ulmer's early work in theatre and set design in large part to emphasize an aesthetic pretense and legitimate his later work. There is no detail about what he did in the theatre and how it concretely remained with him; instead, the operative assumption seems to be that someone who worked in European theatre necessarily gained aesthetic ambitions from this experience that would influence the remainder of the career. (Again, this may or may not have been the case with Ulmer. But typically, the impact of an early theatre experience on the later life is assumed and asserted, rather than argued.)

This narration of a useable artistic background parallels another common gesture in Ulmer criticism: the comparison of him or his films to established artists in order to insert him into a larger aesthetic community. In some cases, the comparison is to figures that Ulmer worked with as if the factual connection logically implies aesthetic inspiration: for example, references to Max Reinhardt, Murnau, Lang or Wilder. In his piece on Ulmer in *Bright Lights Film Journal*, Gary Morris renders the comparative gesture explicit: "[Ulmer's] provenance is impeccable in its early phases." (Here, though, we should note two diametrically opposed strategies in Ulmer criticism. On the one hand, he gains in value by being compared favorably to others he interacted with. On the other hand, the very fact that he didn't have the grand careers they often did also becomes a badge of Ulmer's value as if they were somehow lucky and he wasn't and as if his very lack of fortune proves his artistic superiority. As John Belton puts it in a moment of confession rare among Ulmer cultists for its frankness, "Ulmer's martyrization by the mass of critics has led to his canonization by the few, myself included" [340].)

In other cases, the reference is to a wider great tradition. Some — and only some — of the comparisons for Ulmer are: Goethe, Kafka, Camus, Kurosawa, Courbet, Gide, Edward Hopper, Theodore Dreiser, Stendhal, Antonioni, Peter Handke, and Dario Argento. The operative idea here seems to be that if one can find something similar in the oeuvre of Ulmer and that of some artist or intellectual he is compared to, then Ulmer takes on some of the greatness of the figure he is being associated with. My favorite reference — in part, because it seems to speak of the weird ahistoricity that can characterize auteurism — is Richard Combs's *Monthly Film Bulletin* review of *Detour* which speaks of the film's "Truffaut-like lyricism" (146); having always wondered if Truffaut took the pneumatic tubes sequence in *Stolen Kisses* from the switchboard scene in *Detour*, it is revealing that Ulmer is here presented as anticipating Truffaut.[1]

Once the aesthetic provenance of an artistic career and its oeuvre is established by such strategies, auteurist protocols of reading can set out to confirm particular artistic qualities of individual works within the oeuvre. That is, the assertion that the director is indeed an auteur serves as a prelude to, and enables, detailed engagement with his or her individual films which are now assumed to be stylistic or thematic embodiments of, and demonstrations of, the auteur's general aesthetic vocation. Thus, one typical aesthetic discourse on *Detour* tends toward a valorization of visual style as that which transcends or takes off from a meagerness of content that serves as mere alibi for vibrant aesthetic play. For example, again to quote Tim Pulleine on *Detour* in *Films & Filming*, "The anecdote itself may seem fairly commonplace.... It is the manner of its telling, however, which excites." Or, take David Thomson on *The Naked Dawn* in the *New Biographical Dictionary of Film*, "a wretched Western plot made in a few days, but transformed by Ulmer's camera style" (888).

It is important to note how often stylistic criticism of *Detour* operates to construct it as a work of classical coherence and balance. Aesthetics here valorizes not the experimental work that defies convention but the work that confirms some very traditional precepts about artistic structure and organic unity. Auteurism often seems driven by conventionalized notions of harmony, symmetry, univocality, and so on. There is, for instance, the search for figures or tropes that run through the text as organic and organizing factors and can give it unity — for example, in *Detour*, the motif of rain or what Richard Combs refers as the recurrence of images of telephones to construct a "poignancy-of-communication" theme (146). In like fashion, the notion of the text's unity — nothing is in it that one can't find an interpretation for — leads to a fascination with reading in detail. Reading in detail becomes a kind of tautological process: it proves the text was important and organically coherent enough to merit such reading but it is only because one has decided the work is worthy and coherent that one constructs and employs an interpretive model to process details. To take just one example, for David Coursen in *Movietone News*, "the closest thing to a moment of freedom in the movie (though the character doesn't perceive it as such) comes in the extraordinary sequence in which, working in the nightclub he professes to despise, he plays a brilliant, disjointed piano improvisation, shown largely through close-ups of his crazily moving fingers" (18). Here, the strategy is to select one moment of the film (the close-ups) and see it as part of a larger structure of meaning for which it serves as a concrete support. (In passing, note how the facile reference to an "extraordinary" sequence is another case of an adjective subtly doing the work of assertion of the evident).

The inverse of stylistic appreciation is a thematic criticism that finds in Ulmer films the expression of important meanings and in a coherent, unified, harmonious fashion. Obviously, stylistics and thematics can work together — for example, Coursen's discovery of a detail (a close-up that reveals the dialectic of freedom and constraint) finds it to be about the dialectic of freedom and constraint — but it is also the case that the two discourses can go their separate ways: thus, thematic interpretation can be a productive strategy in Ulmer criticism in some cases insofar as it can admit the stylistic meagerness of the films and yet still find great thematic worth in them.

One important thing to note about thematic criticism in the case of auteurs is the extent to which it generally emphasizes not any themes whatsoever but what we might call the big themes, the seemingly eternal issues: that is, large questions of freedom and fate, destiny and determination and so on. In Ulmer criticism, for example, there is a focus on characters searching for self-will in a structured and structuring universe. There is an optimistic version of such thematics — Ulmer characters find a path to illumination — and a bleak one: we are victims of a malevolent and Godless universe. In the case of *Detour*, its seeming identity as film noir becomes a propitious path to thematics insofar as the genre of noir is assumed by its interpreters essentially to deal with dialectics of fate and freedom and even in its tensions of light and shadow is taken to invoke cinema's fundamental investment in such a dialectic (for instance, Marc Vernet's argument from 1980 that film noir's plays on black and white are as an essential reflection on themes of presence and absence).

Here, again, we are seeing a detouring of history. Insofar as thematic criticism needs to find themes of eternal or universal interest, it can only downplay those aspects of film that seem more rooted in a specific historical context and operate as precise responses to that context. That is, it is rare that the themes auteur criticism unveils are seen as sociological or historical. To my mind, for instance, it is risky to see *Detour* as a work of film noir. To the extent that we romanticize *noir* as a genre of exceptional people in exceptional settings and circumstances — for example, the heroic gumshoe and the seductive femme fatale circulating through fascinating locales like swanky nightclubs and overblown apartments or mansions — *Detour* can only appear decidedly unglamorous, not really invested in exoticism. Outside a few scenes, the film doesn't even look like classic noir. Except for obviously mechanical moments, such as the one in which a bright light picks out Al Roberts' eyes from the inky shadows as he begins to tell his tale of personal doom, *Detour* even avoids the exotic plays of light and dark that typify noir and, for much of its narrative, opts instead for a washed-out look — for example, the harsh brightness of the California sun, the dreariness of the used car lot, and the nondescript blandness of the hotel room in which Al and Vera play out their duet of doom.

To my mind, it is perhaps more productive to think of *Detour* within a very particular trend in postwar cynical crime cinema that film historians Noël Burch and Thom Anderson refer to as "*film gris*" (gray film). The *films gris* reject *noir* glamour and wallow instead in an unremitting bleakness. Where romantic film noir pictures a world of larger-than-life figures, the *films gris* deal with all-too-average losers, everyday American citizens who are caught in the rat race of dead-end career options and desperately try to beat the system by means that are as meager as their dreams. In *Detour*, it is important that Al Roberts's journey propels him westward toward Los Angeles and the radiant blondeness of his girlfriend Sue. In a parody of the foundational American myth of the pioneer quest, Al's "Mecca" turns out to be a hopeless site of broken dreams, lost illusions. We learn, for instance, that even Sue, who has preceded Al and about whom he was sure that success was just around the corner, has become nothing more than a hash-slinger in a commonplace diner.

As a *film gris*, *Detour* immerses us painfully in the world of ordinary characters trapped by the very nature of their human condition. In the most common interpretations of the film, this condition is existential insofar as the film appears primarily to depict people as the inevitable victims of a contagious fatalism that by nature they can never outrun. But it is also possible to take the depiction of the human condition in *Detour* as sociological in its emphasis on irreconcilable differences between the haves and the have-nots in the very definable context of 1940s America. For instance, the film harps unremittingly on the centrally determinant role of money in people's lives: what you can accomplish when you possess it, how much is closed off to you when you don't. Here, Andrew Britton's essay is one of the rare discussions of *Detour* to deal with the film's sociology of ordinary America and the determinant role of money in the 1940s.

However, like other auteurists, Britton reads in detail — in his case, to find signs of the unreliability of Al's narration thereby to imagine him ever more as a money-grubbing figure who is looking out for number one. There is then the risk in such sociological reading that once again the film is constituted as a special aesthetic object — the film becomes not merely the sociologically symptomatic work but the especially revelatory one. That is, Britton assumes that the unreliability of narration in the film gives this film a special ability to comment on a society of acquisitiveness and that such special perception comes from Ulmer's own special position as privileged auteur. Once again it is easy to slide into an auteurism that imagines that Ulmer had a special grasp on his historical moment (perhaps because the conditions of B movie-making gave him his own up-close view of realms of financial constraint).

Perhaps it would be fruitful to move beyond a classical aesthetics that would search in films for the conventional unities — unity of style, unity of theme, unity of style and theme together. For example, like La Capra's *Madame Bovary*—in which the infamous use of *style indirect libre* doesn't in fact fit the trial lawyers' image of the novel as simple and univocal in point-of-view—*Detour* can be seen as a film that confounds categories. For instance, insofar as it doesn't resemble A-film performance, the acting in *Detour* may be readable thematically (for instance, as metaphor of one's deadened submission to fate) but it also can work at a level of undecidability: is it good? is it bad? is it camp? is it deeply resonant? Or does it play across these categories? And to what extent does what the film enacts and enables depend on the viewing protocols within which it is viewed? One of the important implications of this last question has to do with the ways we often make use of a contrast between the Poverty Row film and big studio Hollywood production. Whether this contrast is used to valorize the B-movie or to denigrate it, there is often the assumption that the value of Hollywood is firmly in place, a standard that other practices can judged against. Studio films also emerged from complicated processes of compromise and whatever success or esteem any individual film garners is constructed through a complex history of production and reception. Thus, to make a confession, my opening paragraph about the ways cult audiences react like football spectators to cheesy lines in *Detour* was in fact a deliberate rewriting of the opening to Umberto Eco's essay on *Casablanca* as cult classic (see Eco 197). Cult films — whether from big studios or B-movie companies — aren't born naturally, magically: they are made and received, according to precise and regularized procedures of aesthetic presupposition.

Before any artistic judgment we might want to make about it, the B-movie finds a primary historical value from the simple fact that it existed and reminds us of a complicated diversity of modes of American cultural production. "M.G.M. does a better job of running humanity than God," says the narrator in Martin Goldsmith's novel of *Detour* and the comment reiterates the hold of Hollywood on an American everydayness. The novel, screenplay, and film of *Detour* all interrogate the role of Hollywood dreams in American lives. And the film especially does so not only in its subject matter but in the very ways it takes up a place in the contemporary history of popular culture. Ulmer's *Detour* may best be understood not as some sort of objective work of art but as something relative — relative to other practices of culture such as A-filmmaking and relative to a social history that grants a large and important role to films and the complicated frames within which we receive them.

Note

1. Mea culpa: in my program note on *Detour* for the Melbourne Cinematheque (2002), I compared Ulmer's film to Sartre's *Huis clos*. But I would contend that the comparison is in this case historical rather than metaphorical as it is clear that existential ideas are in circulation in the postwar period and could well show up equally in a play by Sartre and this B-movie.

Works Cited

Anderson, Jeffrey M. "*Detour*: Ulmer's B-Masterpiece." *http://www.combustiblecelluloid.com/detour.shtml*, last accessed 10 December 2007.
Belton, John "Edgar G. Ulmer." *American Directors, volume 1*. Jean-Pierre Coursodon and Pierre Sauvage (eds.). New York: MacGraw-Hill, 1983, 339–47.
Britton, Andrew "*Detour*." Ian Cameron (ed.). *The Book of Film Noir*. New York: Continuum, 1993, 174–83.
Burch, Noël, and Thom Anderson. *Les Communistes d'Hollywood: autre chose que des martyres*. Paris: Presses Universitaires de la Sorbonne, 1994.
Combs, Richard. "*Detour*." *Monthly Film Bulletin* 49 (1982): 145–6
Coursen, David. "Closing Down the Open Road: *Detour*." *Movietone News* (February 1976): 16–9.
Eco, Umberto. "*Casablanca*: Cult Movies and Intertextual Montage." *Travels in Hyperreality*, Trans. William Weaver. New York: Harcourt Brace Jovanovich, 1986, 197–211.
La Capra, Dominick. *Madame Bovary on Trial*. Ithaca, NY: Cornell University Press, 1982.
Morris, Gary. "Edgar Ulmer's *Detour*." *http://www.brightlightsfilm.com/31/detour.html*, last accessed 10 December 2007.
Polan, Dana. "*Detour*." Melbourne Cinematheque Program Note, 2002, *http://www.sensesofcinema.com/contents/cteq/02/21/detour.html*, last accessed 10 December 2007.
Pulleine, Tim. "*Detour*." *Films and Filming* 335 (August 1982): 37.
Rivette, Jacques. "The Genius of Howard Hawks (*Monkey Business*)." Jim Hillier (ed.). *Cahiers du cinéma. The 1950s: Neo-Realism, Hollywood, New Wave*. Cambridge, MA: Harvard University Press, 1985, 126–31.
Sartre, Jean-Paul. *Search for a Method*. Trans. Hazel E. Barnes. New York: Knopf, 1963.
Thomson, David. *The New Biographical Dictionary of Film*. New York: Knopf, 2002, 878–88.
Vernet, Marc. "Clignotements du noir-et-blanc." Jacques Aumont and Jean-Louis Leutrat (eds.). *Théorie du cinéma*. Paris: Editions Albatros, 1980, 223–33.

The Strange Woman: An Analysis with Gilles Deleuze's Notion of the Impulse-Image
JULIA MEIER

> *There is an identical parasitic impulse everywhere.*
> —Gilles Deleuze (*Cinema 1: The Movement-Image*, 1986)

> *Sheena is a champion of self-reliance*
> *As soon as she needs it she knows just where the knife is.*
> —The Horrors (*Sheena Is a Parasite*, 2007)

> *Give me the head of Iokanaan!*
> —Oscar Wilde (*Salomé*, 1893)

The Strange Woman, released in 1946, is one of Edgar Ulmer's bigger Hollywood film productions filmed with a much higher budget than his previous films. The collaboration with the producers of *The Strange Woman*, Hunt Stromberg and Jack Chertok, was not always to Ulmer's content, and he could not realize the movie the way he wanted (see Grissemann 238). The biggest obstacle was that everything had to pass the consensus of a mainstream Hollywood production. At least, Ulmer could convince Stromberg to agree with his choice for the role of the leading actress, Hedy Lamarr, who became a scandalous sex symbol after the release of the movie *Ecstasy* (1933) directed by Gustav Machaty in which she appeared as the first nude in film history.

Shot in black and white, *The Strange Woman* takes place in Bangor, Maine, U.S.A., a rising industrial city in the early 1820s. The center of the story is a beautiful young woman, Jenny Hager (Lamarr) who lives together with her impoverished and violent alcoholic father. Money and libido, one could say, are the two driving forces and decisive factors for her to get through life.

The prologue already forebodes the complex character of Jenny: We see her as a little girl. She stands on a bridge spurring on two children to swim faster. With an unusual, impulsive cruelty and with joyful laughter she then pushes a young boy, who cannot swim into the river and lets him almost drown. When the boy cries for help she even pushes his head down with her feet. What might cause bewilderment in the viewer is that little Jenny's violence is paired with joy — the joy of discovering power, the possibility to act and to change given circumstances, even if the effect of this action is more often than not the destruction of the other person.

Already in the beginning of the movie it becomes clear that Jenny has no pity when it comes to the point to save or to mark her power. Being more beautiful than the other girls she already knows as a little girl of what kind her only power to rise above her pre-designed destiny may be: "I'm going to be beautiful," she promises to herself. The way she strokes her hair makes her decisiveness as well as her awareness about her blossoming sexual power that would stop at nothing eerily clear. She wants to be a winner and not a loser in society. After a time leap depicted in a melodramatic image in which her shivering reflection in the water transforms into the face of a beautiful grown-up young lady, the story begins. A brief plot summary will show the fast rise and fall of the film's central character:

Jenny finds out that one of the richest man in town, Mr. Poster (Gene Lockhart), an old widower, is attracted to her, and she knows how to manipulate situations to become his wife: Jenny uses the heart attack and subsequent death of her father who has beaten her up with a whip just before he died, as a means for her plan: At night she runs over to Mr. Poster to tell him about the father's assault — skipping the fact that he has already died. This assault gives Mr. Poster for his part the justification to marry her. Under normal circumstances this marriage between an old widower and a young girl of lower class would not have been approved by society. When her stepson, Ephraim Poster (Louis Hayward), returns home from studying abroad, Jenny immediately directs her desire towards him. Ephraim cannot resist his father's wife. As it seems obvious, her attraction to Ephraim is not caused by pure love. She might wish for a more appealing and younger man, but her behavior can be understood in terms of monetary motivations: In the more adequate relationship with Poster Jr. Jenny could keep all the money. Her plan is to get rid of Mr. Poster Sr. and she tries to manipulate Ephraim to kill his father during a boat ride. In the end Mr. Poster dies during the ride, however, it was not by the active murder of Ephraim. Instead Ephraim was so anxious because of his fear of water that he caused the boat to capsize by accident and could not save the father from drowning. When Jenny learns this, she is extremely turned off by his weakness. She turns away from Ephraim, and actually blames him for the death of his father. This makes him feel so guilty that he starts to drink and later commits suicide. Subsequently her desire finds another object, John Evered (George Sanders), the fiancé of her best friend Meg Saladine (Hillary Brooke). She pinches Meg's fiancé and marries him. But in the last sequence of the film things change. For the first time Jenny really admires a man and she becomes jealous when she fears that he might return to his former fiancée. In the last scene Jenny rides a carriage and sees them both standing together in front of an isolated cabin. And although her husband and the other woman met in total innocence, Jenny becomes jealous. She whips the horses and races in their direction wanting to kill them both. But the carriage gets out of control and she crashes down a hill. The last image shows her dying in the arms of her husband, saying: "I wanted the whole world, but really all I wanted was you."

In *The Strange Woman* it becomes evident that all of Jenny's crucial actions seem to depart rather from elementary impulses than from contemplative intelligence. Her behavior is often coupled with an unusual pitilessness. As there is no explanation given in the film narrative, her behavior is portrayed out of context for the viewer. Therefore it appears to be somewhat "strange," as is also suggested by the title of the movie. In order to analyze the impulsive dynamism of *The Strange Woman* the work of the French philosopher Gilles Deleuze, *Cinema 1: The Movement-Image*, lends some valuable tools. For *The Strange Woman,* it is important to concentrate on some aspects of the Deleuzian concept of the *impulse-image*, which Deleuze associates with naturalism. His point is, however, that those films which show the *impulse-image* do not narrate a naturalistic plot, but everything in the film — setting, character, story — emanates from a primordial (or "originary") world of drives and forces that are inseparable from the real world of concrete particularities (cf. *Cinema 1: The Movement-Image* 132). The setting of Ulmer's film could be seen as a first indicator of the *impulse-image*, in which, according to Deleuze, the historical and geographic "milieu" serves only as a medium for the originary world (cf. 128f.). The originary world of elementary impulses is tied to an actual milieu — that is, its specific time frame and place: Bangor in 1824. But the actual milieu itself is altered in such a way, "as if it was 'derived' as a secondary effect of a turbulent substrate, (hence the surreal tendencies within naturalistic films [...]" (Bogue 84). Accompanied by an eccentrically dramatic orchestral music, the artificial studio-landscapes, as well as the bizarre (almost surreal) permanent riots of foreign lumberjacks in town, let Bangor seem to occupy this particular space between the real and the primordial world. In *Cinema 1: The Movement-Image* Deleuze gives a short explanation for this kind of milieu:

> The originary world may be marked by the artificiality of the set (a comic opera kingdom, a studio forest, or marsh) as much as by the authenticity of a preserved zone (a genuine desert, a virgin forest). It is recognizable by its formless character. It is a pure background, or rather a without background, composed of unformed matter, sketches or fragments, crossed by non-formal function, act, or energy dynamisms which do not even refer to the constituted subjects [128].

The riots, for instance, are never explained or portrayed in a realistic manner; they can be seen to only serve as a means to render perceptible an atmosphere of turmoil. A milieu, so to speak, in which men have to fight their way in order to save their own skin. This agitation of the outer world brings forth the restlessness in Jenny's character. If we were to understand an actual or real milieu as a social surrounding then Jenny belongs to the underprivileged class of the town. In order to escape her fate of staying poor she instinctively takes advantage of what her surrounding offers her, knowing that her only power to improve her situation is her beauty. This connects the originary world to the real in which the energetic forces of impulses manifest themselves. Deleuze explains this intrinsic power of the impulse as follows:

> The law or the destiny of the impulse is to take possession through guile, but violently, of everything that it can in a given milieu, and, if it can, to pass from one milieu to another. This exploration, this exhaustion of milieux, is constant. Each time, the impulse selects its fragment in a given milieu and yet it does not select it, it takes indiscriminately from what the milieu offers it, even if it then means going on further [133].

When Jenny's father dies she is liberated of his violence, but nevertheless she needs somebody to take care of her. The minute after her father's death she runs over to Mr. Poster to take advantage of his affection for her. But she does not rely on his honorable good will only. In order to make her plan really effective she impulsively uses her erotic power showing him her naked shoulder as that body part which has been whipped by her father. With reference to Deleuze "the nature of the impulse is 'elementary' or 'raw'; it can be as simple as the impulse of hunger, impulses to nourishment, sexual impulses, or the impulse for money" (132). Similarly, one could understand Jenny's behavior in this situation as such an impulse of all of the above mentioned. She wants to go further, to burst the frame of the given social role and law. Therefore, Jenny has to make very quick decisions. She does not have the time to wait for another circumstance or situation; it is always now or never. This urge to use a given situation to its full extent can also be traced on her face. In fact, Ulmer often draws all force and attention onto Lamarr's face, thus making it the predominant site of the film, where most intensity takes place. Many non-verbalized contents that the body manages to hide become visible in the facial expression even if they only show up in small agitations — "tiny local movements" (Deleuze 90); an eyebrow that moves up, "the quivering of the lips" or "the brilliance of a look" (90). According to Deleuze it is especially desire that manifests itself in small agitations, and thus is able to give an "intensive face [that] expresses pure power" (90ff, cf. also Bogue 76). In Jenny's face, it is desire tied up with the impulse for power that becomes visible only through these little solicitations or impulsions that erupt on an almost empty, static, blank, iconic surface recalling all the masked faces of the sublime diva that seems to be detached from reality.

Her facial expression mirrors some typical features of the *femme fatale*, who is very aware about her effect on men. She is able to play the many faces of typical female clichés ranging from desperation to childish naiveté to erotic temptation. She switches from the helpless victim to the power of the seductive culprit in a second. This play of artificial feelings is so much a part of her that it erupts naturally when she needs it. The correlation between the seeming fear of Jenny, her crying and beauty thus heightens the erotic quality of the situation. Mr. Poster is caught — himself like a victim — whose blood gets virtually sucked by a vampire. In the same manner as the horror genre deals with the vampire's impulse or hunger for blood, Ulmer's melodrama makes evident the woman's impulse for power through wealth that has to be satisfied. This driven force of a predatory impulse is elementary. Jenny must seduce men in order to explore the given milieu, to burst its frames and to move from the poor girl to the society lady.

A scene that plays at church shows Jenny's face under high tension for she has to grasp the whole situation in order to use it to her fortune. It is interesting to note that in contrast to the surrounding church community her face appears clearer and brighter, almost like a soft and shining surface. This slight illumination gives her a calm yet powerful aura. Again, there is the need to be accepted by society (when she and her husband entered the church for the first time as a couple the community did not welcome her kindly but rumor started). Being very aware of this enviousness, Jenny again manages to save and to gain reputation in an extraordinary way. When the priest is asking for a money gift by the rich men in town he does not receive any offers. This is when Jenny takes over: She offers $1000; thus she takes on the domain of men, but being clever enough to explain her deed on the grounds of her husband's own wish to let her doing so. This secures her the reputation of the community — equally of men and women. Again, one could argue that her action derives from her desire to heighten her power. At the same time she transgresses the borders of female role in patriarchal society.

This urge to move on, however, never finds its end, for Jenny is not yet satisfied which is shown in the next sequence of the film. In trying to manipulate Ephraim to kill his father, her impulse for power culminates in criminal intentions. The murderous intentions of Jenny's impulse are again visualized through a special lighting of her face.

In film history, the lighting of a scene, as well as the contrast of black and white was the predominant feature of German expressionist film. With reference to Deleuze, Ronald Bogue points out that "[e]ach shade of light is a degree of intensity in relation to darkness (Bogue 60, cf. Deleuze 50f.). Thus, light and shadow can be conceived as "two separate entities in constant conflict" (Bogue 60). Although Ulmer's film does not contrast black and white to the full extreme, as the expressionist film does, several close-ups of Lamarr's face remind of this cinematographic image. As a first interpretation of this scene one could say that the conflict between good and evil looms in Jenny's face. Her forehead and her eyes still shine white and bright, but down from her cheeks the light dives into darkness. Shot as a close-up, which has the capacity to remove the person from social codes and the commonsense coordinates of space and time, the face becomes an image expressing pure affective quality or power (cf. Bogue 78, cf. Deleuze 99). Thus rather than being a statement of a moral judgment between good and evil, the contrast of the dark shadow functions as an "intensifier" of the bright illuminated part of the face, and thereby one could argue, as an intensifier of Jenny's power that stops at nothing in order to satisfy her needs. As Deleuze explains the nature of the impulses:

> they are inseparable from the perverse modes of behavior which they produce and animate: [They can be] cannibalistic, sado-masochistic, necrophiliac, etc. [But,] however low, repulsive or disgusting it may be [...] the impulse becomes a necessity for it is paired with a great joy to rediscover its power of choice. At the deepest level [this power of choice is] the desire to change milieu, to seek a new milieu to explore [Deleuze 132f].

In the case of Jenny's murderous impulse it is important to note that this perverse mode of behavior, therefore, is not meant as a deviation of "normal" behavior, but perversion is itself derived. In this sense it becomes the "normal/necessary" expression in the derived milieu where it appears (cf. Deleuze 132). Thus, one could argue, that the film portrays the human condition of acting out desire (as a philosophical subtext); impulses of sexual desire that is, be that they are coupled with love, be that they are coupled with money. This has been mostly understood in psychoanalytical terms as a negative concept because, in psychoanalysis, desire begins from lack — desiring what we do not have. But read in a different, or maybe more positive manner, desire for philosophers like Gilles Deleuze and Félix Guattari above all is productive, and the expansion, not the repression of desire is what gives rise to power, a power that is necessary to preserve and enhance life (cf. *Anti-Oedipus: Capitalism and Schizophrenia 1* 25). In not repressing but acting out desire, new, or simply other modes of social behavior become possible. Those other modes are not necessarily better, but they underline the fact that all groundings, foundations, or laws are not stable. Thus, what the film shows, is this intrinsic power of going beyond the restrictions of a given milieu via the impulsive actions derived from the desire of Jenny Hager.

At first sight, it appears therefore somewhat strange that the film has to end with a moral cliché: Inevitably, in the end such deviant women always have to die. Therefore, the tragic death of Jenny almost seems like a punishment for her sins. But if one was to read the film with the notion of the *impulse-image*, the death of Jenny becomes a consequential ending, because, as Deleuze observes, the *impulse-image always* ends with the death impulse: "[I]mpulses have the same goal and destiny: to smash into fragments, to tear off fragments, gather up the scraps, from the great rubbish dump and bring everything together in a single and identical death impulse [...]. Here it attains its extreme baseness" (134). The "great rubbish dumb" in this "derived milieu" is both the "trash" as well as the rigid, rich class system of Bangor; and one of Bangor's most vigorous inhabitants is fundamentally occupied with the impulse, which, according to Deleuze,

> by nature, is too strong for the character, whatever his [/her] personality. This violence is within him [/her] and is far from being an appearance, but it cannot be awakened — that is, reveal itself in the derived milieu — without shattering the character at a stroke, or in entangling him [/her] in a becoming which is that of his [/her] own degradation and death [Deleuze 142].

If we were to connect psychological attributes as for instance masochism, schizophrenia, perversion or another mental illness/strangeness to the protagonist of the movie, we are wrong. In his analysis of the *impulse-image* in *Mr. Klein* (1976) directed by Joseph Losey, Deleuze especially stresses the fact that what "is peculiar to *Mr. Klein* is that the violence of the impulses which dwell in him draw him to the *strangest becoming*" (142, emphasis mine). This "becoming" can be a "reversal against the self" (142), or it can take "a course of entropic dissipation" (Bogue 83) — but in all it seems to be more a destiny that is "dictated less by psychological motivations than a physical law of gravity" (Bogue 83). The "strangest becoming" on the part of Jenny Hager is not connected to lack but to an extraordinary vital power that pushes her not only out of the socially fixed frame; she wanted to go so far — and actually set out — to gain the whole world by the forces of her impulses, but in the end, dying in her husband's arms, she even bursts her own frame of self-consciousness in understanding that all she ever wanted was really him. Thus her final "strange" becoming was "becoming-loving."

What makes this film so special is that Ulmer depicts the character of the "strange woman" *without* moral judgment. The film does *not* describe a specific and located "evil," whether that be the "psychopathology" of a desiring, impulsive and aggressive woman, who drives several men into death and despair, or whether that be the patriarchal society, or the milieu of the unprivileged, or privileged. Rather, the film raises the question of who finds himself really in a position of judging or blaming the other?

And this is precisely the question Jenny raises to her second husband when it comes to an argument about her old childhood friend who became a prostitute in town. Before its final end, the film had already come to a crucial turning point in another scene: This sequence sums up the whole quality of the film showing that Jenny's entire existence only follows elementary impulses out of which her personality shapes up. Although Jenny became rich and privileged she shows real empathy to this prostitute and does not renounce her. Her husband asks her to end this friendship, which he does not regard as suitable. But Jenny becomes furious and starts to yell at him. The dialogue goes as follows:

> JOHN: Jenny, I have come to a decision. We are going to put Lena out of your house.
> JENNY: No!
> JOHN: I don't care what she meant to you when you were a child. I'm talking about what she is now. I don't want you to be connected with her.
> JENNY: Why not? In what way is she different from us? Except that she is more honest?
> JOHN: I don't want her sins on your hand.
> JENNY: You good righteous man! You hypocrite! Telling others what they must and must not do while you live in this house with me!

Especially this sequence makes it clear that the clichéd imagery of good and evil does not hold up. Impulses have the same goal everywhere, and the seemingly good person, Jenny's second husband, appears to be just as exploitative as Jenny is (because he also took advantage to marry Jenny, knowing that she caused the suicide of Ephraim). The prostitute turns out to be the only honest person for she does not pretend to be honorable or to take the right to judge upon the other. In fact the film shows that all men that have been connected to Jenny also on their part only took advantage of Jenny's deprived and needy situation and let themselves be seduced by her. Referring again to the title of the movie, it is thus not only Jenny who can be attributed as strange but everybody else behaves as strange as she does. And this is the point where *The Strange Woman* takes an unexpected turn because Jenny, at last, is very conscious about herself, as well as about the others. Her analysis of human behavior is not strange at all but it captures the truth. She does not judge the prostitute as minor being but identifies with her, and more than that, she considers herself to be minor to the prostitute because she herself wears the mask of the privileged. In a sense this scene does not only expose her second husband to be a hypocrite but does expose the viewing audience as well.

Up to this point of the film the viewer is the laid back observer on the safer side of human strangeness: The overtly melodramatic imagery with its eccentrically dramatic orchestral music which touches even the categories of sentimental kitsch and cliché; the misleading title; everything seems to deal with a person who deviates from the "normal," as well as it alludes to a world outside of reality. But at the point where Jenny names the good and righteous a hypocrite is an outbreak of different quality: It is total conviction — a shocking moment of catharsis — of which the audience cannot distance itself any longer. This scene thus has the potential to push the viewer into asking the same question that Jenny asks: In what way does the prostitute differ from us? And moreover: Why are we less strange than Jenny? Maybe life in general follows the same impulses, only that they remain hidden under the layers of our own illusive reality.

Works Cited

Bogue, Ronald. *Deleuze on Cinema*. New York and London: Routledge, 2003.
Deleuze, Gilles. *Cinema 1: The Movement-Image*. London and New York: Continuum, 1986.
_____, and Félix Guattari. *Anti-Oedipus: Capitalism and Schizophrenia 1*. New York: Viking: 1983.
Grissemann, Stefan. *Mann im Schatten. Der Filmemacher Edgar G. Ulmer*. Wien: Paul Zsolnay Verlag, 2003.
The Horrors. "Sheena Is A Parasite." *Strange House*. Loog/Polydor Records, 2007.
The Strange Woman. U.S.A., 1946. Directed by Edgar G. Ulmer.

The Logic of Contradiction and the Politics of Desire in *Ruthless*

Reynold Humphries

Like Ulmer's earlier *Detour* (1945) *Ruthless* (1948) is told in flashbacks, although the main character does not recount the past in the first person but remembers it. For anyone who has not seen the film this distinction does not go without saying. We shall discuss how the flashbacks are presented and the possible significance for the film after a plot summary.

Vic Lambdin (Louis Hayward) and Mallory Flagg (Diane Lynn) visit the palatial mansion of Vic's boyhood friend Horace Woodruff Vendig (Zachary Scott) in order to assist at a very special ceremony.[1] Vendig wishes to work for peace and is turning over his home and grounds, along with an endowment of $25 million, to an association devoted to the cause. When Lambdin introduces Mallory to him, Vendig is taken aback by the resemblance between her and Martha Burnside whom Vic and he knew as youngsters. This meeting leads to the first flashback where Vendig remembers how he saved Martha from drowning when the three of them were out boating. Martha, unlike Vendig, is from a relatively affluent family and her father shows his gratitude by paying for Vendig's schooling. When Martha celebrates her eighteenth birthday, it becomes apparent that it is Vendig, and not Vic, whom she loves. In exchange for Vendig confirming he wishes to marry his daughter, Mr. Burnside offers to pay for his studies at Harvard so that he will progress more rapidly in the insurance business where he has been working for two years, while Vic has been studying at university.

While at Harvard Vendig draws the attention of Susan, whose father is a wealthy Wall Street investor. She invites him to her home where Vendig impresses her father with his knowledge of the world of business and his willingness to take risks to make money. Vendig exploits Susan's being attracted to him sexually to leave Harvard and take up a powerful position on Wall Street. He returns to Boston to see Martha and tells her that she no longer fits into his plans for wealth and power. Then he encourages Vic to try his hand at making a fortune from the growing Latin American market and, thanks to his daring ideas for making vast profits, also persuades a banker, Mr. MacDonald, to trust him and give him a free hand. Vendig is highly successful but bites off more than he can chew when he tries to take over the financial empire of a cunning Southerner, Buck Mansfield (Sidney Greenstreet). Humiliated and thwarted, Vendig refuses to be beaten and sets about seducing Mansfield's wife, a woman some forty years her husband's junior. Once he gets the better of the Southerner, he drops her in order to get on with the business of making money.

Vic and Vendig have drifted apart from the day when MacDonald, faced with enormous debts, commits suicide in Vendig's office because the latter refuses to help him. Vendig dismisses Vic's appeals for generosity: he and he alone made the investments pay massive dividends. Years later, however, Mallory persuades Vic that they should attend the reception at Vendig's home in favour of the Peace Foundation. Both Mansfield and his ex-wife also turn up. In the course of the evening Vendig pledges to take Mallory away from Vic but before his plan can come to fruition he is attacked by the crazed and vengeful Mansfield who pulls him into the river where they both drown. The film ends with Mallory kissing Vic, telling him he has not lost a friend: Vendig "wasn't a man but a way of life."

This presentation shows the role of betrayal in Vendig's behavior, as well as the theme of repetition contained in these acts of betrayal. It also highlights the film's main theme: big business. Despite Vendig's presence from beginning to end and the way the script apparently makes him responsible for everything, things are far more complex and we shall not have to go far to discover that, under the surface, *Ruthless* is less concerned with the portrait of an unscrupulous megalomaniac than with the portrayal of a system where money is paramount and people irrelevant except as pawns to move around the board to win ever more (financial) games in the name of ever-increasing profit.[2] In the context of a film whose structure, right down to such details as looks and individual shots, is profoundly Freudian and Lacanian, it is interesting that two critics should, on two separate occasions, misquote Mallory's remark about Vendig being "a way of life": each time they write "system" (Buhle and Wagner 2002: 332; Buhle and Wagner 2003: 191). Through this slip of the tongue they have, in fact, put their finger on the film's underlying theme: the capitalist system of profit taking precedence over any and every non-monetary value.

Whether for reasons of studio meddling or due to political cunning, the script does not exactly present things so bluntly. After all, this is a Hollywood movie and it was therefore essential to home in on an individual. What *Ruthless* does show, however, is that Vendig is the perfect signifier of financial ruthlessness, its most extreme representative. He is by no means alone, as my summary shows. The entire film is based on an exchange economy. The everyday formula "fair exchange is no robbery" is there to remind us how capitalism exploits ideologically supposedly innocent statements. It evokes explicitly via the word "robbery" the basis of capitalist money-making the better to disavow it and lead people to believe that the money they hand over in exchange for a given consumer item corresponds exactly and naturally to the value of said item. What does *Ruthless* show us? Mr. Burnside is aware that, without Vendig's help, Martha would have drowned and puts Vendig through high school, since his mother cannot afford to. When Vendig and Martha are young adults he makes what he himself calls an "investment": in exchange for marrying Martha, and thus transmitting patriarchal law from one generation to the next, Vendig's tuition fees to study at Harvard will be paid. Put that bluntly, there is surely something indecent in the situation, although Martha is anxious to marry Vendig. The old concept love is turned into a *commodity* to the benefit of everyone. Or perhaps to the profit of the masculine members of the deal/contract. After all, it was once common to evoke a marriage contract, wasn't it?

In fact both Martha and Vendig become commodities within the system represented by Mr. Burnside, but only Vendig is in a position later to turn the situation in his favour (to his profit) by ditching Martha in favour of a woman who sees him as a sort of sexual commodity but who has failed to understand that the decisions are made between men. Significantly, Susan is absent when Vendig meets her father in the presence of a small, select group of businessmen — i.e. businessmen who have selected one another to enhance their bank balances and who select Vendig as the man most likely. Susan is soon discarded in favour of Mrs. Mansfield whose sexual needs cannot be satisfied by her elderly husband. Mrs. Mansfield is forced, without realizing it, to prostitute herself to Vendig, with her own husband's vast fortune as collateral. In exchange for sex, she betrays her husband but Vendig is no more grateful to her than he was to Mr. Burnside for giving him his first chance in the world of business, in exchange for access to Martha's body. This is one form that repetition takes in *Ruthless*.

The irony lies in the fact that Burnside, like MacDonald, is an unwitting victim of the ideology underpinning "fair exchange is no robbery," whereas Vendig is made of sterner stuff. There is no such notion as fairness in a world devoted to robbery. This is perfectly illustrated through the case of Vic who has no desire to remain in stuffy old Wall Street: South America's the place for him, a limitless land that is wide open. Perhaps he thinks it's uninhabited, a favorite capitalist phantasy: a land without people, up for grabs.³ So he returns, rolling in money and positively revelling in it. And yet there is no doubting the sincerity of his horror and disgust when he discovers that Vendig has abandoned MacDonald to his fate. Vic remains the victim of ideology: MacDonald trusted Vendig and did not ask for collateral, except Vendig's word. And Vic is right, for the saying "fair exchange is no robbery" assumes the existence, within capitalist relations, of a certain morality: what you do to help one man, he will do to help you when the time comes. You scratch my back.... But this goes on the lingering assumption that something other than money matters, and what sets Vendig apart in the film — but not in the world of finance — is that such morality is so much idealistic claptrap. Vendig is an early version of our old friend — and friend of fascist dictators in Latin America, starting with Pinochet — Milton Friedman, for whom businesses exist to make money and must not take into account such frivolous matters as democracy, ecology, workers' rights, pension schemes, and so on. The makers of *Ruthless* were lucid and far-sighted men indeed.

In the case of screenwriter Gordon Kahn, far too lucid for his own good. Kahn had the distinction of being one of the Hollywood Nineteen, the men subpoenaed by the House Committee on Un-American Activities (HUAC) to appear before the Committee in Washington in October 1947 to answer question on the influence of Communism in Hollywood and on its films. Finally, only ten were called, refused to answer the Committee's questions in the way imposed by HUAC — "yes or no" to the question "Are you now or have you ever been a member of the Communist Party?"— were cited for contempt of Congress, blacklisted by the industry and finally imprisoned for six or twelve months in 1950.[4] The remaining eight were among scores of Hollywood personalities called to appear before HUAC in the second round of the Hearings, which lasted from early 1951 to early 1953. Some refused to testify and took the Fifth Amendment, which allowed them to avoid prison but which meant immediate blacklisting. Others named names and repudiated their radical pasts. In 1948 Kahn did not only write *Ruthless:* he also published a book, *Hollywood on Trial*, relating the Hearings of 1947 and pillorying the Ten's prosecutors and HUAC's friendly witnesses. Named and blacklisted in 1951, he left for Mexico and never worked in Hollywood again. He died in 1962, aged 60.[5]

The force and subtlety of *Ruthless* lies not only in the way Vendig is shown as the representative of a system that, with the exception of him, refuses to say its name but also *why* he develops as ruthlessly as he does. The keys to understanding the film are to be found in the film's second shot and the information contained in the first flashback, where Vendig saves Martha. We have summed up the manifest content of the film and shown how the latent content, easily accessible to conscious thought processes, questions the individual status of Vendig as the film's only negative character. It is necessary now to turn to the unconscious content of the film which turns on the question of desire and shows Vendig to be a profoundly neurotic person but one whose problems cannot be simply attributed to the psyche of an individual. Hence, the fact that he has three names in the film, as already indicated. On the manifest level of the script, this can be put down to the nature of the friendships between him and other characters. On the unconscious level, the three names symbolize different subject positions adopted by Vendig according to the circumstances determining his subjectivity.

What, then, is the film's second shot? The first shows us a car wending its way up a steep road in the direction of a gigantic home in the far background. Cut to a medium shot of a young woman's face. It is Mallory Flagg, in the back seat of a limousine with Vic Lambdin. Why should the shot show her alone, when the whole point of the scene is the discussion between her and Vic about Vendig? It would be far more rational, within Hollywood logic, to show them seated side by side, then to alternate shots of one or the other with shots of both of them on screen. Such, in fact, is how the scene evolves in the car after this shot. There is an unconscious textual logic inscribed into this shot of Mallory — the first shot of the film showing a leading character — that goes far beyond the logic of insisting on her features: actress Diane Lynn plays both Mallory and Martha, the film's two female characters. Or rather: the two that play the most prominent roles in the script's manifest content. For there are three other important female characters: Vendig's mother, Martha's mother and Susan. It is striking to note, in the light of our remarks on Vendig's three names symbolizing his split subject position in the film, that one actress plays the role both of the first important female character in Vendig's life and of the last female character to exert an influence on him. Diane Lynn is thus "split" like Vendig and Martha and Mallory are each destined to play a dual role in the film: each as herself and as Vendig's *mother*. We shall now see how the film imposes this logic but does not reduce it to the Oedipal complex, however central this is to the film.

It is necessary, then, to analyze how *Ruthless* foregrounds Vendig's attachment to his mother through framing, cutting, and a certain number of remarks that are repeated, much in the way Mallory repeats Martha. When he meets the former during the reception, Vendig cannot believe his eyes, much to Vic's amusement. The script outlines for us in the first flashback a classic Oedipal situation. Vendig's father has been chased from the family home by his strong-willed wife, tired of having to work hard to compensate for his failure to be the bread winner, and has been living across town for the past two years.

Vendig, however, is more attached to him than he is ready to admit to his bitterly resentful mother: not only does he have a large, signed photo of his father in his bedroom, but he disobeys his mother and goes to see him. We can say that Vendig (who is in his early teens) submits to the paternal law by refusing to renounce his love for his father but is also forced to submit to the maternal law. Or rather: the mother has to fill both paternal and maternal functions, bringing her son up alone and earning money as if the man of the family. Due to circumstances she has the phallus, which poses a problem for Vendig: this is his father's function.

When Vendig visits his father, the man gives him some paternal advice that he clearly never followed himself but hopes his son will: "Don't let anything stand in your way; opportunity comes only once." If the symbolism of this remark is soon to become clear when the spectators see for themselves what lengths Vendig will go to in order to succeed, the situation is soon rendered more complex by the brilliant way in which Ulmer exploits the script to present us with a primal scene. Vendig returns home and finds that his mother is not alone: a man is sitting beside her. The lad flattens himself against the wall, to the left of the open door, and listens. We, the spectators, both watch and listen. Neither we nor Vendig learn who the man is: it is his symbolic function that matters. He is in the throes of telling Mrs. Vendig that this is their last chance and that Horace must not be allowed to stand in their way; they cannot take him with them. At first she refuses, then refers to the worthless father. Finally they kiss in close-up. It is precisely at this moment that Vendig peeps into the room. Cut from them kissing to a shot of the boy's horrified face. End of scene.

Several things are going on simultaneously here. Mrs. Vendig has already accused her son of being like his father who squandered money; Vendig promises her he'll make money, a promise he keeps. But not simply because he made a promise. The reference by his mother to his worthless father cannot but place Vendig in the same category, even if this is not conscious. Even more dramatic from the boy's standpoint, however, is the parallel between what his father told him about not letting anything stand in his way and the fact that, for this unknown man, it is Vendig who is standing in the way of him and the mother. Just as the father has been eliminated by the mother, so Vendig has the impression of being eliminated too, excluded from the family home as his father was. This Vendig can grasp consciously but the situation is overdetermined by desire, the boy's unconscious interpretation of the lover's discourse. The man is eliminating Vendig in order to have access to the mother, whom he kisses to show the spectator there is no ambiguity here. In which case Vendig cannot but see in this man his own father, kissing his mother and therefore denying Vendig access to her. He has apparently resolved this Oedipal crisis as far as his father is concerned, but now relives it in the form of a repetition and, as a result, sets in motion a form of psychic regression.

The scene is a version of the primal scene inasmuch as it reactivates pre-Oedipal desire on Vendig's part. We are dealing therefore with an adolescent boy, well aware of the nature of sexuality, being confronted with a real-life situation where he is to be deprived of everything and a phantasy situation where the father deprives him of the mother he loves above all. Unconsciously, Vendig sees himself as having nothing and in later life nothing will stand in his way so that he will have everything. Significantly, his feeling of being deprived of his right to live at home is over-determined by the behavior of the woman with whom his father has taken up. When Mr. Vendig tries to give his son some money to buy a suit, the woman snatches it away from the boy: the father owes her this money. Vendig is literally deprived of his rights here — the phallic rights passed on by his father who turns out to be jovial but *weak*— by a woman. This form of symbolic castration is then repeated in the primal scene sequence which shows that Vendig has only imperfectly resolved his Oedipal complex. Literally and metaphorically, consciously and unconsciously, everything stands in Vendig's way. In later life he will adopt the solution to the dilemma posed by desire: eliminate everyone who stands in his way.

We can now propose an interpretation of the second shot of the film. When the man kisses Vendig's mother, we see the couple framed together in an embrace. Cut to Vendig, alone in the frame, horrified and excluded. Just as he is alone in the frame — which represents his subjective feelings at that moment and will determine his future life where he makes decisions alone, regardless of others — so is Mallory. She occupies therefore the place of the mother, alone but waiting for her suitor. For the manifest content of the film, this suitor is Vic, but on the level of desire it is Vendig she is waiting for. Mallory is thus both herself and the mother. The horror for Vendig the adolescent is that he cannot replace the man whom he sees kissing his mother, whereas for Vendig the adult, master of all he surveys, Mallory is there for the taking. She reminds him of Martha, to whom we shall return presently, and he makes a determined play for her, sure that she will abandon Vic and choose him. Vendig is therefore living through the trauma of the earlier situation where it was he who was abandoned (literally) by his mother who chose another man. This too, we must not forget, takes the form of a repetition for Vendig: just as she once preferred his father before excluding the latter from the household, now she prefers another man and it is Vendig she excludes. By identifying with his father Vendig therefore identifies with a failure on every level: social, sexual and economic. This act of identification must be overcome and overcome it he does.

However, there is another repetition at work here and one which produces a further adolescent phantasy on Vendig's part, one that we are also entitled to refer to as a primal scene. As we have already seen, Vendig earns the gratitude of Mr. Burnside when he saves Martha Burnside from drowning. Although it is not until more than a decade later that he — and Martha — realize it, she was Vendig's first love. Or rather: second love, for his first love was his mother. As Norman Bates said to Marion Crane, "a boy's best friend is his mother."[6] After witnessing the kiss, Vendig slips away (guiltily, as if he had seen something forbidden, whereas what he has seen has *reactivated* something forbidden) and goes over to the Burnsides' home. There he stands outside and looks in, in much the same fashion, but all he sees first is Mr. Burnside alone. Then an upstairs window is thrown open and little Martha (she is several years younger than Vendig and Vic, who was also in the boat when it capsized) appears, combing her hair. Vendig just stares up at her. She does not see him and the Romeo and Juliet reference is patent. Then he looks in at another window where he spies Mrs. Burnside who, on noticing him, ushers him inside. She at once becomes a substitute mother: Vendig tearfully tells her he no longer has a home and a mother. Significantly, he adds: "I don't want to be a man," unconsciously admitting to his desire to remain a child with its mother.

His wish is granted in an extraordinary scene which bears all the marks of a Freudian fantasy. The Burnsides put him up for the night (indeed, they become his foster parents as the real parents disappear entirely from the film) and he is installed in a spare room. We see him in bed, with a bowl of soup, and Martha standing beside the bed. Add a decade or so to each of them in years and you have a tender scene between a loving wife and a sick husband. On the level of phantasy we have a boy being looked after by his mother, a realization of the desire "I don't want to be a man." If marrying Martha is clearly Vendig's conscious wish, and one which seems about to come true when Martha celebrates her eighteenth birthday with all her friends, there is already a troubling sign present: everyone is singing joyously, except Vendig. Clearly this is not because he cannot sing but because, now that Martha is of age and therefore sexually accessible, she becomes out of bounds. Martha is taking on her fantasy role as substitute mother. At the very moment when he can, literally, take hold of her, desire steps in to stop him and launch him again in pursuit of that which can never be obtained: the mother's body.

Vendig's life is one of pursuit, pursuit of the object *a*, object and cause of desire. Patently, this means anyone resembling the mother and who becomes in his fantasies a mother figure. At one point Vendig makes an odd but revealing remark: "All my life I've spent collecting things I can't trust," adding that there's "nothing that's part of me." There is surely condensation at work here on the level of the verbal signifier, particularly trust. How can you trust or not an object? The condensation means that two statements co-exist here unconsciously: "all my life I've spent collecting things that mean nothing to me" and "all my life I've spent making the acquaintance of people I cannot trust." The things come under the heading of the ever-elusive object *a*: either he never obtains what he wants or the thing he obtains is not that which can assuage desire. This is indeed the very definition of desire, an endless search to which only death (or return to the maternal womb) can put an end. We have already seen that betraying colleagues and collaborators is a (repetition) compulsion as strong as discarding the women who come briefly into his life (except for his mother, of course). Thus when Vendig tells Mallory at the reception that he's loved her ever since he was a boy — a revelation as extraordinary as it is meaningless on the literal level, since he didn't know Mallory when a boy — he is admitting to his desire: Mallory = Martha (whom he met as a child) = his mother. We can see in the repetition of "M" the logic of the signifier, the insistence of the letter.

The fact that Vendig feels he can trust nobody is both a sign of paranoia (of which the narcissistic megalomania from which he suffers is an essential component) and of unconscious reversal: it is his acquaintances who should never trust Vendig. Making such revealing remarks is an inherent part of Vendig's psyche: seldom has a script resorted to such questions of language to reveal the pathology of a character. One such statement occurs when Vic, shocked at Vendig's callousness and his ability to discard people like things, informs him that Mr. Burnside is dead. Visibly taken aback, Vendig replies: "He was like my father." Since we know that the Burnsides welcomed him into their home like a son, the remark consciously means "he was like a father to me." Fine, but that is not what Vendig said and what he did say is by no means an equivalent formula on the level of the signified. "He was like my father" means rather "he resembled my father." Now Mr. Vendig and Mr. Burnside were as alike as chalk and cheese, both physically and temperamentally. Vendig's remark is, however, to be taken literally in another way: his father was a failure, Mr. Burnside generous and, to a certain extent, altruistic. Thus both men were wrong in his eyes. Mr. Vendig failed financially, while always giving advice, Mr. Burnside made an "investment" which was wise, but a real businessman, such as Vendig, cannot allow sentiment to stand in his way. Vendig considers that he and he alone can have the phallus, but the true reason for which he wants to have it is a pure fantasy: for the mother. When he says that he has "nothing that's part of me," he is admitting to that fact and recognizing, without knowing it, that his entire existence has been a meaningless failure and that one can never possess the object *a*, except in death, inasmuch as its possession puts an end to desire.

This is hardly how Vendig presents things, either to himself or to his interlocutors: When he ditches Martha, he tells her: "I'm going far, fast — and alone." When denounced by Vic for his sadistic treatment of the banker MacDonald, he insists that it is he, Vendig, and he alone who made the financial empire, thus denying the role of the help from the other financier. To what extent does *Ruthless* go along with this ideology of individual success? We have already shown that the film brilliantly deconstructs this ideology on the level of the script by the simple but intelligent tactic of making Vendig *worse* than the other speculators, not radically different from them. There is, however, another aspect to the film's subversion of the values current at the time and one that is due to Ulmer's direction. Or, to be more precise: his unusual use of a common cinematic code of narration, the flashback. As we shall now see, the film gives the impression of a narration without a narrator, precisely at the moment when it is apparently Vendig recounting his past. It was normal for the *film noir*, when having recourse to a flashback, to present a close-up of the person about to go back in time: Walter Neff dictating his confession in his office in the middle of the night in *Double Indemnity*; Waldo Lydecker in the restaurant with Detective Mark McPherson in *Laura*; the various members of the gang telling Riordan about aspects of the Swede's life in *The Killers*; Jeff Bailey framed by the car window alongside the loving heroine as they drive up to Lake Tahoe in *Out of the Past*. In each case the person about to remember and the person about to hear the account are present. This is also the case in *Ruthless*: Vendig, Vic and Mallory are present as the first flashback begins, Vendig and Vic when the second starts. There is, however, a crucial difference.

The first flashback, which goes into detail concerning Vendig's life from the days he saved Martha from drowning, begins with a close-up, not of Vendig, *but of Mallory*. The second flashback proceeds in an identical fashion: it is Vic who is framed and not Vendig. This, however, is a case of repetition reinforcing what the first manifestation of the device connotes. This use of Mallory's face instead of Vendig's to introduce the flashback — true to a Hollywood tradition, the image goes out of focus, then becomes wavy — is linked in a very particular way to the second shot of the film. For this shot can help explain why Ulmer should return to Mallory to launch the flashback and not to a shot of Vendig. In both scenes, Mallory looks almost, but not quite, into the camera. She is, in fact, looking off-screen right in the direction of Vic (in the limousine) and in the direction of Vendig (at the reception). This importance accorded to Mallory, inexplicable for the second shot of the film and apparently incoherent according to the logic of the signifier as conceived by the dominant Hollywood narrative techniques, implies that we should be skeptical about what we are seeing. As it is clearly not Mallory remembering the past, then we have a narrative without a narrator, a memory without someone remembering. It is not a question of claiming that Vendig's memory is false nor that he is lying. It is in this context that the second shot of the film, that of a close-up of Mallory, becomes meaningful in a new way. During the ensuing conversation with Vic, she suggests that his memory of Vendig is partial. Living in the past can affect one's judgment, she says, adding that he might be exaggerating. The fact that, on the strength of what we see of Vendig, Vic was not exaggerating about his ruthlessness, does not prevent us from concluding that Mallory, on another level of the film's logic, is perfectly right.

There is a profoundly *impersonal* aspect about the flashbacks, as if Vendig were not implicated in them, as if someone else were speaking in his place. I suggest we take this literally: Vendig is speaking but a discourse is speaking *through him*. Vendig's version of things is a phantasy in the sense of being so ideologically colored as to need deconstructing. For it is the ideological big Other who assumes the flashback and Vendig's desire as it is communicated gradually to us throughout the following sequences is one that cannot apprehend the true nature of the social relations being created as characters meet and interact. It is difficult to accept as a mere coincidence that Vendig's life begins with him saving a person from drowning and that it should end when he and his nemesis, Buck Mansfield, drown together. A remarkable chain of plays of words on the verbal signifiers is at work here. In the boat that capsizes are Vendig, Vic and Martha. When she falls overboard, the boys are thrown into the water too and Vendig, a good swimmer, gets to Martha before she goes under. Interestingly, Vendig excels at swimming at university, which brings him to the attention of Susan. This new relationship persuades Vendig to abandon Martha, to let her sink, as it were. At the end Vendig and Mansfield both die. As Vendig has asked Mallory to join him on his yacht and ditch the insufficiently ruthless Vic, we have a form of repetition of the first scene in the boat, but with an ending where Vendig and Mansfield find themselves in the same boat: they both drown. Mansfield has taken Vic's place, leaving Vic and Mallory together.

Now Vendig's ideology is certainly one of sink or swim, one that he applies to everyone and everything. The irony lies in the fact that, just as Martha would have sunk if Vendig had not been there to save her, so Vendig would *not* have sunk if Mansfield had not come along to get his revenge. Just as Vendig took Martha from Vic, then Mrs. Mansfield from her husband, so he has been trying to pry Mallory away from Vic. Moreover, whereas he saved Martha, her father Mr. Burnside saved him. At no time in his life was Vendig ever alone: everything he said and did was determined by a particular social situation of which he was an effect. The whole point of *Ruthless*, then, is this:

that Vendig is *not* an individual who can take the blame for everything, thus leaving the system intact. Vendig's first autonomous act was to save Martha, an implicit rejection of the selfish individualism inherent to capitalist ideology. He then spends his entire life trying to live down this act of altruism, only to suffer at the end the fate from which he saved Martha. The ending is scathingly ironic. Vendig's *alter ego* Mansfield is a surrogate father, punishing Vendig for refusing to submit to patriarchal law. However, he is also punishing him for having shown that one sign of humanity which gives the lie to the extreme individualism represented by Vendig throughout the film.

Ultimately, then, Mansfield is a more perfect representative of what capitalism means by being ruthless.

Notes

1. Vendig is called Horace, Hoss or Woody, according to the person talking to or about him. I shall refer to him as Vendig throughout, but we shall see that these different names are not without significance.

2. I am evoking obviously the chessboard but am also thinking, given the context, of the boardroom.

3. Like "darkest Africa" which was said to be inhabited by beasts of the jungle and cannibals.

4. An eleventh man was also questioned: German writer Bertolt Brecht. As he was a foreigner, he answered the questions put to him, and ran rings round his interrogators, who ended up thanking and dismissing him. He left the United States at once for Germany.

5. Among those who named Kahn as a Communist was writer Richard Collins, who was one of the Nineteen. There is every reason to suppose that Kahn's co-screenwriter, S.K. Lauren (1893–1979), was also blacklisted, although his name appears nowhere in specialized studies: just one of the anonymous victims. Lauren worked in Hollywood regularly from 1932 (he wrote von Sternberg's *Blonde Venus*) until 1943; after that, nothing except for *Ruthless*.

6. On the website *www.imdb.com* an anonymous comment on *Ruthless* reads: "Zachary Scott is chilling in his mentally perverse portrayal of a tycoon that is more in league with Norman Bates than William Randall [sic] Hurst [sic]." This intriguing reference to *Psycho* is more pertinent here than the more obvious one to *Citizen Kane*.

Works Cited

Buhle, Paul, and Dave Wagner. *Radical Hollywood*. New York: New Press, 2002.
_____ *Blacklisted. The Film Lover's Guide to the Hollywood Blacklist*. New York and England: Palgrave MacMillan, 2003.

The Man from Planet X
Matthew Sweney

The Man from Planet X (1951) is further proof of Edgar G. Ulmer's versatility — an atmospheric science fiction film seemingly without precedents, which does not rely on big-budget special effects or horrific situations; instead, while based upon a fairly simple plot, it is thinking-man's science fiction, posing questions about humanity and otherness which cannot be answered.

To its credit, there are no bug-eyed monsters in this film — the alien, as the title states, is a man; one is never quite sure whom to root for or against — the question of who is the "villain" in the film is never resolved.

The script is by Aubrey Wisberg and Jack Pollexfen, who also produced the film; although the bulk of the credit for the finished product must certainly go to Ulmer: *The Man from Planet X* is one of the director's best-paced films, in addition to featuring striking, unforgettable visuals. Bill Warren, in his excellent *Keep Watching the Skies! American Science Fiction Movies of the Fifties, Volume I, 1950–1957* (McFarland, 1982), goes out of his way to single Ulmer out for credit, even adding a mini-essay on Ulmer to his article on *The Man from Planet X*, and repeatedly pointing out its superiority in entries to other films by Wisberg and Pollexfen. That said, the script has its strengths, and even its defects (i.e., lack of dialogue, all the running back and forth from village to tower) work to Ulmer's advantage.

Putting the Pieces into Play

The film begins with a nine-second daytime shot, accompanied by pleasant music, of a beach, which dissolves into a nighttime shot with menacing music of a tower on the moors, the waves of the ocean seeming to have melted into the fog on the moors. In typical Ulmer fashion, the film's ending mirrors this beginning, going from the moors back to the ocean, from nightmare to daylight. In addition, the opening sequence sets up a visual equation (ocean

= fog), which will develop into one of the themes of the film (ocean = fog = space). And it mirrors the audience's experience, going from daylight into the night-time world of the cinema, and back out again.

From here there is a ten-second process tracking shot until the tower is caught in the branches of a leafless tree, then a dissolve into five-second close-up of the tower, one of its windows illuminated, a further dissolve into the tower interior, where a man is pacing before two windows, into one of which a telescope is set. He arrives at the window, looks out.

So far there have been no words spoken. At this point there is a voice-over, and it is actually the film's longest monologue. It is worth quoting in full to see how Ulmer's visual sense punctuates the text:

> [Man paces with his back to us, shot around a column at just above floor-level] "I don't know if she's still alive or not ... they've had her now for the past twenty-four hours. [Cut to medium shot of man, still with back to us, at window, camera at eye-level] I'm equally uncertain as to the fate of her father, Professor Elliot — both are probably dead. The odds are a hundred-to-one I too will be finished before another sun rises, but tonight I'm going to try to fight for my life [he turns to face us, although his face is obscured, walking toward the camera to a writing desk], and those larger issues so perilously at stake, affecting all mankind [camera moves in, he sits, but his figure is obscured by the column, just his hand can be seen on the desk]. If I fail, which seems most likely, [puts pencil to paper, and writes] the consequences to humanity defy the imagination. As the only trained reporter who has been in the position to observe the terror from its inception [cut to close-up of the hand on paper, the man's body facing us now], and as one of the few living humans who has actually met face-to-face the Man from Planet X [pencil breaks, the camera pulls slightly back as the hand rubs eyes, covers face], I will try to set down the strangest story a newspaper man ever covered. [Cut to a shot of a planet and stars in space, round frame] It began, prosaically enough, in a college observatory not far from Los Angeles...." [Cut to the man, taking his eye off the lens piece and we see his face for the first time.]

The actor has not been speaking, it is a voice-over, allowing Ulmer to "tell" the story purely visually. The breaking of the pencil and the cloaking of the man's face create the film's tension, and prepare the viewer for a film where the pencil breaks and the camera takes over, and where it is very difficult indeed to read a man's — or the Man's — face.

And, the scene can be read as a statement on filmmaking — you have a writer writing a script, but the story begins with a scientist looking through a view finder, who then takes a frame of film from the bottom of the lens, and goes to develop it in the laboratory darkroom, not far from Los Angeles.

The downward motion of the scientist's journey down a ladder and a flight of stairs is mirrored later in the observation tower in Scotland, when the characters go from the telescope in the tower down into working quarters and finally into the dungeon (to see what develops).

In three minutes Ulmer has established two visual themes, one of water and fog which will have significance to the plot as mediums for invasion; and one of the tower, which plays a central role in the film as an observatory where things are not always clear. The pieces have been arranged on the board and it will take the next hour to play them out. It is as neat a piece of filmmaking as anything in Ulmer's oeuvre.

Synopsis

The plot is not complex. In the flashback, which takes up 60 minutes of the 71-minute film, we learn that a new planet, Planet X, has been discovered, and what is more, the trajectory of the planet will bring it into contact with the Earth. Its discovery was prompted by "strange radio waves bouncing off the Earth in Burray" (one of the Orkney Islands) and we soon learn that it will make closest contact with the Earth in Burray. The scientist who made the discovery, Professor Elliot (played by Raymond Bond), was responsible for carrying out meteorological studies during the Second World War for American bombers stationed in Scotland. One former pilot is now a newspaperman; he is summoned by the scientist from the U.S.A. to investigate the story. The newspaperman, John Lawrence (Bob Clarke), finds that Professor Elliot's daughter Enid (Margaret Field, mother of Sally Field) is no longer the "gawky" girl that she once was. She brings him to the Broch (an ancient tower), where her father is working with Dr. Mears (William Schallert), who is known to Lawrence; the two men dislike each other. There are hints that Dr. Mears has done something in the past for which he "should have gotten twenty years," later Enid says she wants him out of the Broch, for "he upsets me." Enid shows Lawrence around the grounds outside the Broch, where they find an alien object, later revealed to be a kind of probe. They return with the probe, the manufacture and composition of which fascinate the Professor and Mears, for the metal is superior in strength and lightness to steel — Mears, ecstatic, says it could be worth "millions, millions! ... The man who controls this formula controls the industry of the world!" Enid takes Lawrence to the village to spend the night in the Red Bull Inn, and on the way back she sees strange lights on the moors. Her car breaks down. She investigates the lights and finds a spaceship, made up of a sphere with a cone and antenna on top, in the fog. Peering into the spaceship she sees a man in a glass helmet with a large, though human-like, face. She screams and runs back to the Broch. Breathless, she tells her father what she has seen and the two return to investigate. Dr. Mears, intrigued, follows at a distance, staying in the shadows. The two make contact, and the Professor falls into the path of a ray, which hypnotizes him — as the Professor says, "All I was capable of was obedience." Enid takes him back to the Broch. The next day Lawrence bicycles to the Broch, is informed of the situation, and he returns with the Professor to investigate the sphere on the moors. They have a close encounter for the third time: the Man from Planet X leaves the spaceship, points what looks like a pistol at them, but then collapses, clutching at a gas valve on his spacesuit. The Professor frees the valve and the Man from Planet X puts the pistol away and tries to communicate with them. He follows them back to the Broch. In the castle they make more attempts at communication, unsuccessfully. Then Dr. Mears comes upon the idea of using geometry as a means of communication. They leave him alone in the dungeon with the Man so as not to interrupt. The Professor does not feel well, Lawrence goes to fix the car and drive into town for medicine. He meets the constable (Roy Engel), who is investigating "strange doings going on at the Broch." We cut back to the dungeon, where Mears is burning papers: "This shall be my secret!" He then tortures the Man from Planet X by depriving him of his gas. Enid goes down into the dungeon and screams. Lawrence returns with the medicine and finds she, and the Man, are gone. Lawrence and Mears go to the spaceship, hidden by the fog. Lawrence returns to the Broch to ask the Professor's help, but the Professor is too sick. The local constable and his helper Geordie arrive to investigate the disappearance of two villagers, Geordie stays with the Professor while Lawrence takes the constable to the sphere, which is no longer there, so the constable decides to go to the station to arrange a search party. Geordie arrives at the station, having seen not only Mears taking the Professor away, but having seen "the boogey" as well. The villagers panic, the constable tells them to stay behind locked doors. The constable attempts to call London for help, but the telephones don't work. There is no radio for contact. Lawrence sets off for the Broch by bicycle, when he is jumped by two villagers, but escapes — he returns to tell the constable, who stumbles upon the idea of using heliograph for communication. They flash a passing ship to contact Scotland Yard, but the fog cuts off communication. More villagers are seized, Lawrence discovers the new location of the sphere, which is being "fortified" by villagers with shovels. He informs the constable, Scotland Yard arrives by plane, they have a radio with which they call for military aid. Lawrence is worried about the loss of civilian life, Scotland Yard gives him an hour and a half before they move in. The film, in its sixtieth minute, arrives at the present, with Lawrence in the tower, writing the story and brooding over how to act. He goes to the moors, reaches the sphere, and commands each "slave" to leave the scene. Lawrence overpowers the Man by shutting off his gas supply, and leaves with Mears and Enid. The Man revives himself, Mears comes to his senses: "You can't destroy him, you mustn't!" and returns to the sphere. The two, Mears and the Man, have something in common aside from scientific minds: earlier in the film Lawrence is informed that Mears just "dropped into Burray"—"Drop in? People don't just drop in here, a place on the edge of the world!" But of course they do. And the locals deal with them accordingly: the military blows up the ship, killing Mears and obliterating the Man. Planet X veers towards Earth, and then away again. John and Enid wonder about the true nature of the Man.

Man with a Plan

Plot improvements or moderations aside, Ulmer's contribution comes down to art direction, camera work and cutting. The art direction by Ulmer of the items from outer space is brilliant (on any size budget). They gleam, they seem unearthly, yet they also seem realistic — the found metal artifact/probe is perfect in its geometry, it looks alien yet purposeful, and we are surprised when Lawrence can lift it so easily. This is simple but effective acting and camera work. The spaceship looks real, and the alien looks plausible, not risible, believable — neither his craft (body, cone and antenna) nor his uniform (helmet, suit, breathing apparatus and energy source) are much different from what astronauts and cosmonauts used a mere decade later.

> JOHN: You know what that looks like to me? A big diving bell.
> PROFESSOR ELLIOT: Well, the only difference between water and space is a matter of density.

That last line is one which gets guffaws, but if you change the word "space" to "atmosphere," it is accurate. Again, Ulmer's visual design for the film (in this case, the diving sphere/spaceship) ties the script together. Water, the ocean, was the medium which brought the Vikings (and the Germans) to Burray, and the alien has dived through the fog, the atmosphere, to arrive in the same place. The ocean = fog = space. In *The Man from Planet X* there is not a question of suspension of disbelief as in most science fiction/fantasy films of the period. This is what makes the film a classic.[1]

In addition to Ulmer's eerie moor paintings and the nice miniature work, the film also features a quintessential Ulmer sequence: first encounter with the alien. In most science fiction films this is a cliché, a holdover from horror: a quick shot of the creature, with blasting music to shock the audience. In *The Man from Planet X*, Ulmer has obviously given careful consideration to portraying something never before seen (Kubrick wasn't able to picture it at all!). The sequence is about two and a half minutes long, and takes place already in the second reel—Ulmer *never* cheats his audience—and it is virtually without dialogue. Enid has left Lawrence at the inn, and is on her way from the village to the Broch. The car breaks down (three words are spoken only: "Confound the luck!")—her mode of transportation has landed—and she gets out, sees the lights on the moors and investigates. She is not a passive character, but an active woman, a scientist in her own way, curious. She approaches the lights and sees the object. She rests for a second on a forked tree. Unafraid, she approaches the object, and in the sphere's gleaming shell she sees her own image reflected. She walks around the sphere, and looks into one of its round portholes. She sees the Man, whose spherical helmet echoes the appearance of the ship and porthole—she screams and runs away, all the way to the Broch, where Mears is lurking in the shadows. She has gone from one man to the Man to another man.

But she is not frightened for long, returning to the ship with her father almost immediately. In Ulmer's vision of the encounter, the porthole is a mirror, like the telescope another looking glass, and it takes time for the infant to recognize the face in the mirror as their own. With her father for security, she is unafraid.

The editing of the film keeps the picture constantly in motion. Ulmer's geometry is very clear: in addition to the mirror opening/closing, the mirror observation towers, and the mirror of the spaceship, you have the two sides of the Broch (always on the left) and the village (always on the right), with the moors in between.

The music in the film does not play as significant a role as it does in other Ulmer films (although the "menacing" theme of the moors by Charles Koff is very well done), but one item in the soundtrack is worth noting: the electronic hum whenever the Man from Planet X appears. It is the sound that radio listeners call "interference," an aural synonym for the Man's actions in the film.

Ulmer was notorious for being a "difficult" director, and was not an "actors'" director—so too with Hitchcock. But like Hitchcock, Ulmer tends to bring out good performances in actors—the acting here is solid throughout, and the role of Dr. Mears is superbly played by William Schallert. Roy Engel, appearing in his first major film role, can be somewhat excused for hamming it up as (what else?) the policeman. Although he did not thoroughly enjoy working on the picture, it became one of Robert Clarke's favorite films. Ulmer was able to elicit good performances even with tight producers; according to Clarke, the film was shot in one week, and the principals all received the Screen Actors Guild minimum, $175 for the week, plus some over-time, which came to $208. Pollexfen told Clarke that the total price, negative cost for the film was $41,000 (*http://www.craterkid.com/ck/clarke.shtml*). The picture had good box office, and was even featured in *Life* magazine.[2]

It should be stated that the film can also be read (although I choose not to) as a "Red Scare" Communist allegory, and with better results than *Inva-*

We have seen the enemy and he is us: The film was highly profitable, as shown in this *Box Office* ad from May 5, 1951 (courtesy Arianné Ulmer Cipes).

sion of the Body Snatchers (1956). Of course Ulmer was more cognizant of the changes in his native Czechoslovakia than many other Americans — the Communist putsch there in February 1948 (in its own way, a sequel to the Munich Agreement of 1938) was a very fresh shot heard 'round the world, an atmospheric disturbance picked up by scientists, journalists, politicians, the military, and laymen alike. Many thought that it did represent the next invasion after World War II. Maybe it is no accident that the villagers who come under control of the "green ray" (red star?) — scientist, young woman, policemen, shepherds, fishermen — all pick up shovels and are forced into labor.

Burray and The Bogey

Elsewhere critics have wondered why the film is set in Scotland — it is actually set on one of the Orkneys, Burray. The island gets its name from the Vikings, who called it "Borgarey." "Borg" in Old Norse means "fortification," and the word "Broch" — the tower in which the scientist, Dr. Elliot, is conducting research — is derived from "Borg," as are the English suffixes -borough, -burgh, -burg, etc. Burray in reality has two "brochs" — Iron Age towers — facing the sea. And so the Man from Planet X is not the first stranger to have landed on this island. And as recently as World War II Burray was the site of a German U-boat breach (U–47, 1939) and an Italian POW camp, in addition to housing big guns. Burray is thus a palimpsest of arrival and occupation — the American protagonist in the film was stationed there too during World War II — and so the Broch in the film shares a kinship with the villa in Ulmer's *The Black Cat* as a nexus of invasion and confrontation, both in European history, and with the arrival of Americans in Europe. Wisberg, from Britain, doubtless knew something about the island's history, and has his Man from Planet X building fortifications as well. This behavior is not alien, but in perfect human character.

The village's inhabitants call the Man the "Bogey," and given the island's history, they may not be superstitious. The same word was World War II military slang for unidentified aircraft, best considered enemy until confirmed friendly. The Bogey, or other, is a good a name as any, and they, and the American pilot, have seen him before.

In fact the Burray Man from Planet X has some older Scottish kin: there is the "Burrey Man of Aberdeen," a tradition which dates to the 17th and eighteenth centuries in Aberdeen (and probably long before that): when fishing was bad a man was chosen, and covered in burrs to take the bad luck out of the town with him, he was often chased out of town, beaten and killed.

And then there is the "Burryman of South Queensferry" who is chosen and also covered in burrs (on the second Friday in August, the day before the South Queensferry fair day) and it is said that he brings good luck to those who give him money and or whisky.

Thus the Burrey/Burry/Burray Man can represent good or evil, just as the Man from Planet X. The question is which? And the film does not answer that question. It is a serious question: would a visitor from space bring mankind good, or would they want to colonize us? We will not know, and it will be difficult to determine at first.

Much of the film has to do with reading the alien: is he friend or foe? Ultimately it is impossible to tell. Here again is the mark of the master: Ulmer's design of the alien's face. It looks human, though as Enid says, "dis-

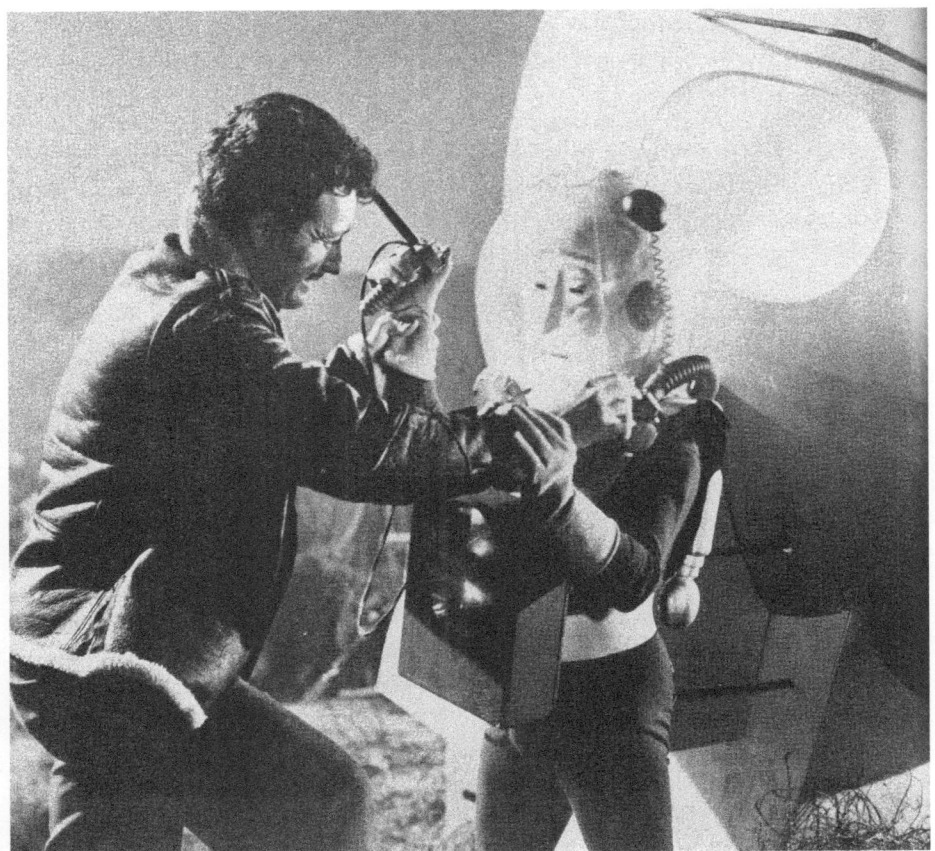

Both men wear flight jackets, but who looks more comfortable? The American (Robert Clarke) tussles with the Man from Planet X (Pat Goldin) in this publicity shot (courtesy Arianné Ulmer Cipes).

torted by pressure." Certainly the alien is under a great deal of pressure, trying to find a new homeland for his race. The face is mask-like, human, but it is not a war mask, to our eyes it shows no emotion whatsoever. The man's face cannot be read, and communication is at first not possible. This is a very serious exercise in semiotics.

Who the Man?

The "Man" from Planet X, not the "Thing" from Another World, nor "It," the Terror from Beyond Space. He is not completely "other"—he is a *man*, and at the same time he is from a planet, not dissimilar from ours, but for which we have no *name*—we call it *X*, the unknown quantity in geometry. We are out of Eden, and cannot name things anymore, paradise has been lost, we are fallen.

Shirley Ulmer, the director's wife and right hand during the production of *The Man from Planet X,* remembered Ulmer's attitude after Hiroshima: "Edgar felt that we were not going in the right direction. As far as the future was concerned, we were off on a wrong road. On a detour. And he was not happy about the idea of the future of the human race. (...) And he conveyed that in his films."

In some quarters the film's fog has been described as a gimmick to hide the sets left over from *Joan of Arc*. But the fog is essential to the film — even the characters complain about the ubiquitous fog, for it makes visual proof difficult. It is hard to see the road, and easy to detour. Planet X can only be seen with a telescope when the fog lifts. The spaceship is not easy to see, even with binoculars. The fog also makes communication difficult—the alien's ship has somehow knocked out the telephone system, so a message of distress is sent to a passing ship by heliograph. However the fog comes in, cutting off communications.

The ambiguity is also reinforced by Ulmer's visual design when showing the size of the alien: when first seen at the spaceship, the point of initial encounter, he appears large and forbidding—yet when confronted in the dungeon of the donjon by Dr. Mears, the Man appears small and weak, and is made helpless. While he has an Achilles heel in the form of the gas valve on his spacesuit (Earthlings share this same flaw in space travel), he is not inferior, for he soon turns the tables on Mears, forcing Mears to do his bidding. Mears has "read" him wrongly. While Mears is greedy to profit from the alien's superior knowledge, he ultimately is not completely bad (Enid at one point says she feels "rather sorry for him"): it is Mears who returns, willingly, to the spaceship when it is being shelled by the British military — hit by "friendly" fire, Mears' last word is "Fools!" Mears is interested in him from a scientific viewpoint (and unlike most genre films, as a competitor to the protagonist, he is not interested here in the girl at all), it is Mears' superior intelligence that makes him able to communicate with the Man, and that intelligence is not wrong when stating the case:

JOHN: What did you do to him back there in the dungeon? ... He showed a definite disposition toward friendliness when I left!
MEARS: Well, how can you talk of him as if he were a human being? How do we know what thought processes run through his head? How can we even assume that he thinks like we do? How can you anticipate what a fantastic organism like that might do or not do?

Friend or foe? We cannot read him, we cannot be sure. From what he communicated to Mears, Planet X is dying and his race needs a new home. Will their New World be one of co-operation or empire? We won't know, for the military solution has dictated the outcome. In addition, it is Lawrence who vanquishes the Man from Planet X by cutting off his gas supply, the same solution arrived at by Mears, but independently. The film ends, not with the screen couple's kiss, but with Enid and John concerned, restating the film's premise:

ENID: You know, I think that creature was friendly — I wonder what would have happened if Dr. Mears hadn't frightened him?
JOHN: Who knows? Perhaps the greatest curse to ever befall the world, or perhaps the greatest blessing.

The film visually has been formally closed, but not thematically. This fits with what the director Bertrand Tavernier has said about Ulmer's films' endings: "This is something which is not very American. I mean the American way of narration wants to solve everything and a lot of Ulmer films, like a lot of Preminger or Lang films, are open."

Notes

1. The film has at least one famous detractor — Harlan Ellison, who singles it out for ridicule in his introduction to *Omni's Screen Flights/Screen Fantasies*: "such abominations as *The Man from Planet X* [1951] and *Invaders from Mars* [1953]. That the fans were desperate is evidenced by the acceptance without a bleat of the former film's extraterrestrial with the tinfoil head, and the latter film's Martians, whose skins had zippers down their backs." (6) This is an odd comment by Ellison, and puts Ulmer in good company, as both films are among the most atmospheric science fiction films of the 1950s — while they both lack large budgets, the art direction [in the latter by William Cameron Menzies, who was also responsible for *The Thief of Bagdad* (1924), *Things to Come* (1936), *Gone with the Wind* (1939), etc., etc.] is exquisite, with unforgettable visuals, and both bear repeated viewing. This reviewer has seen each

over a dozen times, and most science fiction reviewers have a very high opinion of the film — Marty Baumann, author of *The Astounding B Monster Bulletin* and *The Astounding B Monster Book* puts *The Man from Planet X* in second-place of the greatest alien movies ever (*http://www.bmonster.com/scifi16.html*). John Brunas, co-author of *Universal Horrors* (McFarland, 2nd edition 2007), puts it in seventh-place of the greatest science fiction films of all-time, and Gary Don Rhodes, author of two books for McFarland (*Lugosi*, 1997, and *White Zombie: Anatomy of a Horror Film*, 1999), puts it in his top ten (*http://www.bmonster.com/scifi28.html*). And Douglas Melville, in his *A Historical and Critical Survey of the Science-Fiction Film*, incredibly includes the film in his list of 1950s science fiction A-pictures, seemingly not to have realized its budget limitations.

2. Winthrop Sargeant, "Through the Interstellar Looking Glass," *Life*, 21 May 1951, 127–8.

Works Cited

Ellison, Harlan. Introduction, *Omni's Screen Flights/Screen Fantasies*. Danny Peary (ed.). Garden City, NY: Doubleday, 1984.

Melville, Douglas. *A Historical and Critical Survey of the Science-Fiction Film*. New York: Arno, 1975. 1959 M.A. Thesis, USC.

Warren, Bill. *Keep Watching the Skies! American Science Fiction Movies of the Fifties, Volume I, 1950–1957*. Jefferson, NC: McFarland, 1982.

Wilson, Michael Henry. *Interview with Bernard Tavernier*. Transcript of tape dated 7 November 1997, Edgar G. Ulmer Preservation Corporation papers.

_____. *Interview with Shirley Ulmer*. Transcript of Tape #5, Edgar G. Ulmer Preservation Corporation papers.

Camp, Art Film, Classical Hollywood Cinema and *Babes in Bagdad*

HERBERT SCHWAAB

Babes in Bagdad is one of Edgar G. Ulmer's less well known works. Even in Ulmer's terms the film was marked by low production values. It was made in Spain, in Cinefotocolor, a cheap color process of two-strip dye-transfer much inferior to the Technicolor photography of other films from the 1950s. The film is a hybrid form of the genres of epic, spectacle, comedy and melodrama. It is set in ancient Baghdad and tells the story of women kept in a harem who claim their rights for self determination. It offers the visual excesses of exoticism and melodrama, but at the same the film continues the mode of representation of classical Hollywood cinema. The film, which is also known as *Babes of Bagdad* or as *Muchachas de Bagdad,* the Spanish title of the European-American co-production, is more or less completely ignored in Ulmer's *œuvre*. It is mainly known as one of the last films by former Hollywood star Paulette Goddard. The following redemptive reading of this significantly insignificant film owes much to camp and the capacity to convert "the incompetent mistakes of naïve dross into modernist gold" (Hoberman, *Vulgar Modernism* 15). It will prove that it is possible to identify the film as a work of art. The film provokes reflections on authorship, on popular culture, on classical Hollywood cinema, on "ways of world making," and on the boundaries between high and low art.

Ulmer, Art and Auteur Cinema

Critics inspired by auteur theory were first to discover Edgar G. Ulmer's films in the 1950s. Therefore, much of what has been said about the status of

Ulmer as an artist must be seen in the context of auteur theory. In fact, he looks like the ideal object for auteur theory: An artist, repressed by the system, not willing "to be ground up in the Hollywood hash machine" as he told interviewer Peter Bogdanovich in *Who the Devil Made It* (Bogdanovich 592). He was regarded as one of the geniuses who managed to express themselves within a system that suppressed personal expression. There were many reasons why Ulmer never made it to the big studios. Ulmer himself preferred to see his career as a self-imposed exile in film studios such as PRC. Although his films had to be made within extremely tight budgets, he felt he had some freedom there to express his artistic ambitions.

According to Andrew Sarris, the critic who brought auteur theory to America, he was successful: "That a personal style could emerge from the lowest depths of Poverty Row is a tribute to a director without alibis" (Sarris 143). But Sarris regards Ulmer's contribution to film art very ambivalently. In his famous book, *The American Cinema*, Ulmer is listed under the rubric "Expressive Esoterica." He praises him as being one of the "minor glories of the cinema" with a career "more subterranean than most," as "an executioner of the Murnau estate." The films are of interest for those who love films, but in the end they remain peculiarities of cinema: great style but incredibly stupid scenarios (Sarris 143). This ambivalence towards Ulmer's status in auteur theory becomes more apparent in writings of *Cahiers du Cinéma* contributor Luc Moullet. Although the French critic was often credited with the discovery of Ulmer, he notices a disproportion between concept and realization. The films may be astonishing and original, but Moullet misses a "signature:" he is not himself; the genius remains hidden and introverted (Moullet 172).

Moullet's dictum shows that there are discrepancies between Ulmer's approach to film and concepts of authorship. Auteur theory is based on romantic notions of genius and individualism epitomized in directors such as John Ford and Howard Hawks. It preferred male genres such as the western to female genres such as the melodrama. In her survey of the genre of melodrama, Christine Gledhill makes us aware of what is being repressed in auteur theory: It was guided by the aesthetic paradigm of realism; therefore auteur theory disliked excesses in style and narration (Gledhill 18). For a very long time, melodrama remained a neglected genre. Its rediscovery was inspired by semiotic approaches to film interpretation: "Formal contradiction became a new source of critical value because it allowed apparently ideologically complicit films to be read "against the grain" for their overt critique of the represented status quo" (6).

Auteur theory was aware of such formal contradictions in Ulmer's work. John Belton refers to the difference between Ulmer and classic representatives of auteur cinema: "Ulmer's narratives, unlike Hawks's, are characteristically disjointed; he introduces characters and settings without establishing their identity or location; transitions from scene to scene often appear chaotic" (167).

In fact, it was his artistic ambition that lead to an unevenness of style in his films. Ulmer supported the view to be regarded as an artist by putting the spot on recurrent motifs of his films: He suggested that they should be read as morality plays (Moullet/Tarvernier 10). He enjoyed such discussions and invented stories and events to foreground his contributions to film art, claiming that he invented the moving camera for Murnau's *The Last Man* (Bogdanovich 569) and that he was anticipating the neo-realism of Rossellini in *Moon Over Harlem* (591) and *Club Havana* (596). Ulmer desperately wanted to be an artist. He was extremely ambitious to give his films a certain style or at least significant moments that engraved themselves into the memories of their admirers. Eric Ulman refers to his films as a cinema of moments:

> One casual and condescending way of approaching Ulmer is simply to enjoy the vivid moments that punctuate what may be generally lackluster films. These moments may represent excesses of either inadequacy or inspiration — not that it is always easy to decide which, since they are by definition exceptional, and thus extrude disruptively from the general texture.

Due to tight budgets Ulmer was very often condemned to an uneven and contradictory film style and narration. That his films are treasured by cinephiles and film scholars alike comes from his outsider status and his artistic ambition. This is why the films have a quality of campiness. The true nature of Ulmer's art is not exclusively to be revealed by auteurist readings of his films but by camp readings, which are better suited to the formal contradictions embodied in them. The concept may help us to understand the quality of Ulmer's films. But as we will see not everything is campy in *Babes of Baghdad*. Ulmer oscillates between camp and art, between the visual excesses of exoticism and the moderate film style of classical Hollywood cinema.

Ulmer and Camp

Susan Sontag's famous essay "Notes on Camp" from 1964 shows us how camp subverts commonly held notions of art. Sontag lists a great number of aspects to reveal the logic and meaning of camp aesthetics. These aspects can be used as a compass guiding through Ulmer's work.

The essence of Camp is "its love of the unnatural: of artifice and exaggeration" (Sontag 275). Ulmer had an extreme stylish and almost abstract way of using film sets, which was due to the tight budget of his films. Within the small space of his soundstages he created a world of extreme artifice. *Bluebeard* (1944), one of the films he made for PRC, created Paris by using only a few sets and some reproductions of monuments such as the Notre Dame. The minimalism was not intended, but he was using the constraints of limited production value to maximum effect, providing the thriller with a suggestive, claustrophobic atmosphere. Camp art, as Sontag continues, emphasizes "texture, sensuous surface, and style at the expense of content" (277). Ulmer had a strong sense for the composition of images: He gives them visual density by putting objects and materials into the frame. *Bluebeard* creates haunting shadow effects with silhouettes of puppets hanging from the ceiling; *Babes in Bagdad* uses ropes, curtains, ornaments and decorative elements to add some visual quality to the cheaply made sets. Sontag defines camp as "a certain mode of aestheticism." It's not art in terms of beauty but in terms of the degree of artifice and stylization (277). Small sets in *Babes in Bagdad* and other studio-made B-Movies of the 1940s and 1950s involve a certain degree of stylization. Their worlds are totally set apart from reality, which can become a source of endless fascination.

Camps means the interaction of a certain sensibility and of specific qualities of objects: "the Camp eye has the power to transform experience. But not everything can be seen as Camp. It's not all in the eye of the beholder" (277). The judgment "It's too good to be Camp" (278), refers to the fine line between objects suited for camp receptions and objects which fall out of the camp universe. Camp may be bad art and kitsch, but it "merits the most serious admiration and study" (278). Camp reception is based on notions of authenticity, which leads us to the most important aspect of camp: "Camp rests on innocence [...] Camp is either completely naïve or else wholly conscious [...] In naïve or pure, [...] the essential element is seriousness, a seriousness that fails" (283). Campiness in the works of Ulmer does not mean that its qualities are produced by the reader's activity, but they are only revealed taking camp sensibility into account. The musical numbers of *Babes in Bagdad* offer a good example. His attempt to imitate a Busby Berkeley choreography turns into a complete failure. It is clumsy, touching and speaks to the heart of the camp viewer. But films by Godard, Fassbinder and Rivette offer similar imitations of Hollywood musical. Both, Ulmer's *Babes in Bagdad* and European art cinema create some kind of minimalist musical, pointing us to the mysteriousness of the passage from reality to song and dance.

Even if there is some viewer investment involved, Sontag denies that camp simply reverses aesthetic judgment: "Camp taste turns back on the good-bad axis of ordinary aesthetic judgment. Camp doesn't reverse things.

It doesn't argue that the good is bad, or the bad is good. What it does is to offer for art (and life) a different — a supplementary — set of standards" (286). Following Sontag, we could argue that Ulmer's *Babes in Bagdad* is only bad when judged from a traditional aesthetic perspective based on values of high art like "truth, beauty and seriousness" (286). Camp does not reverse these values but it questions the authorities of the social formations identifying with them. Camp means learning to love mass produced objects, to possess them "in a rare way" (289), to reveal hidden qualities. Camp developed out of changes in the cultural households in the twentieth century: "The experiences of Camp are based on the great discovery that the sensibility of high culture has no monopoly upon refinement." (291). To love and to treasure the products of mass culture is the consequence of this transformation. Sontag stresses the "democratic esprit" and the generousness of camp (289), as if camp was anticipating cultural studies' approach to popular culture and the formation of new audiences.

Let us have a closer look at the aesthetic logic of camp and its modification of aesthetic judgment. Inspired by Sontag's camp aesthetics, J. Hoberman explains how it is possible to love bad films:

> There are a number of reasons to consider bad movies. The most obvious is that tastes change; that many, if not most, of the films we admire were once dismissed as inconsequential trash; and that trash itself is not without certain socio-aesthetic charms. Then too, bad movies have a pedagogic use value — the evolution of film form has largely been based upon mistakes. [...] it is possible for a movie to succeed because it has failed [Hoberman, *Vulgar Modernism* 13].

Reading films against-the-grain and opposing commonly held aesthetic values has a long tradition. The surrealists were the first to cultivate an appreciation for bad movies (13). Robert B. Ray refers to surrealism and the concept of photogénie. The surrealist and the early French film theory were both totally fascinated by faces and objects, a phenomenon created by the effect of photogénie: "for reasons that the French could not define, the camera rendered some otherwise ordinary objects, landscapes, and even people luminous and spellbinding" (Ray 4). They were attracted to such effects and not to a cinema of narrative integration. Jean Epstein's famous quote: "The telephone rings and all is lost" complains about the event that initiates action and contains the effects of photogénie (4). André Bréton wandered from movie house to movie house, entering films during their projection "leaving for the next once the plot became apparent" (Hoberman, *Vulgar Modernism* 13). Surrealism and cinephilia coincide in their love for moments created by "photogénie." The cinematic effect of "photogénie" is an important aspect of the ontology of film but also of camp aesthetics.

Genre, Art and Babes of Baghdad

Babes in Bagdad belongs to the campy genre of epic or spectacle. Steve Neale, whose work is of great importance to the genre study, defines spectacle as films with "historical, especially ancient-world setting" (86). It is an important genre in films history because it helped to establish the multi-reel format and dramatically changed the way film were seen and shown. Italian epics of the 1910s and D.W. Griffith's *Birth of a Nation* and *Intolerance* demanded the attention of its viewers and were based on the ambitions to make cinema a part of the respectable, middle-class culture (86). *Babes in Bagdad* falls into the era of the greatest success of the genre in the 1950s and shares its emphasis on "aural and visual spectacle." The use of new technologies such as the widescreen format was an attempt to lure back the audiences from television to cinema. A lot of these films, including *Babes in Bagdad*, were made in Europe as American-European co-productions. Hollywood produced epics as an opportunity to gain access to overseas subsidies, to cheap plant and personnel and to deploy blocked overseas income (89).

The genre's success was often credited to the 1950s cold war ideology of conservatism and anticommunism. Biblical epics like *The Ten Commandments* were stories that focused on authority, power, and freedom. But Neale reveals the ambiguities, complications and contradictions of the genre, using a quote from film scholar and critic Robin Wood: "The great scenes in these films, the reasons for our being in the cinema at all — the orgies, the triumphs, the gladiatorial games — all belong to the oppressors. The palaces, the costumes, the pomp are all theirs" (90).

The genre's engagement with contemporary culture is very important for our reading of *Babes in Bagdad*. Cecil B. de Milles *Cleopatra*, one of the few epics from the 1930s, put the spot on issues of modernity, sexuality and the new woman (88). There are even subversive elements of gender reversions in epics. The display of male muscled bodies, which turned Victor Mature into a male pin-up model, was inaugurated by DeMille's 1949 *Samson and Delilah*. Italian epics of the 1950s and 1960s displayed an eroticized female body as symbols of the threats of hedonism and unbridled sexuality, but some of them also endorsed "female pacifism, sexuality and power" (91).

Orientalism, Gender and Ideology

The setting of *Babes in Bagdad* allows the film to be read along the lines of Edward Said's concept of Orientalism. Matthew Bernstein points us to the strong ties between early Hollywood cinema and the nineteenth century ideology of colonialism:

> Western narratives and ethnographic cinemas of the late nineteenth and twentieth century inherited the narrative and visual traditions, as well as the cultural assumptions, on which Orientalism was based, and filmmakers discovered how popular Orientalism could be. In Holllywood, for example, the representations of the East — typically titillating viewers with the thrills of unbridled passion, miscegenation, and wild adventure in a raw and natural setting — were by the teens conventional constructions [3].

One element of Orientalism is the projection of repressed desires and sexuality onto foreign culture. The Orient became the locus "of irrational primitivism and uncontrollable instinct" in nineteenth century representations and in film (Shohat 32). The objective status of these projections was used as an excuse to represent sexuality, which in Hollywood cinema of the Production Code era was only allowed to be represented when absolutely essential to the plot (46).

Visual and narrative stereotypes of Orientalism also gave the films an air of campiness. The 1942 Technicolor-extravaganza of Universal's 1942 *Arabian Nights* lead to a subgenre of films starring Maria Montez. Jack Smith's famous essay published in the Journal *Film Culture* in the 1960s turned her 1944 *Cobra Woman* into a camp classic (Bernstein 11). It is significant that Jack Smith's praise of the aura of artifice and the excessive display of exoticism was written twenty years after the film's distribution, proving Sontag's observation that "time liberates the work of art from moral relevance, delivering it over to Camp sensibility" (Sontag 285). The films are born within specific cultural conditions, reproducing the moral of an era and sustaining a stereotype of a sexualized Orient, but at the same time they become objects of immense adoration.

Let us have a look at how *Babes in Bagdad* reflects the ideology of the decade. Surprisingly, the Orient of Baghdad and its images of a harem are as much the product of the 1950s ideology of conservatism as they reverse it. *Babes in Bagdad* is an exoticist comedy creating a world of artifice and imagination, similar to films such as *Arabian Nights* or the 1944 William Dieterle *Kismet* and the musical remake by Vincente Minelli from 1955. All these films used the Oriental background to tell a comedic tale far removed from narratives of power, freedom and authority for which the epic of the 1950s was known. They displayed a playful exoticism and set a totally different tone to the seriousness of Cecil B. De Mille's epics and other opulent dramas about Christian fate.

The 1954 *The Ten Commandments*, filmed in cinemascope and Technicolor, had an old-fashioned pictorial approach to film making. It was a relapse into the long take cinema of some of the earliest silent spectacles, resulting in a slow and static narration. These films were truly exotic as they were totally alien to the developments of film narration and visual style in cinema in the 1930s and the 1940s. Although William Wyler was known for his innovative use of depth of field and long take cinema in the 1930s and 1940s, his 1959 *Ben Hur* is static and old fashioned. *Ben Hur* is truly campy, not only because of its anachronistic visual style but because of its representation of repressed homosexuality in the relation between Ben Hur (Charlton Heston) and his Roman friend and rival (Stephen Boyd). But *Babes in Bagdad* is not a narrative of repression. Unlike *Ben Hur* it uses the epic setting to tell a story of women's liberation in the patriarchal world of a harem.

In her essay on the gender aspects of Orientalism in cinema, Ella Shohat refers to the Hollywood stereotype of the harem: "The Western obsession with the harem [...] was not simply crucial for Hollywood's visualization of the Orient but also authorized the proliferation of sexual images projected on an otherized elsewhere" (47). This misinterpretation of the paternalistic nature of the harem is contrasted with the picture of a historical harem that depicts the complex familial life and strong network of female communality:

> Whereas Western discourse on the harem defined it simply as a male-dominated space, the accounts of the harem by Middle Eastern women testify to a system whereby a man's female relatives also shared the living space, allowing women access to other women, providing a protected space for the exchange of information and ideas safe from the eyes and the ears of men [50].

Ulmer's film seems to be based on this view of the harem. Women talk to other women and reflect on the nature of repression, forming a protest against this paternalistic world. The Paulette Goddard character opts for her rights of self-determination, and she finds her love in the arms of the caliph's son. The film apparently preconceives the woman's lib movement of the 1960s.

In an essay on the genre of melodrama, film philosopher Stanley Cavell points us to the capacity of the genre to create a woman's space in which the screen becomes a field of communication (Cavell, *Cities of Words* 279). Ulmer's *Babes in Bagdad* is a mixture of musical, comedy and melodrama and fully accomplishes the goal of creating a field of communication. It obeys in many ways the aesthetic logic of Orientalist representations in cinema. Ulmer attempts to give the film visual opulence and a rich texture of sets decorated with signs and materials. But Ulmer either didn't have the money or the intention to make a genuine epic.

Babes in Bagdad *and* Classical Hollywood Cinema

Ulmer knows how to achieve a convincing aesthetic style in his recreation of worlds on film, letting them appear real and imagined at the same time. This is the source of the fascination for the reconstruction of the shtetl world in his ethnic films of the 1930s, especially in *The Light Ahead* (1938). J. Hoberman refers to the film as the most expressionistic of Ulmer's Yiddish talkies "With its crazy angles and skewed lampposts, Glubsk suggests the confluence of Marc Chagall and The Cabinet of Dr. Caligari" (Hoberman, *Bridge of Light* 303). Its *mise-en-scène* oscillates between realism and illusion, trying to achieve a convincing aesthetic vision of a world lost and gone, speaking to the hearts of Ulmer and the targeted audience. In a similar way, *American Matchmaker* from 1940 is both, an imitation of classical Hollywood cinema and the genres of romantic comedy and musical, and an extremely low budgeted reconstruction of metropolitan Yiddish culture. And although the sets are so small that the camera almost never moves, the visual style is elegant and dynamic. It turns the film into an entertaining comedy about love and split Jewish identities torn between American and European culture. Nothing of this may play any role in the naïve exoticism of *Babes in Bagdad*. But all of them establish a specific visual style and create an autonomous reality.

Ulmer's *mise-en-scène* in *Babes in Bagdad* is smooth, elegant and dynamic the way classical Hollywood cinema was. Whereas the epic and spectacles of the 1950s used new forms of addressing their audiences, with wide-screen formats and high production values to renew and update the cinematic experience (Neale 89), *Babes in Bagdad* remained within the frames of classical Hollywood continuity form of narration. It's pure studio style Hollywood cinema with an almost abstract use of the sets and only few location shots of the Baghdad market place. Everything is enclosed within a small space, visualizing the Orient as a chamber drama. This lends the film an aura of privacy totally alien to other epics and spectacles. The film belongs to the genre and reflects in many ways the social and cultural conditions of the 1950s — the crisis of the film industry, its struggle with television and its new approach to audiences, the cold war, the moral conservatism of the era — but it moves into another direction and confirms the artist's outsider status. It's surprising to note that although the film offers many campy elements it turns out to be less campy than the big studio productions of *The Tenth Commandment* or *Ben Hur* and their pretentious dialogues, static narration, Christian pathos and display of male bodies.

Looking closer at *Babes in Bagdad* may force us to reverse our judgment of its campiness. It's an artwork that continues the classical Hollywood cinema mode of representation. Ulmer uses only a few panning and tracking shots in the film but he reveals a great sense for cinematic space and for matching cuts. At first, the film seems a bit static, but it finds its own rhythm and establishes its own visual order. In all its limitations caused by the low production values, the film has a certain kind of dynamic and smoothness. The film may cause a feeling of claustrophobia as it never leaves the comparatively small sets of the harem and the palace. It's simply not enough room for musical numbers in the style of Busby Berkeley or of Vincente Minelli, which lets them, as already noted above, appear both, clumsy and touching. Ulmer tries to give this film some visual beauty. He uses many ornaments, the columns and walls are painted with figurines and symbols, abstract patterns are used to fill the frame. But at the same time he never foregrounds the aural and visual spectacle. *Babes in Bagdad* is different to the Orientalism described by Ella Shohat: "The spectator is subliminally invited on an ethnographic tour of a celluloid-'preserved' culture, which implicitly celebrates the chronotopic magical aptitude of cinema for panoramic spectacle and temporal voyeurism" (Shohat 32). *Babes in Bagdad* contrast this with a toned down version of exoticism.

Entertainment and Art

Orientalism makes us aware of how films construct cultural stereotypes of the East. But films in general create symbolic realms rather than mirroring the world. *Babes in Bagdad*'s reconstruction of the orient must be seen in the light of cinema's capacity to give us access to worlds set apart from reality. Richard Dyer speaks of an Utopianism embodied in escapist Hollywood genres like the musical:

> Entertainment does not [...] present models of utopian worlds, as in the classic utopias of Sir Thomas More, William Morris, et al. Rather, the utopianism is contained in the feelings it embodies. It presents, head-on as it were, what utopia would feel like rather than how it would be organized. It thus works at the level of sensibility, by which I mean an effective code that is characteristic of, and largely specific to, a given mode of cultural production. The code uses both representational and, importantly, non-representational signs [Dyer 373].

Dyer refers to classical Hollywood cinema and the genre of the musical, not necessarily to what attracts camp reception. It could be argued that the films inspire escapist thoughts because they invoke a totality and closure of their worlds. According to Stanley Cavell there is a reflexivity of the medium of film itself that involves distance. The world enfolds as if there was no viewer, it needs no participation and is present to us by accepting our absence from it (Cavell, *The World Viewed* 23). Cavell's works try to comment on the loss of this "natural condition of film viewing" in the 1950s. The loss was caused by several aspects, for example by the modernism of the *nouvelle vague* that demanded attention from the audience for the fact that films were made by artists, or by the new technologies used in Hollywood cinema to compete with television. The wide-screen camera formats of the 1950s were created to achieve immersive effects and more participation from the audience. *Babes in Bagdad* avoids these immersive effects and grants the viewer some distance.

But the film is more than a continuation of the classical Hollywood mode of narration. Unlike other "more campy" films by Ulmer such as *The Black Cat,* whose digression from the path of conventional cinema stimulate our imagination, *Babes in Bagdad* is too much classical Hollywood cinema to offer such digressions. *Babes in Bagdad* surprisingly turns out to have not enough campyness to stimulate our imagination immediately. Therefore, it calls for patience and attentiveness to bring to light what is significant about the film.

J. Hoberman points us to the capacity of bad movies to invite thoughts on the nature of cinematic representation. Hoberman refers to Oscar Micheaux, a black filmmaker whose films from the 1930s and 1940s had by far lower production values than Ulmer's and are notorious for their incredibly inaccurate story telling. But at the same time the films tell us something about the "institutional mode of narration" (a concept by film scholar Noël Burch) of classical Hollywood cinema:

> Micheaux constructed an anti–Hollywood out of rags and bones on some barely-imaginable psychic tundra. The spectacles he fashioned of blacks playing whites constitute a ruthless burlesque of the dominant culture. [...] Micheaux took the "institutional mode of representation," up-ended it, and turned it inside out. He demystified movies as no one has ever done and performed this negative magic for an audience that [...] was victimized by Hollywood's mechanical dreams. It is his futile attempt to imitate the "institutional mode of representation," the mode of narration in classical Hollywood film drama, that gives his films a quality of subversiveness [Hoberman, *Vulgar Modernism* 15].

In the case of a filmmaker who belongs to an ethnic minority this subversiveness is tied to the reality of repression of Blacks in the 1930s and 1940s. But it has an aesthetic value, as it makes us aware of how films are narrated or of where exactly narration ends.

Ulmer's film is interesting for similar reason. But Ulmer succeeds in continuing the "institutional mode of narration." Although the film is delimited to a very small, closed and rather claustrophobic space, the film is dynamic. It feels like an experimental film testing the limits of abstraction and artifice: how much can be left out before we cease to accept the film's representation of a world. There are, as J. Hoberman is indicating with his concept of vulgar modernism, some crossing points between B-Movies and between art film, blurring the boundaries of high and low art. Amos Vogel's important book, *Film as Subversive Art*, transcends these boundaries convincingly. Popular films, B-Movies, experimental and avant-garde cinema, European art cinema, all are given the same attention as films which attack capitalist society and question our beliefs and convictions (Vogel). Another proof for the close link between popular culture and art cinema can be found in Joan Hawkin's essay on the canons and cultural hierarchies of trash cinema. In mail order catalogues for lovers of trash cinema, masterpieces of European art cinema are listed on the same pages with films such as *Zontar, the Thing from Venus* (1966) or *The Yeti and the Werewolf* (1975). Her observation sheds some light on an aspect "generally overlooked or repressed in cultural analysis, namely, the degree to which high culture trades on the same images, tropes, and themes which characterize low culture" (Hawkins 15). This close link between high and low art explains how it is possible to find some abstract and subversive qualities in *Babes in Bagdad*. It helps us to identify its peculiar visual style as some kind of narrative minimalism, as abstractions and as reflections on film conventions.

In a similar experiment, in *Mélo* from 1986, Alain Resnais was taking thought on the nature of theatre and film and the boundaries between them. The film creates an atmosphere of extreme claustrophobia. It has a delimited narrative space, uses only a few sets and very long takes. The longest take is a 5 minute tracking shot that slowly approaches a character during his monologue until his face is in close up. The film may be boring and demanding, but with a little patience Resnais' *Mélo* establishes its own order of narration and turns out to be a rewarding experience. Art films afford some investment by their audiences to display their effects. In the same way, camp reception stimulates viewer investments and attention. With a little more patience even the significantly insignificant *Babes in Bagdad* establishes its own order of narration and turns out to be a rewarding experience of a slightly different nature — as a camp film by an "introverted" auteur, as a continuation of classical Hollywood cinema, as an epic avoiding visual excesses and stereotypes in its representation of women and the Orient, and as an art film that invites thoughts on the nature of cinematic representation.

Works Cited

Belton, John. *The Hollywood Professionals, Vol. 3.: Howard Hawks, Frank Borzage, Edgar G. Ulmer*. London: Tantivy, 1974, 149–80.

Bernstein, Matthew. "Orientalism and the Construction of Gender: Introduction." Bernstein and Studlar, 1–18.

_____, and Gaylin Studlar (eds.). *Visions of the East: Orientalism in Film*. New York: I.B. Tauris, 1997.

Cavell, Stanley. *Cities of Words: Pedagogical Letters on a Register of Moral Life*. Cambridge Mass.: Belknap Press of Harvard University Press, 2004.

_____. *The World Viewed. Reflections on the Ontology of Film. Enlarged Edition*. Cambridge Mass.: Harvard University Press, 1979.

Dyer, Richard. "Entertainment and Utopia." During, Simon (ed.). *The Cultural Studies Reader, Second Edition*. London/New York: Routledge, 1993, 317–81.

Gledhill, Christine. "The Melodramatic Field: An Investigation." Gledhill, Christine (ed.). *Home Is Where the Heart Is: Studies in Melodrama and the Woman's Film*. London: BFI, 1987, 5–39.

Hawkins, Joan. "Sleaze Mania: Euro-Trash and High Art." *Film Quarterly* 53.2 (Winter 1999/2000): 15–29.

Hoberman, J. *Bridge of Light: Yiddish Films Between Two Worlds*. New York: Schocken, 1991.

_____. *Vulgar Modernism. Writing on Movies and Other Media*. Philadelphia: Temple University Press, 1991.

Moullet, Luc. "Edgar Ulmer." *Cahiers du Cinéma* 25.150–1 (December 1963/January 1964): 172.

_____, and Bertrand Tavernier. "Entretien avec Edgar G. Ulmer." *Cahiers du Cinéma* 21.122 (August 1961): 1–16.

Neale, Steve. *Genre and Hollywood*. London/New York: Routledge, 2000.

Sarris, Andrew. *The American Cinema. Directors and Directions 1929–1968*. Chicago: University of Chicago Press, 1985.

Shohat, Ella. "Gender and Culture of Empire: Toward a Feminist Ethnography of the Cinema." Bernstein and Studlar, 19–66.

Sontag, Susan. *Against Interpretation and Other Essays*. New York: Farrar, Straus & Giroux, 2001.

Ulman, Eric. "Senses of Cinema, Great Directors." *http://www.sensesofcinema.com/contents/directors/03/ulmer.html*, last accessed on 27 March 2008.

Vogel, Amos. *Film as Subversive Art*. New York: Random House, 1974.

The Pleasures of the "Not-Quite Movie": *Murder Is My Beat* and *Daughter of Dr. Jekyll*

EKKEHARD KNÖRER

This discussion focuses on two Ulmer films grouped together by chance rather than analytic design. This, of course, is rather appropriate where a work is concerned that is not so much an oeuvre than it is a hodgepodge assembly of qualitatively rather varied movies. These movies, then, are not what — in the French nouvelle vague lingo — an *auteur* has willed into being, but they are rather the breathtaking and sometimes breathtakingly awful result of ever new mixtures of chance, delusions of — as, to some extent, also actual — grandeur, and sheer defiance. It's hardly an exaggeration, even, to say that chance was Edgar G. Ulmer's most consistent, albeit also extraordinarily fickle collaborator. It is important to develop ideas for something like an Ulmer aesthetic, or, rather, a notion of what the lack of such an aesthetic may entail for the pleasure of watching his films.

The genres, the settings and the moods of these two films are different enough. There is some connection at second sight, though, in the fact that London-born Aubrey Wisberg, producer and screenwriter of *Murder Is My Beat* and Jack Pollexfen, author of *Daughter of Dr. Jekyll*, had collaborated and would further collaborate as authors, producers and even directors in the fifties. The most famous and also most pertinent example here is, of course, Ulmer's *Man from Planet X* from 1951, but Wisberg and Pollexfen were also churning out pulp titles like *Dragon's Gold* (from 1954). A short summary (from IMDB) goes like this:

A bonding company sends an investigator (John Archer) to China to find out if one of its clients actually stole $7,000,000 worth of gold as claimed by the supposed owner. He is soon involved in a series of murders and intrigues involving a man posing as the client, the client's wife (Hillary Brooke) and the man who claims ownership of the stolen gold.[1]

In 1955 — the same year *Murder Is My Beat* was made — they were responsible for the screenplay of *Sinbad's Son*, produced by Howard Hughes and featuring Vincent Price as well as, quoting again from IMDB, "a bunch of scantily clad harem girls."[2] In 1952 Wisberg and Pollexfen had written the first postapocalyptic movie in film history, which Howard Hughes, who was again the producer, titled *Captive Women*. It "is set in a post nuclear holocaust world where three warring tribes, 'The Norms,' 'The Mutates,' and 'The Upriver People' battle each other for supremacy in and around the ruins of New York City and its environs in the year 3000." Let me add that Aubrey Wisberg went on to eternal fame by in 1970 writing the screenplay for *Hercules in New York* (aka *Hercules Goes Bananas*), the movie which gave a first title role to a struggling young Austrian actor named Arnold Strong — the speaking name Strong, as you might guess, being an ever so slightly adapted version of the not so speaking and highly unpronounceable real name "Schwarzenegger."

This is a scant sketch of the exploitational context into which Edgar Ulmer's two films, written by Wisberg and Pollexfen respectively, are situated without quite belonging to it.

Generic Variations

Let's now look at the question of genre and context a bit more systematically. The first of these questions: How generic is *Murder Is My Beat*? Or, put differently: How easily is it recognizable as belonging to a genre? This, however, at once produces another question: What genre? Which genre does — or could — *Murder Is My Beat* belong to? The American Cinematheque retrospective places the film — beyond the shadow of a doubt — into the *noir* genre (or cycle or style or as whatever you whish to regard *film noir*). To quote from the cinematheque website: "Next to DETOUR, this is Ulmer's finest *noir*."[3] Stefan Grissemann in his Ulmer-monograph *Mann im Schatten* also groups *Murder Is My Beat* with *Detour* as a "hardboiled fantasy" and "film *noir*." But this is not certain.

Film noir as a genre or, as Michael Walker put it, a "generic field" (Cameron 8), is far more easily recognizable than definable (this is a reformulation of what James Naremore says in the first sentence of the first chap-

Murder Is My Beat: How noir is it? (courtesy Edgar G. Ulmer Preservation Corporation).

ter of *More Than Night*, arguably the most important book on Noir).⁴ Naremore, of course, elegantly avoids the kind of positivism that tries to define film noir as something describable by a list of common traits, and shifts the attention to the retrospective construction of a historical consciousness. This completely reasonable theoretical movement, however, does not really help with the questions. *Murder Is My Beat* is not listed in any film *noir* books (or any other books, excepting those specifically concerned with Edgar Ulmer. The movie is even so obscure that a CD that collects music and dialogue snippets from noir movies, although titled *Murder Is My Beat*, does not include anything from Ulmer's film).⁵ But again: "How *noir* is it?" The movie surely shows some of the traits we are used to connect with film *noir*, beginning with the flashback structure and certainly not ending with the emergence of Barbara Payton as a *femme* that seems *fatale* enough in the beginning. It very soon begins to mutate into a rather ordinary whodunit, though. The femme is not fatale after all, the cop is doing mostly his job — however ineptly — and it all leads to a perfectly happy ending. One murderer is caught, the other one commits suicide, and the central couple are on the way to their wedding. The beginning, and actually large parts of the movie, do not prepare us for this ending. *Murder Is My Beat* begins with images of a man driving a car on a generic American road, reminding us at once of Ulmer's *Detour*. But this reminiscence is soon interrupted, when the car, before meeting any kind of detour, stops at a motel, in which a man (Paul Langton) who turns out to be the movie's hero has got stuck. The confrontation between the two men, the one who arrives and the one on his bed in the motel, triggers the kind of flashback narration that is so typical of the noir style. The man on the bed, we learn from his narration, is a policeman who has got stuck in this motel with a case he cannot solve and with a murder suspect — the seeming femme fatale — he believes is innocent. And although Ulmer gets his plot moving, backwards first by flashback narration, and although we will see the frantic movement of a train's wheels quite a few times, *Murder Is My Beat* on the whole turns out to be a movie not about movement, but a movie about getting and being stuck.

The crucial and actually dubious phrase in this last sentence, however, is *on the whole*. It is completely justified to ask: "How much of a whole is *Murder Is My Beat*?" Movies, or texts of any kind, are not ever "wholes" in the sense of what classical aesthetics imagined as texts structured by a central idea, symbol (or whatever) that reigns supreme over the text's meanings, movements, seeming contradictions etc. And yet there are different ways of not being whole in the world of works of art. Put very simply: Some texts and works of art hold together and others fall apart. There are, no doubt, beautiful ways of falling apart, but what prevails are the exasperating ones, especially in the kind of Ulmer style low-budget-independent-filmmaking we are concerned with here. Only in very few cases do the far less than perfect conditions of production allow something as unified as *Detour*, which undoubtedly — and in spite of its technical flaws and bumps — adds up to a sum that is much larger than its parts, i.e. to a rather homogeneous whole in mood, style, setting and vision.

But there is also something like a paradox buried here: What holds together the "generic field" are those genre pieces that achieve a certain kind of purity and unity and thereby find their place in the center of a genre. The paradox being that these pieces, like, in the case of *noir*, Billy Wilder's *Double Indemnity* or John Huston's *Maltese Falcon* are the least generic, in a way, quite simply because they will be observed as changing the rules they follow. Exactly by being one of their kind, they encourage and engender all kinds of generic products that imitate and vary these models, more or less successfully. In industrial contexts, generic fields are opened, agendas are set by what not without reason are then called seminal movies. Genre history consists in their engendering, unknowingly, beautiful variations and mutations that shape our perception of the generic field. The works that will be regarded as the epitome of a genre in hindsight, are what constitutes this hindsight, which then makes them what they are: classics in the history of a genre. *Detour*, as an eminent example, came to be regarded as a seminal noir movie only late after the fact. But this fits with the logic John Naremore described as a logic of the formation of a generic field in hindsight; and it is the general logic of writing — and rewriting — history, the paradoxical logic of metalepsis. We posit that which we posit as that which has always been exactly the way we describe it; *as if unposited.*

The Pleasure of Texts Falling Apart

In every generic field works on the fringes fall by the wayside, as does a corpse in Ulmer's *Detour*. *Murder Is My Beat* surely is a film that has almost completely fallen by the wayside of genre history. But certainly for a reason; it is not a masterpiece, far from it. Still, it is not entirely bland, either; it — like a lot of Ulmer's films — is something we can enjoy not for the presence but for the absence of a certain kind of perfection and wholeness. *Murder Is My Beat* very surely lacks the unity of *Detour*, the kind of unity we in more "successful" cases either ascribe to the function in the process of film production we call the director, or alternatively to, for example, the genius of the system. But what if a film lacks this unity; what if it falls apart? What do we make of it? How do we describe it and how and why do we enjoy it, if we enjoy it? What kind of pleasure and satisfaction do we get from the unsatisfactory? This is not necessarily the pleasures of camp and trash here, which might be the correct category for stuff like *Hercules in New York*, but not for the "better" parts of Ulmer's work. And how is this pleasure related to the pleasure of genre as the pleasure of a coming back and coming home to what we more or less know, of a revisiting of something we seem to remember, although perhaps differently? What are, in other words, the pleasures of falling apart, the pleasures of being lead astray to the fringe of a generic field, to a place where perhaps this field itself fizzles out, mutates into something of uncertain shape and contour? And what are, as in the case of *Murder Is My Beat*, the pleasures of getting stuck in a text that fleetingly reminds you of generic motifs, but does not get a grip on the however fuzzy rules of a genre?

Let's answer these questions starting out from the perspective of somebody who loves moments and sequences in quite a few of Ulmer's films, but most of the time does not manage to love the films as a whole. So let me tell you about *my* moments of pleasure in *Murder Is My Beat* and also in *Daugh-*

ter of Dr. Jekyll, a movie that, in a way, is placed as awkwardly in the generic field of horror as is *Murder Is My Beat* in that of *film noir*. My first moment of pleasure I obviously share with Michael E. Grost who on his online website on Edgar G. Ulmer's films describes particularly one sequence in *Murder Is My Beat* as, "coming out of nowhere."[6] (This idiomatic expression sums up the kind of pleasure perfectly, as a pleasure derived from being caught unawares, coming from places you never assumed did exist.) It is the scene in which the hero moves from a sunny Californian afternoon into a mountainscape and finally a cabin shrouded in snow. This is amazing, even baffling in the way only things you at first can't account for are amazing. You can't even say that it doesn't work, because when you look at it from the screenwriter's point of view it makes perfect sense. He wants to get his hero and his heroine to get stuck together for a while. So what solution could be more obvious than shrouding them in huge amounts of Californian snow. Still, it comes out of nowhere. Then it stays there, nowhere that is, for quite a few minutes, only to be forgotten as soon as the heroine and the hero have become a little better acquainted.

Another moment of pleasure: In *Daughter of Dr. Jekyll* we have a — quite beautifully directed — murder scene which for no obvious reason leaves the somewhat haunted house the rest of the film is located in (or around); we are quite suddenly transported to what seems like a different film, a different genre, say, a Hitchcock thriller or an urban noir movie or perhaps one of those rather campy German Edgar Wallace films. Abruptly leaving the very artificial fog (the B-movie maker's best friend — something you can see even in a film as ambitious but impecunious as Hans-Jürgen Syberberg's *Hitler*), a fog that hovers in the foreground of most of the scenes that play outside the house, we are transported to a brightly lit room, where music is playing on an Edison Standard Phonograph, which is shown in a close-up. We see a scantily clad woman moving in this room. A phone is ringing, we see the horror in the victim's eyes, we also see the Mr. Hyde-figure at the window, already mutated into a werewolf. The woman is killed, we see her lying on the floor, but it is not at all a gory scene. It is directed with the refinement that so regrettably lacks in most of the rest of the movie. And then we are back in the fog and back in the haunted house and back to the rather routine unspooling of a silly horror story.

In a way watching a movie like this is like living a life in which you have lost your long term memory and only remember the last ten minutes of what happened. What you seem to realize is that there are motifs you know from a certain kind of film: flashbacks and femmes fatales and werewolves and a lot of artificial fog and corpses and bizarre camera angles. But they somehow don't exactly add up. And *quite a few* sequences seem to come out of nowhere.

Above: Daughter of Dr. Jekyll: a "not-quite" movie (courtesy Edgar G. Ulmer Preservation Corporation). *Right:* Death and the Edison Standard Phonograph, from *Daughter of Dr. Jekyll* (courtesy Image Entertainment).

There certainly is something like a continuous narrative, but it seems of little consequence, as it is disrupted by more or less blatant non-sequiturs. Or perhaps one should rather say "not-quite-sequiturs." This might even be a perfect term for this kind of film: The "not-quite" movies; movies that do not quite fit into a generic field, movies that do not quite make sense, movies that are to be taken not quite seriously, but are not quite ridiculous either. There must be then, I think, something like the pleasure of the "not quite," the pleasure of the intriguing imperfection; but not much has been written about it. (And, it should be added, the majority of serious writers on film will actually not even know it, or at least won't admit to it.)

This pleasure might be a pleasure born out of frustration. Because the film does not lead us where we are expecting it to lead us, it does not surprise us the way we wish to be surprised, it does not twist our expectations we hoped they would be twisted. In fact, we pretty soon feel at a loss because our attempts at stitching together a continuous and unified text of meaning and sense get us more or less nowhere, or get us, at least, more or less stuck. So perhaps we give up these attempts, which at first is an uneasy thing to do; especially for people (like us) trained as readers of texts that give us the pleasure of answering our efforts of interpretation more or less eagerly. What we have to learn is to appreciate a text falling apart in front of our eyes and despite our attempts of holding it together. Or perhaps we will never really give up trying to stitch it together, which would make our pleasure a very special kind of *angstlust*, that is not quite a pleasure, rather a clinging to something we feel we should give up for the real pleasure to begin.

But what kind of text is the "not quite movie"? A text, I should say, that holds together as much as it is falling apart. Outright disasters — the Ed Wood kind of movie — are for the trash and camp *aficionado*. *Murder Is My Beat* is not camp or trash (*Daughter of Dr. Jekyll* is closer, but not exactly it, either). Perhaps it could be said that these texts do *not quite* achieve the suspension of disbelief that is necessary for us to get fully into the text, to lose ourselves in the fictional world of werewolves and cops and beautiful blonde dames. We do not watch what we see with the outright distance by which the sophisticated appreciation of camp is characterized. In camp it is the very distance, or rather the act of distancing ourselves, that gets us back and close again to what we know is ridiculous — it re-enables us to love what we do not take seriously at all. This, however, is not what happens when we watch movies like *Murder Is My Beat*, at least it is not what happens when I watch them. We will not, in a complete turnaround of critical judgment, appreciate the most what aesthetically satisfies the least. My pleasure here is a pleasure of moments; it surges and then ebbs away, to resurge again after a stretch of boredom or indifference. Perhaps you could say that my pleasure also "comes out of nowhere," almost as if the movie has done nothing to earn my enjoying it; there is no build-up here, as is in all kinds of suspense and melodrama. It is not the character development or the story arc that have more or less subtly prepared me for my moment of satisfaction and enjoyment. In this kind of movie, the sequences of pleasure are rather disruptive or interruptive. They disrupt — without following from it — only the most generic telling of a story. The "not quite movies" are something like a variation of a "cinema of attractions" and perhaps its sequences of pleasure only work because the movie does not manage to construct a convincing build-up. Its incompetence might be exactly what achieves to catch me and my pleasure unawares.

Let me talk about other moments of pleasure in *Murder Is My Beat*. These are the sequences of the most unconvincing rear projection I know. Rear projection as such is, of course, a conventionally accepted means of creating the illusion of people — very often in cars — moving through an outside world, when in fact they never leave the studio. We sometimes find it a bit jarring, but in general we have no problem really to invest in the suspension of disbelief that is needed to accept the illusion as fictional reality. In *Murder Is My Beat* there are, however, scenes where the difference between the figures in the foreground and the street scene in the background is so blatantly obvious that I feel completely incapable of forgetting that what I am watching is a rear projection. And my pleasure is caused exactly by my not being capable of forgetting it. I am doubly involved in these scenes, following, on the one hand, the movements within the fictional world, and, on the other hand, quite clearly observing the rift between foreground and background, that is: observing the rear projection *as* rear projection. I assume that, in a way, this is what we always do, that this is exactly what we mean when we talk about fiction: the creation of a world in which we invest our belief without ever quite forgetting that in fact we have to invest in the *suspension* of *disbelief*. What makes virtual worlds feel real for us is that we know about our investment, but that we don't realize that we know. My moment of pleasure in the rear projection sequences in *Murder Is My Beat* is a moment exactly of the *realization* of this knowledge. It is a very gentle realization, though. The film — in contrast to all kinds of avant-garde works — quite obviously does not want to produce this realization. It wants to hold together but is, against its intentions, falling apart. Perhaps, as a reaction to that, I laugh, but perhaps I don't. I am in two places at the same time, inside and outside, and my pleasure seems to derive from a strangely mixed experience. This, I think, is as close as I get to my describing the rather strange pleasure of texts falling apart.

The Director's Place in Texts Falling Apart

This pleasure is not the same as the aesthetic satisfaction of watching movies that are unified wholes. It is *not* what we experience when we are in the hands of a master in complete control of his material — which, of course, does not mean that there are no mistakes, gaffes or goofs even in this case. It rather means that these goofs usually don't make us suddenly realize what we always know: that in the movies fictional worlds are created out of rear projections, montage, fog and thin air. What it, on the other hand, takes for the pleasure of the "not quite" variety is a certain kind of daring on the writer's and/or director's side. The blandly generic wouldn't make possible the pleasure caused by a text falling apart against its intentions. And the result, although certainly something of a failure, must not be ridiculous, either. I am quite sure that it takes a certain kind of director and a certain kind of circumstances to unintentionally produce this kind of text and this kind of pleasure. A director with daring and with ideas, but no money at all. A director who makes possible the impossible without quite succeeding in what he envisions. In a lot of cases Edgar G. Ulmer is exactly this kind of director. There are movies in his career, *Detour* or *Ruthless*, where it all comes together, and there are movies that are bad enough to be trash or camp. But then there is the middle ground — and *Murder Is My Beat*, perhaps even *The Daughter of Dr. Jekyll* belong to it — in which Edgar Ulmer proved to be not quite a master, but certainly a master of the "not quite."

Notes

1. *http://www.imdb.com/title/tt0207433/plotsummary*, last accessed April 10, 2008.
2. *http://imdb.com/title/tt0048642/usercomments*, last accessed April 10, 2008.
3. *http://www.americancinematheque.com/archive1999/edgargulmer1999.htm*, last accessed April 10, 2008.
4. Naremore's wording: "It has always been easier to recognize a film noir than to define the term" (Naremore 10).
5. Cf. *http://www.musicweb-international.com/film/2000/feb00/murder.htm*, last accessed April 10, 2008.
6. *http://home.aol.com/MG4273/ulmer.htm*, last accessed April 10, 2008.

Works Cited

Cameron, Ian. *The Movie Book of Film Noir*. London: Cassell, 1994.
Naremore, James. *More Than Night: Film Noir in Its Contexts*. Berkeley, Los Angeles, Oxford: University of California Press, 1998.

Products of Circumstances
STEFANIE DIEKMANN

This essay will focus on three topics — or issues? — which have resurfaced so frequently in writings on Ulmer that they might be specific to his work, in the sense that they tell us something about the challenge it constitutes to academic comment and to certain concepts that are usually applied when a cinematic work is undergoing the kind of re-evaluation that Ulmer's work has been undergoing (and still *is* undergoing). The three topics are the concept of authorship, the concept of signature and that of the body of work. The fact that these may be called, more specifically, "Ulmer issues," owes to the observation that in the case of this film director all three concepts seem a little conflicted and de-stabilized. And while this may be true of many cinematic works to a certain extent, Ulmer is a director with whom the conflict becomes more obvious than with others. This is a case of contested authorship, of interfering and interacting signatures, and a body of work in which the fragmentary plays a role that is too significant to be overlooked.

Authorship

For all we know, Ulmer himself had a rather conservative idea of authorship in general, and a very strong idea of *his* authorship in particular. This is obvious in the much-quoted interview[1] by Peter Bogdanovich in which Ulmer not only clearly enjoys himself in the role of a master-director discussing his work but in which he also appropriates a good part of Weimar cinema, films and technical innovations alike. (As Alexander Horwath points out in his text on Ulmer's *Strange Illusion* (1945), the Ulmer/Bogdanovich interview constitutes a somewhat problematic source, alternating between anecdotal narrative, bold claims, plain exaggeration, and accounts that cannot be verified or falsified, because there exists so little documentation of Ulmer's work, be it in Hollywood or elsewhere) (see Horwath 297).[2]

From Curt Boese's/Paul Wegener's *Der Golem, Wie Er in die Welt Kam* (1920) to Robert Wiene's *Das Cabinet des Dr. Caligari* (1920), from Fritz Lang's *Die Nibelungen* (1924), *Metropolis* (1927) and *Spione* (1928) to Friedrich Wilhelm Murnau's *Die Finanzen des Großherzogs* (1924) and *Der Letzte Mann* (1924), Ulmer presses his claim to fame and communicates that, as a production designer of these films, he played a decisive part in the making of almost every masterpiece from this period.[3] These claims are underlined by his explanation that directorial work in those days was usually the work of two artists: one in charge of the actors and the other responsible for the more cinematographic aspects of filmmaking. "At that time, up to the coming of sound, there were two directors on each picture: a director for the dramatic action and for the actors, and then the director for the *picture itself*, who established the camera angles, camera movements, et cetera. There had to be teamwork" (Bogdanovich 546).

Teamwork it may have been, and it may also be true that the main credit for the films went to others. There is, however, no misunderstanding as to which part of the directorial work should be considered essential for the artistic success of the film and it seems clear which of the two parts must have been Ulmer's. With regard to his later work in New York and Hollywood, the history of which is somewhat better documented, we know that even if Ulmer was by now in charge of the actors *and* in charge of the "picture itself," he repeatedly worked with certain artists who may have contributed significantly to certain features for which Ulmer's work was later praised by cinephiles and B movie lovers alike. This applies in particular to the famous "primacy of the visual" (see Meisel) in Ulmer's films and his achievements in *mise-en-scène* which may be as much his own work as that of Eugen Schüfftan, a camera man who never managed to become a member of the Hollywood Union but was nevertheless in charge of the light and the camera work in much-praised Ulmer films like *Bluebeard*, *Strange Illusion*, and *Club Havana*.

We also know that Ulmer's idea of authorship was closely connected to that of High Art and cultural sophistication. What his films betray is not so much the vast cultural background and knowledge he almost certainly would have claimed to have, but a rather serious effort to *appear* cultured, i.e. to communicate, by a number of hints and allusions, that he was an educated or even erudite director. (His appropriation, later in life, of the title Dr. Ulmer points into the same direction.) This effort is most obviously at work in Ulmer's film *The Black Cat* (1934): the title itself refers to a tale by Edgar A. Poe, otherwise not very recognizable in the plot, while the film's master villain Poelzig bears the name of a famous German architect, and the master villain's villa bears a strong resemblance to Bauhaus architecture (while the real Poelzig is generally listed as a representative of Neue Sachlichkeit).[4] Add to this the recurring tune of a piano concerto by Mozart which acquires a vaguely sinister and threatening quality, some not too-well researched allusions to the Nietzschean concept of *Übermensch*, references to World War I and a number of borrowings from Nineteenth Century Gothic fiction, and you end up with a rather wild collection of fragments from the history of European culture which Ulmer, no doubt, held in very high esteem. However, it may be more interesting to discuss *The Black Cat* and a number of other Ulmer films in terms of camp and appropriation instead of those of the forgotten masterpiece.[5] And while Ulmer himself may have fully subscribed to the notion of the director-*auteur* who is to be regarded as the artistic master of his work, the cultural references could also be seen as somewhat overdetermined and indicative of an effort to stabilize a difficult authorial position.

That Ulmer's position as a director was difficult, we know. It was difficult in New York where he made his ethnic and educational pictures. It was very difficult in Hollywood where he barely kept afloat as a director of B-movies. And it continued to be difficult in later years when he worked in Mexico and Italy and right until his last film *The Cavern* (1965). Most texts on Ulmer, especially those written by his admirers in the 1970s, inevitably open with a remark about the very low budgets and the very tight schedules on which his movies were made,[6] always including a reference to the four (or six or eight or ten) days it took to him to make films like *Club Havana* (1945), *Detour* (1945) or *The Naked Dawn* (1955). According to Ulmer himself, the ratio in most of his film projects was 3:1 or 2:1, sometimes as fractional as 13/4:1 (*Grine Felder*, 1937); there was little or no room for tryouts or errors, and his crew usually consisted of those who were willing to work for very little money (and in some cases, especially the ethnic movies, no money at all). It seems that artistic freedom and authorial control would be the last words to come to mind when we take a closer look at these working conditions; still, some of Ulmer's admirers tend to interpret them exactly that way. In an obituary published in 1972, Myron Meisel writes:

> What is little understood about the Ulmer of the 1940s and 1950s ... is that he did not make these films as a hack director on salary, on commissioned assignments. Ulmer *chose* to make these films, frequently serving as his own producer when the ubiquitous Leon Fromkess of PRC was elsewhere. Ulmer employed absurd scripts and monotonal acting to reach the kind of controlled expression he felt compelled to create [Meisel 149].

If the auteur theory as it has been rendered (or devised) by Andrew Sarris proposes that the Hollywood studio system imposed potentially beneficial constraints on its directors, then Meisel's obituary indicates that Ulmer, way down the line in the ranking of studios and studio people, was not only one of those film makers for whom constraints worked well but one who *made them work* in the sense that he sought them actively — and who even preferred them at their most difficult and unattractive. Some remarks in the Ulmer/Bogdanovich interview point into the same direction, and like Meisel's, they appear as a somewhat radicalized and even exaggerated version of the *auteur* concept, to say the least. On the other hand, it is certainly too simplistic to regard Ulmer's attempts to cast himself in the (changing, interacting) roles of author, artist, scholar as downright compensatory or as an effort to disguise his lack of success. What we encounter here is a rather stubborn conceptualization of filmmaking as artistic, intellectual work. And although this conceptualization is essentially conservative there is still something very intriguing about the eclectic and erratic way in which it was defended.

Signature

The concept of signature is, of course, closely connected to that of authorship. In Ulmer's work signature presents itself not so much as the imprint of one authorial figure but rather as a constellation of signatures, i.e., influences that have left their mark on the films. Generally speaking, an Ulmer film does not only bear the mark of Ulmer, the director, but quite a few others as well.

One of these other signatures could be called the signature of circumstances, i.e., the fact that the very difficult conditions under which many of Ulmer's films were made, literally inscribe themselves into certain scenes. A prime example of such an inscription is the breakfast scene with the passing cars from *Daughter of Dr. Jekyll*. This scene, we have been told, was shot in a garage or a run-down studio near the Sunset Strip in Los Angeles. As a result of this, the window in front of which the breakfast table is placed clearly shows a number of passing cars on the street, while the action of *Daughter of Dr. Jekyll* is supposed to take place in a not-too-clearly-defined late Nineteenth Century setting, Victorian mansion, countryside, and a family vault included. Apparently, the film was made in too much haste to notice that the action *behind* the window had found its way into the film as well, and if Ulmer discovered it later, the budget did not allow him to re-shoot the scene at the studio or at a different (and more appropriate) location.

If this is one case of circumstances not only leaving their mark but also actually introducing themselves into the film, others are not too difficult to find. To point out just a few would include the extremely diverse styles of acting and non-acting which are brought together in *The Cavern*, the blank (i.e., undecorated) walls in front of which Ulmer often placed his actors/characters, or the rather surprising change of scenery and climate which Ekkehard Knörer has described for some episodes in the Ulmer *noir Murder Is My Beat*.[7] While in some cases, including that of the breakfast scene in *Daughter of Dr. Jekyll*, these scenes may be regarded as an example of the circumstances working *against* the director, the concept of opposing forces seems less plausible in others. In the films of Edgar G. Ulmer, the circumstances quite often produce effects that turn into a specific quality, and even into something approaching a signature trait. (This may apply to the blank walls that appear in so many films, or to Ulmer's insistent and very straightforward use of rear-screen projection.) In a very literal sense, these films can be called products of circumstances just as much as they can be called products of Ulmer's. And, again, this affects our notion of authorship because what are we to make of circumstances which acquire authorial force?

Other, more sociological, examples of competing signatures are Ulmer's ethnic and educational pictures. Both would be excellent material for any scholar of social anthropology or cultural studies because of the many parties and agendas that were involved in the making of these movies. Take, for example, the Yiddish films made between 1937–1939 (*Grine Felder, The Singing Blacksmith, Let My People Live,* and *The Light Ahead*). Among the forces and actors that played a role in their production you will find: an immigrant community which was not so much a community but a number of groups of very different people who probably did not share much more than their religious beliefs (and sometimes not even these as they may have differed on questions of religious practice and orthodoxy); the representatives of this immigrant community who acted as commissioners of the films; the sponsors, sometimes from the community, sometimes with a different background; the owners of the film theaters where the pictures where shown; the film director Edgar G. Ulmer; other directors who were hired before Ulmer but later replaced by him; film people from the West coast; theater people from the East coast; professional actors, amateur actors, etc. All in all, this makes for a rather breathtaking scenario.[8] It also gives us an idea that sometimes the production of an Ulmer film may have been more interesting than the film itself, and that the films are also interesting insofar as they bear the imprints and traces of various agendas that were active in their production.

The Body of Work

As with so many marginalized filmmakers, much of the early research on Ulmer has been dedicated not to the study but to the recovery and restoration of his work: an effort which has been essential (and quite simply indispensable) to facilitate any subsequent study. However, we cannot help noticing that there exists a certain tension between the effort to restore the work as a whole and the tendency to look at a very limited number of very short clips whenever the value or the interesting aspects of Ulmer's films are discussed.

We are thus dealing with two different tendencies. The first is the effort to work towards restoration, towards completion, against the fragmentary, against the limitation of dealing with remnants, i.e., bits and pieces of discarded film. (The filmmaker Michael Palm, in his documentary on Ulmer, has linked this tendency to the concept of resurrection — a resurrection and reanimation of the body of work.) The second tendency takes us towards fragmentation, towards a fetishist attitude, towards the cutout, the framing of a single shot or scene. In our dealings with of Ulmer, these two tendencies coexist, and I would like to suggest that they coexist necessarily, because they depend on each other: one enforces and legitimizes the other.[9]

One thing that can be said about the fragmenting, fetishist approach is, of course, that it is by no means restricted to the evaluation of Ulmer's work. Herbert Schwaab and Ekkehard Knörer have both described it as essentially cinephile.[10] As a practice, it is also essentially academic. To show just one or two short clips or a few stills is what you usually do when you lecture on a film. We are dealing here with a specific form — the film scholar's equivalent, so to speak — of quotation.

The specific about Ulmer, however, is that his work seems to facilitate and to justify this approach far more than that of many other filmmakers. This is only partly due to the fact that much of this work is not exactly A-class filmmaking. It also has a lot to do with the particular disconnectedness between the scenes and the rest of the work. As it has frequently been described, we find, in many Ulmer films, one scene (sometimes two or three) that stands disconnected from the rest of the picture, or a shot that seems to come out of nowhere, or several scenes that do not really come together, etc.

This brings to mind Knöerer's idea of a best of DVD of Ulmer clips. It would be easy to fabricate such a DVD, because in a sense practically all of the films present themselves as pre-fragmented. And I think we would all agree that such a DVD could give the impression of a brilliant filmmaker, unjustly forgotten, and of a great *œuvre* which merited every effort to restore it. What the DVD would not show, of course, are the hours and hours of middle-brow filmmaking which Ekkehard Knörer has so aptly described in terms of the not-quite (not quite convincing, not quite successful, not quite coherent, not quite plausible, etc.).

We are such left with the question of the relation between the scenes which we all know so well and which we have been shown so very often, plus a film like *Detour*, so short that it could almost be compared to the structure of the clip, and the vast territory of rather bleak storytelling and image-making by which they are surrounded. (This brings to mind Andrew Sarris' formula concerning the appreciation of B pictures: "good moments in bad films" ("Beatitude" 50). If Ulmer's are not necessarily bad, they are, for the most part, still far from being good.) We should keep this question in mind for future discussions of his work. And we should oppose any attempt to establish these clips as those parts of Ulmer's work in which we finally confront the true genius of the filmmaker. What will certainly not work for Edgar G. Ulmer is the standard idea of the talented director hemmed in by harsh working conditions and sometimes triumphing over the difficult circumstances.[11] On the contrary, Ulmer's films may be most interesting when the workings of the filmmaker and that of the circumstances come together, and to ignore this seems to me the one approach that would *not* do them justice.

Notes

1. Much-quoted largely because, as Bogdanovich remarks, the three interviews he conducted with Ulmer in 1970 and 1972 "seem to be the only ones of any length that have survived" (Bogdanovich 542). This, of course, presupposes that there *were* a number of other interviews and other interviewers, which, given the not too successful development of Ulmer's career, is a rather bold assumption. The only one I know of is Ulmer's "Entretien" (Moullet and Tavernier).

2. See also (Nau 122).

3. The same claim is then extended to other well-known films of the 1920s, for example to the early Garbo pictures *Gösta Berlings Saga* by Mauritz Stiller (1924) or *Die Freudlose Gasse* by W.G. Pabst (1925), and later to Erich von Strohheim's *Merry-Go-Round* (1923), Ernst Lubitsch's *Lady Windermere's Fan* (1925) or Cecil B. DeMille's *King of Kings* (1927) on which Ulmer, according to his own statements, collaborated either as a production designer or art director. Most of these contributions are listed as "uncredited" in Ulmer's filmography at the Internet Movie Database. http://www.imdb.com/name/nm0880618, last accessed on April 10, 2008.

4. "It was very much of my Bauhaus period" (Bogdanovich 559).

5. For a different outlook on Ulmer and camp see Meisel. Meisel praises *The Black Cat* precisely for the film's achievement to "effectively neutralize the inherent camp tendencies of the horror genre" (Meisel 148).

6. "Ulmer worked on the lowest depths of Poverty Row, far beyond the pale of the B film onto the seventh circle of the Z picture, shooting his films in dingy studios on makeshift sets, on lightning-swift schedules" (Meisel 148).

7. See Ekkehard Knörer's essay in this volume.

8. One cannot help to be intrigued by Ulmer's own account (later revised and extended in the biography by Stefan Grissemann) of his work on *Natalka Poltavka* (1937), made on commission from the Ukrainian community in the United States. It seems that the community was at that time largely represented by the New York branch of the Window Washers Union (the window washers being mostly Ukrain-

ian) while the film project's main manager and representative was a dancer called Vasily Avramenkov. Add to this a Russian film director, formerly connected with the Moscow Arts Theatre, a university professor from New Jersey who acted as adviser on Ukrainian history, more window washers, representatives from the Greek Orthodox Clergy, a Ukrainian group from the Finnish Carpenters Union who built the set, Russian singers form the Metropolitan opera, Ukrainian folk dance groups from all over the U.S. and Canada, Ulmer who first acted as a production designer and later replaced the Russian director, plus a hurricane, a broken projector and a competing film project by the Russian firm "Tsofkino" in New York, and cannot help wondering what a wonderful story/script/film could be based on the making of *Natalka Poltavka*, itself one of Ulmer's less interesting films.

9. Two different but related tendencies are described by Andrew Sarris in a text about B pictures first published in 1974: "There are at least two ways of looking fondly at any given B picture. One is the way of the trivia hound, and the other is the way of the treasure hunter. Whereas the trivia hound loves all B pictures simply because they are B picture, the treasure hunter loves only certain B pictures because they have somehow overcome the onus of having started out as B pictures. Thus, the trivia hound tends to be encyclopaedic, and the treasure hunter tends to be selective" ("Beatitudes" 49).

10. See Schwaab and Knörer's essays in this volume. Compare Roland Barthes' remarks about the theft of the Odessa staircase scene from a copy of *Battleship Potemkin*.

11. This describes more or less Bogdanovich's approach which is expressed in his introductory remark on Ulmer's work: "a miracle against heavy odds" (Bogdanovich 541). A similar approach is to be found in Meisel's obituary that closes with the remark that "Ulmer had chosen the most impossible of terms and had functioned as a true artist. To disregard Ulmer is to miss the affecting experience of the triumph of the essential over the impossible" (Meisel 152).

Works Cited

Barthes, Roland. "The Third Meaning." *Image—Music—Text*. Trans. Stephen Heath. New York: Hill and Wang, 1977, 52–68.

Bogdanovich, Peter. "Edgar G. Ulmer." *Who the Devil Made It? Conversations with Film Makers*, New York: Alfred A. Knopf, 1999, 541–85.

Horwath, Alexander. "Das Shining: *Strange Illusion* von Edgar G. Ulmer." Christian Cargnelli, Michael Omasta (eds.). *Schatten. Exil. Europäische Emigranten im Film noir*. Vienna: PVS, 1997, 296–309.

Meisel, Myron. "Edgar G. Ulmer: The Primacy of the Visual." Todd McCarthy and Charles Flynn. (eds.) *Kings of the B's: Working within the Hollywood System: An Anthology of Film History and Criticism*. New York: E.P. Dutton, 1975, 147–52.

Moullet, Luc, and Bertrand Tavernier. "Entretien avec Edgar G. Ulmer." *Cahiers du Cinéma* 122 (January 1961): 1–16.

Nau, Peter. "Das Geheimnis der Form in den Filmen Edgar G. Ulmers." *Aufbruch in Ungewisse: Österreichische Filmschaffende in der Emigration vor 1945*. Eds. Christian Cargnelli, Michael Omasta. Vienna: Wespennest-Film, 1993, 117–31.

Sarris, Andrew. "Beatitudes of B Pictures." Todd McCarthy and Charles Flynn. (eds.)

Kings of the B's: Working within the Hollywood System: An Anthology of Film History and Criticism. New York: E.P. Dutton, 1975, 48–53.

_____. "Notes on the Auteur Theory in 1962." Gerald Mast and Marshall Cohen (eds.). *Film Theory and Criticism.* Oxford: Oxford University Press, 2004, 650–65.

The Naked Dawn: Production, Sources, and *Mise-en-Scène*

BILL KROHN

Production

Much of the research for this article was done in the archives on *The Naked Dawn* at the University of Southern California's Universal Collection. Because the film was an independent production which Universal distributed, the studio documents only concern the marketing. The file also contains two identical scripts. One has the title *The Bandit* and the name of the original producer, Josef Shaftel, on its title page; the other, which had the name *The Naked Dawn* slapped on at the last minute, is Shirley Ulmer's copy of the script.

Shirley Ulmer was the script supervisor on almost all of her husband's films, and the script at USC is the so-called lined script which she annotated during production and turned over to the editor. The numbered lines drawn on the script pages are shorthand for shots, indicating where they start and end. Facing them on the backs of pages are notations about how many takes were done of each shot and the qualities of each. The horizontal black and white type on each page is the script. The multicolored vertical lines are shorthand for Ulmer's direction of it. The graph they form is the film, but only if we complete the metaphor by adding the crucial third dimension — the actors, about whom Ulmer made some interesting remarks in an interview with the *Cahiers du Cinéma* conducted by Bertrand Tavernier and Luc Moullet.

With no production files to guide us, other aspects of the making of *The Naked Dawn* are murky. Arianné Ulmer Cipes says that the original producer, Josef Shaftel, couldn't get the picture financed, so it was sold to another producer, James Radford, who made it after signing a negative pickup deal with

Universal. This meant that it ended up being released, ironically, by the studio that blacklisted Ulmer in the '30s. But Radford is as much a phantom as the screenwriters, Nina and Herman Schneider, and his only credit is associate producer.

Some care was devoted to developing two ad campaigns, one to sell the film as a straight western, and one to sell it as a love story with an action background. Much thought was given to renaming the film, which for a while was called *I Love a Stranger*. Some of the titles proposed were *The Bandit Affair, The Peso and the Gun, Sombre Interlude, Violence Below the Border, A Man Named Trouble, The Root of All Evil, Gunmen Are Doomed, Gunmen Have No Future, Gunmen Have Two Hands, Lust, The Farmer's Wife, A Bed of Her Own, No Bed of His Own* and *Never Trust a Stranger*. As the date with the lab drew near, two titles appeared on separate lists—*In the Naked Dawn* and *Ride the Naked Dawn*—and after the title we know was extracted from them, both authors were rewarded with checks for $25.

Universal had been planning to open the picture in Los Angeles on the bottom half of a double bill with a Tony Curtis costume picture, but Universal sales manager and vice president Charles Feldman told them to open it in Philadelphia, where it could play top half. "Only then," he wrote, "will we be satisfied that we have given the picture a chance." It opened in Philadelphia on Halloween 1955 and made $3,188 its first week, but did poorly in other cities. Eventually only half its projected $25,000 promotional budget was spent, and it played Los Angeles on the bottom half of a double bill with *Lady Godiva*.

But there was one more twist of fate ahead. A Spanish picture picked for the Venice Film Festival wasn't going to make it because the subtitles weren't going to be done on time. The head of Universal's distribution for Italy, who liked the picture, proposed it as a "Spanish" picture that didn't need subtitles, and it was accepted. When it subsequently opened in Paris, Francois Truffaut and Jean Domarchi wrote about it for *Arts* and *Cahiers du Cinéma*.

Whatever the other details of the production may have been, Ulmer appears to have enjoyed considerable freedom on this project. For example, the score is by Herschel Burke Gilbert, who in the late Forties had composed scores for films produced by PRC and its subsequent incarnation, Eagle Lion. Did his path and Ulmer's cross on this picture by chance? We can only guess, but Burke's score for *The Naked Dawn* is very good and very Ulmerian — that is to say, unconventional in a way that recalls the conventions of another musical art, opera. Did Ulmer have any control during post-production? Again, we don't know, so let's turn to the areas where some light can be shed on this mysterious film, after first posing one question: Who is the hero of this story?

Sources

The script for *The Naked Dawn* was written by a blacklisted writer named Julian Zimet living in Mexico. Zimet used his sister and brother-in-law as fronts so that it could be sold to Josef Shaftel, a producer of low-budget films, for $5000—"no questions asked." Zimet reports in an interview published in Patrick MacGilligan and Peter Buhle's collection of interviews with blacklisted screenwriters that he and his lifelong friend Bernard Gordon started developing the idea in Hollywood before they both fled the blacklist. Ulmer, who was presumably brought in by Shaftel when he still owned the property, never met Zimet and probably didn't know who "Nina and Herman Schneider" were.

Zimet's original idea for the script came from the first published short story by Maxim Gorky, "Chelkash." There are basically only two characters in "Chelkash"—a tramp who lives by stealing, and Gavrilla, a peasant who has been doing farm work in the south to earn money to buy a farm, and has now come to the city on the way back to his village, empty-handed. Because Chelkash's usual partner in crime is indisposed, he enlists Gavrilla to help him pull a job. After the robbery they quarrel and Gavrilla almost kills Chelkash. Chelkash contemptuously gives him all the money, and they part: "Not a sign was left on the deserted shore," Gorky concludes, "to testify to the little drama enacted here between these two men."

Once settled in Mexico, Zimet revived the project, setting it in his adopted country and making Chelkash the ex-revolutionary Santiago, and Gavrilla a full-blooded Indian peasant named Manuel, who already has a little farm. Instead of involving Manuel in a robbery, Santiago pays him 50 pesos for the use of his truck to deliver the goods to an untrustworthy fence, thus putting Manuel on the wrong side of the law and tempting him with the prospect of money. Manuel needs money to build a well and make other improvements to his farm, which he has to irrigate with water from a distant spring. Zimet also gave Manuel a wife who hates him, Maria, and made the story a triangle in which Santiago vacillates between wanting Maria and wanting to make Manuel his surrogate son, because he sees in him the young man he once was, before he joined the Revolution in hopes of getting his own piece of land.

Originally Zimet had intended to call the script *Tierra*, which would have put the focus on economics, but he changed it to *The Bandit* after writing it as a character study of an embittered revolutionary not unlike himself. Before being blacklisted, he had been booted out of the Party for being in analysis, and he told MacGilligan that his seven years in Mexico taught him "to value feeling above all." All of this went into his creation of Santiago, but in most respects Zimet stuck close to Gorky's character and the dynamics of the relationship between the two men. It is doubtful that Ulmer, when he was handed the script for *The Bandit*, knew that it was based on Gorky, but like Zimet, who imposed a sentimental Freudian interpretation on the story, he was faced with the task of interpreting characters who had essentially stepped out of Gorky's pages, and his interpretation differed from the screenwriter's.

The other inspiration for *The Naked Dawn* is four key films of Ulmer's mentor Murnau in which a couple are threatened by a sinister figure—Nosferatu, Tartuffe, the father in *City Girl*, the priest in *Tabu*—who destroys their couple, or tries to. Zimet's script, when presented to Ulmer, would have been likelier to evoke this mythic template in Ulmer's mind than anything out of Freud, and in other Ulmer films — *The Black Cat, Moon Over Harlem, Strange Illusion, Daughter of Dr. Jekyll* — evil nosferatus do try to break up couples, and always fail. Santiago, moreover, is enough of a nosferatu to fit the template, because of the peculiar history of the story that inspired the script.

When Gorky wrote "Chelkash" he was not yet a revolutionary, he hated the Russian peasantry for their backwardness and greed, and he was under the influence of Nietzsche, whose ideas he may have been embodied in Chelkash. But he subsequently revised the story several times, and his political evolution would have required him to turn it into a critique of his Nietzschean tramp. In a famous letter to a colleague in 1910 he wrote:

> I love people who are active and vigorous, who value and adorn life, even if only a little, by a small something, if only by the dream of a better life. In general, the Russian tramp is a character more terrible than I succeeded in saying; this man is terrible first and foremost in his implacable despair and in the fact that he negates himself, expels himself from life.

So even if Chelkash was Zarathustra incarnate when he first burst upon the Russian literary scene, in the only version of the story that has been translated into English — the one that Zimet and Gordon would have known — he is guilty of the nihilism Gorky later ascribed to all the tramp characters in his early fiction. In fact, a Nietzschean reading of "Chelkash" is still possible, even after Gorky made Chelkash the villain — one that would make the struggle between the two men an expression not of contrasting attitudes toward money, but of each man's will to power: Chelkash lords it over the country bumpkin, getting him drunk for no good reason before the robbery and enjoying his terror during the commission of it, while Gavrilla struggles blindly to preserve his dignity, finally striking out against his oppressor and nearly killing him.

When Julian Zimet turned Chelkash into Santiago, he gave him a motive to explain his irrational actions — the yearning for a son — but he kept the dynamic of the strange alliance in Gorky's story, to which Maria is more or less irrelevant. She says so in the kitchen scene: All Santiago cares about is protecting Manuel. Even when Santiago's anger at Manuel's treachery pushes him to take her with him when he leaves, the prose in Zimet's script repeats what Maria has said. As Maria and Santiago ride away, "Santiago's face is grim, as if he would rather have had Manuel shoot him than do this.... He looks at her as if he wished there were some way out other than this. But he is committed." In the scene as filmed none of these regrets is even hinted at by Arthur Kennedy's performance.

Mise-en-Scène

When the growing reputation of *The Naked Dawn* sent Pierre Rissient and later Patrick MacGilligan in search of Julian Zimet, he told them that Ulmer had changed nothing in his script — a statement that expressed his rare pleasure at this, as a writer accustomed to massive tinkering by the studios, and an implicit gripe — not unwarranted — about Ulmer getting all the credit. For in fact, only small changes were made during production, with two big exceptions.

One very small example first: After collecting his money from Guntz, the fence, Santiago buys tacos for himself and Manuel, tips the taco lady ten pesos and gives her another ten to buy tacos for the railroad watchman, who is sporting a bandage where Santiago socked him in the head the night before. The moment is played for humor, but Santiago is being surprisingly generous to the man who killed his best friend. Later, when Guntz arrives at Manuel's farm to take vengeance, he sees Manuel's truck and tells his henchman, "That's the one the taco lady described." The detail may have been added to explain how Guntz found Manuel, but it certainly undercuts the warmth of the scene with the old taco lady, and her final wish that "God will bless" her generous customer, thereby adding an extra touch to the portrait the film paints of a harsh world where it would seem that no good deed ever goes unpunished.

Reverence for the script was unusual for Ulmer, simply because he was so often handed bad material that he had to either rewrite it or work around it, whereas Zimet's script for *The Bandit* was very good: In addition, Ulmer knew what studios expected. "When you work for a studio," he told the *Cahiers*, "you had better shoot what is in the script." Accordingly, the fact that Shirley Ulmer's numbered lines all seem to reflect the numbered scenes in the script should not blind us to the fact that Ulmer was constantly rewriting with his camera.

The biggest example of this, which Zimet commented on to Tavernier, is Tita's musical number in the cantina. This striking sequence, which blossomed from two brief shot descriptions in the script — one where she sings, and one where she "is selling her number with a little dance step." Of course the producer knew what Ulmer was doing — he may even have insisted on it. What is interesting is how, even here, the director allowed the script to suggest the structure of the number — one long master for the song, and another for the dance.

The same binary rhythm is imposed on the script in Ulmer's rendition of Zimet's extraordinary scene between Maria and Santiago in the kitchen. Although Zimet often indicates montage effects, here he frames this very long scene — scene 183 — as a single medium shot, leaving the blocking up to the director, as screenwriters often do in dialogue scenes. Legend has it that Ulmer actually shot a 9½ minute take that the studio forced him to cut into, and in the *Cahiers* interview he supports this notion, which many people believe to this day. Elsewhere in the same interview, when Ulmer wasn't being allowing himself to be drafted into the religion of the long take, he made his esthetic position clear: While color and Scope have made long takes more fashionable, he says, montage "has not only a practical advantage, but an artistic one: You can impart a visual rhythm to the film which isn't possible with the famous 'Ten Minute Take.' A long take is still theatre, even if the camera is moving."

Accordingly, in the kitchen scene Ulmer shot two "masters" (the script supervisor's notation) which were designed to be linked by a shot-reverse shot of Maria and Santiago when, appropriately enough, he describes the way eyes speak in Vera Cruz, and she responds by asking him to take her with him. Then he filmed "drop-in close-ups" (Shirley's notation again) of Santiago reclining on the steps that divide the kitchen from the bedroom, to serve as punctuation for the second long take, which ends when Santiago flees. The first long take is Santiago's aria — only one take was needed for Kennedy. The second, which took three, is Maria's.

This binary structure shows that Ulmer had not forgotten the lessons of Murnau, as summed up by Jacques Ranciere in an essay on *Tartuffe*: "To say the opposite of what one shot says, you need another shot that completes and reverses what the first one began." The same principles of *mise-en-scène* structure all the sudden reversals in the film, like the one near the end which Jean Domarchi described in his *Cahiers* review, the scene when Manuel impulsively confesses that he planned to kill Santiago: "If Santiago rejects him it is because he has had the brusque revelation of a cowardly, greedy soul at the very moment when it is another Manuel who is speaking to him," Domarchi writes.

"One of the film's merits is to make this turnabout, which will be followed by others, perfectly plausible. Murnau's *Sunrise* had already accustomed us to such turnabouts.... The genius of Dostoevsky is to have shown these brusque mutations of conscience.... On the formal level, they require the author (novelist or filmmaker) to pass from tragic to comic and back. This was the talent Dostoevsky and Murnau possessed in the highest degree, and Ulmer is no slouch in this regard — quite the contrary."

The scene where Manuel confesses and Santiago almost kills him, which comes right out of Gorky, is typical of the dramaturgy of the story, even after Zimet tried to rationalize it into what filmmakers today call "the curve of the character" with Freudian psychology. Rejecting that interpretation, Ulmer simply filmed these sudden reversals without any explanation, as Gorky first described them, but each scene of this kind required the full arsenal of rhythmic techniques to realize its potential, which would have been spoiled by the writer's often corny ideas of *mise-en-scène*.

The dramatic texture of the film also evolved based on Ulmer's work with the actors. Contrasting himself to Murnau, the "super-technician," Ulmer told the *Cahiers*: "I have one big fault: I fall in love with a character or a situation, and I improvise from that. In *The Bandit* I fell in love with the young man. We had no hope for him until he arrived on the set — I didn't think he could play the part. But suddenly he woke up, and Kennedy gave him a hand."

Eugene Iglesias' performance is not only comic — he has as big a range of emotions to play as Kennedy — but the comic side of Manuel's personality continually shifts the film from somber to gay, when he faints during the hanging of Guntz, for example, or when he hurriedly takes the 50 pesos after Santiago becomes furious because he has claimed to be a respectable man — Burke even underlines the shift with a few bars of comic music. In the cantina, Manuel takes the money Santiago offers soberly and thanks him. At this point Zimet wanted him to cry, seeing which Santiago would be "deeply moved," while the soundtrack would have evoked "the music theme of Santiago's childhood," before revolting against his own emotions and throwing himself into a dance with Tita. But in the film the mariachi band just starts playing a waltz, and Santiago revolts against *that*: "Who are we burying?" he grouses, downing his drink, and challenges Tita to a flamenco dance.

Here is Zimet's prose description of the scene where Santiago dances with Tita — played by the fabulous Charlita:

> There is a wild, defiant spirit loose in Santiago now. He is defying age and loneliness, desperately asserting his pride in his vigor and courage; above all denying the once buried longing for another way of life that has made him identify with Manuel as a son.... Tita senses his spirit. Though young, the

odds on her own survival are so slim that she, too, can be reckless with defiance, and the two of them, thief and whore, do their dance as if spitting in the face of death.

This is the most elaborately lit and edited sequence in the film — shots of feet, and shots of feet framed by other feet (repeated from details in other parts of Zimet's script) — pink lights, yellow lights, fast cutting, pounding boot heels on the soundtrack. The idea of death is nowhere reflected in the expressions of the dancers, in their movements, or in the *mise-en-scène*, and Manuel's delighted and increasingly drunken reactions are there to ensure that we react accordingly.

Ulmer added that he was able to improve the next-to-last scene because Iglesias was so good. The script would have sent the shattered farmer, as his wife rides away, back to the hut, where he would have caressed Santiago's sombrero and drawn strength from it. Seeing his burro in the cornfield he would have run out just in time to be caught by Guntz, who would have set fire to both house and field before attempting to hang the owner. But whereas Hitchcock could spend $5200 ($200 more than Zimet got for his script!) planting a whole cornfield for *North by Northwest*, Ulmer had only a few stalks of the stuff to stick in the ground and wasn't about to burn down the hut, which was probably part of the Universal ranch. Economies aside, the larger effect of the improvisation is to shift the focus, as Zimet himself had done when he changed the title, from the land to the characters, and their endless capacity for surprising us.

Viewed in this way, it is easier to understand Truffaut's famous remark that *The Naked Dawn* showed him it would be possible to film a certain novel called *Jules and Jim*. He was thinking not just of the triangle, which bears little resemblance to the one in *Jules and Jim*, but rather of the endless series of sudden irrational turnabouts that structure the plot of the novel and the film he eventually made of it, embodied in the capricious figure of Jeanne Moreau's Catherine.

The reigning deity of *The Naked Dawn*, however, is Maria: Bored and miserable, she is toying with a minnow when Santiago finds her by the spring where she has gone to gather water, as if she hoped to catch a fish with it. When Santiago follows her home, she realizes she has caught a big one. The famous bath scene is part of her purposeful preparations to persuade him to take her away with him, and her sudden demand is premeditated: "I don't care where you take me," she says when he berates himself for painting romantic pictures of Vera Cruz. "I was ready before, waiting for you." The script says that she indicates her dress when she says this line, but in the film she just says it, meaning perhaps that she was waiting for him before he ever rode into view.

After this scene she will control the cascade of events, first pleading with Santiago to spare Manuel so that she can feel free to leave with him, then leaving her husband with a curt "adios" (Ulmer cut all the niceties: "I hope it will go well for you.... Too much has been said.... Perhaps you can be happy with another.") After the shootout with Guntz she chooses Manuel because he has shown he can change by refusing the money, because Santiago wants her to choose him, and because she knows that Santiago is dying. She is anything but capricious, however — that quality is symbolized by Tita, and by the contrast between Maria's hut (the crucifix in the wall) and Tita's cantina (the bullfight fresco, which supplies the metaphor for Santiago's dance with her). Maria is purposeful, all-seeing and inflexibly moral, like destiny, and like destiny, she has been waiting for Santiago for a long time.

When Ulmer told Moullet and Tavernier that he liked sudden reversals, he was defending the film's ending, which legend ("printed" by Ulmer in that interview) says Universal imposed. What really happened is more interesting. "Manuel is the real hero," Ulmer told his interviewers, "Of course, Kennedy tries to revolt to preserve his moral integrity, but his revolt comes from an egocentric vision of the world, and he uses the money he steals only for pleasure, not to change a world living under oppression. Manuel, however, will discover true happiness, and do more good in the world than the bandit." The moral of the film, he says, is: "If you refuse the few acres of land you're entitled to and take justice into your own hands by stealing, you will automatically end up leaning against a tree trunk while your life drains away....' Kennedy passes judgement on himself and does so with great severity."

So Santiago does become the nosferatu after all at the end, and Manuel and Maria ride away to an uncertain future on one horse, having refused the money he offered them. Manuel's final address to him as "padre" is moving and doubly appropriate, but it doesn't sum up the meaning of Santiago's life, as the script would have it. Zimet had written an ending where the couple, after days of riding, would look down from a high bluff at the seashore and a beautiful new land waiting for them below. Apparently Ulmer filmed this shot, but he also filmed Santiago's point of view on them riding away twice, with "two lights" (noted the script supervisor): the daylight we see in the farewell scene, and the golden light known to filmmakers as Magic Hour, when the sun is about to go down. Then he — or someone else who knew the ending of Fritz Lang's *You Only Live Once* very well — looped Santiago's speech ending with the line, "Vicente, here is your land," over the closeup of Santiago dying, and cut from it to the golden shot of the couple about to ride over the hill, to a burst of gay mariachi music and cries of joy.

Works Cited

Barret, Andrew. "'Chelkash:' Games Tramps Play," in *The Early Fiction of Maxim Gorky: Six Essays in Interpretation*. Nottingham: Astra, 1993.

Domarchi, Jean. "Un nouveau romantisme." *Cahiers du Cinéma* 58 avril 1956.

McGilligan, Patrick, and Paul Buhle (ed.). *Tender Comrades: The Backstory of the Hollywood Blacklist*. New York: St. Martin's, 1997.

Moullet, Luc, and Bertrand Tavernier. "Enteretien avec Edgar G. Ulmer." *Cahiers du Cinéma* 122, août 1961.

Rancière, Jacques. "Tartuffe muet," in *La fable cinematographique*. Paris: Editions du Seuil, 2001.

Truffaut, François. *The Naked Dawn*, Arts 559, 1956, reprinted in *Les films de ma vie*. Paris: Flammarion, 1975.

The Effects of the Displacement of Home in *Daughter of Dr. Jekyll*

Michal Peprník

Displacement

Edgar G. Ulmer displaced his birthplace so successfully that until recently he was believed to be born in Vienna. Although Bernd Herzogenrath, who provided clear evidence that Ulmer was born in Olomouc, has already clarified the probable reasons for this displacement (Herzogenrath), the consequences on Ulmer's film art still deserve a close examination.

The theoretical framework for the process of displacement was provided by another Moravian native, Sigmund Freud, who was born some 50 km northeast of the city of Olomouc. Freud presented one of the most famous formulations of this process in his paper "The 'Uncanny'" ("Das Unheimliche," 1919), published in the time when young Ulmer was in Vienna. Freud in his linguistic analysis of the meaning of the word discloses several fields of denotations and links them with specific processes: in the first meaning it refers to the process of defamiliarization, in which the familiar and agreeable is transformed (metamorphosed) into its opposite, the unfamiliar and disagreeable. In the second meaning of the word, with reference to Schelling, the uncanny is defined as that which "ought to have remained secret and hidden but has come to light" (Freud 345). The process by which the hidden contents come to light can be called *disclosure*. Another source of the power of the uncanny springs from an unexpected repetition or *recursive pattern*. In psychoanalytical theory it is believed that what is repressed, returns with a vengeance, its force increased for all the accumulated energy.

Freud also explored another path to the understanding of the concept of the uncanny, a linguistic analysis. Drawing on Grimms' dictionary, Freud specified the meaning of the "heimlich" as free from fears, and what is particularly important for our purposes, "a place free from ghostly influences." If a heimlich place is free from ghosts, then an unheimlich place, being its opposite is in fact the place with ghostly influences, in other words, a haunted place, a meaning which it acquires in several languages, as Freud argues.[1] With the concept of haunted place we have driven home, home to the haunted place of Ulmer's imagination, Ulmer's birthplace Olomouc, repressed and displaced, and replaced in a public gesture by insisting on Vienna, as his place of origin. Like a true immigrant, he decided to reinvent himself and change his past. Even though he was not so far from truth because it was in Vienna where his career started, nevertheless one's imagination is formed from early experience, as Freud emphasized, so his deep roots are in Olomouc. But what is repressed is bound to come back in another form, Freud believed. In Ulmer's case it was the recursive motif of *the haunted house* or place.

Even though Arianné Ulmer Cipes claimed during the Ulmerfest in Olomouc (2006) that within his family he did not hide the truth and talked about Olomouc in positive terms as a beautiful and cultural town, the public displacement of Olomouc was almost too effective and suggests some sort of discontent.[2] Bernd Herzogenrath explains that Ulmer saw himself as "a representative of European High Culture and that he almost 'naturally' felt the urge to repress provinciality." This is true to some extent, the presence of the archbishop and his cannons (officials) encouraged the practice of classical music, a habit adopted by the burgers as well. According to *Leitmetzer's Olomouc chronicle,* from 1778 to 1829 there were often two concerts in a single week. The theatre was also much attended. However, compared to Vienna, the social and cultural life in Olomouc must have had a provincial character.

In spite of its provincial air, Olomouc does not miss a very distinctive spirit of place, its power stems less from people one could meet here, but more from the almost magic configuration of the place. It has been inhabited for at least 4,000 years. Its late Renaissance and Baroque architecture, engrafted upon the medieval layout, must have left a deep impact on Ulmer's imagination. The historical center of the old town still maintains its medieval layout, and as Bernd Herzogenrath pointed out, the crooked lanes, bad light, uneven cobblestones, houses that slant inside and seem to be very slowly falling out, are reminiscent of expressionist aesthetics (Herzogenrath). The impact of the city on child's imagination could be perceived in yet another perspective: the image of the town that is trying to break free from the confines of the city walls, expanding into the edges of a green void. The green void because child's known world is a small one and what is beyond, is hidden in a fog, which he liked to employ so often.

Transformation of Home

No matter how we justify Ulmer's public denial of his affiliation to Olomouc, the offence has been given, the spirit of the place needs rites of appeasement.

It is well known that among the strategies of dealing with abandoned homeland is nostalgic idealizing as well as demonizing. In the demonic transfiguration, the home can take the form of a haunted castle or haunted house. Haunted house is one of the favorite topoi in the gothic tradition. While in the Eighteenth Century gothic novel the haunted castle or house was used merely as a formal element of composition, in romantic literature the setting was exploited from a psychological perspective as symbolic construction — apart from being a melodramatic stage, it also operated as an external analogy for the internal states of mind, as it is often the case in E.A. Poe tales. In his films Ulmer followed on this romantic tradition in his artistically ambitious projects, *The Black Cat*, *Bluebeard*, or his less arty productions such as *Strange Illusion*, or *Daughter of Dr. Jekyll*. In these films we find variations on the haunted house motif. In *The Black Cat* a modernist house is literally engrafted upon the military fortress, in which thousands of soldiers died during the World War I. In *Bluebeard* the whole city of Paris is haunted by a sinister serial woman killer. In *Strange Illusion*, for the young protagonist, his *heimlich* home is transformed into an *unheimlich*, uncanny place, after he discovers his father was murdered and his murderer is taking his place. In *Daughter of Dr. Jekyll*, the young heroine, an orphan, coming back home after a long absence discovers the house is haunted by sinister past, by the dark legacy of her father Dr. Jekyll.

In all those places we can observe a similar pattern — a place familiar and safe becomes a place unfamiliar and dangerous. Even though such a transformation was no novelty in films of that period, yet its distinctive variant (the place does not have a sinister appearance at first sight, unlike the dilapidated houses and castles in gothic novels), homes turning into a sight of nightmare must have had a special and personal appeal to Ulmer and allowed him to play out his ambivalent relation to his birthplace. If the transformation or metamorphosis of the heimlich into the unheimlich is one track we will follow, we will also explore the return of the repressed in the strange case of *Daughter of Dr. Jekyll*.

The Haunted House in Daughter of Dr. Jekyll

Daughter of Dr. Jekyll (1957, script Jack Pollexfen),[3] a retake (see Eco 94) of R.L. Stevenson's famous mystery tale, *The Strange Case of Dr Jekyll and Mr*

Hyde (1886), is not generally regarded as a very good film. It is however an interesting example of the ways in which Ulmer, a perfectionist and fine film stylist, a man in love with both the high culture of the Old World and the popular culture of the New World, appreciative of the American democratic social and political climate, engaged the material tailored to the tastes and desires of the masses.

The topic is one of formulaic American stories: an innocent young American from the New World entrapped in the devious web of the Old World of England, a type of story immortalized by E.A. Poe in "The Fall of the House of Usher." This young brave American hero is George Hastings, fiancé of Janet Smith, who is to discover that she is a daughter of the notorious Dr. Jekyll. Janet Smith grew up in England but having left home a long time ago and acquiring an American fiancé, she has become Americanized to some degree. Nevertheless, the generic conventions of a sensational tale did not leave much space for exploration of the concept of the exile, as discussed by Noah Isenberg. Drawing on Edward Said, Isenberg argued that an exile is a

A lobby card for *Daughter of Dr. Jekyll* (courtesy Edgar G. Ulmer Preservation Corporation).

person, who still occupies two worlds, having a "plurality of vision" (Isenberg 3) and this plurality lends such a person a intensity of seeing, the power of contrast, because the past always interferes with the present. This is, however, less applicable to Janet Smith. First, she has come home, instead of arriving to a new world, where she would have to struggle make ends meet. Second, instead of double consciousness, she simply switches from one consciousness to another. And third, she does not seem to gain any privileged, more complex point of view. She is cast in the role of a hapless victim. After the revelation of her true origin (Dr. Jekyll's daughter), she allows herself to be trapped in this old (World) identity and the script does not offer any clash of identities.

Nevertheless Ulmer's film chooses another strategy for introducing plurality of choices. The plurality of vision is ontologically grounded. The film raises the classic romantic question, recycled in postmodernist works: in which world am I living, which of them is real or true? (see McHale 10).

To reach a better understanding of the ontological issues of the film narrative, a close analysis of the narrative structure is needed.[4] For a sensational movie, the film narrative has a surprisingly fine structure. The film narrative is framed by the brief opening and closing scene with a close-up on a hideously disfigured face with animal fangs. The opening frame makes the necessary intertextual allusion to Stevenson's story, recounted by the voice of the narrator.

The narrator's last hopeful words that "the evil will never prowl again" are undermined by the croaking words of the hideous monster, which slowly turns to a face close up: "Are you sure?" extended into a demoniac giggle. Stevenson's careful reader can notice two important changes in the structure of Stevenson's story: the transposition of the setting from an urban one to the countryside, and classification of Hyde as a werewolf.

The narrative opens with an extreme long shot of the English manor house enveloped in fog.[5] The architecture of the house works as a metaphor for the uneasy blend of the modern (a comfortable manor house), and the archaic (the medieval part with a Gothic round tower), or more exactly it gives the impression of a hybrid formation, where it is difficult to say whether the new is simply added to the archaic, and thus coexisting with it in a symbiotic relation, or whether the archaic is contained within the modern structure.

A track-*in* movement follows an arriving car, and the extreme long shot of the whole building comes down to a long shot detail of the modern part, dominated by nice and comforting round curves of an Art Nouveau door. This feels like what it is, coming home. The car has brought a young couple, Janet Smith and her American fiancé, George Hastings. Janet is coming home after a long absence to celebrate her twenty first birthday and to introduce her fiancé to her guardian, Dr. Lomas. From this sequence familiarizing and defamiliarizing sequences take turn, setting the rhythm, pace, and dramatic tension, conceived as a conflict between the country superstition and modern city rationality. The image of the comforting main entrance is contrasted with the image of the huge, rude, silent servant Jacob, who opens the door and looks like Frankenstein's monster. The monster's rude conduct is quickly compensated by the second character, which comes to meet the young couple, a housekeeper Mrs. Merchant, warm-hearted, friendly and caring.

Of key importance is naturally the master of the house, Janet's guardian, Dr. Lomas. Like the house itself, he is double, a part of him Gothic monster, another part modern and civilized. Although he is the villain, the film plot (*sujet*) effectively hides his shadow side for the most part of the film. From the very beginning Dr. Lomas offers the viewer all the reassuring signs of a kind uncle. His reasonable, rational and helpful conduct is in sharp contrast with country superstitions. He assumes the role of a generous, law-abiding guardian, as evident from his readiness to inform the young couple that he is not the owner of the estate but only the executor and because Janet reached the age of 21, she is now the sole inheritor of the whole property. But he has also a dark family secret to reveal the next morning, a revelation which definitely change Janet's familiar home into a place haunted by the ghosts of the evil past, reaching into the present.

Ulmer handles the revelation of the secret in a very effective manner. It happens offstage and we

Gloria Talbott stars as Janet Smith, the daughter of Dr. Jekyll (courtesy Edgar G. Ulmer Preservation Corporation).

are presented only the desperate Janet, who abruptly announces to her fiancé that wedding is now impossible. The degree of her frustration is a good indicator of the terrible secret, which we, the viewers, knowing the title of the film, suspect. Perhaps the secret is revealed too soon but its early revelation is in harmony with the simplicity of the structure. Since she agrees to share her secret with George, Dr. Lomas unveils the dark secret. Thus we learn (what we suspect) that her father was Dr. Jekyll, Dr. Lomas' friend, who having metamorphosed in the monster Hyde committed some unspeakable crimes and was not only "torn to pieces" by the angry villagers but also pierced with a spike because he was believed to be a werewolf. (Nothing of this sort is ever even hinted in Stevenson's novella because he tries to maintain the frame of science. In the novella Hyde/Jekyll commits suicide). Janet fears that her father's unspecified infliction may be hereditary. In Freud's words, she fears "involuntary repetition" (359) and the loss of control over her self, in other words a dissociation of the self, a split. When Dr. Lomas is asked for his view he at first says nicely that there is no evidence in support of such a possibility, and then, with well-measured pause, adds nicely but with an edge, there is also no evidence that it need not happen.

The revelation of the secret is again configured within the trope of the architecture of the house. There is no doubt that the film makers drew inspiration from E.A. Poe's tale "The Fall of the House of Usher," where he very effectively developed a number of parallels between the architecture of the house and the mind. The discovery of the secret chamber, a chemical laboratory obviously long out of use, by Janet's perceptive American fiancé, is an analogical anticipation of the hidden secret of Janet's true origin.

Understandably, after this awful disclosure of the displaced piece of her past Janet cannot fall asleep and her ever helpful uncle hypnotizes her with a candle flame. In the following, visually beautiful sequence the spirit of the girl leaves her bed. Her nasty expression leaves no doubts about her intentions as she walks lightly through the forest, accompanied by the sounds of eerie music, pursuing the unfortunate maid servant on her way home, and kills her. Then comes a cut, Janet wakes up screaming and finds bloody stains on her arms. The next news validates the scene — the maid was found dead in the forest.

We do not have to continue with the plot summary — it is enough to demonstrate that the familiar place has become unfamiliar, changed into a haunted place because an archaic formation, hidden and repressed, is coming to light. Now it becomes apparent that Janet's *heimlich* home has become *unheimlich* (uncanny) and what was hidden, has come to light.

And once again the architecture of the place provides useful analogies. All the major gothic topoi are interconnected, the house, the burial vault in the garden, and the forest. The room of the young couple has a secret door to the laboratory, from the laboratory leads a secret passageway to the burial vault in the garden. And from the vault one can reach the forest.

Recursivity, Ontological and Semantic Ambivalence

The uncanny has a disturbing, often frightening effect because anything that is repressed turns into a source of anxiety, no matter how familiar it once had been, and whether it was an object of fear or desire. One of the most important features of the uncanny is its recursive character, its unexpected repetitions, which deprive us of the sense of control over our mind and life.[6]

The uncanny is "something repressed, which recurs ... this uncanny is in reality nothing new or alien, but something which is familiar and old-established in the mind and such has become alienated from it only through the process of repression" (Freud 363–4). "The constant recurrence of the same thing" [can] involve "the repetition of the same features or character-traits or vicissitudes, of the same crimes"(356). And this is what is a real issue in the film narrative. Janet fears the repetitions of the crimes of her father, and in fact duplicates them, but fortunately only in her dreams. Dr. Lomas, however, duplicates Jekyll in real.

Freud also identified another important aspect of the uncanny apart from *recursivity* and *disclosure* of a familiar secret. This aspect is the *ontological* and *semantic ambivalence*— ontological because we hesitate to call it supernatural or natural, animate or inanimate; semantic because the object which produces it tends to become a symbol—"an uncanny effect is often and easily produced when the distinction between imagination and reality is effaced, as when something that we have hitherto regarded as imaginary appears before us in reality, or when a symbol takes over the full function of the thing it symbolizes, and so on" (367).

The ontological context of the film narrative is not a fantasy world of a fairy tale in which the supernatural cannot have the uncanny effect because it is simply a "natural," integral part of such a world. In Ulmer's film narrative the context of the reality is quite clearly established — it is set in Britain, in the modern era, indicated by the presence of the car and telephone. The intrusion of the imaginary and the demonic has then a truly disturbing character. The problem is that the script does not allow much opportunity for ontological ambivalence. The metamorphosis of Dr. Lomas is not presented as a result of a scientific experiment but is treated as a sensational supernatural event. Dr. Lomas turns into a kind of werewolf, a supernatural creature, which cannot be killed by ordinary means and is killed, like a vampire, with a stake. The script firmly roots the plot in the supernatural ontology, making Dr. Lomas a werewolf. Original Stevenson's pseudoscientific ontological frame is abandoned, the process of metamorphosis does not need any chemical drugs any more, it is rather subject to natural processes and forces such as the influence of the moon.

Ulmer was however too sophisticated to accept such a simple outline of the supernatural ontology and strove to achieve the ontological ambivalence by other means. As usual in a mystery tale it is important to control the flow of vital information. The narrative has to create gaps in understanding and has to establish enigmas and mysteries. I have already shown how nicely Ulmer withheld for a while the revelation of the family secret, Dr. Jekyll's crimes. At first we see the effects of the news, only then the news is broken. Even more clever it is the haunting dream sequence, in which the wicked spirit of Janet is shown to leave her body and pursues the innocent maid and murders her in the forest. The whole scene is beautiful done, Ulmer uses the double-exposure technique (of two overlapping layers) to produce the uncanny effect. He also shoots the scene in the forest from an unnatural slanting angle, giving the impression of a twisted deformed perspective.

The whole scene is a splendid example of the uncanny — not only the fear of an archaic animal side of the self is aroused, the whole scene also does not lack the ontological uncanny as well as the effect of recurrence. Janet seems to repeat what her father did, releasing her dark double. While we are led to believe that the murderous sequence is real, we discover only later on that it was a dream hallucination induced by Dr. Lomas' hypnosis. But for a long time the ambiguity is maintained and we are held in the dark. We are unsure whether it was a dream or not, and whether Dr. Lomas is helping Janet or abusing. Only towards the end of the film, we are finally taken behind the scene and can observe the real culprit, Dr. Lomas in action.

Nevertheless the framing device, the scene with the demonic laughter of the monster at the beginning and at the end, against subverts and undermines the traditional resolution of the conflict as a closure, and produces the effect of the uncanny by means of recursive pattern. In this case the monster's sentence "Are you sure?" suggests that a new round of the "sprawling" evil may be expected. The uncanny cannot be destroyed; it can be only deprived of its power over us by rational analysis of the causes of its repetitions.

Conclusion

It is highly significant that the confrontation of the demonic Old World and the American Brave New World represented by the young couple is brought about by the motif of homecoming. The homecoming is a nostalgic but also fearful process because it releases the angry spirits of the place, which have been repressed and return with force of a vengeance. For Ulmer, as for most immigrants, his hometown aroused a complex feeling of nostalgia, fear, guilt and denunciation. In the world of modern America the crooked streets of Olomouc and its cultural life generated nostalgia, though its provincialism must have annoyed his cosmopolitan mind trained both by the classics and the great moderns. Also the existing political circumstances, the Communist rule in Czechoslovakia, conspired against any outward reconciliation and discouraged him from a return or even a mere visit.

The motif of troublesome homecoming and demonic figuration of the place helped him to play out his ambivalence about his place of origin.[7] It is however good to note that in spite of the sinister frame with metamorphosis, in the narrative the old ghosts are exorcised and home is made safe, even the local people are appeased. If we extend the analogy a little further, we can say that this is what is going on right now. Ulmer has finally come home and the offended spirits of his publicly displaced home are set to rest.

Notes

1. Freud also notices that in usage the meanings of "heimlich" and "unheimlich" sometimes merge: "Thus heimlich is a word the meaning of which develops in the direction of ambivalence, until it finally coincides with its opposite, unheimlich" (Freud 347).

2. Cp. Arianné Ulmer Cipes' comments on Edgar G. Ulmer's relation to Olomouc at the occasion of the *ulmerfest* 2006. See *www.uni-koeln.de/phil-fak/englisch/ abteilungen/berressem/herzogenrath/ulmer/index.htm*

3. Jack Pollexfen (1908–2003) was a scriptwriter and producer of Ulmer's earlier SF film, *The Man from Planet X* (1951). Before *Daughter of Dr. Jekyll* he wrote a script for *The Son of Dr. Jekyll* (1951).

4. I use the term narrative in the way proposed by Seymour Chatman in his *Story and Discourse: Narrative Structure in Fiction and Film* (Ithaca, NY, and London: Cornell University Press, 1988).

5. The technical film terminology is adopted from David Bordwell and Kristin Thompson. *Film Art: An Introduction* (Reading, MA: Addison-Wesley, 1979).

6. Freud relates the pattern of strange repetitions is to the process of doubling, having its origin in the narcissistic gaze of child into a mirror and the animistic belief in the omnipotence of thought. The duplication of the self in this primitive stage of development is seen as an expression of desire for immortality. Even though we may not accept this particular explanation, there can be no doubt about recursive patterns in the film narrative. See (Freud 356).

7. Ambivalence is regarded as a very strong structural feature of Ulmer's films. See for instance George Lipsitz, *Time Passages: Collective Memory and American Popular Culture* (Minneapolis, MN, and London: University of Minnesota Press, 1994), 194.

Works Cited

Bordwell, David, and Kristin Thompson. *Film Art: An Introduction*. Reading, MA: Addison-Wesley, 1979.
Chatman, Seymour. *Story and Discourse: Narrative Structure in Fiction and Film*. Ithaca, NY, and London: Cornell University Press, 1988.
Eco, Umberto. *The Limits of Interpretations*. Bloomington and Indianapolis: Indiana University Press, 1994.
Freud, Sigmund. "The 'Uncanny.'" *Art and Literature*. The Penguin Freud Library. Vol. 14. Ed. Albert Dickson. Harmondsworth: Penguin, 1990, 335–76.
Herzogenrath, Bernd. "Put the Ulmer back in Ulmermouc." *Cult Fiction and Films*. Olomouc: Palacký University, 2008.
Isenberg, Noah. "Perrenial Detour: The Cinema of Edgar G. Ulmer and the Experience of Exile." *Cinema Journal* 43: 2 (Winter 2004): 3–25.
Leitmetzerova olomoucká kronika z let 1778–1829 [Leitmetzer's Olomouc chronicle of the years 1778–1829]. Olomouc: Memoria, 2001.
Lipsitz, George. *Time Passages: Collective Memory and American Popular Culture*. Minneapolis, MN, and London: University of Minnesota Press, 1994.
McHale, Brian. *Postmodernist Fiction*. London and New York: Routledge, 1987.
Příspěvky k charakteristice a poznání hlavního města a pohraniční pevnosti Olomouc od Jana Alexia Eckbergera [A Treatise on the Character of the Capital and Border Fortress Olomouc by Johann Alexius Eckberger]. 1788. Olomouc: Memoria, 1998. 147.
Tichák, Milan. *Když padly hradby: Olomouc na přelomu dvou století* [When the City Walls Fell Down: Olomouc at the turn of the nineteenth century]. Burian a Tichák, 2005.

What You See Is What You Get: Ulmer and the Nudist Picture

PETRA HANÁKOVÁ

Ulmer's nudist film *The Naked Venus* will be approached as representative of a genre in which body, its social meanings and control through display and/or censorship become the site for negotiation, contestation and performance of the politics of the visual. The nudist film is torn within a paradoxical conflict between what is being said about its images and what is actually shown and offered for specific purposes. It is critical to investigate how these two levels interact and struggle. The genre of the nudist film is here read as a flawed palimpsest, in which the process of scraping away the original images is not fully achieved and far from fully overwritten by the text of the film's communicated message. Furthermore, *The Naked Venus* goes in some respects beyond its genre — rewriting the exploitation film as a moral tale and an implicit critique of the perverse nature of a certain type of American family.

The phenomenon of the nudist film is an integral part of the history of cinema that is situated within a broader history that legitimizes looking at the human (and prominently female) body.[1] Historically, with the coming of the modern regime of looking, the body becomes a locus of exploration, research and control — and with the advent of photography and film, this process of examination even intensifies.[2] The body is approached as an apparatus, commonly broken down to poses or even organs, that both help to know it and demystify (or "mechanize") it, to strip away its mystique, including its sexual allure.[3] On the other hand, it is precisely this discarded sexual dimension of the body that, while considered superfluous by researchers (or *Somatikòs*-graphers), returns with unexpected (but generally appreciated) force in what is in film theory referred to as the "implantation of perversions."[4]

While it is true that film introduces a new visual regime surrounding the body, the problematic status of the nude in visual representation is present already in previous artistic media[5] and only increases in film.

Together with the arrival of cinema as the apparatus of the body and eroticism *par excellence*, there is also the emergence of attempts to regulate the eruptive potential of the medium. Gertrud Koch reminds us that "the history of film is also the history of its limitations, supervision, regimentation, judicial constraint, and examination of norms" (Koch 3). Two strategies are generally used to enforce the norms of at least superficial "decency." First of all, certain types of images of the body and the erotic are legitimized with the advent of narrative cinema, particularly with regard to the newly imposed authority of the fixed voyeuristic position of the spectator.[6] The second (but in fact older) strategy is to create specific niches and marketing contexts in which the production and screening of the "indecent" films is legalized and tolerated. (This is primarily seen in the creation of circuits for pornographic production). The genre of the nudist film draws on both traditions.

We can approach this shared history of the superficially decent (be it scientific, instructive, or aesthetic, i.e. voyeuristic) and the openly immoral (or, consensually exhibitionist) representation of the body as a trajectory towards the gradual legitimization or at least public tolerance of the latter. The nudist films reflect this trajectory, revealing the complex strategies of legitimization (since the nude images in them are ostensibly only a representation of a lifestyle) while at the same time playing an open double game (the same nude images are also images that can be consumed and exploited as erotic). How this double game is structured and implemented will be especially evident in the case of Ulmer's *The Naked Venus*.

The Discourse of Nudism vs. the Discourse of Voyeurism

Nudity in film was no novelty at the time of the boom of nudist pictures in 1950s and '60s. From the early striptease or bathing films and the production of companies such as the Viennese Saturn[7] to the later artsy skinny dipping scene in Machatý's *Extase* (these are examples from my own Central European context, other countries have other films *scandaleux*), nudity in film has always been used both as a marketing strategy and as a provocation for moral reformers. Clearly, from the American perspective, the imposition of the Production Code in the middle of the 1930s rather successfully pushed nudity to the margins of the film industry. Nudist and naturist films, produced and marketed as a representation of a life-style and thereby presented as documentary or educational, are probably the most visible genre to break through the Hays blockade.

At the same time, these films were blatantly intended not for the purposes of enlightening the spectators, but for the exhibition and commercial exploitation of female nudity. Although there is some presence of the naked male body in nudist film, the active, well-built masculine figures are mostly ignored both in the plot and by the camera. Their presence is motivated by other objectives — namely to provide the expected images that show mixed-sex groups engaged in asexual leisure activities. (The exploitation of the male body as an object of the look and erotic stimulations comes only later, especially with the coming-out of gay cinema after Stonewall.) Paradoxically, the nudist film was significantly cultivated by the female filmmaker and producer Doris Wishman, probably the most active woman director of all time. It has even implied that it was she who "revolutionized and suggested how to almost legitimize the adults only sexploitation."[8]

The nudist films often claim in their commercials and trailers that they only aim to present the freedom of body and mind in their natural splendor and portray a lifestyle of perfect harmony between healthy mind and healthy body. Nudity is here proclaimed as the natural condition of the human race, and clothing as a symbol of civilization and its corrupting power.[9] The discourse of nudism extols the physical and mental benefits of sunshine and fresh air, which epitomize its healthy philosophy. Physical fitness, exposure to sunlight and clean air supposedly contribute to mental and psychological strength, overall good health, and a superior, moral life view.[10] Thus, the main character Stacy in *The Diary of the Nudist* can, once successfully converted to nudism, exclaim that she is "feeling completely alive" for the first time in her life, and can express admiration for the "healthy suntans" of all the people around her. (Curiously, this impression on her is not spoiled by the fact that some of the actors are obviously so called "cottontails," meaning that their buttocks are paler that the rest of their body, visual evidence of wearing a swimsuit in real life).

Asserting that nothing about the body is immoral (or in itself sinful or obscene) and that immorality is merely an effect of the mind, the images from nudist camps came to be composed as pastoral scenes, conjuring the idea and vision of the return to the Garden of Eden. The reference to Eden is quite often directly evoked within the films or in the discourses surrounding them. As one advertisement for Wishman's *Hideout in the Sun* exclaims, "Escape to a modern Garden of Paradise where Nature's sun-kissed daughters walk forth in all their natural beauty!" Max Nosseck's 1954 film actually bears the title *The Garden of Eden*.

In the emblematic scene of a nudist camp, nude people, mostly women (the films openly claim to present particularly the beauty of the female form "at play and rest"), pose by the swimming pool or in the recreation area, sunbathe, and engage in sports such as volleyball, basketball, and archery. (The underwater title sequence in Wishman's *The Diary of a Nudist* depicting a naked underwater swimming champion is quite exceptional, almost having the feel of an experimental film). As full frontal nudity still remains a taboo, most of the characters pose unnaturally, chastely covering themselves with towels, hats, newspapers, or standing behind trees or shrubs. The scenes of nudist communion are clearly pastoral and sometimes have an almost religious or political feel. (In one of the first scenes in *The Diary of a Nudist*, the naked discussion group poised on a set of stairs invokes the image of the meeting of a perfect polis). The pastoral, bucolic atmosphere even includes scenes of a nudist wedding, which again stresses the presence of traditional values in the camps. The infantile visions of happiness and wholesomeness of the body in its natural form sometimes achieve an almost surreal feel — such as in the scenes of nude groups sipping tea or coffee and chatting at the table in a very constrained manner, more fitting to a snobbish club or party. These fantasy visions are so awkwardly posed and choreographed that their very arrangement ironically contradicts the discourses of freedom, vivacity, and a truthful lifestyle.

At the same time, the nudist films cannot but show that nudism is there to be explored and observed with a supposedly moral and scrutinizing gaze. In Doris Wishman's *The Nude of the Moon*, this literally takes the character of an anthropological observation. In this film, we follow two scientists on their expedition to the Moon, where, we might say, they encounter a return of the repressed (namely, the misplaced libido of the younger scientist). The Moon is surprisingly green, having vegetation and thus an atmosphere. (The scientists ruminate that "perhaps this is the part of the Moon that is never seen.") The moon is also inhabited by semi-nude creatures with weird antennae that communicate purely telepathically. Although the visitors from the Earth scrutinize the place and its creatures scientifically, they overlook the resemblance of the Moon vegetation to that of the Earth and make no thoughts about the presence of an atmosphere. Their exploration of the Moon is based on sight and scientific distance. The nudity of the moon-beings does not shock them; they see these creatures as simply another species (not as naked humans) to be anthropologically studied. Their look remains the gaze of a scientist and even when the younger scientist starts to feel attracted to the moon-queen (or, that "lovely creature," as he says), his feelings are "pure" and not that of sexual stimulation. At the beginning of *The Diary of a Nudist*, a hunter-reporter (and, as we later find out, the editor in chief of *The Evening Times*), out on a hunting trip, discovers a nudist camp and immediately considers exposing this scandalous site. His thoughts are communicated by an inner voice commentary that is domineering and completely antagonistic to nudism. His exclamation, "This is outrageous, I will do something about it!" stands in stark visual contrast to the almost obtusely decent pastoral scenes from the nudist camp he observes.

The initial encounter with the nudist camp (or: nudist community in the case of the Wishman's sci-fi film) usually demands that desire and pleasure are suppressed. This is typically achieved by imposing the law, be it moral, legal or investigative, by means of the gaze. In *The Diary of a Nudist*, the undercover reporter chosen for the job of the nudist expose and sent to a nudist camp is surprisingly a woman. Yet, she appears unable to possess the necessary gaze, being too easily initiated and converted to the lifestyle of the nudists. (She makes a swift transition from the multiple reiterations of denial at the beginning of the mission: "You expect me to join one of those camps? Oh no, I couldn't! I wouldn't! As a matter of fact, I won't!" to what she calls "a girl sold on nudism" at the end). Actually, during her first days in the earthly paradise, she nearly forgets her mission and neglects her writing. It is only the voice of the "law" (a telegram from the editor) that reminds her of her task. Yet, by this time, the expose she writes cannot be anything other than a positive defense of nudism. At this moment, the male gaze of her boss must interject to verify her real insider information. After joining the camp, he maintains both his gaze and his swimming suit. When the female reporter is fired and he takes her place, we are reminded of another gendered exchange early in the film when the editor asks the reporter to do the nudist expose, saying it needs a good reporter, male or female. Aware of the consequence of his words, she reacts: "Sometimes I'd like to be thought of as a woman, not as a reporter." Yet, it is precisely her position as a woman, unable to keep her gaze and distance from the lifestyle (or image) that is held up for scrutiny in the end.[11]

The classical theory of the gaze[12] presupposes a grounding complicity between the controlling gaze of the film protagonist and that of the male spectator. This relay of looking grants the spectator easy access to the pleasures of looking and control over the images of women in the film. In the nudist film, however, this is not the case. In order to enjoy the images as erotic, the spectators must *avoid* the trajectory of the protagonist's gaze, which is suppressing precisely this erotic dimension of looking and replacing it with a moral or scientific gaze. The spectator does not require the protagonist to serve as bearer of the gaze; on the contrary, he must look outside the gaze and attain direct rapport with the images in order to gain the promised pleasure from them. We can claim that the nudist film is avoiding the regime of looking that is typical for classical cinema in favor of a more direct version of voyeurism, not covered by the alibi of the protagonist's enjoyment. In short, the proper way to consume a nudist film is to follow the saying: What you see is what you get.

The Legal Gaze and the Family "Romance"

Ulmer's *The Naked Venus* (which he made under the pseudonym Ove H. Sehested) exposes the paradox of the gaze that obstructs the spectator enjoyment. The director recasts the nudist genre as a legal drama, significantly personalizes the central nudist protagonist, and in the end, puts on trial the perverse gaze of the hypocritical American family and its misuse of the legal system. Here, the stark contrast between images and their status as evidence is laid out and presented as the main theme of the film. Furthermore, nudism here is not the initiator of the main conflict, but merely a side effect and an aggravation for the main character, French model-nudist Yvonne. More than a nudist film, *The Naked Venus* is yet another representative of an ambiguous morality play so typical for Ulmer's oeuvre.[13]

The film's prologue may be rather misleading in this respect, but it is not actually connected to the story of the film. Following the caption "somewhere in France," we are taken on a tour of the very familiar terrain of the typical nudist film — the terrain of male voyeurism masquerading as a moral gaze. We see two heavily dressed reporters (in absurdly hot outfits, complete with hats and jackets) spying on young women bathing in the river. To aid their viewing, the men are further equipped with a phallic-looking camera. The naked girls trifle by the boat, strike alluring poses, smile, and generally perform for the camera.

The next shot takes us to Paris, which is, rather logically, presented here not so much as the city of the Eiffel tower, but as the city of the Moulin Rouge. The narrative shifts to a domestic scene that introduces the main couple of the film. The husband, an American named Robert, is gaining fame in Paris as a painter and his loving wife, Yvonne, works as an artist's model. They are facing a major change in their life — after the death of Robert's father, they are at the point of leaving Paris to help Robert's mother in California, who does not really know that her son is married with a child of his own. Yvonne reluctantly agrees to go to California, despite the fact that she is scared to death to meet her mother-in-law. We may presume that her fears will prove true, as Robert not only became painter against the will of his parents, but as it later becomes clear, his mother also had also other plans regarding his choice of life partner.

From the beginning, the easy-going, bohemian atmosphere and rather humble conditions of the couple's life in Paris are contrasted with the elegant, stiff and highbrow American world of Robert's mother. Already in the first moments, Yvonne's fears appear to have been warranted. Her first encounter with her mother-in-law has rather the appearance of an interrogation and the mother-in-law seems to be especially shocked by the fact that her son's wife had worked as a painter's model. Yvonne's feeble defense ("there is nothing bad about being nude") is quickly reduced to terms of national and social difference ("we have different views, you French are having your ideas"). Although the mother keeps acting rather nicely on the surface, she is quickly revealed as domineering and perversely fixated on her son, declaring his decision to marry Yvonne a "haste marriage." From this point, the film turns into an investigation of the Oedipal triangle and perverse fixation in the family. It is this dimension of the family that will be revealed and broken down in the court where, quite originally, the nudist lifestyle is put on trial.

The mother decides to get rid of Yvonne and take control over her son's life and family, as he "needs a wife, not an artist's model." Her game of manipulation begins by making Robert believe that he is deluding himself, "afraid to face (the) reality" of his marriage. The representation of the relationship between mother and son in *The Naked Venus* is thus in some respects closer to *Psycho* than to a "normal" nudist film.[14] Significantly, the decision to divorce is not communicated directly between the couple, it is presented by a representative of the law, who was directly hired by the mother to arrange the annulment. The American and European views of relationships are contrasted when Yvonne claims that marriage is not for sale, whereas the lawyer turns this economic allusion around in his claim that Americans do not believe in commercialized nudity. He further announces that because the American moral code differs from hers, he can threaten to take away her child. Moral standards are thus contrasted with the supposedly immoral practice of earning a living, and this, paradoxically, by a lawyer who is evidently beyond all moral judgments.

As is often the case in nudist films, Yvonne runs to a nudist camp, refusing to surrender her fight.[15] (Significantly, her recommendation for the camp came from Paris.) She hires an ambitious young female lawyer, who is, at first, a very stereotypical "professional woman" complete with glasses and cigarette, yet later in the film is presented in surprisingly positive light. (The lawyer was played by Ulmer's daughter Arianné). Together they agree to fight not only the mother-in-law, but also to "battle vigorously the prejudice in the courtroom." The following scene, in which we see the mother, Robert and his "girlfriend from childhood" Scherie by their swimming pool stands in stark contrast to the relaxed and welcoming atmosphere of the nudist camp.

Here, the people in the swimsuits and bathing gowns plot "dirty tactics" to get rid of Yvonne. The mother evidently plans to replace her with a "decent girl," the neighbor's daughter.

This scheme is evident in the first of the subsequent court scenes. The prospective "replacement" girl is also one of the key witnesses, expressing shock that her childhood sweetheart married an artist's model, and claiming that Yvonne is a gold-digger that "will do anything to get a nice American boy." The situation becomes only more aggravated when a private detective hired by the mother presents additional evidence. Yvonne is judged not only on the grounds that she posed in the nude; the fact that she joined a nudist organization in France is also considered scandalous. The evidence from the camp (intended to support the absolute necessity for the divorce and a sole custody of the child for Robert and his mother) is screened as a "film within a film," as a distanced view for the "legal" and moral public.

On the other hand, nudity as a pure ideal is defended in court by a museum curator that provides the picture of the Naked Venus that Robert painted, and for which Yvonne modeled. He presents an enlightened and unbiased viewpoint, standing for the belief that ignorance and prejudice have always been the enemies of civilization and art, and should therefore be contested. For him, the painting is an exceptional "expression of the times," and, being art, it is beauty and thereby pure, never morally questionable. He stresses the fact that Rembrandt's wife posed for her husband and that posing has been a way of participating in the creation of art since antiquity. For him, the practice of nudism is a person's private business (arguing that it is not necessary to ask if Dante was a nudist to assess the value of his work).

In this way, nudism and the social practice of nudity are defended and shown as more moral than the dirty tactics of the domineering mother and her allies. There are virtually two happy endings — the first is the victory of Yvonne in the courtroom, the second the final reuniting of the central couple in the epilogue, (unsurprisingly back in Paris, away from the corrupting power of the American society.) Thus, nudism is again totally legitimized at the end of *The Naked Venus*, yet only in the context of a broader social acceptance, in which nudity in itself is not seen as immoral. This acceptance is connected to the valorization of the open-minded bohemian Europe as opposed to deceitful America, the pitting of artistic freedom against hypocritical morality, and the contrasting of a loving young marriage with the perverse economy of the traditional Oedipal family. Furthermore, by providing the central character with her own history and issues to fight for, thereby providing a much broader context for her exposure as a nudist, the film "spoils" much of the direct voyeuristic pleasure derived from looking at her nude body.

While the right to freedom is in the nudist films very often connected to the vision of the American dream (which is very present in Wishman's films, both in overall context and behind her compulsion to make "unruly" films[16]), for Ulmer, this freedom is illusory, and the space of the American family is as terrifying as the places of his horror films. In this context, the nudist goals of heath and total relaxation together with the fact that "nudism looks at sex the way we look at nature and life itself" are confronted with many more difficulties, they are more directly linked to the accompanying sensationalism, voyeurism and exploitation of female nudity. So, we may read *The Naked Venus* as Ulmer's commentary on the genre itself, exposing the paradox inherent in the overt message of the films — namely, that the hypocritical public has too many preconceived notions to recognize the truth. On the contrary, he seems to argue, the only truth the public receives is visual stimulation — the public knows what they want, and this is what they see.

Notes

1. See Lynda Nead. "STRIP. Moving bodies in the 1890s." *Early Popular Visual Culture* 3:2 (September 2005): 135–50. "The historiography of cinema studies has been dominated by the triumph of the eye; by framing the cinematic experience in terms of a kind of disembodied looking, driven by the pleasures of scopophilia. In their present, mature phase, cinema audiences, it is claimed, have grown out of their early uninhibited physical responses and are concerned with the indulgence and management of the gaze. Cinema, it is suggested, has abandoned its sensory promiscuity and has realized its definitive function as an ocular form of representation and mode of address" (136).

2. The coming of the modern regime of looking was extensively analyzed by Jonathan Crary in his *Techniques of the Observer: On Vision and Modernity in the Nineteenth Century* (Cambridge, MA: MIT Press, 1992). For the exploration of the human body through photography and film, see the work of Jean-Martin Charcot, Étienne-Jules Marey, Eadweard Muybridge, Aleksej Gastev and others.

3. For a description of the public autopsy as an almost cinematic way of researching the body see Guiliana Bruno, "Spectatorial Embodiments: Anatomies of the Visible and the Female Bodyscape," *Camera Obscura* 28 (1992): 238–61. The body's status as a site of evidence is also evident in the practice of exhibiting corpses in the Paris Morgue at the end of the 19th century, see Vanessa R. Schwartz, "Cinematic Spectatorship Before the Apparatus: The Public Taste for Reality in *Fin-de-Siècle* Paris," in Leo Charney and Vanessa R. Schwartz (eds.), *Cinema and the Invention of Modern Life* (Berkeley: University of California Press), 1995.

4. Building on Foucault's claim about the intensification of the body as an object of knowledge, and thus object of power relations, Linda Williams applies his term "implantation of perversion" to describe cinema during its emergence in the second half of the 19th century: "nowhere has the deployment of sexuality, with its attendant implantation of perversions, been more evident than in the visible intensification of the body that came about with the invention of cinema" (Williams 508). For Williams, the cinema apparatus is both the instrument of power over bodies, "machinery of observation and measurement," but also one that investigates the body with a

surplus of meaning (514), and brings forth a "powerful fantasization of the body of the woman" (532).

5. As Linda Nead states: "The nude, and most particularly, the female nude, has always been a troublesome subject for fine art. This is precisely the point of the nude: to test the boundaries of morality and artistic propriety; to play with convention and sensation at once" (144).

6. For a discussion of the transition from early cinema to the classical narrative film and the subsequent channeling of the spectator's look into the regime of the keyhole, and the shift from exhibitionist to voyeuristic cinema, see Miriam Hansen, "Adventures of Goldilocks: Spectatorship, Consumerism and Public Life" *Camera Obscura* 22 (1990): 51–71.

7. For more information on Saturn, the company that actually initiated the regular production of films in Austria, see Michael Achenbach, Paolo Caneppele, Ernst Kieninger (eds.). *Projektionen der Sehnsucht. Saturn. Die erotische Anfänge der österreichischen Kinematographie* (Wien: Filmarchiv Austria), 1999.

8. On Wishman as a "gutter-level Fellini," see Christopher J. Jarmick "Doris Wishman," *http://www.sensesofcinema.com/contents/directors/02/wishman.html*, last accessed April 10, 2008, and Andrew Leavold, "Bad Girls Go To Dildo Heaven: An All-Nude Tribute To Doris Wishman," *http://www.sensesofcinema.com/contents/02/23/doris.html*, last accessed April 10, 2008.

9. Quite often the nudist discourse makes reference to history, especially to antiquity. For example, we are reminded that the terms "gymnasium" and "gymnastics" are derived from the Greek word "gymnos," meaning "nude," because athletics in Greece were routinely performed naked.

10. In reality, this philosophy often remains purely a figment of wishful thinking. The notable presence of activities that go against the bodily acceptance program and turn the female body into a spectacle (i.e. beauty pageants and lingerie parties, which are seen as more sexualized than "naked fun") is definitely damaging to the image of the nudist clubs. A recent study also shows that the environment of the nudist camps may indeed be far removed from the utopian ideal of their fundamental philosophy. Ellen Woodall from the University of Florida, who studies nudist communities, has claimed that "the naked truth about the American nudist movement is its failure to live up to the ideal that everyone is treated the same, despite social standing or the shape of their bodies." See Cathy Keen. "UF Study bares contradictions about American nudists," *http://news.ufl.edu/2001/10/18/nudism/*, last accessed April 10, 2008.

11. The final happy ending is based on the logic of nudist life as a site of truth: only after seeing Stacy "completely alive" (and naked) in the camp, does the editor reveals his true feelings and admiration for her not only as a reporter, but his love for her as a woman.

12. I refer here to the classical scheme of the gaze as outlined by Laura Mulvey in the 1970s, which describes the complicity of looking between the male spectator and the male protagonist as his representative in film. See Laura Mulvey. "Visual Pleasure and Narrative Cinema," in Constance Penley (ed.), *Feminism and Film Theory* (London: Routledge), 1988.

13. "Whether the focus is on the psychology of individuals, on contexts of creation and exploration, or on broader images of culture and society, Ulmer creates ambiguous 'morality plays,' as he himself asserted." See Peter Bogdanovich, *Who the Devil Made It* (New York: Knopf), 1997, 601–2.

14. Yvonne's lawyer claims later that the weaker side of Robert is dominated by his mother. In many respects, the mother posits herself as a lover to her son. For the recurrence of this theme in American cinema, see Molly Haskell's claim that to a high degree "American woman's feeling for son and lover are identical." Molly Haskell, *From Reference to Rape: The Treatment of Women in the Movies* (Chicago: University of Chicago Press), 1973, 171.

15. The nudist camp as a refuge, an open space of freedom, stands in contrast to the Ulmerian dark threatening interiors, such as the trademark "vicious villa" in *The Black Cat*: Ulmer's "interiors frequently become traps or potential graves ... which his characters seek to escape.... Even Ulmer's exteriors suggest atmospheres similar to his interiors." John Belton, *Cinema Stylists* (Metuchen, NJ: Scarecrow), 1983, 154–55, quoted in Erik Ulman. "Edgar G. Ulmer," *http://www.sensesofcinema.com/contents/directors/03/ulmer.html*, last accessed April 10, 2008. The metaphoric position of this enclosed interior is here taken on by the family, which is dominated by an overwhelming mother.

16. Wishman is expressing her belief in freedom also in her famous slogan: "After I die I will be making movies in hell!" See Christopher J. Jarmick, "Doris Wishman," *http://www.sensesofcinema.com/contents/directors/02/wishman.html*, last accessed April 10, 2008.

Works Cited

Achenbach, Michael, Paolo Caneppele, and Ernst Kieninger (eds.). *Projektionen der Sehnsucht. Saturn. Die erotische Anfänge der österreichischen Kinematographie*. Wien: Filmarchiv Austria, 1999.

Belton, John. *Cinema Stylists*. Metuchen, NJ: Scarecrow Press, 1983.

Bogdanovich, Peter. *Who the Devil Made It?* New York: Knopf, 1997.

Bruno, Guiliana. "Spectatorial Embodiments: Anatomies of the Visible and the Female Bodyscape." *Camera Obscura* 28 (1992): 238–61.

Crary, Jonathan. *Techniques of the Observer: On Vision and Modernity in the Nineteenth Century*. Cambridge, MA: MIT Press, 1992.

Didi-Huberman, Georges. *Invention of Hysteria: Charcot and the Photographic Iconography of the Salpetriere*. Cambridge, MA: The MIT Press, 2003.

Hansen, Miriam. "Adventures of Goldilocks: Spectatorship, Consumerism and Public Life." *Camera Obscura* 22 (1990): 51–71.

Haskell, Molly. *From Reference to Rape. The Treatement of Women in the Movies*. Chicago: University of Chicago Press, 1973.

Jarmick, Christopher J. "Doris Wishman." *http://www.sensesofcinema.com/contents/directors/02/wishman.html*. Last accessed April 10, 2008.

Keen, Cathy. "UF Study bares contradictions about American nudists." *http://news.ufl.edu/2001/10/18/nudism/*, last accessed April 10, 2008.

Koch, Gertrud. "The Body's Shadow Realm." *October* 50 (Autumn, 1989): 3–29.

Leavold, Andrew. "Bad Girls Go To Dildo Heaven: An All-Nude Tribute To Doris Wishman." *http://www.sensesofcinema.com/contents/02/23/doris.html*, last accessed April 10, 2008.

Lyon, Elisabeth. "Unspeakable Images, Unspeakable Bodies." *Camera Obscura* 24 (1992): 169–93.

Mulvey, Laura. "Visual Pleasure and Narrative Cinema." Constance Penley (ed.). *Feminism and Film Theory*. London: Routledge, 1988.

Nead, Lynda. "STRIP. Moving bodies in the 1890s." *Early Popular Visual Culture* 3:2 (September 2005): 135–50.
Schwartz, Vanessa R. "Cinematic Spectatorship Before the Apparatus: The Public Taste For Reality in *Fin-de-Siècle* Paris." Leo Charney and Vanessa R. Schwartz R. (eds.). *Cinema and the Invention of Modern Life*. Berkeley: University of California Press, 1995.
Ulman, Erik. "Edgar G. Ulmer." *http://www.sensesofcinema.com/contents/directors/03/ulmer.html#23*. Last accessed April 10, 2008.
Williams, Linda. "Film Body. An Implantation of Perversions." Philip Rosenp (ed.). *Narrative, Apparatus, Ideology: A Film Theory Reader*. New York: Columbia University Press, 1986, 507–34.

Geocinema and Geophilosophy: *The Cavern*
PHILIPP HOFMANN

This essay will use the geophilosophical approach of the French writers Gilles Deleuze and Félix Guattari developed in their book *A Thousand Plateaus* for a reading of Edgar G. Ulmer's last movie, *The Cavern,* from 1964. We'll tentatively label this film as "geocinematic," a term designating movies in which the geological state of affairs of the earth motivates and influences the action. In the movie, which is set during the second World War, a group of seven people are captured in a cave whose entrance/exit has been destroyed by a bomb. Through the violent forces of war, a fundamental structural and spatial change takes place for the protagonists: One kind of space gives room for another one as they suddenly find themselves being cut off from the outside, entombed in an underground world. To secure their survival, the protagonists have to re-organize the social structure of the group as well as adapt their lives to the geological givens of the cave.

The subterranean setting of the film is a feature that *The Cavern* shares with Ulmer's previous movie, *Journey Beneath the Desert* (1961), which tells the story of the underground city of Atlantis. In the early '50s, American popular culture picked up a long literary tradition of fantastic tales of the underground and developed an increasing interest in the worlds below, as for example in Henry Ridder Haggard's *She* or Edgar Rice Burroughs' *Pellucidar*. Pulp magazines such as *Weird Tales* and *Amazing Stories* thrived on underground science-fiction stories, one of the most famous of them probably being "The Shaver Mystery." A further popular example is Raymond Bernard's book *The Hollow Earth* in which Bernard confronted the reader with the "fact" that "the Earth is hollow and is not a solid sphere as commonly supposed, and that its hollow interior communicates with the surface by two polar openings" (17). Bernard's fantastic account of the real geological state of affairs of the earth culminates in a wild conspiracy theory and the suggestion that "it is very possible that the mysterious flying saucers come from an advanced civilization in the hollow interior of the earth" (18).

Considering the increased interest in underground worlds by American culture in the 1950s (partly inspired by a long tradition of the hollow earth motive in European literature from Dante to Casanova) it seems fair to say that Ulmer's two movies pick up a theme that had been popular in literature, but not yet in cinema and that is essentially geological in nature. Considering the number of films that have been produced since the late '50s with themes revolving around subterranean worlds and underground adventures, it might not be immoderate to speak of the development of a new filmic subgenre that might be termed "geocinema," a subgenre to which Ulmer has certainly added the earliest, and thus, founding films. Among other movies with a geocinematic theme one can find *Unknown World* (1951), *The Land Unknown* (1957), the 1968 episode of *Star Trek* "For the World Is Hollow and I Have Touched the Sky," *At the Earth's Core* (1976), *The Core* (2003) as well as various film versions of Jules Verne's *Journey to the Center of the Earth* such as *Fabulous Jour-*

Above and page 250: English and French-language posters for *The Cavern*, Ulmer's final film (courtesy Edgar G. Ulmer Preservation Corporation).

ney to the Center of the Earth (1988). Geocinematic films that are less concerned with topology than with the catastrophic release of geological intensities are *Earthquake* (1974) or *Dante's Peak* (1997).

The notion of geology has not only been an important one for Edgar Ulmer. In their book *What Is Philosophy?*, the French writers Gilles Deleuze and Félix Guattari explain that, in their philosophical approach, the earth constitutes a fundamental concept since it "is not one element among others but rather brings together all the elements within a single embrace, using one or another of them to deterritorialize territory" (*What Is Philosophy?* 85). Consequently, in the introduction to their recent book on Deleuze and Guattari, Mark Bonta and John Protevi state that "if you open *A Thousand Plateaus* at any page you'll find terms such as 'plateaus,' 'deterritorialization,' 'rhizome,' 'cartography,' and so on. If you would then say to yourself that this is a 'geophilosophy,' you'd be right" (Bonta vii).

In the final chapter of *A Thousand Plateaus*, Deleuze and Guattari describe two philosophical key concepts which they express in the geological terms "striated" and "smooth" space, while simultaneously relating them to the notion of what they call "the war machine." These two kinds of spaces can also be found in *The Cavern*, and much of the film's dynamics is grounded in the tension between the smooth and the striated and in the resulting force-field that the protagonists find themselves in.

Even though Deleuze and Guattari stress that the relationship between the smooth and the striated does not consist of a simple opposition but is marked by a complex interplay, for the sake of my argument I will treat them as a being basically opposed. The two philosophers describe striated space as "the space instituted by the State apparatus" (*Thousand Plateaus* 474) that is highly organized by centralized, hierarchical and metrical structures. It "intertwines fixed and variable elements, produces an order and succession of distinct forms, and organizes horizontal ... lines and vertical ... planes" (*Thousand Plateaus* 478). Striated space is filled with meaningful forms and static power relations which are defined by external properties such as length and volume creating fixed positions. Striated space is the space of law and order, it is rectangular, rectilinear State-space in which fixed forms organize matter: the grids of suburban city-planning, a crossroad of highways, a chess board, Cartesian space.

In contrast, smooth space is topological, it is "an *amorphous*, nonformal ... continuous variation [and] development of form; ... the pure act of drawing of a diagonal across the vertical and the horizontal" (*Thousand Plateaus* 477–8). In smooth space, "the line is ... a vector, a direction and not a dimension or metric determination" (*Thousand Plateaus* 478). Deleuze and Guattari stress that smooth spaces, the desert, the ice, the sea, "always possesses a greater power of deterritorialization than the striated" (*Thousand Plateaus* 480).

As Adrian Parr explains, the process of deterritorialization "can best be understood as a movement producing change. ... So, to deterritorialize is to free up the fixed relations that contain a body" (67) and he concludes that "the principle insight [is]: deterritorialization shatters the subject" (69). Bonta and Protevi give a similar description when they claim that deterritorialization is "the process of leaving home, of altering your habits, of learning new tricks" (Bonta 78). Deleuze and Guattari themselves define deterritorialization as "the movement by which 'one' leaves the territory. It is the operation of the line of flight" (*Thousand Plateaus* 508). However, it is important to note that deterritorialization goes hand in hand with reterritorialization, and their relationship "must not be construed negatively; [deterritorialization] is not the polar opposite of territorialization or reterritorialization (when a territory is established once more)" (Parr 67).

Even though the smooth and the striated intersect and fold into each other, they can be distinguished by one important characteristic: striated space is an "aggregate with a whole number of dimensions ... for which it is possible to assign constant directions" (*Thousand Plateaus* 488). In contrast, "smooth space is constituted by the construction of a line with a fractional number of dimensions greater than one, or of a surface with a fractional number of dimensions greater than two" (*Thousand Plateaus* 488). Smooth space is constantly striving towards an additional dimension without ever reaching it, such as a fractal line that is infinitely curved and tends to fill out a plane without ever reaching this "higher," second dimension. An example for such a fractal line that is created by the infinite iteration of a pattern within itself on a smaller scale is Von Koch's curve.

By infinitely repeating the operation of replacing the straight line by a triangular one, the one-dimensional line starts to fill out a two-dimensional surface without ever actually becoming a plane.

A further difference between the smooth and the striated is the relation they have to the war machine. Deleuze and Guattari stress that the war machine is "the constitutive element of smooth space, the occupation of this space, displacement within this space" (*Thousand Plateaus* 417). Bonta and Protevi describe it as "the counterforce to the state's stratification machine" (Bonta 165) operating against "hierarchical, centralized, and overcoded social formations" (Bonta 165). Therefore, the war machine actually is a "smooth" machine.

Even though the term sounds militaristic, it does primarily *not* describe a military apparatus, but designates "a nonsubjectified machine assemblage" (*Thousand Plateaus* 353),

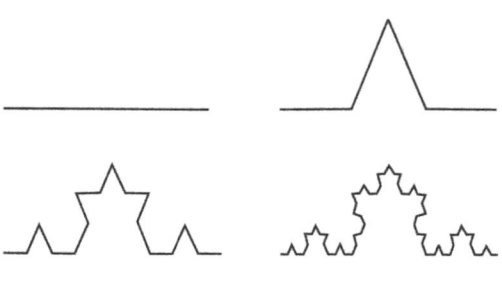

Van Koch's curve.

"a kind of rhizome, with its gaps, detours, subterranean passages, stems, openings, traits, holes" (*Thousand Plateaus* 415). The State apparatus — as occupying striated space — is of another order, another nature and another origin than the war machine. For Deleuze and Guattari, the State "is defined by the perpetuation or conservation of organs of power. The concern of the State is to conserve" (*Thousand Plateaus* 357) and therefore it is not really interested in the war machine's dynamical force that operates *against* the conservative State by "irruption[s] of the ephemeral and the power[s] of metamorphosis" (*Thousand Plateaus* 352). Since the State is principally critical towards the war machine, it "*has no war machine of its own*; it can only appropriate one in the form of a military institution" (*Thousand Plateaus* 355). However, it is when "the State apparatus appropriates a war machine that the war machine takes war as its object, and that war becomes subordinated to the aims of the State" (*Thousand Plateaus* 418) with the result of an "institutionalized, regulated, coded war with a front, a rear, battles" (*Thousand Plateaus* 353). A structure of discipline and order is imposed upon the machine, striating its disruptive powers and turning it into a State war machine. Counterintuitively, then, "discipline is [not] what defines a war machine: discipline is the characteristic required of armies after the State has appropriated them" (*Thousand Plateaus* 358).

The mode of moving through and in the striated differs decisively from that of moving in the smooth: As Deleuze and Guattari point out, "what distinguishes the two kinds of voyages is ... the manner of being in space, of being for space (*Thousand Plateaus* 482). It is this manner of "being in space, of being for space" of the protagonists of *The Cavern* that we will focus on.

Ulmer's 1964 film was the last motion picture he directed. It was produced for Twentieth Century–Fox starring, among others, the young Larry Hagman, his later *I Dream of Jeannie* and *Dallas* fame still to come. In the beginning of the film we see a State war machine at its full force: In 1944, a group of Allied soldiers is captured by the Germans in the Italian mountains. When a group of American airplanes attacks and starts to bomb the road, the Germans and their prisoners seek shelter in a cavern that is used as a secret supply storage. They are not the only ones doing so: An Italian soldier, a peasant woman, and a Canadian Air-Force officer had the same idea. When the entrance to the cavern is blown up, only seven people survive: The two American soldiers Captain Wilson and Private Cramer, the British General Braithwaite, the Canadian Peter Carter, the Italian soldier Mario, his friend Anna and the German soldier Hans Beck. This heterogeneous group of people (in terms of nationality, gender, age, social status and military rank) finds itself locked deep within the belly of the mountain. Luckily, they have an almost unlimited food supply and a generator that provides them with electricity.

The film describes how they approach the two major problems of organizing their survival and social life and of finding a way out of the cave.

When the entry of the cavern is blown up, we see how the striated, ordered space is turned into smooth space. The explosion is literally an "act of drawing of a diagonal across the vertical and the horizontal" (*Thousand Plateaus* 478). When the structure of wooden beams that has supported the entrance in horizontal and vertical ways is destroyed, the camera shows the wood tumbling across the screen in diagonals. The entrance collapses under the pressure of the mountain and by that destroys the dimension of the outside.

Even though the protagonists find themselves caught in the closed, and at first seemingly confined and narrow space of the cavern, this very space shows attributes of smooth space, which the camera underlines by showing structures that work according to a different logic than that of the wooden beams that had supported the entrance: The noisy and violent explosion is abruptly ended by a similarly violent and sudden jump cut when the breakdown of the man-made structure is juxtaposed with the natural structures of the cave as the film introduces the viewer to the new location by panning in an uncannily silent shot across places deep within the cave. As Deleuze and Guattari state, a characteristic of smooth space is "when, independent of metrics, determinations arise that ... are connected by processes of frequency or accumulation" (*Thousand Plateaus* 485). This is exactly what the camera is showing since the inside of the cavern is filled with structures — such as stalactites and stalagmites — that have been literally formed by processes of frequency (frequent dropping of water) and accumulation (of sedimentary particles).

There are more hints that the protagonists have left the striated space of the State war machine and entered a smooth space since the film hints to the fact that the cavern is of a fractal nature. When the group tries to asses the situation after the blast, Mario, the Italian soldier confirms that there are no maps or plans of the cavern that would represent its extension or forms and, as Captain Wilson claims, the tunnels are potentially infinite and "you could go on forever" exploring them. Although the cavern seems to be infinitely porous and tunneled, it never reaches the additional dimension of the outside. Even when the protagonists start to dig a new tunnel, all they reach is just a neighboring cave: the smooth space always folds back upon itself. This fractal nature is underlined when the protagonists start to create quarters for the night out of the wooden storage-boxes. These quarters are little small-scale caves that are related to the large cave which envelops them by a relation of similarity.

At first the protagonists are overwhelmed finding themselves in this unfamiliar kind of space. They do not know how to be in this space and be for this space and therefore they immediately start to striate the smooth space of the cave by organizing it: General Braithwaite orders that "a complete check must be made of all stalls and equipment" to get an overview over the supplies there are. In addition, the space they move in during the first half of the film (the front part of the cavern) differs from that of the second half of the film when the action is taking place deeper within the cave. In the front part, the natural walls are hardly visible because they are blocked by rows of boxes that create artificial walls in front of them. These walls are not only striating because their boards create a rigid horizontal and vertical grid structure, but also because they're literally representing metrical systems, such as a calendar.

Therefore, right from the start the protagonists try to reterritorialize themselves by ordering and structuring space and by maintaining the discipline of the State war machine. The biggest concern of the General is the hierarchical chain of command. As he explicitly says it is even more important to him than food.

The protagonists try to maintain the discipline of the state war machine. Brian Aherne, left, Peter Marshall, John Saxon, Nino Castelnuovo and Rosanna Schiaffino (courtesy Edgar G. Ulmer Preservation Corporation).

BRAITHWAITE [to Carter]: Good Heavens, man. What's that you're eating?
CARTER: It's powdered, dehydrated vegetables, Sir. Delicious! [Offers him some powder] Here, Sir, have a carrot.
BRAITHWAITE: No, no, thank you. I'm afraid we have more important business at hand, Carter!
CARTER: More important than eating, Sir?
BRAITHWAITE: Yes, yes. It is a matter of command. We're all in a pretty sticky situation here. And if order's to be maintained, well, someone has to be in charge.
CARTER: You're quite right, Sir. Very, very important!
BRAITHWAITE: Do you agree, Captain Wilson?
WILSON: Yes, absolutely. Who do you think it should be?
BRAITHWAITE: Well, this sort of thing is generally determined by rank, isn't it?
WILSON: Yes, ordinarily. But there is the question here of whether a retired General serving as a war correspondent outranks a Captain on active duty.
BRAITHWAITE: What?
WILSON [to everybody]: Who do you think?
CRAMER: Who do we think should be in charge?
WILSON: That's right.
CRAMER: The best man for the job.
WILSON: Right!
CRAMER: I think I'd be the best man for the job.
BRAITHWAITE [snickers]: A Private? Quite impossible!
CARTER: Wait just a moment Sir. Why not hear his reasons? After all he was asked to speak out....
WILSON: All right, Cramer, what are your reasons?
CRAMER: It figures, that's all. The general hasn't seen combat for over twenty years. The lieutenant [Carter] here is an Air Force officer, doesn't know anything about ground command. And those guys are supposed to be our prisoners.
WILSON: And me?
CRAMER: You're not a soldier, Captain, you're a public-relations officer.

However, no attempt to introduce striating structures will keep the State war machine from becoming destratified. As Bonta and Protevi explain, destratification (an, again, geological term) denotes "decentralizing an organism or other hierarchical structure by pushing it past a 'crisis' threshold of its intensive properties to allow the components to find their own arrangements rather than submit to the overcoding of the stratifying agent" (Bonta 78). And this is exactly what happens in the course of the film. The protagonists are pushed past a crisis threshold by being caught in the cavern, and it soon becomes clear that the rules and structures of the outside world have become irrelevant. The grid of the striated State space starts to crack up when the principle of military ranks is questioned. Instead of depending on the external stratifying agent of military ranks the arrangement of the group follows immanent properties (the man in charge should be "the best man for the job"). Also, the hierarchizing and striating differences between captor and captured, between nationalities and even between gender have lost their structuring/territorializing powers to such an extend that Anna, the peasant woman, finally insists: "There is *nothing* about me, Excellency, except that I *am*."

> GENERAL: We've all got to work together to get out of this blasted hole and being our prisoners, you are naturally under our orders.
> HANS BECK: We all are prisoners, General. Prisoners of the mountain.
> CRAMER: Sir, two willing pair of hands extra could only help, maybe we ought to declare armistice until we dig ourselves out, and once we're out, it could be every man for himself.
> GENERAL: Hm, very well, then. We shall all work together and absolutely forget about nationalities. [To Hans Beck] But I warn you! I know you Germans through and through, and I shall stand for none of your Prussian tricks!
> HANS BECK: Yes, Sir!
> GENERAL [to Anna]: Now, what about you, young woman?
> ANNA: What about me? There is nothing about me, Excellency, except that I am.

The protagonists have entered the cave as part of a State war machine, but being cut off from State power, this machine is slowly becoming destratified, changing back into a smooth war machine. Not only are the protagonists deterritorialized in terms of nationalities and rank, also the discipline is starting to come apart. As it turns out, General Braithwaite and Captain Wilson are alcoholics. Luckily for Wilson, he stumbles over cases of brandy which he decides not to share with the others. When the General discovers this secret, Wilson persuades him not to mention the alcohol to the others, pretending that his only concern is the discipline in the group. The General, feeling that he is slowly "cracking up" without a decent drink, admits to covering up the story, even though he stresses that this secrecy is against his "principles":

> WILSON: I'm an alcoholic, General. I have been for years.
> BRAITHWAITE: No excuse!
> WILSON: No, I'm not giving you excuses. I'm telling you facts.
> BRAITHWAITE: But it's the whole principle of the thing. I mean, one can't live like that, absolutely out of the question!
> WILSON: The principle of the thing? You mean I should share this bonanza with them out there?
> BRAITHWAITE: What else?
> WILSON: No, no, no, General, you don't understand! There are cases of this

stuff! Now you just take a look at this men out there, Mario and Cramer and that Kraut, shut up in a place like this for months and the nerves shut with all the liquor they can drink and the girl to fight over? Oh General, they'll be killing each other within three days.
BRAITHWAITE: But the whole terrible secrecy of the thing!

As Deleuze and Guattari state, the smooth war machine brings "secrecy against the public" (*Thousand Plateaus* 352), and in this scene the secrecy of the two men does in fact start to subvert the discipline and order of the striated space.

As mentioned before, the first plan to escape from the cavern by digging the way out fails because the only place the protagonists reach is just another cave within the cave. It can be argued that this plan had to fail, because it depended on the wrong mode of orientation, namely that of reproduction, which only works in striated space. According to Deleuze and Guattari, "reproducing implies the permanence of a fixed point of view that is external to what is reproduced" (*Thousand Plateaus* 372). Ironically, in the case of the captured protagonists, the very point is that they are *not* external to the cave; still they reproduce an imaginary form of the cave that they try to shortcut by breaking through the material. However, in smooth space, lines are vectors that express intensities rather than metric determinations, therefore a reproductive model depending on fixed lines and properties will necessarily lead to a distorted image. Consequently, the tunnel is not actually leading to where they think it would and they have to realize that smooth space requires a different mode of orientation.

But Private Cramer comes up with a new plan. He intends to follow the underground stream that is flowing through the cavern to see where it leads to. This idea is much more in accordance with how Deleuze and Guattari define orientation in smooth space because, instead of being based on reproduction, it is literally based on "following:" "[F]ollowing is something different from the ideal of reproduction. Not better, just different. One is obliged to follow when one is in search of the 'singularities' of a matter, or rather of a material, and not out to discover a form; when one escapes the force of gravity to enter a field of celerity" (*Thousand Plateaus* 372). By jumping into the river, Cramer does indeed escape the field of gravity and instead enters an intensive field in which the speeds and slownesses of the currents of the water become important. Unfortunately, the forces of the subterranean river are so strong that it becomes impossible for Cramer to find out whether it will eventually lead to the outside, and he is forced to return.

In the following, the group diminishes slowly: Captain Wilson, in a state of complete drunkenness, stumbles into the river and drowns. So does Carter during a second attempt to explore the river using a makeshift diving mask to breathe under water. Hans finds an even more ironic end: While searching the endless tunnels of the cavern he eventually discovers an exit to the surface. Unfortunately for him (and for the others) once he has left the smooth space of the cavern in which his nationality and uniform have become meaningless, he is reterritorialized immediately: As Deleuze and Guattari point out, the striated "is defined by the requirements of long-distance vision" (*Thousand Plateaus* 494). This very long-distance vision of striated space is adopted by the camera (it imitates binoculars), it reduces Hans to the signs and emblems of his German uniform and the State war machine brings back his nationality with a vengeance. He is shot by Italian partisan soldiers (who happen to spot him leaving the cavern) before he can get back to the others to tell them about his discovery.

With each day spent inside the confinements of the cavern the remaining protagonists are increasingly cracking up. The General is starting to suffer from dementia, and with the dwindling food and power-supply, the hopes of Cramer, Anna and Mario to escape from the cave are vanishing, too. In the final scene, when all order and discipline has eventually been eroded by desperation, the General is turning the war machine against himself. Wit-

Rosanna Schiaffino and Nino Castelnuovo in *The Cavern* (courtesy Edgar G. Ulmer Preservation Corporation).

nessing how Mario and Cramer are fighting over Anna, and seeing that the last remnant of discipline has been eroded, he takes a hand grenade and decides to kill himself. When the others realize what he's about to do they try to stop him, but the General is determined to end his life and bends over the exploding grenade, his last words being "Please let me die like a soldier." Faced with the crack-up of the other characters he is thus reterritorializing himself. This instance of returning to the striating structures of a State war machine within the smooth space opens up the smooth to the additional dimension of the outside. The explosion triggers a chain reaction that creates an exit to the striated space, and in the final scene, the three surviving protagonists stumble into the sunlight again.

Conclusion

Deleuze and Guattari warn the reader at the end of *A Thousand Plateaus* that, "[o]f course, smooth spaces are not in themselves liberatory" (*Thousand Plateaus* 500). Instead of advocating to counter the stratifying powers of the striated by the pure destratifying forces of the smooth, Deleuze and Guattari refer to a third kind of space: "Transpierce the mountains instead of scaling them, excavate the land instead of striating it, bore holes in space instead of keeping it smooth, turn the earth into Swiss cheese" (*Thousand Plateaus* 413). The true "counter-action to striation" (Bonta 145) is creating a holey space, an "'underground' space that can connect with smooth space and be conjugated by striated space" (Bonta 95).

Ulmer's *Cavern* is such a holey space in which the protagonists are forced to oscillate between the smooth and the striated. Being suspended in this dynamic force field requires them to find new modes of being in space and for space, it pushes them past a crisis threshold and exposes them to intensities that have the force to crack them up, to completely de-organize the subject, such as the alcoholism of Wilson and Braithwaite. The State war machine, as part of which they have entered the cave, is becoming destratified, leading to deterritorializations and new couplings. Unlikely friendships among and beyond nationalities and political parties emerge and by the end of the film, Mario's friend Anna has fallen in love with Private Cramer. Thus, Ulmer's geocinematic film expresses the same geophilosophical warning that Deleuze and Guattari express in the last sentence of *A Thousand Plateaus*: "Never believe that a smooth space will suffice to save us" (*Thousand Plateaus* 500).

Works Cited

Bernard, Raymond. *The Hollow Earth*. Secaucus, NJ: Lyle Stuart, 1969.
Bonta, Mark, and John Protevi. *Deleuze and Geophilosophy*. Edinburgh, Scotland: Edinburgh University Press, 2004.
The Cavern. U.S.A., 1964. Directed by Edgar G. Ulmer.
Deleuze, Gilles, and Félix Guattari. *A Thousand Plateaus*. Minneapolis, MN: University of Minnesota Press, 1987.
_____. *What Is Philosophy?* New York: Columbia University Press, 1994.
Parr, Adrian. "Deterritorialization/Reterritorialization." Adrian Parr (ed.). *The Deleuzian Dictionary*. New York: Columbia University Press, 2005, 66–69.

Ulmer in the Aquarium
Adrian Martin

The Big But

There is still a tendency in articles about Edgar G. Ulmer — as there is in articles about Joseph H. Lewis or Jack Arnold, as there used to be in articles about Samuel Fuller or Phil Karlson — to hinge all praise on a *but*. It takes various linguistic forms: *despite* poor scripts and bargain-basement resources, Ulmer managed to express himself ... *although* the actors were dreadful and the projects not of his choosing, Ulmer somehow stamped his distinctive style on the material ... most of the films are meaningless, ridiculous even, *but* Ulmer's delirious sensibility shines through....

It is a big *but*. A defensive, qualifying move that, no doubt, concedes far too much to middlebrow, conservative, conventional taste. Do we really think so highly, so automatically, of traditionally well-made, well-shot, subtly acted, solidly scripted, smoothly edited, handsomely resourced cinema? For this is exactly what that *but* implies, over and over, every time it is uttered: that the exception exists but the rule insists, indomitably; and that this rule informs, even determines, all our judgments of value and taste. Ultimately, all such statements boil down to the horrid, casual remark heard, years ago, from a university student making a serious presentation on the films of Seijun Suzuki: *really, he was a bad filmmaker, but his movies are crazy and fun*. A posture that can only ever invite a form of superior laughter on the part of the spectator.

In short, the big *but* is an expression of normative thinking, normative aesthetics, normative criticism. In my opinion, we will never come to terms with Ulmer without first thoroughly defusing the minefield of such normative artistic and cultural attitudes — and then seeing what is left on the ground, or what needs to be planted or replanted there, in order to proceed with another kind of criticism. This essay is a consideration of such methodological and theoretical questions (about Ulmer considered as an auteur, and about

B cinema), a prolegomena to a proper study of Ulmer — taking as its sole illustrative figure (out of the many interwoven cinematic figures in Ulmer) the idea of the Ulmerian *aquarium*.

For the moment, however, we must return to the consideration of that big but — the default position in which so much Ulmer criticism (and, beyond him, so much supposedly eccentric B cinema) gets caught. The strangest spectacle of all is to hear this default position espoused by those who set themselves up as champions of a certain other, different, alternative cinema — a sub-popular cinema inside and against the mainstream: B cinema, exploitation cinema, Poverty Row cinema, *cinéma bis* ... It is what I have elsewhere diagnosed as the *nerd reflex* in film criticism: the nerd with a taste for horror or action movies, *The Black Cat* (1934) or *Detour* (1945), who makes a show of appreciating what is inventive, crazy or sublime in the work they trumpet — but, unfailingly, brings this work to the bar of normative aesthetic values (see Martin). The film is almost ruined by the cast! If only the script were better! It falls down in Act 3, alas! But, despite it all, there are signs of our *maudit* master, flashes of a sensibility, touches of his or her style....

There is a mindset haunting nerd criticism which smacks of what Jacques Lacan once called the *non-dupe* position, a term that Serge Daney loved to use to diagnose the paralyzing double-binds of film culture everywhere (see Krohn, "Les *Cahiers*"). The non-dupe attitude to B cinema is highly rational, economic, professional in its aspiration: the nerd lover dreams of doing it himself or herself, and doing it better, with a bigger budget, trained actors, good lighting, and the backing or Miramax or New Line. This is, today, the Tarantino School of slicked-up exploitation (*Death Proof* [2007]: the would-be quota-quickie made with unlimited money, promotional tie-ins and Cannes premiere) which, for instance, includes the masterminds of the *Blair Witch* franchise or (more recently) the *Saw* cycle.

What, in Ulmer, can truly survive this normative sifting procedure? Some nutty camera angles, maybe, some spots of expressionist lighting, or a florid use of familiar classical music. Inventive touches that reach only to the decorative: pure surplus value for the well-made (or not so well-made) product, surface sheen, clever packaging. Economic, assembly line, corporate thinking again prevails; artistic "production for use," as Marilyn Campbell once wrote of the classical Hollywood cinema (her example being Hawks' *His Girl Friday* [1940]) at its most ruthlessly efficient (see Campbell). And this is exactly what is recycled in what we might call the wanna-B cinema of our time: a type of proud, sub-baroque fiddling that forces its way to the surface under the smelting blast of tight budgets, short shooting schedules and formulaic templates — but that leaves the traditional substance of the project utterly intact. The young American filmmaker Morgan J. Freeman (not to be confused with the actor) epitomizes this approach when, on the typically over-earnest, self-aggrandising auteur audio commentary to his weak assignment *American Psycho II: All-American Girl* (2002), he remarks of a fussy shot taken for no particular dramaturgical or formal reason through colored, frosted glass: "It was an aesthetic decision!" And such aesthetic decisions mark the self-conscious development of B cinema in the era inaugurated (for good and for ill) by Roger Corman, less as a director himself (the ones he signed are fairly classical) than as producer, impresario and purveyor of young film-school talent since the early 1960s. It is precisely this attitude, devouring film history retroactively, that tends to be expressed apropos of Ulmer in the documentary *Edgar G. Ulmer—The Man Off-Screen* (2004): what remains of the zany wreckage of his career are only the fussy, nutty, aesthetic decisions, punctual, eye-popping or ear-blasting.

The big but of nerd criticism obsesses itself, anxiously, over budget, schedule and shooting ratio. We read that this or that immortal Ulmer film was shot in three, five or seven days, that the money wouldn't stretch to this set or that prop, that scenes were executed in a minimum of takes — as if the gumption, or the recklessness, or the ultra-professionalism of this is really all that matters. But truly — from a certain angle of artistic evaluation — why should we care (beyond the anecdotal background level) about such information? Do we inquire into how many days it took to shoot Dreyer's *Gertrud* (1964) or what the precise budget of Hawks' *Monkey Business* (1952) was? Raúl Ruiz — a great fan of Ulmer, whom he considers a cinematic father-figure long unknown to him — at least raised this species of admiration to another, more avant-garde level by endeavoring to shoot conceptual-art quickies like *The Territory* (1981) and *The Roof of the Whale* (1984) as swiftly and with as many separate camera set-ups as possible (see Ruiz). But Tag Gallagher is right when he complains:

> What does it matter that *Green Fields* (1937) was shot in five days, for $8,000, or that Ulmer hadn't had even twice as much negative to shoot with as his finished film would be, or that he had to share a bed with his assistant and they had all hocked their furniture to raise money? What do these things matter, unless to prove that money is bad for art, since nearly every movie ever made has cost more than *Green Fields* and looks impoverished alongside it [Gallagher].

"Take the questions of justice, beauty, happiness, and perhaps even truth," Jean-François Lyotard once ventured. "Why is it necessary to believe in competence and authority in these matters, when there is none?" (38) The questions of cultural taste and judgement, certainly, need further probing in this context, in the light of an infamous pop-pedagogical example. Lyotard's expressed scepticism (too often mistaken for an anything-goes relativism) could have been taken to underlie *J'Accuse*, an early 1990s television series from Channel 4 in Britain. Each episode started with a touch of drama in the credits — a hand chiseling the defiant words "'j'accuse" into a slab of stone bearing the names of great artists from Eliot and Joyce to Charlie Parker and The Beatles. The idea of the series was to offer a platform, each week, to a brave, dissident critic who challenges the previously unquestioned assumption that a particular artist or work is truly great and deserving of its place in the canon of art. In the first episode, Fay Weldon accused Jane Austen, and in the second Robert McKee, world-famous how-to-write-a-screenplay guru, took on Orson Welles' *Citizen Kane* (1941).

J'Accuse did not practice the traditional critical arts of exploration, interpretation or appreciation. Nor, unfortunately, did it exhibit the radical sense of critical openness for which Lyotard called. Rather, *J'Accuse* heralded a newer style of criticism which has since become massively prevalent in the mass media and specialist coverage of the arts alike — criticism as righteous exposé, oneupmanship, brutal discernment. And it is this mindset which, paradoxically, underlies even the prevalent discussions of a filmmaker like Ulmer.

The suspicion expressed by *J'Accuse* was healthy enough: why trust the experts, why parrot the canons? But the critique offered by the program was itself disturbingly authoritarian in its eagerness to denounce certain artworks as merely the latest instance of the Emperor's New Clothes — regarded highly only by those very stupid, trendy people who are susceptible to hype and mystification (and, of course, to anything even slightly avant-garde). Accordingly, the show practiced — and encouraged in its eager cohort of viewers and reviewers — a style of impatient, indignant, philistine dismissal. You thought Jane Austen was a great writer? She's just dressed up Mills and Boon!

It is possible to discredit every great or interesting artwork in the universe by reducing it to an absurd theorem, and then mocking what remains: in the case of Ulmer, this task is exceedingly easy. Robert McKee, a master of rhetoric, talked over the top of certain shots from *Citizen Kane* in his *J'Accuse* episode — pointing out, with affected weariness, the symbolism of mirrors, shadows, empty rooms — all the while punctuating his remarks with outbursts like 'Gimme a break!' This is a good example of a journalistic style which reigns in places like the slick American film magazine *Premiere*, and is today everywhere on the Internet: smart ass and swaggering to the end, it gets in its mean little death blows as quickly as possible, ever eager to denounce any new movie event as derivative, formulaic, silly, overblown....

One of the most deeply disturbing elements of this style of critique is, once again, how conventional, how utterly normative its standards and criteria actually are. McKee's case against *Citizen Kane* in *J'Accuse* rests on booming assertions that include: "The ideal in art is to create a seamless unity in which style never calls attention to itself," "we want emotion from a great film — rich emotion, not the easy sensations of violence or sentimentality," and "there's a great principle underlying all fine storytelling, known as show, don't tell." A great wall of rules, injunctions and norms that deny any measure of greatness to a work of art where style exhibits itself shamelessly, emotion is shallow, or stories are baroque — qualities which describe quite a lot of mass culture, and certainly B cinema.

It can be quickly verified that the vast majority of film reviewers/critics — whether in newspapers, magazines, blogs or academic journals — exercise their right to praise or damn on the basis of unspoken principles quite close to McKee's. The workaday film review regularly manifests quite spurious assumptions and imagined standards about what constitutes a well-structured script, proper rules for a specific genre, a correct style of screen acting, and so on. Words like overlong, risible, incoherent and implausible are the stock-in-trade of any proudly judgmental reviewer. Films are regularly damned for "not knowing what they want to be," or for unwisely attempting to do two different things at once. Yet the general, cultured consensus on what constitutes a good film — noble theme, psychologically deep characters, believable story, seamless continuity and so forth — is ridiculously rigid and overprescriptive, able to do justice to less than probably ten per cent of the wonders of world cinema. Such an evaluative system inevitably draws a blank, indeed, on Orson Welles who, before he was even eighteen, published a series of radically condensed promptbook editions of Shakespeare's plays that carry this fine piece of showbiz advice: "Remember that every single way of playing Shakespeare — as long as the way is effective — is right." Ulmer, with his unique take on the classics, could have related to that.

There's something particularly nerdy about a culture buff who alights on popular art — obviously drawn to it because it is often undervalued, misunderstood or unsung — and then proceeds to enforce, like a maniac cop, the standards that he or she has unquestioningly inherited from the dominant culture. It's the same smug sense of superiority that underwrites the derisive laughter of primed audiences at screenings of supposedly bad movies like *Robot Monster* (1953) or Hong Kong action films like John Woo's *The Killer* (1989), the whole Golden Turkey phenomenon born in the 1980s: an assumption that everyone knows what a good or quality film is, and that anything which deviates from that norm is worthy only of our contempt and ridicule. William D. Routt has rightly called such scornful taste "an apotheosis of constriction, criticism as constipation, in which anything that speaks of risk is condemned as foolish, loose and uncontrolled, prodigally stupid or inept" ("The Menace" 70).

So what of all this bad popular art, which so many of us, at some time, will find ourselves loving — even if, at another time and place, we will struggle to downplay, rationalize, or repress the intensity of that love? *Citizen Kane* is — paradoxically, because of its classic status — a good place to start in the search for Ulmer and his artistic compatriots. Both *Kane*'s supporters and its detractors have argued down the decades as to what exact sort of aesthetic beast it is, trying to definitively claim it as a Hollywood film or an art film, a modernist work or a conventional one, an ironic comedy or a reflective drama, as profound or shallow. McKee — smelling a film with awful pretensions to art — savagely adjudicates: "It's pure Hollywood: energy, extravaganza, technical razzle dazzle, but ultimately all glitz and no guts." But the glory of *Citizen Kane* is that it is such a hybrid of a movie — it shamelessly mixes up all sorts of very distinct styles and impulses and refuses to opt for any single category. In the parlance of no-bullshit reviewing, it is indeed a film that can't make up its mind what it wants to be. But what's wrong with that?

Serge Daney once remarked that he loved the American cinema "in spite of itself — and in spite of the way it wanted to be loved" (qtd. in Krohn, "Les Cahiers" 35) As a critic, Daney championed what he saw as the most despised part of popular art: the accused part that even its makers are sometimes quick to disown. He tells the story of how, as a young film buff, he made a pilgrimage to Hollywood to interview his favorite directors. "I remember in 1964 we saw George Cukor and confided in him that *Wind across the Everglades* [Nicholas Ray, 1958] was one of the most beautiful American films. He broke out in a peal of laughter where all the contempt he had for this little film could be read. We were very wounded, but we have never changed our minds" (35).

Daney's sensibility is not based upon a perverse attachment to material deemed so bad that it's riotously funny; it expresses a spontaneous, even childlike embrace of what can sometimes be sublimely ridiculous, florid, excessive, silly, sentimental, confused or incoherent in popular art. (*Wind Across the Everglades*, by the way, is a swamp opera with Burl Ives, Christopher Plummer and Gypsy Rose Lee. Leonard Maltin's tag: "Oddball cast in even odder story.") To cultivate such a sensibility is to develop a fine appreciation for what Raymond Durgnat once called pulp poetry — marvellous apparitions that sometimes escaped the conscious design of their maker (see Durgnat). I am reminded of Roger Tailleur's assessment of Frank Tashlin's movies such as *The Girl Can't Help It* (1956): "His poetry ... is the poetry of the comic books, of children, of the pure, the mad, of Jerry Lewis" (10).

Jerry Lewis is, in fact, a key case in the history of accused popular art. Still today, uncharitable exposé writers in smart American gossip magazines like *Spy* make a big deal about the silly French critics (such as Tailleur) who deluded themselves into finding magnificent virtues in the movies Lewis directed in the 1960s (like *The Nutty Professor* [1963] and *The Ladies' Man* [1961]) — when the plain truth is there on the screen that the films are simply horrible, unwatchable, BAD! Even Lewis fans in the Anglo world of criticism have to regularly readjust their mental sets when they encounter the passionate homages of those French (and other European) movie lovers who beheld the art of Jerry Lewis and then unapologetically offered up (in Paul Willemen's description) "frenzy, madness, neurosis, extravaganza, monstrosity" as "positive values" in a work of art (9).

Of all those who have struggled in defense of the cultural accused, filmmaker Martin Scorsese is among the wisest. His own films have long been elevated to the rank of serious art, yet he fearlessly testifies to his passion for certified trashy directors in popular cinema history like Jerry Lewis or Sam Fuller — not forgetting the lurid or sensational aspect of more respected figures like Welles or Michael Powell. It may well have something to do with his personal, ambivalent struggle with Catholicism, but Scorsese in interviews is the model of a popular culture fan who sees everything — both what is deemed good and what is deemed bad — in the works he loves. On emerging from *The Killer*, for instance, he is reported to have said: "'It's hysterical — and also very beautiful."

Scorsese's appreciation of the force and significance of certain films is bound up completely with his sense of how they oscillate between the poles of aesthetic goodness and badness — and what is unleashed as a result of that tussle. His films, too, explore an acute awareness of the social drama involved in the avowal of bad art: he cast Jerry Lewis in *The King of Comedy* (1983) — the film par excellence of excruciating bad manners, humiliation and embarrassment — because he remembered how in a TV appearance of the 1950s the comedian "walked on and just put his mouth on the lens. Ate the camera. It was bad. Vulgar. But the surrealism of it ... it just worked. It was total anarchy. It destroyed television as we know it" (qtd. in Houston 65).

To destroy the canon of art as we know it should not mean, as it did on *J'Accuse*, doubling the effort to police badness and rid the world of anything that seems suspiciously unfamiliar, ill formed or wrongheaded. It should mean — as it has for many true lovers of popular culture — publicly expanding the definition of what is good, interesting, important and beautiful art. But this is always a struggle and Scorsese, for one, knows it. He admitted during a television interview of the mid-'90s: "I guess I'm still a little cowed by the tyranny of art with a capital A," he admits, reflecting on his admiration for films such as *All About Eve* (1950) which have "a sense of dignity because of their literary background." But then he recalls his enjoyment of King Vidor's Western *Duel in the Sun* (1946): "I thought that was just phenomenal. Granted, it's trash down to the very bone, the very core, the very marrow, but wonderful, just wonderful. I prefer the excess and the hysteria there." His adieu, however, is rueful: "The literary will always have the upper hand here. It always will."

Frenzy, madness, neurosis, extravaganza, monstrosity ... ultimately, it is a question of grasping, understanding — and redefining — the very notion of the *sublime* in art. And never more so than in the case of Ulmer. What would it mean to call his work sublime, beyond a simple swooning reflex (it's great, I loved it!), or the exhibition of some hyper-sophisticated twenty-first century irony (the kind that loves to call Steven Seagal movies sublime, thus both earning a laugh and gaining the nod from the new cognoscenti of the cultish sub-popular)? Let us look at one of Ulmer's finest and most admirable commentators, the French critic Jacques Lourcelles — both for the substance of his appreciation of Ulmer, and for the terms (descriptive, intellectual, rhetorical) in which he phrases it. The subject is *Club Havana* (1945):

> One of the most perfect, and most typical, films of this director. In sixty minutes, with the help of a pathetic budget (one rightly thinks of a poor *Grand Hotel*), Ulmer presents twenty principal characters and films five musical numbers, the entirety atop a pleasing rhythm which accords to each character his time of speech, his fragment of destiny. A reduced — even miniaturised — human comedy, it is truly here the occasion to speak of a microcosm. This miniaturisation marvelously expresses Ulmer's viewpoint on the world: always the viewpoint of Sirius or Mars. Earth seen from the planet Mars, like in all Ulmer's films. Men and women are these pathetic (in both senses) marionettes who make three little turns and then come back around again, under the sympathetic but faraway gaze of this Murnau disciple. The angel of the bizarre appears not so much in this or that aspect of the intrigue, nor the genre to which it belongs. It is present everywhere: in the distance of the filmmaker's regard as much as in this heteroclite entanglement, this express-inventory of human passions (cynicism, despair, tender love, murderous love, etc.) [307–8].

Note: hardly a word here about the budget, and, at any rate, nothing defensive or apologetic about it. Lourcelles adopts a shamelessly *cosmic* tone or vision that can be associated with the loose school of 1960s criticism that he first came to notice with: the MacMahonist circle, with its organ *Présence du cinéma*, which championed the greats like Preminger, Losey and Lang, but also Blake Edwards, Allan Dwan, Don Weis, Richard Quine ... a MacMahonism to which Serge Daney always respectfully genuflected when he returned to fetish-objects like Lang's late-period Indian extravaganzas, so derided by official taste. "Earth seen from the planet Mars, as in all Ulmer's films": this artist is defined first and foremost by a *regard*— meaning both an attitude and a gaze — and not by a genre, or a production context, or a cul-

Critic Jacques Lourcelles adopts a shamelessly cosmic tone when applauding *Club Havana* (courtesy Edgar G. Ulmer Preservation Corporation).

turally-bound subject matter. Of course, here Lourcelles (like much of the MacMahonist criticism) risks a certain abstraction of all materiality of time and place, risks an outrageous "transcendentalising" of the material in this film, this lowly little *Club Havana*, an item which in other contexts of reception elicits only a faint, brief, forgetful, camp giggle. But why not take this risk?

The B Question

Another fine comment from the (relatively small) critical annals on Ulmer, by the American critic Bill Krohn:

> Shirley Ulmer was to perfect her craft [as a script supervisor] under the tutelage of a director with a passion for heterogeneity., who would frequently change the lighting or the background of a shot over her protests and in flagrant violation of all the laws of continuity on the pretext that it was "right for the feeling" or that "no one notices these things anyway" ["King of the B's" 61].

A passion for heterogeneity: this excellent phrase can only really be understood within a context of a certain strain in film theory as it developed between the 1960s and the '80s, and as it was eagerly imbibed by a critic like Krohn who for many years wrote a column for *Cahiers du cinéma*, initiated by Serge Daney. Heterogeneity: difference, intervals, gaps, ruptures, discontinuities, excess; a film with a variegated texture, completely on display, all seams showing. The dead opposite of the Classical Hollywood style, which aims for smoothness and invisibility, steady functioning, control of tone and purpose. The cinema of Werner Schroeter, Marguerite Duras, Jean-Luc Godard. But also: Jerry Lewis, Sergio Leone ... and Edgar G. Ulmer. Although it was not really grasped as such at the time, the passion for heterogeneity — among critics as much as filmmakers — was, as much as an avant-garde trope, also a stirring defense of the ways and means of B cinema. This is exactly what Krohn expressed, in 1983, when he displaced the passion for heterogeneity from the Marxist-Lacanian discourse of *Cahiers* to an article on Ulmer in *Film Comment*.

It is a delicate matter to situate Ulmer within the context of the B movie. Because, all over again, we must fight for a new standard of taste, a new way of seeing, that is endemic to the form. And even some of the most perceptive commentators on B cinema have fallen into a few traps: either celebrating B cinema as a kind of *anti-cinema* — an oppositional gesture which always ends up, inevitably, reaffirming conventional cinema in its dominance, even as one rails against it; or making the move to separate out certain, special directors (such as Ulmer, Joseph Lewis, Karlson, even Ed Wood) from the general B pond, to elevate them as artists above the mere conventions. And part of the problem here, certainly, is that it is impossible, finally, to cleanly separate A from B cinema — many conventions and tendencies (aesthetic as well as industrial) are indeed shared, carried over, handed down.

Nonetheless, it is, once again, worth taking the risk to define B cinema as its own kind of cinema. One of the most important guides in this task is another Ulmer scholar, the American-born, Australia-based William Routt, (see his "The Old Wild Men of the Movies") already cited above in his dead-on critique of the "loving bad movies" cult. What matters for Routt about B cinema is not simply that it undoes, on every level, the homogeneity of classical cinema — spatial and temporal continuity, cause-and-effect plot connectives, naturalistic acting, and so on — but that it compels our attention to another, different, new kind of cinema: a kind of neutral *literalness* (a literalness of gesture, image, event), a certain kind of flatness or sheer evidence that brings with it both an antidote to conventional dramatic interpretation and the challenge of thinking amorally, beyond the standard moral calculus of fiction (see his "Bad for Good"). In his article on the least artful gangster-crime films of B cinema, Routt writes:

The cinema appears to present a facile opportunity to approach pure denotation, while pure denotation in literature is something which belongs to the avant-garde. Doubtless this cinematic facility arises from the medium's kinship with other printing technologies — the sense in which cinema is not seen to "create" but only to "reproduce"— and of course that semblance is open to question. Nonetheless, as with other forms of printing, the question of reproduction, thus of literalism, is at the heart of the question of the cinema in a way that it cannot be in purely verbal discourse (discourse, that is, which represses its medium, its technology).

Among gangster films, *Inside the Mafia* (Edward L. Cahn, 1959) is an example of what edges nearest to the literal. Nothing in *Inside the Mafia* (until the last sequence) remains unexplained — no volitions, no competencies demand to be inferred, for they are spelled out explicitly, leaving the imagination nowhere to roam. Characters move stolidly without discernible intent through a series of mundane acts, about which the film says absolutely nothing except that they have occurred. Beside this, the films of Andy Warhol seem to seethe with undercurrents and connotations, not to say absurd pretenses and refinements. This is paracinema, a film from beyond cinema: raw film which pleases no one, which everyone calls "bad" or "boring," but which, despite that, is one of the few places where our orphan of the nineteenth century actually encounters the period in which it has grown up, one of the few places where the cinema appears an art of today rather than of yesterday ["Todorov Among the Gangsters" 113–4].

Routt admires Ulmer films including *The Black Cat, Jive Junction* (1943) and *St. Benny the Dip* (1951). But it is to *Strange Illusion* that I wish to briefly turn in order to mention one special feature of the B movie approach and aesthetic. In this frankly psychoanalytic film which fits into the Hollywood cycle which includes Alfred Hitchcock's *Spellbound* (1945), Fritz Lang's *Secret Beyond the Door…* (1948) and Jacques Tourneur's *Experiment Perilous* (1944), Ulmer revels — as he would also in *Detour, Ruthless* (1948) and *The Naked Dawn* (1955) — in a profoundly non-psychological form of characterization in cinema. This is not to sure that psychological states and affects are missing — indeed, they are everywhere, in a dizzying profusion — but that these states and affects are never tied to the coherence of what conventional dramaturgy considers a proper, stable, coherent, "three dimensional character," who is coherent even in their innermost conflicts and contradictions. And yet the standard way of describing B cinema modes of characterization — as a recourse to clean and clear, highly economic character *stereotypes* — also misses the mask, for it inscribes, at a lower, simpler level, the same hierarchical judgement based on the notion of character coherence and solidity.

In Ulmer, and B cinema more generally, we witness a different sort of picturing or dynamic *figuring* of the human personage. The identity of characters wildly shifts from scene to scene, plot plateau to plateau, shot to shot

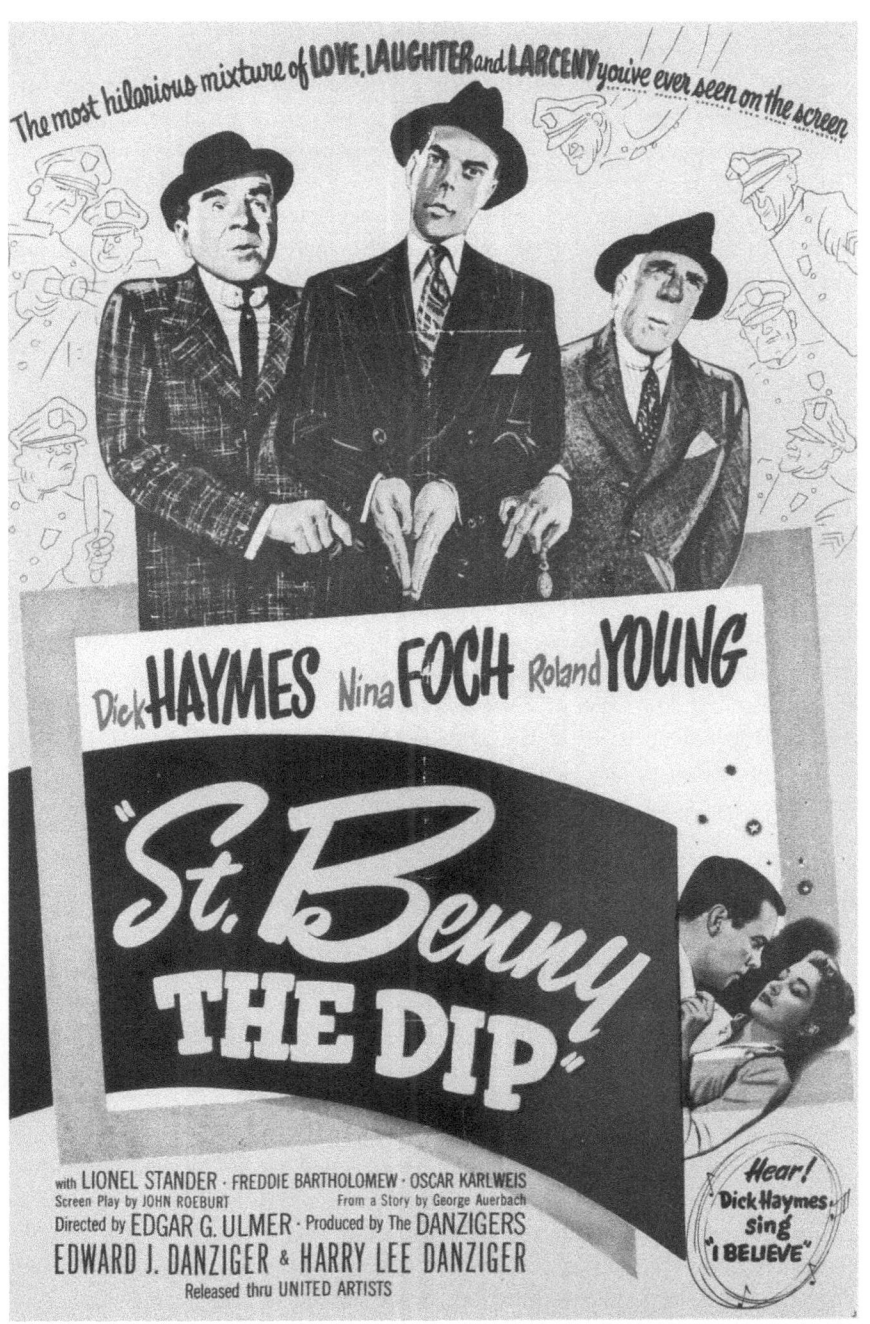

A poster for *St. Benny the Dip* from 1951 (courtesy Edgar G. Ulmer Preservation Corporation).

and even moment to moment. As Raúl Ruiz reminds us, in his own work and elsewhere, this is a property of both avant-garde fiction and of many popular traditions of storytelling (Mexican melodramas, Spanish *telenovelas*, Chilean folklore). The girl who is a beggar at the start of a tale is suddenly a princess, a singing star, or a notorious "honeymoon killer"—and then, just as suddenly, is deposited back on the street corner to beg, as if nothing had ever happened to her. She is neither older nor wiser, more cynical or less full of illusion; she simply *is*, a vehicle for pure fiction. There is less a moral to this kind of zany story than, simply, a vertigo of displacement, and a swift change in identities, more superficial than profound—recall Lourcelles' just evocation of the characters in *Club Havana* as "marionettes who make three little turns and then come back around again." Nanni Moretti pays homage to this truly Surreal storytelling tradition in his *Caro Diario* [1994] when, glancing up at a TV playing in a bar, he spies Silvana Mangano first playing as a nun, and then, when he looks again, singing seductively like Gilda in a nightclub—an entire lifestyle change accomplished in a single cut, fade or flashback cue. And Ulmer is the master of this kind of perpetual transformation of self, this furious and yet serene process of unknowable metamorphosis. It is that quality of serenity—even in the midst of the noir convolutions of *Detour*, where the femme fatale at one point emerges from sleep to utter the anti-hero's exact worst nightmare—which gives Ulmer's *oeuvre* that sense (again from Lourcelles) of "Earth seen from the planet Mars."

In the Aquarium

In *Isle of Forgotten Sins* (1943), we can note a particular penchant of Ulmer—to cram as many people in the picture at once: three, five, ten ... all perfectly composed and contained in his frame. In *Club Havana* (as Lourcelles reminded us earlier) "Ulmer presents twenty principal characters"—reminding us of how Luis Buñuel topped that total by one, proud of conceiving his *The Exterminating Angel* (1962) as a film about twenty-one characters unable to leave a large but very crowded room. The more we look for this visual notation of figure in Ulmer, we literally find it everywhere—including in films with not such as large casts, like *Strange Illusion* (1945). Gallagher notes: "In movie after movie, Ulmer will track and pan following a hero or heroine in constant position in the frame" (Gallagher). In fact, it is more, usually, than a single hero or heroine: it is a couple, a trio (think of the opening and closing dream sequences of *Strange Illusion*) or a whole pack of bodies. Ulmer goes to great pains to keep his characters together in very

John Carradine, left, Sidney Toler and Gale Sondergaard in *Isle of Forgotten Sins* (courtesy Edgar G. Ulmer Preservation Corporation).

many shots. And think — considering, for once without the usual caveats, his budget — of the effort this would have required, the effort of will on Ulmer's part to impose this stylistic *parti pris* on his crews, who were probably much more used to the same old, analytic, master shot/counter shot set-ups and (in post-production) cutting.

There is a name for this unusual visual and cinematic configuration. It is another contemporary French critic, Alain Bergala, who has best defined the kind of thing Ulmer is doing when he places so many figures in a frame at once. He calls it an *aquarium shot*. Bergala distinguishes "*aquarium* filmmakers from *interval* filmmakers — for me, the two extreme poles of cinema" (28). Interval filmmakers are all about the distance between characters — and how editing articulates, exacerbates or resolves the fraught intervals placed between figures as laid out within the *mise-en-scène*. Aquarium filmmakers, on the other hand, "are filmmakers of the compressed arrangement of bodies, in a closed space. Bodies are piled up, folded, twisted, interlinked and positioned so as to enter this aquarium" (28). The prototype of

A lobby card from *Isle of Forgotten Sins* (courtesy Edgar G. Ulmer Preservation Corporation).

this form of cinema — where the principal of the aquarium shot is extended to a holistic aesthetic — is Vigo's *L'Atalante* (1934); and its descendants include Jean Epstein, Roberto Rossellini (his *Fioretti* is "a film of the agglomeration of bodies") and Philippe Garrel (especially his aptly titled *La Concentration* [1968]). Bergala continues:

> Aquarium filmmakers are afraid of the distances where characters can get lost or get away. By contrast, they are unafraid of deploying the "elastic" between actors, who come near to each other or far from the camera — above all, without a cut. Doubtless, the agony for aquarium filmmakers is the thought that the characters might escape them altogether [28].

How do we categorise the aquarium shot within an appreciation of Ulmer's work? A signature-effect, like Mario Bava's zooms or Max Ophuls' craning-and-tracking shots? A dramatic-stylistic motif, like the mirror-images and window-frames in Douglas Sirk? An obsession, like the shadows with a life of their own in Ruiz? Gallagher, for instance, advances a thematic reading, complete with its matching stylistic inversion:

There is a constancy of self despite a change of place or desperation to escape. In contrast, when Ulmer keeps the camera still and makes the person move within the stable frame, we understand that the world stays the same while the person is changing, and perhaps that the world and change are out of the person's control [Gallagher].

This is a logical system, but it cannot hope to cover all the crowded frames we will find in Ulmer once we begin looking for them.

This raises the problems that Ulmer poses for yet another classic gesture within the study of film: auteurism. That Ulmer is, in the most banal and taken-for-granted sense, an auteur — that he expressed something of himself in his work, and that any suitably primed spectator can easily come to recognize the material signs of this — is beyond contestation. But what does it mean, finally, to trace an auteur within his or her body of work? Raymond Durgnat once put it very simply but very powerfully: when we talk of an auteur, we are talking about *recurring material* from one film to another signed by that person. (24) That recurring material can be stylistic or thematic; it can be the matter of a felt attitude or approach (even if that attitude is eclecticism or the approach chameleon, rather than some absolute consistency in self-fidelity); it can reside in the smallest details or the loftiest levels of metaphysics. But recurring material is deceptive: it does not necessarily take us to the beating heart of the work, its most secret logic, or its most formative strategy. Psychoanalysts know that the story that is avowed most frequently, and always in the same words on the couch — the sad story of a primal childhood trauma or a first lost love — is probably just a cover-story (even if it happens to be perfectly true), something rehearsed and repeated to evade other currents, other intensities, other encounters and truths. This is the case, for instance, with Brian De Palma's line on his early family problems, or Scorsese's riff on his Catholic mean-streets upbringing: do these accounts really tell us anything that matter about the films made by these individuals? Rather, they become a kind of handy shorthand for exegetes and journalists, a sop to the age of generalized self-analysis and telling one's own life story.

Ultimately, Ulmer's auteur vision as expressed in the aquarium shot might best be understood as a matter of artistic *will*, in a strong and powerful philosophic sense. Deeper than a signature, more varied than an *idée fixe* obsession, and far more prevalent than a simple "touch." The aquarium shot is Ulmer's *regard*, in that double sense of vision and attitude — the regard that, in virtually in any production circumstance, hospitable or inhospitable, he was able to impose, guide, modulate and control. Lourcelles speaks of that "angel of the bizarre" which visits Ulmer's films from on high — and here we must take special precautions in using words (as I have again done here) on the order of strange, crazy, zany, oddball, Surreal ... but this elevated, angelic, metaphysical vision of the Bizarre is, once again worth risking. For Lourcelles, this quality of the bizarre is not a matter of narrative content, or genre. Perhaps we could argue — a little to one side of Lourcelles' purer auteurism — that it may be, indeed, a matter of this form of cinema unto itself, the B cinema, at its highest level of alternative possibility. When we understand that form of cinema better, we will be a little closer to taking the true measure of Edgar G. Ulmer.

Works Cited

Bergala, Alain. "L'intervalle." Jacques Aumont (ed.). *La mise en scène*. Bruxelles: De Boeck, 2000, 25–35.
Campbell, Marilyn. "*His Girl Friday*: Production for Use." *Wide Angle* 1:2 (Summer 1976), 22–27.
Durgnat, Raymond. *Films and Feelings*. London: Faber and Faber, 1967.
Gallagher, Tag. "All Lost in Wonder: Edgar G. Ulmer." *Screening the Past* 12 (2001), *http://www.latrobe.edu.au/screeningthepast/firstrelease/fr0301/tgafr12a.htm*, last accessed April 02, 2008.
Houston, Beverle. "*King of Comedy*: A Crisis of Substitution." *Framework* 24 (1984): 60–70.
Krohn, Bill. "Les *Cahiers du cinéma* 1968–1977: Interview with Serge Daney." *The Thousand Eyes* 2 (1977): 31–40; on-line at *http://home.earthlink.net/~steevee/Daney_1977.html*, last accessed April 02, 2008.
_____. "King of the B's." *Film Comment* (August 1983): 60–64.
Lourcelles, Jacques. *Dictionnaire du cinéma: Les Films*. Paris: Robert Laffont, 1992.
Lyotard, Jean-François. "An Assessment of Television." *Framework* 11 (Autumn 1979): 37–39.
Martin, Adrian. "Responsibility and Criticism." *Cinemascope* (January 2007), *www.cinemascope.it/Issue%207/Articoli_n7/Articoli_n7_05/Adrian_Martin.pdf*, last accessed April 02, 2008.
Routt, William D. "Bad For Good." *Intensities* 2 (November 2001), *http://www.routt.net/bill/badforgood2007.html*, last accessed April 02, 2008.
_____. "The Menace." *SubStance* 55, 17:1 (1988): 67–76.
_____. "The Old Wild Men of the Movies." *American Film* 1:10 (1976): 35–40.
_____. "Todorov Among the Gangsters." *Art and Text* 34 (1989): 109–126.
Ruiz, Raúl. *Poetics of Cinema*. Paris: Dis Voir, 1995.
Tailleur, Roger. "Frank Tashlin." Paul Willemen and Claire Johnston (eds.). *Frank Tashlin*. Edinburgh Film Festival, 1973, 10–16.
Willemen, Paul. "Frank Tashlin: A Proposition." Paul Willemen and Claire Johnston (eds.). *Frank Tashlin*. Edinburgh Film Festival, 1973, 5–9.

About the Contributors

Marcel Arbeit is an associate professor in the Department of English and American Studies, Palacký University, Olomouc, Czech Republic. His main fields of research are contemporary Southern literature, American and Canadian independent cinema, and popular culture. He is the author of a monograph on the novels of Fred Chappell and Cormac McCarthy published in 2006 (in Czech), the main editor of the three-volume *Bibliography of American Literature in Czech Translation* (2000), and the co-editor of *America in the Course of Human Events: Presentations and Interpretations* (Amsterdam 2006). He has published essays on Robert Altman, Tod Browning, David Gordon Green, Hal Hartley, and the South in film. He also co-edited a Czech anthology of contemporary Southern short fiction. He is the president of the Czech and Slovak Association for American Studies.

Stefanie Diekmann is a media and theater scholar from Berlin, Germany. Among her publications are a book about the discourse on photography in the nineteenth century (*Mythologien der Fotografie*, Fink, 2003), a number of articles on film, photography, theater and comics that have appeared in journals like *Fotogeschichte*, *Texte zur Kunst*, and *Kritische Berichte*, as well as four co-edited volumes and journals on photography in narrative and documentary film, on the concept of latency, and on comic books. Her second book is on representations of theater in narrative film, *Backstage: Konstellationen von Theater und Kino*, 2007. While working as assistant professor at the European University Viadrina from 1999 to 2006, Diekmann was also invited to teach as a visiting lecturer and professor at University College Cork (Ireland) in 2005 and at the University of Texas at Austin (USA) in 2006. She is a visiting professor at the Institute of Theater Studies, University of Berne, Switzerland.

Stefan Grissemann has published an extensive German-language survey of the life and work of Edgar G. Ulmer entitled *Mann im Schatten* in 2003. His other books include works on Michael Haneke, Elfriede Jelinek and Robert Frank. A film critic since 1988 in various international publications, Grissemann works as head of the arts section of *profil* magazine in Vienna, Austria. His latest publication is a 300-page study of Ulrich Seidl's life and career, *Sündenfall (Original Sin)*.

Petra Hanáková is an assistant professor in the Film Studies Department, Faculty of Arts, Charles University in Prague, Czech Republic. Her main research is on gender and film, theories of film and visual culture, and the representation of national identity in Czech cinema. She has co-edited the collection *V bludném kruhu: Mateřství a vychovatelství jako paradoxy modernity* (Motherhood and education as the paradoxes of modernity, Slon 2006), wrote *Pandořina skřínka aneb Co feministky provedly filmu?* (Pandora's box or What did the feminists do to cinema? Academia 2007) and is the editor of *Výzva perspektivy: Obraz a jeho divák od malby quattrocento k filmu a zpět* (The Challenge of Perspective: Image and Its Spectator from Quattrocento Painting to Film and Back, Academia 2008).

Bernd Herzogenrath is a professor of American studies and teaches American literature and culture at the University of Frankfurt and the University of Cologne, Germany. He is the author of *An Art of Desire: Reading Paul Auster* (Rodopi 1999), and the editor of *From Virgin Land to Disney World: Nature and Its Discontents in the USA of Yesterday and Today* (Rodopi 2001), *The Films of Tod Browning* (Black Dog 2006), and *The Cinema of Tod Browning: Essays of the Macabre and Grotesque* (McFarland 2008). His fields of interest are nineteenth and twentieth century American literature, critical theory, and cultural/media studies. He has just finished *Deleuze/Guattari & Ecology* and future publications include a collection of essays on *Deleuze/Guattari & Ecology*, an anthology on *Intermedia[lity]*. Bernd is also the organizer and founder of the *ulmerfest*, a bi-annual conference series on the work of Edgar G. Ulmer that takes place in Ulmer's hometown of Olomouc in the Czech Republic (see www.uni-koeln.de/phil-fak/englisch/abteilungen/berressem/herzogenrath/ulmer/index.htm). After years of digging through various archives, he also managed to locate Ulmer's birth home in Olomouc. There are two plaques on this house — one for Ulmer, one for Bernd.

Philipp Hofmann has earned his M.A. at the University of Bielefeld, Germany, and his Ph.D. at the University of Cologne, where he is teaching in the American Literature and Culture Department. He has published on Gilles Deleuze, Leonard Cohen, and digital media and chaos theory.

Reynold Humphries is a student of Christian Metz and wrote his thesis on a corpus of Fritz Lang's American films as *Fritz Lang: Genre and Representation in His American Films* (1989). He has since specialized in the horror genre, publishing *The American Horror Film: An Introduction* (2002) and *The Hollywood Horror Film, 1931–1941: Madness in a Social Landscape* (2006) and contributing to *Monstrous Adaptations* (2007), forthcoming anthologies devoted to Tod Browning and the modern American horror film, as well as to special horror issues of *Post Script* and *Paradoxa*, and to the online journal *Kinoeye*. He has published essays on David Cronenberg and Michael Powell and is co-editor of *Horror Stud-*

ies. An Interdisciplinary Journal. His other publications include essays in *Film Noir Reader 4, Gangster Film Reader, Docufictions* and anthologies devoted to Kubrick and Huston, as well as articles on Hollywood, blacklisting and the Cold War in French publications, seven contributions to *501 Movie Directors* and essays in French on Joseph Losey, Kenji Mizoguchi and Jacques Tourneur. His latest book is *Hollywood's Blacklists: A Political and Cultural History* (2008).

Ekkehard Knörer is a film and literature scholar as well as a film critic. He has written his dissertation, "Entfernte Ähnlichkeiten," on *wit* and *ingenium* in seventeenth and eighteenth century poetics and aesthetics from Baltasar Gracián to Jean Paul. He has published articles on desert movies and Tod Browning, on Robert Bresson's aesthetics of transubstantiation and various aspects of Hollywood movies. Hundreds of reviews and essays can be found in Jump Cut (*www.jumpcut.de*), the online movie magazine he has been editing since 1998. He is currently working on a book-length study on (seemingly) identical copies and remakes. He lives in Berlin.

Bill Krohn is the author of the award-winning *Hitchcock au travail* and of *Luis Buñuel: Chimera*, which have been published in several languages, and co-director, -producer, -writer of *It's All True: Based on an Unfinished Film by Orson Welles*. He has been the Los Angeles correspondent of *Cahiers du cinéma* for 30 years. He also reviews films for *The Economist*. He recently published French monographs *Alfred Hitchcock* and *Stanley Kubrick* and is completing *Serial Killer Dreams* for Reaktion Books, London, and translations of five "cinepoems" by Jean-Luc Godard that were originally published by P.O.L., Paris.

Petra Löffler, Ph.D., has been teaching at the Department of Media Studies, Information Sciences, and Cultural Studies at the University of Regensburg since 2005. She studied German philology, art history, and Slavic philology at the University of Cologne, worked from 1999 to 2004 on early cinema and media theory, at the Research Center for Media and Cultural Communication in Cologne, and has published numerous books and articles as well as art criticism in *Texte zur Kunst* and *Springerin*. Recent publications include *Medientheorien 1888–1933: Texte und Kommentare*, Frankfurt a.M. 2002 (with Albert Kümmel); *Affektbilder: Eine Mediengeschichte der Mimik*, Bielefeld 2004; and *Gesichter des Films*, Bielefeld 2005 (with Joanna Barck).

Gregory William Mank is the author of such books as *It's Alive! The Classic Cinema Saga of Frankenstein, Women in Horror Films, 1930s* and *Women in Horror Films, 1940s*, and his most recent book, *Hollywood's Hellfire Club*. His upcoming book *Bela Lugosi and Boris Karloff* (McFarland) will feature more material on *The Black Cat*.

Adrian Martin is senior research fellow in film and television studies, Monash University, Melbourne, Australia. He is the author of *Raul Ruiz: Sublimes Obsesiones* (2004), *The Mad Max Movies* (2003), *Once Upon a Time in America* (1998) and *Phantasms* (1994). He is the co-editor of *Movie Mutations* (2003) and the online film magazine *Rouge* (www.rouge.com.au). He has won the Byron Kennedy Award (Australian Film Institute), the Pascall Prize for Critical Writing and the Mollie Holman Award. He has written in many journals including *Trafic*, *De Filmkrant*, *Film Quarterly*, *Cahiers du Cinéma*, *España*, *Sight and Sound*, *Tren de sombras*, *16:9* and *Film Comment*. His forthcoming books include studies of Terrence Malick and Brian De Palma and a collection of essays on film theory, history, culture and analysis, *The Artificial Night*.

Frank Mehring is an assistant professor at the Department of Cultural Studies of the John F. Kennedy Institute for North American Studies at the Free University Berlin. He studied English and American literature, history, and musicology at the Justus Liebig University of Giessen, where he received his Ph.D. in 2001. With scholarships from the German National Academic Foundation, the German Academic Exchange Service (DAAD) and the German-American Fulbright Commission, he has been a visiting scholar and visiting fellow at the University of Wisconsin–Madison (1995-96) and Harvard University (1997-98 and 2004-05). His book publications include *Between Natives and Foreigners: Selected Writings of Karl/Charles Follen* (Lang, 2007); *Karl/Charles Follen: Deutsch-Amerikanischer Freiheitskämpfer*, *Studia Giessensia* (Universitätsverlag der Verlag Ferber'schen Buchhandlung, 2004); *Sphere Melodies: Die Manifestation Transzendentalistischer Ideen in der Musik von Charles Ives und John Cage* (Metzler, 2003); and *Sight & Sound: Naturbilder in der Englischen und Amerikanischen Romantik* (Tectum-Verlag, 2001). Various of his articles have appeared in *Zeitschrift für Anglistik und Amerikanistik*, *Frankfurter Zeitschrift für Musikwissenschaft*, *Cambridge Opera Journal*, *MusikTexte*, *Positionen*, *American Studies/Amerikastudien*, *Glossen*, and encyclopedias such as *Gemany and the Americas: Culture, Politics, and History* (2005), *Encyclopedia of the African and African American Experience* (2006), and *Encyclopedia of Africa and the Americas* (2007).

Julia Meier is a Ph.D. candidate in English and comparative literature at Leibniz University of Hanover, Germany, where she also taught at the Department of English/American Studies. She was a lecturer and visiting research scholar at the Department of Comparative Studies at Stony Brook University, New York, and was awarded a doctoral fellowship with the German Academic Exchange Service (DAAD) (2004-2005). She also worked as a curator for contemporary art at the Kestner Gesellschaft, Hanover, Germany (2003). Meier has published essays and articles on contemporary art, music, and film. Her dissertation examines the films of David Lynch in relation to Gilles Deleuze's logic of sensation.

Michal Peprník is an associate professor of American literature and literary theory at the Department of English and American Studies at Palacký University, Olomouc, Czech Republic. He published two books in Czech, *Metamorfóza jako kulturní metafora: James Hogg, R.L. Stevenson a George MacDonald* (Metamorphosis as a cultural metaphor, Olomouc University Press, 2003) and *Topos lesa v americké literatuře* (The topos of the forest in American literature, Host, 2005). His main fields of research are nature in the nineteenth century American literature and the literature of the fantastic. He is the secretary of the Czech and Slovak Association for American Studies.

Dana Polan is a professor of cinema studies at New York University. He is the author of seven books in film and media studies including the recent *Scenes of Instruction: The Beginnings of the U.S. Study of Film* (University of California Press, 2007) and *The Sopranos* (forthcoming, Duke University Press).

Sharon Pucker Rivo is the co-founder and executive director of the National Center for Jewish Film, a film library created in 1976 to collect the cinematographic records of the Jewish experience. Located on the Brandeis University campus, the center holds over 12,000 cans of film, gathered from all over the world, which preserve images of Jews from 1903 to the present. The Center has restored (with new English subtitles) 37 Yiddish feature films, including Ulmer's *Green Fields, The Singing Blacksmith, The Light Ahead,* and *American Matchmaker. www.jewishfilm.org*. An adjunct associate professor in the Department of Near Eastern and Judaic Studies at Brandeis, Ms. Rivo has received numerous awards, most recently the Zvi R. Cohen Leadership and Legacy Award from the Boston Center for Jewish Heritage for her contribution, vision, and commitment to preserving Jewish cultural life, and the Distinguished Humanist Award, "in recognition for her scholarship which helped to create and to shape the field of Jewish film studies" from the Melton Center for Jewish Studies at the Ohio State University.

Herbert Schwaab teaches literature, film and media studies in Dortmund and Lüneburg. He holds a Ph.D. in film studies from the Department of Media Studies at the Ruhr-University Bochum. His dissertation focused on the film philosophical works of Stanley Cavell and on concepts of popular culture, experience and the ordinary. His main fields of research are television series, popular film, concepts of cinephilia, theory of criticism and interpretation, and film philosophy. He is working on an introduction to media philosophy based on readings of the sitcom *King of Queens*.

Matthew Sweney is an assistant professor in American studies and Irish literature at Palacký University in Olomouc, Czech Republic, where he also organizes the international poetry festival Slova Bez Hranic (Words Without Borders). He is a translator from Czech to English. His most recent publication is *The Drug of Art*, the first English edition of the Czech-British *poet maudit* Ivan Blatny. In addition to film studies, he also trawls the depths of 1950s American paperback fiction.

Arianné Ulmer Cipes is the daughter of Edgar G. Ulmer. She was an actress and has worked in the film business for many years. Today she runs the Edgar G. Ulmer Preservation Corporation in Sherman Oaks, California.

Index

American Matchmaker 5, 11, 107, 112, 115, 116, 117, 191
Anderson, Thom 147
auteur 3, 12, 16, 17, 21, 138–140, 183, 193–195, 208–209, 213, 262–263, 277–278
authorship 16, 17, 43, 44, 206, 210, 211, 277

Babes in Bagdad (also *Muchachas de Bagdad*) 6, 14, 15, 183, 185, 186, 187, 188, 189, 190, 191, 192, 193, 194
bad films 187, 212
Baumann, Marty 182n1
Belton, John 140–141, 144, 184
Berlin, Irving 130, 133
The Black Cat 3, 6, 10, 14, 15, 23, 27–28, 30, 33–34, 40, 89–103, 106, 126, 178, 193, 207, 208, 212, 218, 227, 246, 263, 272
Bluebeard 5, 6, 30–34, 36, 40, 44, 101, 103, 126, 186, 207, 227
body of work 16, 17, 43, 44, 206, 210, 211, 277
Bogdanovich, Peter 93, 94
Bond, Raymond 173
Brecht, Bertolt 12, 15, 119–121, 123–125, 133–136, 170
Breen, Joseph 96–97, 99, 101, 142–143
Britton, Andrew 147
Browning, Tod 92
Brunas, John 28, 37, 182n1
Burch, Noël 147
Burray (island) 13, 173, 175, 178, 179

camp and campiness 3, 14, 15, 30, 148, 183, 185, 186, 187, 188, 189, 190, 191, 192, 193, 194, 200, 201, 203, 205, 208, 212, 270
capitalism 40, 53, 54, 121, 161, 162, 170, 194
Carradine, John 102
Cavell, Stanley 190, 193, 195, 283
The Cavern 5, 19, 46, 208–209, 248–260
Clarke, Robert 45, 173, 176–177, 179

Classical Hollywood Cinema 9, 15, 103, 185, 190, 191, 192, 193, 194, 263, 271
Combs, Richard 144, 145
Coursen, David 145

Damaged Lives 9–10, 23, 41, 63–86
Daney, Serge 263, 267, 269, 271
Daughter of Dr. Jekyll and Mr. Hyde 15, 16, 17, 18, 43, 196
Deleuze, Gilles 7, 13, 19, 150, 152, 153, 154, 155, 156, 248, 250, 251, 252, 253, 254, 258, 259, 260
DeMille, Cecil B. 188, 212
Detour 3, 5, 6, 9, 12, 36, 39–48, 103, 117, 126, 128, 137–148, 159, 197, 199–200, 205, 208, 212, 263, 272, 274
Dietrich, Marlene 100
documentary 1, 5, 9, 10, 37, 39, 40, 43, 49, 50, 52, 55, 62, 63, 64, 78, 127, 133, 211, 238, 279; style 39, 40, 43, 49, 50, 52, 55, 133, 238

Eco, Umberto 148
Ellison, Harlan 181n1, 182
Engel, Roy 174, 176
entertainment 12, 51, 53, 54, 56, 59, 73, 74, 107, 119, 121, 125, 126, 130, 134, 192
exploitation 24, 28, 55, 207, 246, 248, 254, 273

femme fatale 94, 146, 154, 199, 274
Field, Margaret 173
flashbacks 14, 31, 34, 43, 159, 162–163, 168–169, 173, 198–199, 201, 274
framing 13, 163–164, 211, 244n1
Freud, Sigmund 6, 18, 24, 25, 26, 27, 30, 37, 218, 225, 226, 231, 232, 234, 235
Fromkess, Leon 33, 208

Gallagher, Tag 264, 274, 276–277
gaze 28, 51, 125, 133, 135, 244, 249–251, 254, 255, 279

genre 8, 9, 11–12, 15, 18–19, 27, 33, 50, 66, 117, 124–125, 130, 134, 136, 146, 154, 181, 183–184, 188–190, 205–207, 212, 236–238, 241, 244, 249, 266, 269, 278–280
Goldin, Pat 179
Goldsmith, Martin 12, 40, 48, 140, 141–142
Gone with the Wind 181n1
Green Fields 5, 11, 40, 105–118, 264
Guattari, Félix 19, 156, 248, 250, 251, 252, 253, 254, 258, 259, 260

haunted house 201, 226, 227
Heywood, Donald 12, 119, 121, 130, 133
Hitchcock, Alfred 43, 141, 176, 201, 210, 222, 272, 281
Hoberman, J. 14, 24, 37, 68, 88, 110,, 118, 183, 187, 191, 193, 194, 195
horror 3, 11, 13–14, 19, 27–28, 34, 37, 43, 74, 89–91, 126, 135, 150, 154, 158, 162, 165, 182, 201, 212, 244, 263, 280–281

impulse-image 150, 152, 156–157
Invaders from Mars (1953) 181n1
Invasion of the Body Snatchers (1956) 172–173
Isle of Forgotten Sins 15, 274–276
It! The Terror from Beyond Space (1958) 180

Jive Junction 41, 126, 272

Karloff, Boris 89, 90, 91, 92, 95, 97, 98, 99, 100, 101, 102
Koff, Charles 176
Kracauer, Friedrich 9, 49, 50, 53, 54, 55, 56, 57, 58, 60, 61, 62
Krohn, Bill 270–271
Kubrick, Stanley 28, 176, 281

La Capra, Dominick 137–138
Laemmle, Carl 90, 91, 95, 100, 101, 102
Laemmle, Carl, Jr. 91, 92, 95, 101, 102
Lamarr, Hedy 13, 44, 46, 150
Lang, Fritz 5, 54, 59, 144, 181, 207, 223, 269, 272, 280
leisure 9, 50–56, 238
Life (magazine) 177, 182n2
The Light Ahead 5, 11, 40, 107, 110, 113, 115, 191, 210
lighting 140, 155, 263, 270
Lourcelles, Jacques 269–270, 278
Lugosi, Bela 89, 90, 91, 95, 98, 99, 100, 101, 102
Lund, Lucile 96, 98, 99, 100, 102

The Man from Planet X 14, 171–181, 234
Melville, Douglas 181n1

Menschen am Sonntag (*People on Sunday*) 5, 9, 40, 49–60, 127
Menzies, William Cameron 181n1
Meyrinck, Gustav 93
minimalism 40, 41, 186, 194
modernity 8, 9, 34, 43, 54, 62, 188, 244, 246, 280
money (lack of, role of) 3, 31, 40, 147, 155, 160–162, 164, 205, 208, 263–264
Moon Over Harlem 5, 11–12, 42–43, 119–135, 185, 218
Morris, Gary 144
Moullet, Luc 184, 185, 195, 212, 213, 215, 223, 224
Murder Is My Beat 15–16, 196–205, 210
Murnau, Friedrich Wilhelm 4, 5, 9, 17, 28, 40, 54, 55, 56, 94, 144, 184, 185, 207, 218, 220–221, 269

The Naked Dawn 6, 17, 46–47, 145, 208, 215–223, 272
noir 6, 14, 15, 41, 117, 126, 146, 147, 149, 168, 197–199, 201, 205, 210, 213, 274, 281
nudism 28, 55, 247–250, 253, 255–256

object *a* 166–167
Olomouc 2, 4, 5, 6, 7, 18, 20, 21, 25, 105, 118, 213, 225, 226, 227, 234
ontological ambivalence 18, 232, 233

Peary, Danny 21, 182
Pollexfen, Jack 15, 171, 177, 196, 197, 227, 234n3
PRC 5, 30, 31, 33, 42, 103, 143, 184, 208, 216
Preminger, Otto 181, 269
primal scene 25, 164–166
primitivism 26, 125, 135–136, 189
Pulleine, Tim 140, 145

recursive pattern 233, 18
Reiss, Winold 128–131, 135, 136
repetition 15, 18, 68, 143, 160, 161, 165–166, 167, 168, 169, 225, 231, 232, 233, 234n6
Resnais, Alain 29, 194
Rivette, Jacques 140
Routt, William D. 266, 271–272
Ruiz, Raúl 264 274
Ruthless 6, 13, 37, 44, 159–170, 205, 272
Ruttmann, Walter 50, 54, 127

Sargeant, Winthrop 182n2
Sarris, Andrew 3, 21, 40, 184, 195, 208, 212, 213, 214
Sartre, Jean-Paul 139

Savage, Ann 9, 39–44, 46, 48
Schallert, William 173, 176
Schüfftan, Eugen 5, 16, 49, 55
Scorsese, Martin 268–269, 277
Screen Actors Guild (SAG) 176
signature 16, 17, 21, 184, 206, 209, 216, 276, 277
The Singing Blacksmith 5, 105–118, 210
smooth space 19, 251, 252, 254, 255, 258, 259, 260
Sontag, Susan 15, 185, 186, 187, 189, 195
Stevenson, Robert Louis 18, 227, 229, 231, 233, 283
The Strange Case of Dr. Jekyll and Mr. Hyde 18, 227
Strange Woman 12–13, 15, 44, 46, 150–158
striated space 19, 251, 252, 253, 254, 256, 258, 259, 260

Tavernier, Bertrand 6, 15, 44, 181, 182, 195, 204, 212, 213, 215, 220, 223, 224

The Thief of Bagdad (1940) 181n1
The Thing from Another Worlde (1951) 180
Things to Come 181n1
Thomson, David 145
trash 8, 14, 23, 33, 37, 187, 194, 200, 203, 205, 268, 269

The Uncanny 225, 227, 231, 232, 233

voyeurism 29, 45, 46, 192, 237, 241, 243–245

Warren, Bill 171, 182
Weill, Kurt 12, 119, 121, 123–125, 133–136
Weimar Republic 9, 12, 51, 52, 54, 56, 57, 60, 119, 120, 125, 134
Wilson, Michael Henry 182
Wisberg, Aubrey 15, 171, 178, 196, 197
Wishman, Doris 248–250, 254–256
Wood, Ed 3, 203, 271
Wyler, William 102, 190

www.ingramcontent.com/pod-product-compliance
Ingram Content Group UK Ltd.
Pitfield, Milton Keynes, MK11 3LW, UK
UKHW041928140426
5217IPUK00014B/361